THE CLEAVEN DYKE AND LITTLEOUR MONUMENTS IN THE NEOLITHIC OF TAYSIDE

GORDON J BARCLAY & GORDON S MAXWELL

To Liz and Kathleen,

for putting up with the Cleaven Dyke

Frontispiece and cover illustration: A speculative reconstruction painting by David Hogg of the Cleaven Dyke in its landscape, during construction. (*Crown Copyright: Historic Scotland*)

THE CLEAVEN DYKE AND LITTLEOUR

MONUMENTS IN THE NEOLITHIC OF TAYSIDE

GORDON J BARCLAY & GORDON S MAXWELL

with

KENNETH BROPHY, CHRISTOPHER BURGESS, DONALD DAVIDSON,
KEVIN J EDWARDS, BILL FINLAYSON, IAN C GRIEVE, PAUL JOHNSON,
DEBORAH J LONG, CLIVE RUGGLES, ALAN SAVILLE, LORNA SHARPE,
ALISON SHERIDAN, IAN SIMPSON, BILL STARTIN, ANDREW TYLER
AND GRAEME WHITTINGTON

and contributions by

CIARA CLARKE, MICHAEL CRESSEY, ALAN DUFFY, DAVID HOGG,
TIM HOLDEN AND RUTH PELLING

ILLUSTRATIONS

SYLVIA STEVENSON
and
MARION O'NEIL

SOCIETY OF ANTIQUARIES OF SCOTLAND
EDINBURGH 1998

MONOGRAPH SERIES 13

SOCIETY OF ANTIQUARIES
OF SCOTLAND

MONOGRAPH SERIES

EDITOR ◆ ALEXANDRA SHEPHERD

Elements of the project were funded by

HISTORIC SCOTLAND

who have provided grant aid for those parts of the publication.
In addition,
Historic Scotland provided further generous sponsorship towards the publication.

British Library Cataloguing-in-Publication Data

A catalogue record for this publication is available from the British Library

ISBN 0 903903 13 X

Produced by Past Historic, Kings Stanley, Gloucestershire
Printed in Great Britain

CONTENTS

Acknowledgements	ix
List of Contributors	x
List of Illustrations	xi
List of Tables	xiii
Introduction	xv
Notes to the publication	xvi

1	Setting the scene		1
	1.1	The Neolithic and Early Bronze Age in Tayside: a brief history	1
		Burial and ceremonial monuments	1
		The significance of aerial photography	2
		Recent excavations	3
		The archaeology of the Inchtuthil plateau	5
	1.2	The palaeoenvironmental background: pollen studies at Rae Loch Kevin Edwards & Graeme Whittington	5
		Methods	6
		Vegetational history	9
		Discussion and conclusions	12
2	The Survey and excavation of the Cleaven Dyke		13
	2.1	The history of the investigation of the Cleaven Dyke	13
		The monument: an introductory view	13
		The Cleaven Dyke's more recent past	14
		Previous surveys of the Cleaven Dyke	22
		Archaeology in the immediate area	22
	2.2	The 1993-1997 surveys	24
		General observations	24
		Description and detailed analysis	27
	2.3	Excavations on the Cleaven Dyke: 1993 and 1995	30
		Strategy	30
		Area I: the main trench in the arable field	30
		Area II: the slots excavated to locate the SE terminal	31
		Area III: the cross-section cut in 1993	31
		Area IV: the axial section cut in 1995	35
	2.4	Palaeosols of the Cleaven Dyke Ian Simpson & Donald Davidson	36
		Methods	36
		Results and discussion: soil types	36
		Conclusions	42
	2.5	Soil pollen beneath the Cleaven Dyke Kevin Edwards & Graeme Whittington	42
		Methods	43
		The pollen diagrams	43
		Interpretation	45
		Conclusions	46
3	The Cleaven Dyke - Construction and design		47
	3.1	Dating the construction of the Cleaven Dyke	47
	3.2	Mensuration and design	47
		Patterns of construction	48
		Questions of alignment	49
		Possible barrows within the bank	50

	3.3	The possible astronomical alignment of the Cleaven Dyke Clive Ruggles	50
	3.4	Estimating the labour required to build the Cleaven Dyke Bill Startin	52

4 Excavation at Littleour 53
    4.1   Background 53
    4.2   Results of excavation 54
            The main structure 54
            Additional pits and posts 58
            Dating 58
    4.3   The nature and date of the Littleour monument 60
            A roofed structure? 60
            The analysis of the structure 62
    4.4   The pottery from Littleour Alison Sheridan 62
            The pots 62
            The daub-like pieces 67
            Discussion 67
    4.5   The charred residues on the Littleour Grooved Ware vessels Deborah J Long 68
            Methods 68
            Results 68
            Discussion 69
            Conclusion 70
    4.6   The flint from Littleour Alan Saville 70
            The pieces 70
            Detailed description 70
            Raw material 71
            Microwear examination Bill Finlayson 72
            Sieved residues 72
            Discussion 72

5 Survey Methodology at the Cleaven Dyke and Littleour 74
    5.1   Contour models and digital terrain modelling in archaeological survey: the development of approaches to the Cleaven Dyke Christopher Burgess 74
            Purpose & methodology 74
            Conclusion 76
    5.2   Geophysical survey on the Cleaven Dyke and Littleour Lorna Sharpe & Paul Johnson 77
            Implications of the area's geology for geophysical survey 77
            Surveys at Littleour 78
            Surveys at the Cleaven Dyke. 80
            Summary 83
    5.3   Estimating soil loss from cropmark sites: using the Caesium 137 methodology at Littleour Andrew Tyler, Donald Davidson & Ian C Grieve 83
            Materials and methods 85
            Results 86
            In situ derived erosion rates estimates 88
            Discussion 90
            Conclusions 91

6 Cursus monuments and bank barrows of Tayside and Fife Kenneth Brophy 92
    6.1   The cursus monuments 92
            What is a cursus monument? 92
            The cursus monuments of Tayside 94
    6.2   The bank barrows 103
            What is a bank barrow? 103
            Kilmany: a bank barrow in Fife 103
            The bank barrows of Scotland 104
    6.3   Discussion 107

7	The Cleaven Dyke and Littleour: Context, form and purpose		109
	7.1	Cleaven Dyke: the construction of the monument	109
		The building sequence	109
		The choice of terrain and alignment for the Dyke	110
		The environment of the Cleaven Dyke's construction	111
	7.2	The Cleaven Dyke in its context of cursus monuments and bank barrows	112
		Function and purpose	113
	7.3	Other Neolithic monuments relating to the Cleaven Dyke	115
		Round and oval mounds	115
		Long mounds	116
		'Long Mortuary Enclosures'	120
	7.4	Comparanda for Littleour: the Balfarg structures	120
	7.5	Other timber structures relating to Littleour	123
	7.6	The Littleour Grooved Ware: a contribution to the Scottish picture	124
8	Postscript		126
		Site conservation issues	126
		...and finally	129
References			131
Foreign language summaries			139
Index			143

ACKNOWLEDGEMENTS

We are grateful first of all to the trustees of the Meikleour Estates, particularly the estate factor, Lady Robert Mercer Nairne, for their permission to excavate, and their interest in, and assistance to, the project.

Many people gave of their time and labour on site: Davy Anderson; Tim Blackwood; Kenny Brophy; Abigail Daly; Rosemary Feilden; Julian and Sandra Fryer; Ann Miles; Jim Rideout; Sarah Ritson; Chris Russell-White; Lorna Sharpe and Julian Thomas. We are grateful for all their hard work, particularly to the long-stay patients: Kenny, Rosemary, Ann, Jim, Chris and Lorna. Philip Nappi, chairman of Blairgowrie Civic Trust, not only worked on site and acted as quartermaster but helped considerably with local liaison and support.

Our great thanks also to our fellow contributors, who have given freely of their time and expertise, making this publication far more rounded. Our thanks also to Sally Foster and Jack Stevenson for generously providing information on Auchenlaich in advance of their own publication.

Funding was generously provided by a number of organisations: the Society of Antiquaries of Scotland (1993; 1994; 1995; 1996); the Society of Antiquaries of London (1993; 1995); the Russell Trust (1995; 1996); the British Academy (1995; 1996); the Prehistoric Society in the form of the Bob Smith Award in 1993.

Historic Scotland undertook the survey of about half of the length of the Dyke, as part of its casework on the monument in areas to be cleared of trees; it also funded the analysis of the Grooved Ware residues as part of its larger project in conjunction with the National Museums of Scotland, and provided film, tools, radiocarbon dating and a grant towards the publication of parts of the report. We would also like to acknowledge the assistance and encouragement provided by Historic Scotland staff, particularly Gordon Barclay's colleagues in the Inspectorate of Ancient Monuments and the Photographic Section. Patrick Ashmore's advice on matters relating to radiocarbon dating was particularly valuable. Gordon Barclay would like to offer particular thanks to David Breeze.

We are grateful to the Royal Commission on the Ancient and Historical Monuments of Scotland (including the National Monuments Record for Scotland) and its staff (particularly David Cowley, Lesley Ferguson, Angela Gannon, Strat Halliday, Peter McKeague and Ian Parker) for their considerable assistance to the project, in the provision of information on comparable sites, archive material and photographs, and to Marilyn Brown, who located the Littleour site from the air. In particular we are grateful for the RCAHMS survey of Herald Hill, in time to be included in this report. We are also grateful to all the colleagues who provided encouragement and support, acting as referees for our funding applications, and for the final text: Richard Bradley, Ian Kinnes and Roger Mercer. Our thanks also to Mark Hall of Perth Museum for his encouragement and help.

We would also like to acknowledge the invaluable editorial input of Jackie Henrie and Alexandra Shepherd.

Finally, our thanks for their support and forbearance to our wives, Elizabeth Goring and Kathleen Maxwell.

SPECIALIST ACKNOWLEDGEMENTS

Edwards & Whittington
Thanks are due to Mr S Moncur of Leys of Marlee who granted permission to work on Rae Loch, to Mrs L Wood who undertook the pollen preparations, and to Historic Scotland which provided the radiocarbon dates conducted by Dr G Cook at the Scottish Universities Research and Reactor Centre, East Kilbride.

Sharpe & Johnson
We would like to thank Professor Brian Bluck and Dr Alan Hall of the Department of Geology and Applied Geology, University of Glasgow, for information and help with various aspects of this study. Thanks must also go to the people

who helped with various aspects of the fieldwork: Kenny Dunlop; Jerry Hamer; Janet Hooper; Debra Walsh; Elaine and Thomas Wilson, and last, but not least James Wright.

Sheridan
Trevor Cowie is thanked for permission to cite the unpublished Wellbrae report.

Simpson & Davidson
Thanks are due to Muriel MacLeod for preparing the soil thin sections, and to Bill Jamieson and David Aitchison for preparing the tables.

LIST OF CONTRIBUTORS

Gordon Barclay, Historic Scotland, Longmore House, Salisbury Place, Edinburgh EH9 1SH
Kenneth Brophy, Department of Archaeology, University of Glasgow, Glasgow G12 8QQ
Christopher Burgess, 22 Comiston Terrace, Edinburgh EH10 6AH
Ciara Clarke, Centre for Field Archaeology, University of Edinburgh, Old High School, Infirmary St, Edinburgh EH1 1LT
Michael Cressey, Centre for Field Archaeology, University of Edinburgh, Old High School, Infirmary St, Edinburgh EH1 1LT
Donald Davidson, Department of Environmental Science, University of Stirling, Stirling FK9 4LA
Alan Duffy, AOC (Scotland) Ltd, 4 Lochend Road, Edinburgh EH6 8BR
Kevin Edwards, Department of Archaeology and Prehistory, University of Sheffield, Northgate House, West Street, Sheffield, S1 4ET
Bill Finlayson, Centre for Field Archaeology, University of Edinburgh, Old High School, Infirmary St, Edinburgh EH1 1LT
IC Grieve, Department of Environmental Science, University of Stirling, Stirling FK9 4LA
David Hogg, 3 Glanville Place, Edinburgh EH3 6SZ
Tim Holden, Headland Archaeology, Albion Business Centre, Unit B4, 78 Albion Road, Edinburgh EH7 5QZ
Paul Johnson, Department of Archaeology, University of Glasgow, Glasgow G12 8QQ
Deborah Long, Department of Environmental Science, University of Stirling, Stirling FK9 4LA
Gordon Maxwell, 'Micklegarth', 72a High Street, Aberdour, Fife KY3 0SW
Marion O'Neil, c/o National Museums of Scotland, Chambers Street, Edinburgh EH1 1JF
Ruth Pelling, University of Oxford, per Centre for Field Archaeology, University of Edinburgh, Old High School, Infirmary St, Edinburgh EH1 1LT
Clive Ruggles, School of Archaeological Studies, Leicester University, Leicester LE1 7RH
Alan Saville, National Museums of Scotland, Chambers St, Edinburgh EH1 1JF
Lorna Sharpe, Department of Archaeology, University of Glasgow, Glasgow G12 8QQ
Alison Sheridan, National Museums of Scotland, Chambers St, Edinburgh EH1 1JF
Ian Simpson, Department of Environmental Science, University of Stirling, Stirling FK9 4LA
Bill Startin, English Heritage, 23 Savile Row, London W1X 1AB
Sylvia Stevenson, 44 Regent Street, Portobello, Edinburgh EH15 2AX
Andrew Tyler, Department of Environmental Science, University of Stirling, Stirling FK9 4LA
Graeme Whittington, Department of Geography, University of St Andrews, St Andrews, Fife KY16 9ST

LIST OF ILLUSTRATIONS

	Frontispiece: A speculative reconstruction painting by David Hogg of the Cleaven Dyke	
1	Location map.	xiv
2	A view of the south-easternmost portion of the Cleaven Dyke.	xv
3	Aerial photograph of the Littleour structure before excavation.	xvi
4	Plan of the 'long mortuary enclosure' at Inchtuthil.	3
5	The Neolithic enclosure at Douglasmuir, under excavation.	5
6	Summary pollen data, loss-on-ignition (LOI) and deposition time for the Rae Loch profile.	6
7	Selected percentage pollen and spore data from Rae Loch.	7
8	Selected percentage pollen and spore data from Rae Loch.	8
9	Time-depth curve for Rae Loch.	9
10	Selected percentage pollen taxa from Rae Loch for the period 5750-4100.	11
11	View of the area of the Cleaven Dyke cleared of trees in 1991.	13
12	McOmie's map of 1784.	14
13	Photograph showing the location of Richmond's two cross-section and single axial trenches (1939) at the SE end of section B of the bank of the Cleaven Dyke.	16
14	The idealised cross-section drawing of the Cleaven Dyke published by Richmond.	16
15	A view of one of the cross-sections through the Cleaven Dyke cut by Richmond.	16
16	The hypothetical original course and extent of the Cleaven Dyke, as proposed by Richmond.	17
17	Adamson's section through the Cleaven Dyke, redrawn from the site archive.	18
18	The plan of the Cleaven Dyke published as figure 3 by Adamson & Gallagher.	19
19	An extract from the new contour survey of the Cleaven Dyke showing Adamson's trench in its correct location.	20
20	Aerial photograph of the NW terminal of the Dyke showing the three hollow ways cutting down the steep drop to the valley in the foreground.	21
21	The modern metalled road immediately to the west of the cropmarks shown in illustration 20. The road is a hollow way.	21
22	The plan prepared by RCAHMS of the area between segment-boundary A10 and close to the SE end of section A of the Dyke.	23
23	Map showing the main subdivisions of the Cleaven Dyke.	25
24	Cleaven Dyke: diagram showing the height of the bank and the ditch bottoms in relation to Ordnance datum.	25
25	View along the NW part of the bank of the Dyke, looking towards the terminal.	26
26	Cleaven Dyke: plan and sections of the ditch in excavation area I/1.	29
27	Cleaven Dyke: sections of the ditch in excavation area I/2.	30
28	Cleaven Dyke: a view to the SE along the portion of the southern ditch in section E (excavation area I/1).	31
29	Drawn section of the bank and northern ditch of the Cleaven Dyke in excavation area III.	32
30	Cleaven Dyke: view of the NW face of the cross-section trench in excavation area III.	33
31	Plan of features below the bank of the Cleaven Dyke in the cross-section cut in excavation area III.	33
32	View from the NE of the axial section cut along the length of the bank of the Cleaven Dyke in excavation area IV.	33
33	Drawn section of the bank of the Cleaven Dyke revealed by the axial section in excavation area IV.	34
34	View from the NW towards the SE along the bank of the Cleaven Dyke during the excavation of the axial section at segment-boundary A10 (excavation area IV).	35
35	Plan of excavated features below the bank of the Cleaven Dyke in excavation area IV.	35
36	Cleaven Dyke: location of micromorphology thin section and soil pollen samples in excavation area III.	36
37	Cleaven Dyke: location of micromorphology thin section and soil pollen samples in excavation area IV.	37
38	Selected pollen and spore data from Cleaven Dyke soil pollen profile P1 (• indicates <2% TLP; x10 exaggeration curves on charcoal samples).	43
39	Selected pollen and spore data from Cleaven Dyke soil pollen profile P2 (• indicates <2% TLP; x10 exaggeration curves on charcoal samples; note the 'reversed' order of the phases).	44
40	Selected pollen and spore data from Cleaven Dyke soil pollen profile P3 (• indicates <2% TLP).	44
41	A 'Hi-spy' photograph of the Littleour structure close to the end of the excavation in 1996.	53
42	Plan of the identified pits and postholes at Littleour.	54

43 Section drawings of the excavated postholes in the boundary of the Littleour structure.	55
44 Littleour: posthole L15 before excavation.	56
45 Contour plan of the cleaned subsoil surface at Littleour, and the boundaries between fluvio-glacial sands and gravel.	56
46 Section drawings of pits and postholes at Littleour.	57
47 Littleour: cross-section of the axial posthole L9.	58
48 Littleour: cross-section of pit L23, showing some of the Grooved Ware.	58
49 Littleour: Grooved Ware Pot *1*, from pit L23.	63
50 Littleour: Grooved Ware Pot *2*, from pit L23.	64
51 Littleour: Grooved Ware Pots *3* and *6*, from pit L23.	65
52 Littleour: Grooved Ware Pots *4, 5, 7* and *8*, and fragments of daub, from pit L23.	66
53 Littleour: flint from pit L23.	71
54 Suggested key line conventions for use in labelling contour surveys.	75
55 The portion of the Cleaven Dyke to the east of the A96, as depicted on the 1:2500 Ordnance Survey map. (a) the most recent published paper edition of 1977; (b) the current electronic Ordnance Survey data.	76
56 A final interpretation of the results of both seasons of geophysical survey at Littleour.	78
57 The location of the profile lines and an interpretation of the results at the NW end of the Cleaven Dyke.	79
58 Cleaven Dyke: the results of the six resistivity profiles across the southern ditch.	80
59 Resistivity profiles at the NW end of the Cleaven Dyke.	81
60 Resistivity profile across the extant section of the Cleaven Dyke.	82
61 Resistivity section across the cropmark portion of the Cleaven Dyke in the arable field, just to the SE of the wood.	83
62 Sample locations at Littleour.	84
63 ^{137}Cs activity distributions observed in the samples collected along the 1995 pilot Transect.	86
64 Variation in the vertical distribution of ^{137}Cs activity.	86
65 Soil erosion rates.	87
66 Mass depth distribution profiles of ^{137}Cs activity.	88
67 An example of an in situ spectrum collected at Littleour.	89
68 Relationship between full soil core and in situ derived ^{137}Cs activity estimates.	90
69 Distribution map of cursus monuments and bank barrows in Scotland.	93
70 Plan of the enclosure at Douglasmuir, Angus.	95
71 The cursus monument at Balneaves.	96
72 Milton of Guthrie cursus monument: a) view and b) plan.	97
73 Plan of the cursus monument at Inchbare.	98
74 Plan of the cursus monument at Star Inn.	98
75 Plan of the cursus monument at Kinalty.	98
76 Plan of the cursus monument at Barnhead, also known as Old Montrose.	99
77 The cursus monument at Blairhall: a) view and b) plan.	100
78 Plan of the cursus monument at Bennybeg.	101
79 View of the cursus monument at Milton of Rattray, defined by two lines of widely-spaced pits.	102
80 Plan of the cursus monument at Mains of Gourdie.	102
81 View of the probable bank barrow at Kilmany.	104
82 A three-dimensional representation of the southern terminal of the Tom's Knowe bank barrow.	105
83 View of the possible bank barrow at Muirton, Moray.	105
84 View of the extremely long cairn at Auchenlaich.	106
85 Extract from the RAF vertical aerial photograph of Cleaven Dyke flown 26 September 1947.	109
86 The distribution of certain classes of Neolithic burial and ceremonial monuments in Tayside.	116
87 The Herald Hill long barrow: a) three-dimensional view; b) contour survey.	118
88 View of the Herald Hill long barrow.	118
89 A photograph of the long barrow at Longmanhill, taken probably in the 1920s.	119
90 Plans of the long mounds at Longmanhill, Banffshire and Blue Cairn of Balnagowan, Aberdeenshire and the NW end of the Cleaven Dyke.	119
91 Comparative plans of Neolithic timber structures in Britain and Ireland.	122
92 Aerial photograph of the 'Littleour type' structure at Fortingall.	123
93 Grooved ware pot *6 in situ* in pit L23 at Littleour.	124
94 The 'mythical' and more normal distribution of tree roots.	127
95 The effects of subsoiling using a normal and a winged tine subsoiler.	128
96 The side of the ditch of the Cleaven Dyke in excavation area I/1 removed by channels cut by two parallel episodes of subsoiling.	128
97 The bank of the Cleaven Dyke, shrouded in trees.	129
98 The NW portion of the contour survey of the Cleaven Dyke.	foldout
99 The SE portion of the contour survey of the Cleaven Dyke.	foldout

LIST OF TABLES

1	Radiocarbon dates quoted in the text.	xvii
2	Radiocarbon dates for the Rae Loch deposits.	9
3	Cleaven Dyke Type 1 soils: buried land surface.	38
4	Cleaven Dyke Type 1 soils: turf lines and dumps.	39
5	Cleaven Dyke Type 2 soils: podsolised soils.	40
6	Cleaven Dyke Type 3 and 4 soils: ditch-fill and sands/gravels.	41
7	Lengths of sections and segments of the Cleaven Dyke	48
8	Location data for the astronomical analysis.	51
9	Alignment data for the astronomical analysis.	51
10	Dimensions of postholes and pits of, and associated with, the Littleour structure.	57
11	Summary of the nature and location of carbonised macroplant remains from Littleour.	58
12	Radiocarbon determinations from Littleour.	59
13	Summary of pollen preservation.	68
14	Palynological results of residues.	68
15	^{137}Cs activity estimates and erosion estimates using the directly proportional and Kachanoski's power function models.	88
16	Results from the Littleour pilot study into soil erosion.	89
17	Dimensions of some of the mounds mentioned in discussion.	117

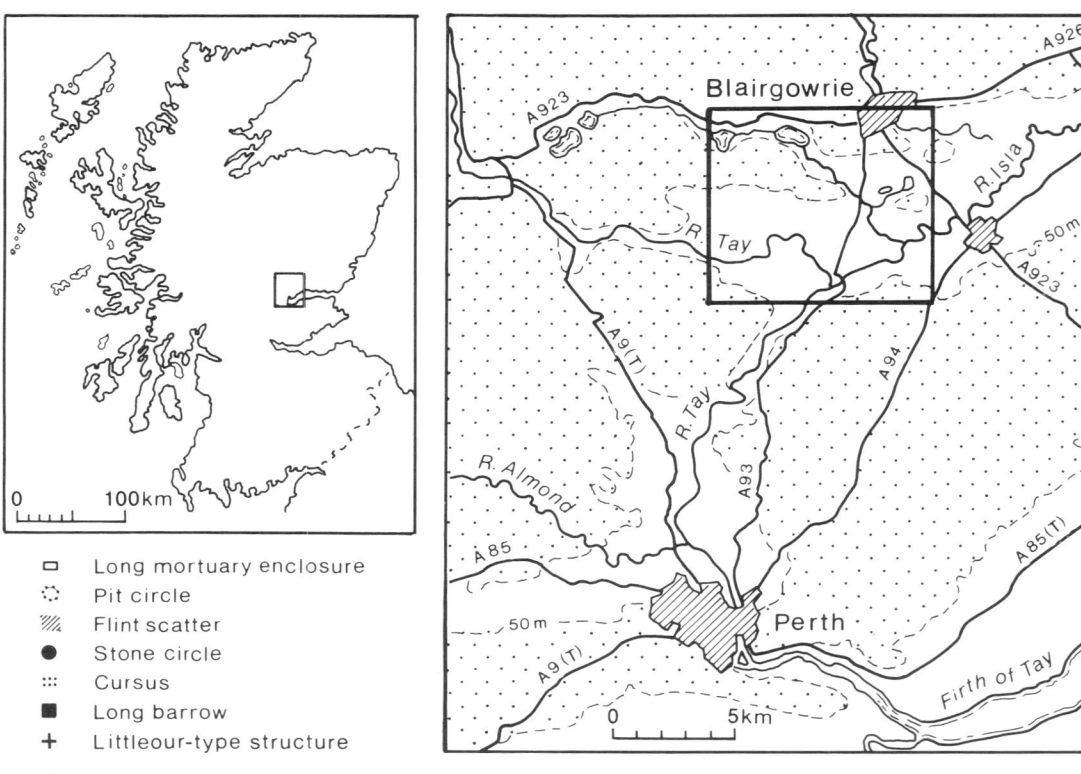

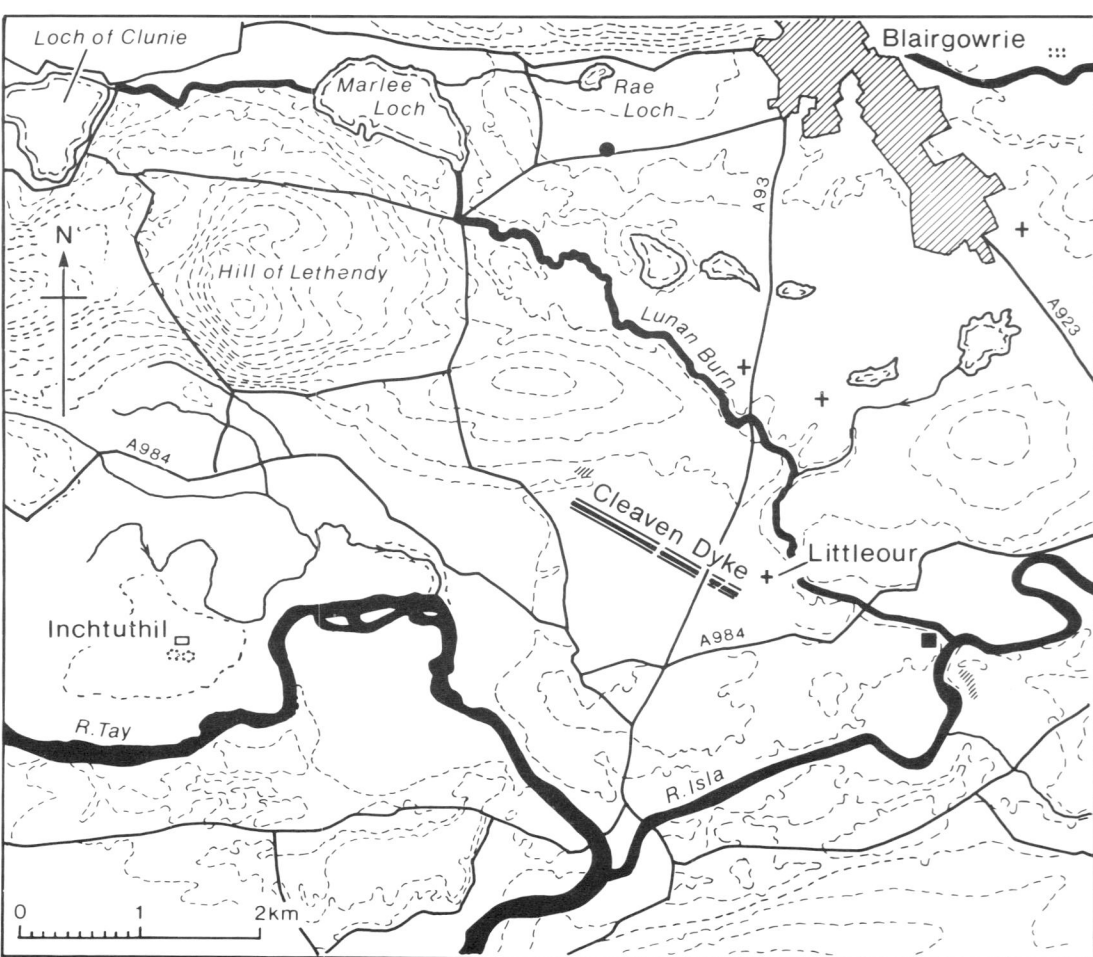

Illus 1
Location map. (*Based on the Ordnance Survey map with the permission of the Controller of her Majesty's Stationery Office.* © *Crown Copyright MC/98/172*)

INTRODUCTION

'I stand beneath the trees, lost in thought.' Wilhelm Müller, *Winterreise* tr Lois Philips 1979

The Cleaven Dyke is a complex linear earthwork comprising a pair of widely-spaced parallel ditches flanking a central bank, running for around 2km through dense forestry plantation and arable fields, north of the village of Meikleour, near Blairgowrie in Perthshire (illus 1). The Dyke appears to terminate on the NW near the edge of the wood in which it lies, and on the SE on the low hill where the cropmarks of the ditch are last visible (illus 2). For 200 years it was confidently identified as a Roman monument, related to the legionary fortress at Inchtuthil (Marshall 1776; Richmond 1940). There has never been, however, explicit archaeological evidence for its interpretation as a Roman work, nor for any extension beyond its presently visible terminals (Pitts & St Joseph 1985, 258). One of us (Gordon Maxwell) first challenged the Roman interpretation in 1983 (Maxwell 1983a) and the interpretation of the monument as related to the cursus monuments of the Neolithic period gained currency through the 1980s (Pitts & St Joseph 1985). The Dyke appears to combine a number of features and

Illus 2
A view of the south-easternmost portion of the Cleaven Dyke. The ditches have never been recorded beyond the point marked 'X'. The Herald Hill long barrow is at 'Y'. (*Crown Copyright: RCAHMS*)

characteristics of burial and ceremonial monuments of the Neolithic: a round or oval barrow, a long barrow, a cursus and a bank barrow.

The way in which the investigation of the Cleaven Dyke has been conducted in the past has been conditioned to a great extent by the assumption that the monument was first, a Roman military earthwork, and second, 'perfectly straight' (Abercromby *et al* 1902). Most previous survey has been at low resolution, incapable of detecting the smaller scale variations in the monument, and excavation has been limited to narrow slots across bank and ditches (Abercromby *et al* 1902; Richmond 1940; Adamson & Gallagher 1986). This has tended to reinforce the perception of the monument as broadly uniform and regular, although the irregularity of aspects of the layout and construction of the monument has been acknowledged for many years. The newly-undertaken survey shows just how complex and varied the monument is.

As part of the project, the opportunity was also taken to examine a cropmark structure, which we believed might be contemporary—a pit-defined enclosure—discovered nearby at Littleour during the course of aerial survey (RCAHMS 1994a, 28). The Littleour structure (illus 3) is one of a group of apparently similar features located by aerial photography in Perthshire in recent years. It had a superficial resemblance both to probable mortuary structures of the Neolithic (cf Balfarg Riding School in Fife: Barclay & Russell-White 1993) and, in scale, to a roofed building of the same period at Balbridie in Kincardineshire (Fairweather & Ralston 1993). The excavation of the Littleour structure suggests it had ceremonial rather than domestic functions (**4**, **7.4** and **7.5** below).

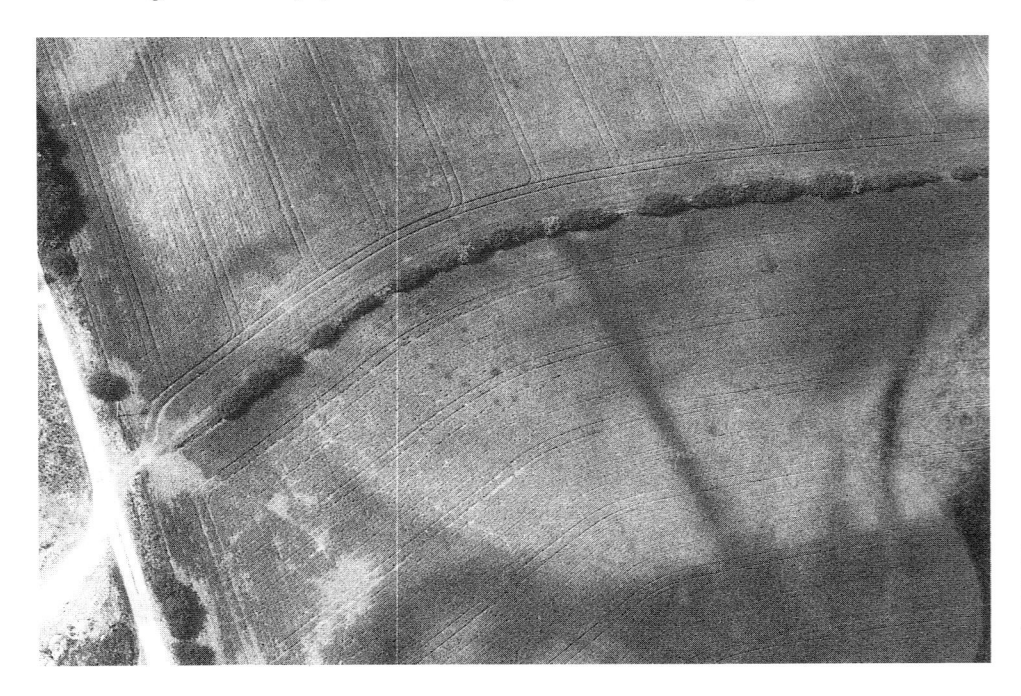

Illus 3
Aerial photograph of the Littleour structure before excavation. (*Crown Copyright: RCAHMS*)

NOTES TO THE PUBLICATION

Nine years ago, Ian Hodder complained in the pages of *Antiquity* (1989) about the bland nature of many excavation reports, singling out for censure their 'impersonal, abstract, timeless and [spuriously] objective prose'. Although we may differ from Hodder in identifying the cause of this malaise, as well as its cure, we agree that we should all try to provide a lively and direct, as well as an accurate, account of our own areas of work. We have attempted to find a balance between, on the one hand, over-detailed presentation of evidence, and on the other, interpretation without adequate supporting data. We hope we have succeeded.

A number of interim reports have been published: Barclay & Maxwell 1993; Barclay *et al* 1995; Barclay & Maxwell 1995; Barclay & Maxwell 1996; Barclay & Maxwell forthcoming. The account published here supersedes all earlier statements.

CALIBRATION OF RADIOCARBON DETERMINATIONS

All radiocarbon determinations, other than those for the Loch Rae pollen column, have been obtained using the OxCal program (version 2.18), working on the 1986 calibration curve of Stuiver and Kra. All calibrated ranges are at the 95% level of confidence. For further explanation of the radiocarbon method and the process of calibration see Ashmore (1996, 15-18). The errors attached to radiocarbon determinations from Glasgow University with a laboratory number lower than GU-1500 have been multiplied by 1.4 and, if then less than 110, have been taken to be 110 (Ashmore 1997); the errors attached to determinations prior to the early 1980s from other laboratories are also likely to be understated, and should be treated with caution (Ashmore, pers comm). Calibrated ranges have been rounded to the nearest five years. As an aid to the discussion sections within the volume, radiocarbon dates for sites mentioned in the text are gathered together here in table 1.

The radiocarbon determinations for the Loch Rae pollen column have been calibrated using the 1993 curve of Steiver et al; however, the way in which the calibrated ranges have been used (to calculate deposition rates for the Loch) make the slight differences between the calibration curves irrelevant. We are grateful throughout to Patrick Ashmore for his advice on radiocarbon dating matters.

Site Name	Context (sample charcoal unless noted)	Laboratory No	Raw determination, cf Ashmore 1997	Calibrated range (95%)	Reference
Balbridie, Aberdeenshire	Carbonised grain from building.	OxA-1768	5010±90BP	4000-3640	Fairweather and Ralston 1993
Balfarg Henge	Mainly *Alnus* charcoal incorporated in fill of posthole.	GU-1160	4180±110BP	3050-2450	Mercer 1981
Balfarg Henge	Mainly *Alnus* charcoal incorporated in fill of posthole.	GU-1161	4035±110BP	2900-2250	Mercer 1981
Balfarg Riding School	Heavily charcoal impregnated later in henge ditch, associated with Grooved Ware.	GU-1904	4385±55BP	3310-2900	Barclay and Russell-White 1993
Balfarg Riding School	Fill of Grooved Ware pit.	GU-1902	4250±85BP	3100-2550	Barclay and Russell-White 1993
Cleaven Dyke	Charcoal from hearth below bank (predates construction by 200-800? years).	GU-3912	5550±130BP	4750-4000	This volume
Creag na Caillich	Peat formed at time of rapid ?human induced change.	GU-2975	4770±50BP	3500-3100	Edmonds, Sheridan and Tipping 1992
Creag na Caillich	Peat at lower debitage layer.	GU-2976	4240±60BP	3030-2610	Edmonds, Sheridan and Tipping 1992
Creag na Caillich	Peat immediately below upper debitage layer.	GU-2977	3820±70BP	2490-2040	Edmonds, Sheridan and Tipping 1992
Douglasmuir, Angus	Charcoal from throughout posthole BDD.	GU-1469	4895±110BP	4000-3350	Kendrick 1995
Inchtuthil, Perthshire	Burnt fence.	GU-2761	5070±50BP	3990-3780	Barclay and Maxwell 1991
North Mains barrow, Perthshire	Old land surface under mound.	GU-1134	3805±140BP	2900-1800	Barclay 1983
North Mains henge, Perthshire	From primary packing of henge posthole A/7.	GU-1353	4102±110BP	2950-2350	Barclay 1983
North Mains henge, Perthshire	From primary packing of henge posthole A/5.	GU-1354	4040±110BP	2900-2300	Barclay 1983
North Mains, ring ditches	Pit predating ring-ditches, containing EN pottery.	GU-1546	4650±65BP	3650-3100	Barclay 1983
Pitnacree, Perthshire	On top of soil above mortuary enclosure pits.	GaK-601	4810±270BP	4300-2900	Coles and Simpson 1965

Table 1
Radiocarbon dates quoted in text.

1

SETTING THE SCENE

'By the word "information" we denote all knowledge which we have...; therefore, in fact, the foundation of all our ideas and actions. Let us consider the nature of this foundation, its want of trustworthiness, its changefulness, and we shall soon feel what a dangerous edifice [it] is, how easily it may fall to pieces and bury us all in its ruins.' von Clausewitz, *On War*, 1832, chapter VI (tr JJ Graham, 1908).

1.1 THE NEOLITHIC AND EARLY BRONZE AGE IN TAYSIDE: A BRIEF HISTORY

The projects reported on here were undertaken in Tayside, used here to encompass the area of the now reinstated counties of Perthshire and Angus. The topography is very varied: broad rolling fluvio-glacial gravels, incorporating one of the largest single areas of good agricultural land in Scotland, backed by the foothills of the Grampians, in which sheltered valleys offer different, but also good, opportunities for settlement. It is effectively formed by the catchments of the rivers Tay, Earn and Isla in its western part, the broad valley known as Strathmore—happy hunting ground of Romanists on foot and in the air—the coastal plain to the south and the arable landscape of Angus, mainly the catchment of the South Esk, to the east.

This part of eastern Scotland, best seen in the paintings of local artist McIntosh Patrick, is extraordinarily beautiful, far more pleasing to the eye of the lowland Scot than the acclaimed grandeur of the mountainous west. Nineteenth-century painters of the Scottish landscape conformed with, and encouraged, the romantic notions of a Highland Scotland evoked in the novels of Sir Walter Scott and his imitators, depicting a landscape 'entirely populated by sheep, woolly cattle and antlered beasts who stood proud against the snow, rain and fiery sun of this mountainous land ... deserted by [the inhabitants] who had finally admitted to their defeat by the elements' (Billcliffe 1987, 8). Much of the traditionally recognised Neolithic of Scotland lies in landscapes not far removed from this sorry 'ideal'. Patrick, in contrast, painted a landscape 'which has offered man an opportunity to co-exist, a countryside which has not spurned his husbandry but which has openly responded to his care' (*ibid* 1987, 8). Perthshire and Angus seem to have been 'openly responding' for over 5000 years.

BURIAL AND CEREMONIAL MONUMENTS

In the absence of easily identifiable settlement evidence, published consideration of the Neolithic period in Perthshire and Angus, as in every part of Scotland, has concentrated on chambered tombs and the distribution of artefacts. Of paramount importance to the cataloguing of the past in Perthshire, as in the rest of the country, is the work of the former Archaeology Division of the Ordnance Survey, unpublished, yet the foundation of all sites and monuments records. Their work has now been superseded in the substantial parts of Tayside that have since been surveyed in detail by the Royal Commission on the Ancient and Historical Monuments of Scotland (RCAHMS 1990; 1994a; 1994b). In other parts of the area new monuments have been located only by small-scale archaeological fieldwork or by accidental discovery. The capacity for even the densely populated arable lowlands of Perthshire still to provide surprise discoveries is remarkable; for example, two substantial burial mounds of similar proportions to the early Neolithic round barrow at Pitnacree, near Aberfeldy (Coles & Simpson 1965–see below) have recently been located in arable areas of Perthshire, one on the outskirts of the village of Dunning, the other within sight of the Perth to Crieff main road (Barclay 1992a, 73).

Between 1954 and 1966 Audrey Henshall undertook the fieldwork on Perthshire chambered cairns that was published in volume 2 (1972) of her *magnum opus*. Her consideration of the Neolithic beyond the tombs was necessarily limited as little was then known. She listed seven probable chambered cairns in Perthshire: Clach na Tiompan (Clyde group, long); Kindrochat (Clyde group, long); Rottenreoch (?Clyde group, long); Cultoquhey (Clyde group, round?); Derculich (unclassified);

Fortingall (long cairn); Cairnwochel (?long cairn). Three of these had been excavated by the time the volume was published: Kindrochat (Childe 1930); Clach na Tiompan (Henshall & Stewart 1956) and Cultoquhey (Stewart 1959). Since 1966, fieldwork has added further examples (eg the cairn at Edinchip: Davidson, JL & Henshall 1983) and the 350m-long cairn at Auchenlaich (Foster & Stevenson forthcoming, and note below). In 1992, the Afforestable Land Survey of RCAHMS located four hitherto unrecorded chambered tombs in the Braes of Doune area (RCAHMS 1994b), effectively filling the gap in the distribution noted by Henshall (1972, 28-9).

Dr Margaret Stewart's published consideration (1959) of Strathtay in 'the second millennium' (in those effectively pre-radiocarbon days, from chambered tombs to Beaker and Food Vessel burials) logged a limited number of known sites. The interpretative structure and the concerns of the paper were very much of their period and as a result it has not dated well. Dr Stewart considered the date and affiliations of the large round earthen mounds of Strathtay and Strathearn and drew the (at that time inevitable) conclusion that they were an early Bronze Age phenomenon belonging to 'an intrusive culture penetrating inland from the east coast'.

Perhaps as a result of Dr Stewart having drawn attention to the Neolithic remains in the area, the mid 1960s saw a considerable, if brief, upsurge in excavation activity in upper Strathtay, around Aberfeldy. In 1964 John Coles and Derek Simpson undertook a research excavation on one of the round mounds that Stewart had speculated about, at Pitnacree, in Strathtay, demonstrating that that example at least had been constructed in the earlier Neolithic; a sample of charcoal from the old land surface produced a calibrated radiocarbon date (using revised errors–Ashmore 1997) of 4300-2900 cal BC (GaK-601) (Coles & Simpson 1965). The life of the monument was broken down into three phases:

1 Two large (?split-trunk) posts were erected at either end of a mortuary structure of 'linear zone' type (Kinnes 1979; Scott 1992).

2 An elongated ring-bank of stone and soil was built, with a formal entrance to the east, associated with cremation burials; the enclosed area contained a rectilinear drystone structure. During the later part of this phase the mound assumed its familiar bowl-shape.

3 A cremation and cist burials were inserted, and a standing stone was erected on top of the mound.

In 1965 the same excavators undertook a brief rescue excavation on a group of pits on a second site, on the opposite side of the Tay at Grandtully (Simpson & Coles 1990). Two phases of activity were represented: deposition of later Neolithic impressed-ware pottery, and Bronze Age cremation burial.

Also in 1965 Piggott and Simpson undertook excavation at the Croft Moraig stone circle (Piggott & Simpson 1971). They discovered that the monument had three phases:

1 A penannular setting of posts with outliers, and a slight ditch.

2 An oval of free-standing stones on much the same plan as the preceding posts, and an enclosing stony bank.

3 A stone circle lying outside the oval but within the stone bank; the circle has two outliers beyond the bank.

Earlier Neolithic pottery was recovered from the ditch of phase 1, with undiagnostic 'flat rim ware'. It is characteristic of Scottish prehistoric studies of the period that the timber structure below the Croft Moraig stone circle (Piggott & Simpson 1971) was interpreted as a *'provincial version'* [our emphasis] of the structures being discovered at Durrington Walls, Wiltshire.

In 1973 Stewart published a further general survey of Perthshire in the 4th to 3rd millennia BC (Stewart 1973). The interpretation of the 'tomb' excavated by Stewart at Dull is unresolved; Henshall believes (1972, 479) that it was actually a corn-drying kiln.

During the investigation of the Roman fortress at Inchtuthil (Pitts & St Joseph 1985) Richmond and St Joseph examined a pre-Roman rectilinear enclosure, interpreted at the time of excavation as a Bronze Age domestic structure. Later investigation (Barclay & Maxwell 1991) showed that the irregular, ditched, trapezoidal enclosure, measured 50m in length and between 10.1m and 8.4m wide, and belonged to quite a different period and classification (illus 4). A fence erected in the ditch was burnt; it was radiocarbon-dated to 4000-3780 cal BC (GU-2760 & 2761 combined). The monument has been interpreted as a mortuary structure, because of its close similarities to such sites in other parts of Britain (Kinnes 1992b).

In 1970 and 1971 Coutts published two summaries of the prehistoric monuments and artefacts of Tayside (1970; 1971). The latter volume contains a more rounded presentation of the monuments, taking in a larger area, and reflecting the dating evidence provided by Pitnacree.

THE SIGNIFICANCE OF AERIAL PHOTOGRAPHY

We have described elsewhere the general part played by aerial photography in revolutionising our understanding

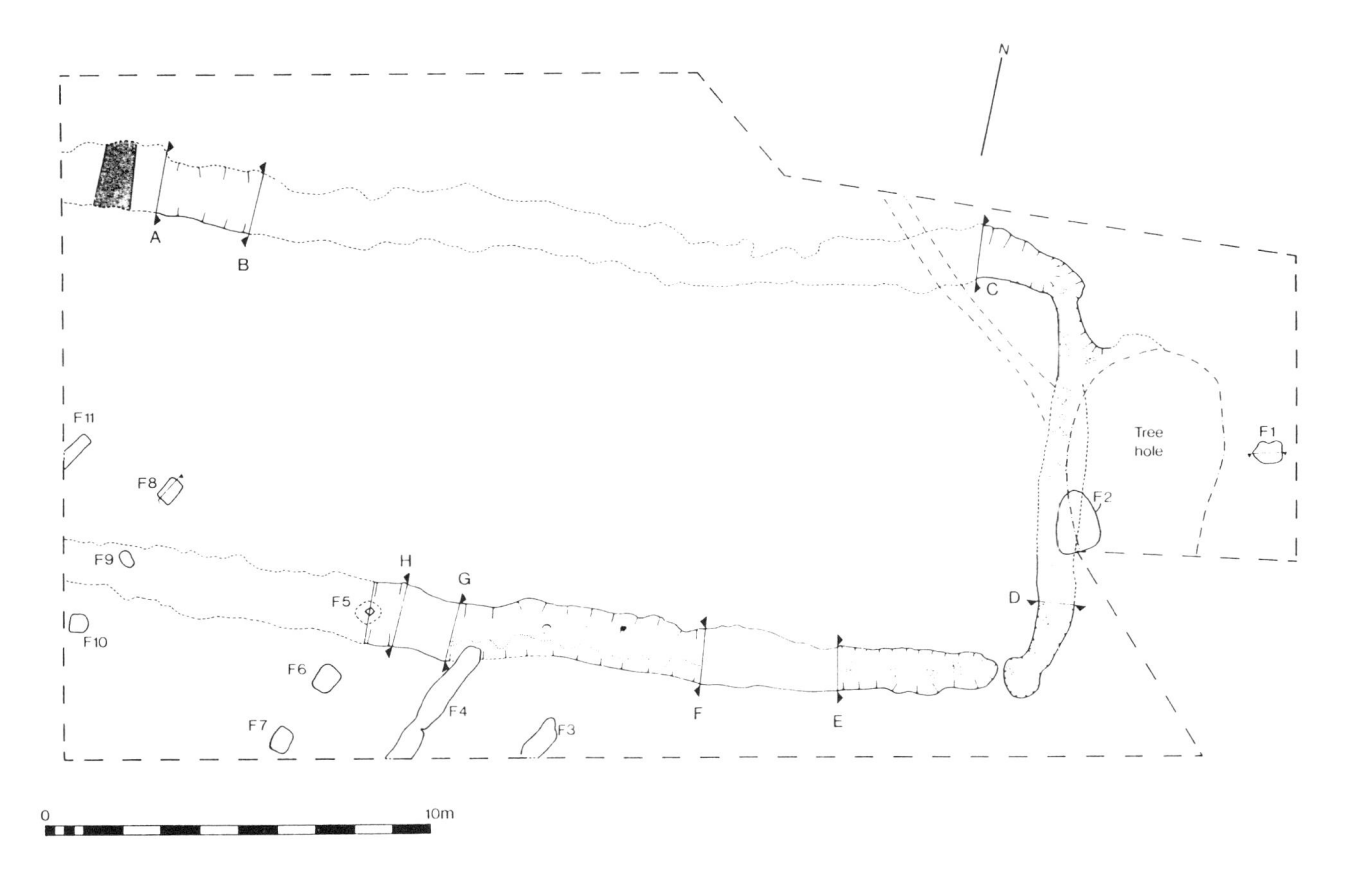

Illus 4
Plan of the 'long mortuary enclosure' at Inchtuthil.

of the prehistory of lowland Scotland (Maxwell 1983b; Barclay 1992b). In particular, aerial photography has made a striking impact on our knowledge of Neolithic monuments of the Tayside area. The last 40 years have seen the density of the distribution of Neolithic or potentially Neolithic monuments in Tayside transformed in a way that can hardly be paralleled: from being an area with a very sparse distribution of monuments of the period, it has become one of the most densely populated in eastern Britain.

At least 16 cursus monuments (both ditch- and pit-defined) or enclosures of related type have been discovered in Tayside from the air (Brophy below), as well as many sites that can be interpreted as henges or hengiform enclosures (eg Barclay 1997a).

RECENT EXCAVATIONS

From the mid 1970s the effects of the expansion of the state-funded rescue archaeology programme began to be felt in Tayside, as in the rest of Scotland (Barclay 1997b). In the early days there were two false starts in adding to our knowledge of the Neolithic of the area. In 1977 the supposed cursus at Huntingtower on the outskirts of Perth proved to be a post-medieval road (Barclay 1982) and in 1978 a second Perthshire round mound, at North Mains, Strathallan (Barclay 1983), proved on excavation to date from later than Pitnacree, the radiocarbon date from the old land surface being 2900-1800 cal BC (the 1σ calibrated range is 2470-2040 cal BC; GU-1134), firmly in the earlier Bronze Age (although if revised, higher, errors are built into the calibration process, the calibrated ranges for Pitnacree and North Mains at 2σ now abut). The adjacent henge at North Mains, excavated in 1979, was radiocarbon dated to 2900-2300 cal BC (GU-1354) and 2950-2350 cal BC (GU-1353) (Barclay, 1983, 133), in its main phase of use. A pit containing earlier Neolithic pottery was located nearby, adjacent to later ring-ditches and cut by one of them. The pit was radiocarbon dated to 3650-3100 cal BC (GU-1546) (*ibid*, 243).

The rescue excavation of a pit-defined site at Douglasmuir in Angus undertaken in 1979 and 1980 (Kendrick 1995) revealed it to be a complex palisaded enclosure associated with the cursus tradition (**6** Brophy below) (illus 5) radiocarbon dated to 3950-3350 cal BC (GU-1210), 4000-3350 cal BC (GU-1469 and GU-1470). In pits close by, an assemblage of early Neolithic pottery

Illus 5
The Neolithic enclosure at Douglasmuir, under excavation, from the north. (*Crown Copyright: Historic Scotland*)

was discovered. The excavation in 1989 of a burial mound at Beech Hill House, in Coupar Angus, close to the Cleaven Dyke, recovered Grooved Ware from a land surface buried beneath an early Bronze Age burial mound (Stevenson 1995).

This excavated material has been put in context, and our knowledge and understanding of the archaeology of eastern Perthshire transformed, by the publication of the RCAHMS surveys of north-east and south-east Perthshire respectively (RCAHMS 1990, 1994a), the Cleaven Dyke lying in the latter area. The discovery of four hitherto unknown chambered cairns, to the west in the Braes of Doune, has already been mentioned (RCAHMS 1994b).

More recently, there have been two further Historic Scotland-supported excavations on round mounds in Angus, at Fordhouse (Peterson & Proudfoot 1997) and Maryton Law (Dalland 1997); interestingly, both had been the victims of hitherto unrecorded 18th-century antiquarian trenching. The former site has produced evidence of a complex history, from Neolithic beginnings (burnt timber structures, a circular stone chamber set into the subsoil (unparalleled in the area) and a low earthen mound) a Bronze Age ring-bank, later filled in to form a mound, which was then coated with stone (cf North Mains), and secondary burials (Peterson pers comm).

Research excavation has continued to play a significant part in broadening our understanding of the period in the area. The main authors of this volume conducted an excavation on a possible Neolithic long mortuary enclosure within the Roman fortress at Inchtuthil (this chapter, below; Barclay & Maxwell 1991). The National Museums of Scotland project of survey and excavation at the stone quarry site at Creag na Caillich (Edmonds *et al* 1992) has provided valuable information on the processes and organisation of stone extraction for axe-head manufacture. Radiocarbon dating suggests the activity spanned the period 3030-2610 cal BC (GU-2976) to 2490-2040 (GU-2977). In addition, a radiocarbon date of 3500-3100 cal BC (GU-2975) was obtained for peat which formed on the site at a period of rapid (human-induced?) change–the latter suggested accelerated soil erosion, decline of elm and birch and increased evidence of fire. Trevor Cowie's recent survey of Neolithic pottery (1993) has provided a valuable and up-to-date review of material from Perthshire and Angus, as well as Fife and parts of Stirlingshire and West Lothian. As Cowie notes, Callander (1929) could point to only one assemblage in this area: now there are 30, although admittedly of considerably varying size. The paper also cites the only occurrence of earlier Neolithic pottery close to the Cleaven Dyke, at the fortress of Inchtuthil (Abercromby *et al* 1902; Cowie 1993, 32). The excavated sites already mentioned, Pitnacree and Croft Moraig, produced contemporary assemblages from further up the Tay. Cowie also discussed the date range associated with this material; the calibrated dates from the Cleaven Dyke and the nearby site at Littleour fall within the range of the currency of these styles.

In 1994 Richard Bradley carried out survey in upper Strathtay (Bradley 1994). Extensive arable fieldwalking, combined with survey of rock art in the area, recovered evidence of a quartz industry. The results provided a measure of support for interpretations of prehistoric rock art based on its siting in the landscape, but they also suggest that the more complex carvings may have followed, or even marked, the outer limits of the settled land.

THE ARCHAEOLOGY OF THE INCHTUTHIL PLATEAU

Although not specifically part of this project, the excavation of the long mortuary enclosure at nearby Inchtuthil in 1989 (Barclay & Maxwell 1991) must be considered here (illus 4), not least because it marked the origin of our joint interest in the Neolithic of east Perthshire. The passage of nine years has also served to enhance our appreciation of the context and significance of both the excavated structure and its setting.

The long mortuary enclosure occupies the summit of a low ridge situated near the centre of the Inchtuthil plateau, an isolated table of fluvio-glacial sands and gravels similar to, but less than half as extensive as, the ground traversed by the Cleaven Dyke. It is most unlikely that Neolithic use of such a desirable topographic niche, on well-drained soils beside the River Tay, would have been restricted to the construction of a single funerary structure, but the report on the extensive exploration of the 20ha Roman fortress which overlay the enclosure could point (Pitts & St Joseph 1985) to only two cinerary urns and a bronze axe as further evidence of pre-Iron Age activity on the site, although a single sherd of Neolithic pottery was found during Abercromby's work (Cowie 1993). Consideration of the cropmark evidence (Barclay & Maxwell 1991, illus 5; RCAHMS 1994a, 28-9) pinpointed two circles of pits near the SW corner of the fortress as possibly yet more indications of funerary or ritual practices in the Neolithic period, and indeed the case is additionally strengthened by the fact that pit-circles and Neolithic structures are known to be near neighbours at other sites in Perthshire (eg Leadketty in Strathearn, and Carsie Mains, a short distance to the north of Littleour; see below). Without excavation, such structures cannot be indubitably assigned to this early period, but the wide spacing and massive scale of the post-pits in the larger (16m diameter) pit-circle at Inchtuthil make the identification very attractive.

Moreover, detailed scrutiny of the accruing mass of aerial photographic material suggests that further candidates for consideration are not lacking - in addition, that is, to the random scatters of pits, the presence of which on a Roman legionary or Neolithic ritual/funerary site would be equally appropriate. The first, already noted in the fortress report (Pitts & St Joseph 1985, 261), but ascribed to the Iron Age, is an oblong enclosure measuring 32m by 16m and apparently defined by a narrow post-trench; aligned roughly E-W, it lies within the Roman labour camp to the west of the fortress, and its intermittent outline may be the result of disturbance occasioned by the Roman works. Attached to its southern side is a curvilinear annexe, which gives the composite structure a lobed appearance. Only a handful of such 'lobate' enclosures has so far been identified in the course of aerial survey in Scotland, and, as with other rectilinear ditched enclosures, it is not easy to decide whether they belong to the 3rd or 4th millennium BC or to the Early Historic period. Nevertheless, as well as certain structural affinities with known Neolithic monuments (for instance, dimensions, shape, and proportions), their tendency to display an E-W alignment means that the earlier context is perhaps more apposite.

There are, however, at least two other elongated subrectangular structures at Inchtuthil that merit closer inspection. The first, lying barely 15m SE of the larger pit-circle, is represented by intermittent cropmark traces (on CUCAP prints CDB59-60), showing an enclosure measuring 18m by 6m within a post-trench and aligned NE-SW. The second, lying c 100m NW of the SW angle of the fortress, is more faintly delineated (on CUCAP prints CDC13-14); it comprises two straight parallel ditches, set c 6m apart and extending for at least 15m on an E-W alignment; the west end appears to coincide with two large pits. Neither structure has been previously identified or discussed in print, but in the context of other features at Inchtuthil for which a Neolithic date has been proposed they deserve more than a passing mention. If of Neolithic origin, they may mark the sites of accompanying mortuary enclosures or even burial mounds of the same general class as those discussed in section **7.5** below, their presence amplifying the already impressive evidence for the area-grouping of such monuments by the Neolithic communities of the middle Tay.

1.2 THE PALAEOENVIRONMENTAL BACKGROUND: POLLEN STUDIES AT RAE LOCH

Kevin J Edwards & Graeme Whittington

Today the Strathmore area of Perthshire is a highly cultivated landscape. That part of the strath which lies between the southern edge of the Grampian hill mass and the River Isla, for which the town of Blairgowrie-Rattray provides a focus, is no exception. The area is floored by strata of Old Red Sandstone (ORS) age overlain for the most part by alluvium and gravels. Distributed to the west, south and east of Blairgowrie is a string of lochs and mires. Relatively little is known of the progress of the landscape of the area from its condition at the end of the last ice age to its current state. This means that the important prehistoric and historic exploitation of this area lacks any contemporary environmental context.

The existence of the lochs and mires does provide the potential to remedy this situation. Care has to be exercised as to the choice of site for any palaeoenvironmental investigation due to the disturbances of the sediments in the larger lochs resulting from the trawling for marl in the 18th century (Brodie 1796). One major palynological record is available for the area, based on a marshy area adjacent to Stormont Loch (Caseldine 1980). Unfortunately, there are no radiocarbon dates associated with that investigation. Dated sites in the wider area are those of North Mains, Strathallan (Hulme & Shirriffs 1985) and Carn Dubh, near Pitlochry (Tipping 1995), but they are too distant to be of practical use. Thus a new site was needed; Rae Loch, 4km north of the Cleaven Dyke, was chosen because of its small size, lack of marl-trawling and restricted catchment area.

METHODS

Rae Loch (NGR NO159446) measures 300m by 200m in size and is located 1.5km west of Blairgowrie at an altitude of 61m (illus 1). A core, 6m in length, was obtained with a Russian corer from the open waters of the loch. Water depth at the point of sampling was 1.8m. The sediment was visually unvarying detrital lake mud (gyttja) apart from the basal 0.11m which consisted of silty gyttja.

The sediments were sampled at every 40mm for assessment of organic carbon content (by loss-on-ignition [LOI], illus 6) and pre-treatment for pollen analysis. The latter was undertaken with NaOH, HF, HCl and acetolysis (Faegri & Iversen 1989). Samples were mounted unstained in silicone oil of viscosity 12,500 cSt.

Pollen and spore counts were undertaken to a minimum counting sum of 500 total land pollen (TLP). Over 100 pollen and spore taxa were

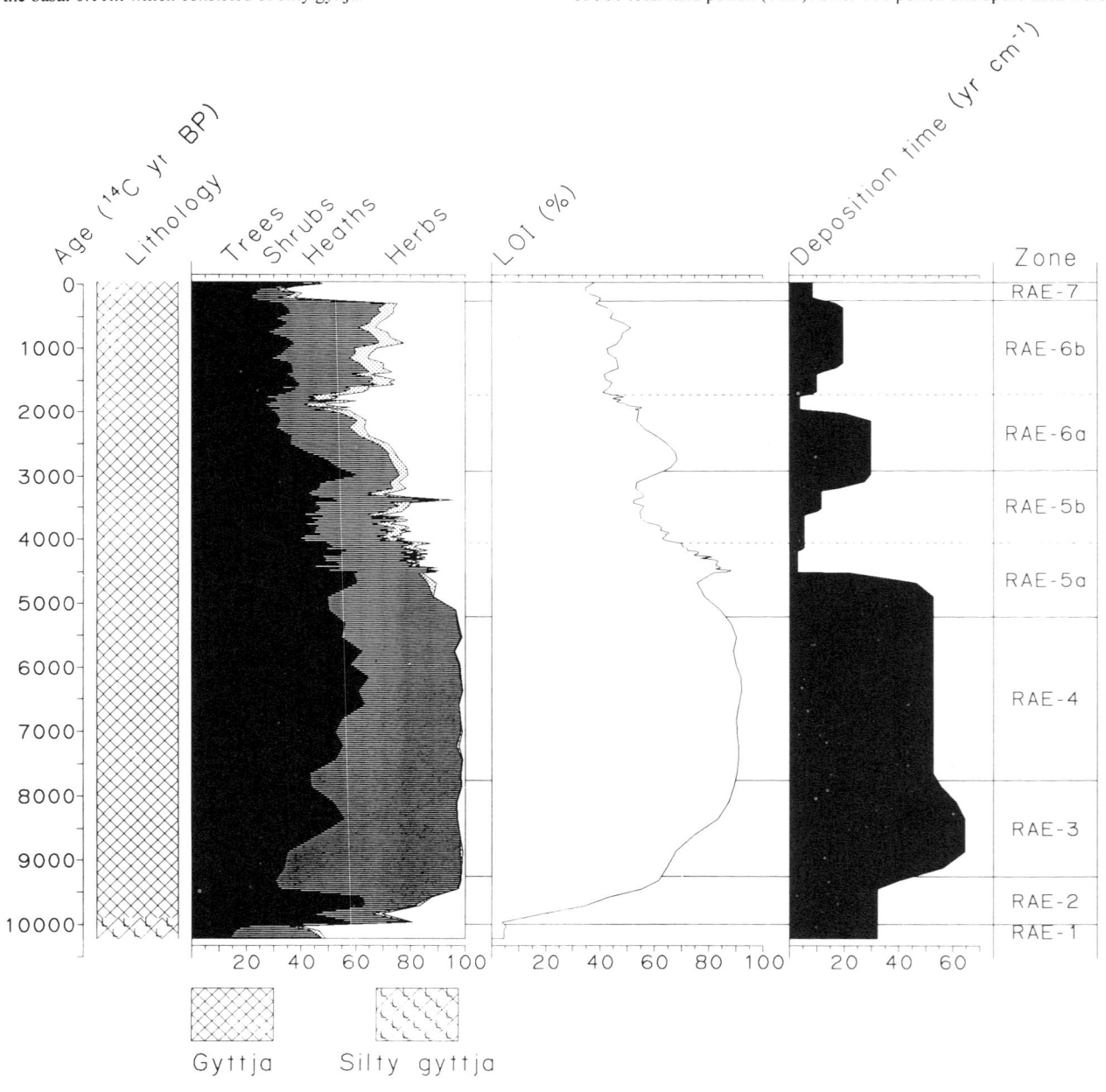

Illus 6
Summary pollen data, loss-on-ignition (LOI) and deposition time for the Rae Loch profile (y-axis=time).

THE PALAEOENVIRONMENTAL BACKGROUND ◆ 7

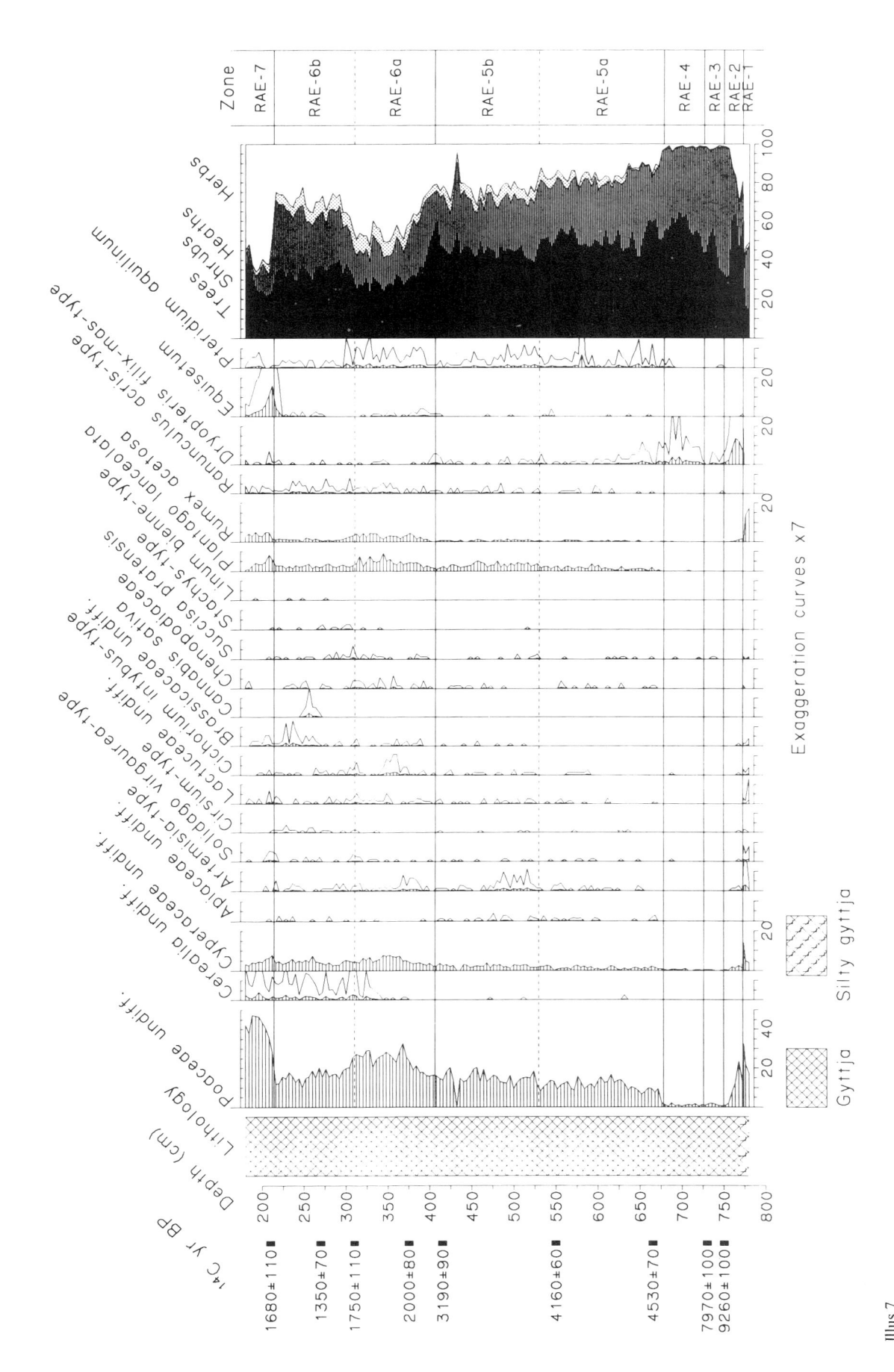

Illus 7
Selected percentage pollen and spore data from Rae Loch (y-axis=depth).

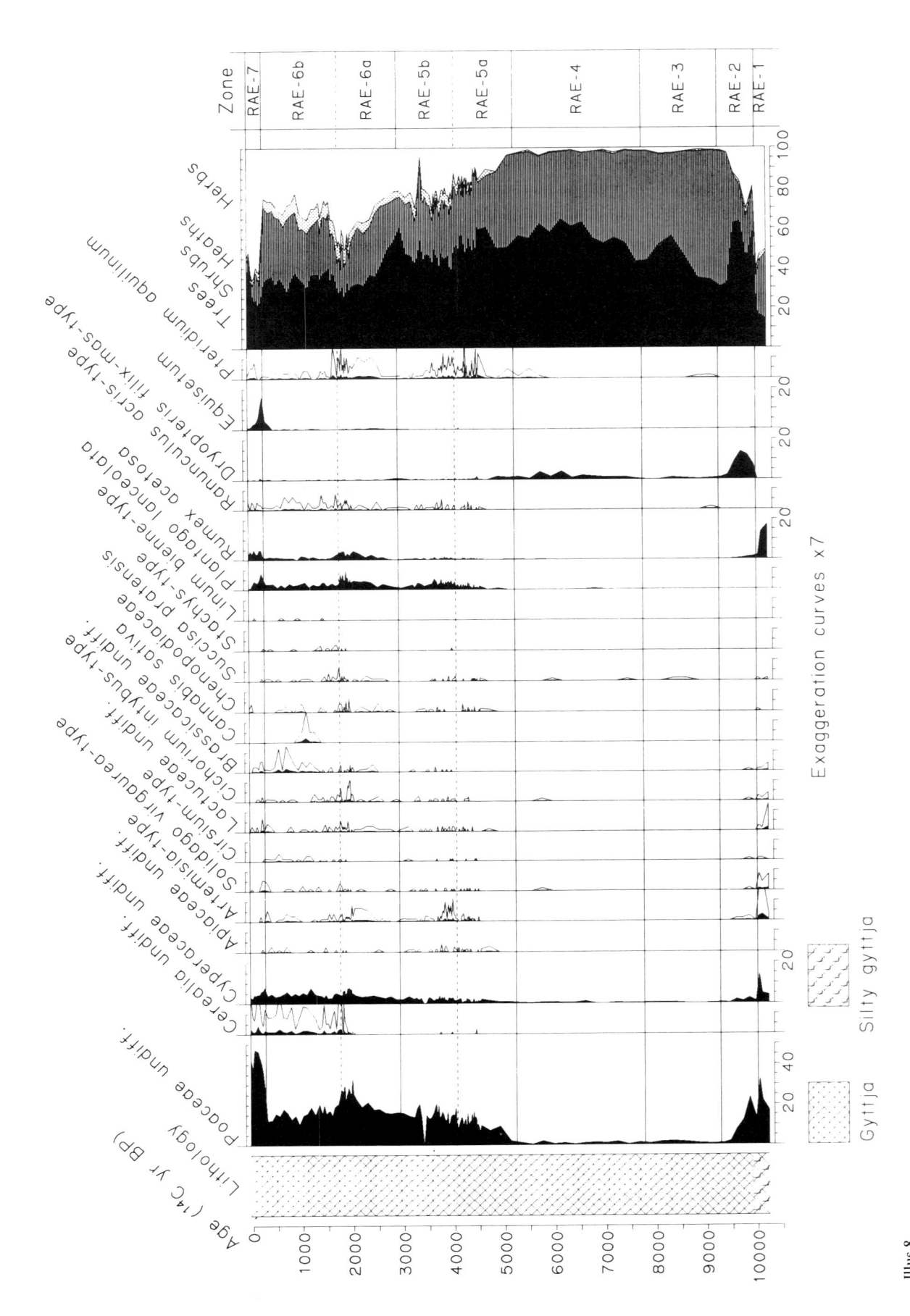

Illus 8
Selected percentage pollen and spore data from Rae Loch (y-axis=time in radiocarbon years).

recorded from the site, indicating its rich potential for reconstructing vegetational and environmental history. Pollen type and plant nomenclatures follow Bennett (1994) and Stace (1991) respectively. Microscopic charcoal was present in trace amounts only. The pollen diagrams presented here (illus 7 and 8) show selected taxa only. The diagrams are divided into seven local pollen assemblage zones (RAE-1–7, two of which are subzoned further). Computations and diagram construction were achieved using the computer programs TILIA and TILIA•GRAPH (Grimm 1991).

Laboratory Code	Depth below water surface (cm)	^{14}C (yr BP)
GU-4770	205-215	1680±110
GU-4769	265-275	1350±70
GU-4768	305-315	1750±110
GU-4767	370-380	2000±80
GU-4766	410-420	3190±90
GU-4765	445-455	3600±70
GU-4764	545-555	4160±60
GU-4763	660-670	4530±70
GU-4762	725-735	7970±100
GU-4761	745-755	9260±100
GU-4760	759-769	Insufficient carbon

Table 2
Radiocarbon dates for the Rae Loch deposits.

Ten radiocarbon (^{14}C) dates were obtained (table 2) which allowed the dating of critical events by means of the construction of a time-depth curve (illus 9). The uppermost date (1680±110 BP uncal) is 'reversed', a well-known phenomenon in loch sediments which have received erosional inputs containing old carbon from catchment soils (eg Edwards & Rowntree 1980). This date was ignored in constructing the time-depth curve and a date of AD 1700 is employed at that point in the profile (0.214m) where palynological evidence for agricultural improvements occurred. A date of 10,000 BP was assumed for the silty gyttja/gyttja interface, taken to be the Late-/Post-glacial boundary on bio- and litho-stratigraphic grounds. Estimated dates, based on straight-line extrapolation between ^{14}C dates, are presented in units of radiocarbon years before present (BP; where present = AD 1950), followed, for dates younger than 10,000 BP, by dendrochronologically calibrated dates (after Stuiver & Reimer 1993) in parentheses, expressed as calibrated years BC/AD. All dates are quoted to the nearest 10 years. A pollen diagram constructed with time as its vertical axis (illus 8; see illus 6) overcomes the compression imposed by slow sediment accumulation rates where depth is used for the y-axis (illus 7). This provides an alternative perspective on events, though temporal fidelity in illustration 8 is achieved at the expense of clarity in the upper part of the pollen profile, which now becomes compressed as a function of the increased sedimentation over the last 5000 radiocarbon years. Deposition time (^{14}C years per cm of deposit) is depicted in illustration 6; this is a reciprocal of deposition rate (cm of deposit per ^{14}C year).

VEGETATIONAL HISTORY

LATE-GLACIAL VEGETATION

Prior to an estimated date of 10,000 BP, the pollen spectra of zone RAE-1 are indicative of Late-glacial (Loch Lomond stadial) conditions. The dominance by willow (*Salix*), dock family (*Rumex* spp), sedges (*Cyperaceae*) and grasses (*Poaceae*), and the presence of *Koenigia islandica*, indicate the final climatic stage before the strong rise in temperature which occurred at the start of the Holocene (Post-glacial). At this time the landscape would have presented an open vista with probably no woodland presence, as the birch, shown in zone RAE-1, was probably of the dwarf variety (*Betula nana*). The basal silty gyttja has an organic content of about 5%; the soils around Rae Loch were clearly low in carbon content, bearing a strong signature of their glacial origin.

THE EARLY HOLOCENE IMMIGRATION AND SUBSEQUENT ESTABLISHMENT OF TREES AND SHRUBS (10,000-5220 BP)

The organic content of the sediments dating from an estimated 10,000 BP rose to 90% by 7750 BP (6520 cal BC). This reflection of soil development within the catchment was a natural consequence of the sudden climatic amelioration from the start of the Holocene, with temperatures at least as warm as those today within several decades of final deglaciation (Whittington & Edwards 1997). Increased summer temperatures enabled the immigration of warmth-loving trees and shrubs from further south (cf Birks 1989).

Thus, zone RAE-2 sees the arrival of birch (*Betula*) in the area. It is unlikely that the birch provided a completely closed canopy as zone RAE-2 also reveals strong representation of the shade-intolerant juniper (*Juniperus communis*), grasses (*Poaceae*) and the fern *Dryopteris filix-mas*-type. The Rae Loch site also conforms to the early Holocene vegetational history of Scotland in that this zone witnessed the eclipse of the dominant position held by birch in the pollen diagram due to the rapid rise of *Corylus avellana*-type (generally taken to have originated from hazel) from c 9650 BP (8950 cal BC). It is noticeable that, by the end of the zone, that taxon had obtained a level of 65% TLP. A further feature of note is the poor representation of Scots Pine (*Pinus sylvestris*) pollen, a situation which continued until very recent times. Zone RAE-1 showed a paucity of herbaceous taxa and, indeed, those already present, like grasses and docks, went into decline in RAE-2. This resulted from the closing of the canopy and the establishment of a more stable soil cover following upon the in-migration of *Corylus avellana*-type.

During zone RAE-3, hazel began to decrease in its representation as other tree species colonised the area. The greater warmth-demanding and slowly-migrating oak (*Quercus*) and elm (*Ulmus*) became established at 9260 BP (8310 cal BC) to be followed from 7760 BP (6540 cal BC) by alder (*Alnus glutinosa*). By this date the Blairgowrie area and the Isla floodplain would have presented a fully forested appearance, though the sporadic occurrences of ash (*Fraxinus excelsior*) indicate that some natural openings in woodland were

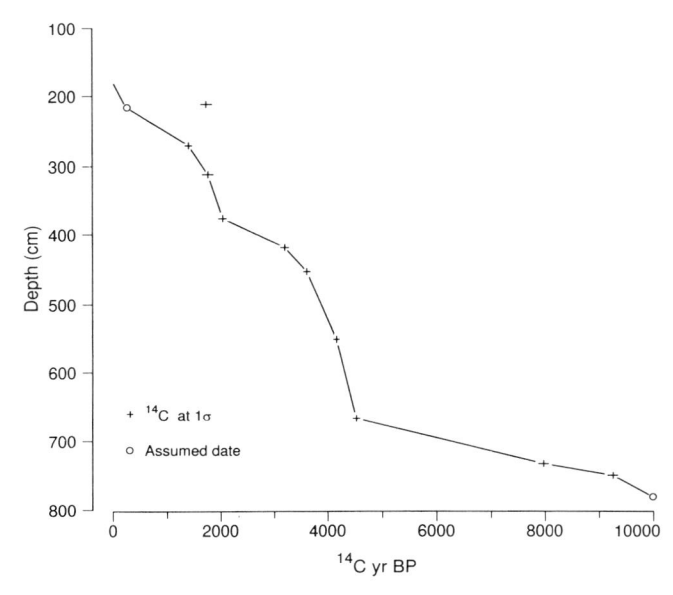

Illus 9
Time-depth curve for Rae Loch (note the by-passed 'reversed' date at the top of the profile).

available for ash to colonise. This situation continued during zone RAE-4. Over the period of this zone, birch and *Corylus avellana*-type had declined, the former reaching a stable condition, while the latter presented a more oscillatory pattern. In contrast, oak continued to expand and elm and alder remained steady.

The end of zone RAE-4 is dated to 5220 BP (4010 cal BC), thus almost 5000 radiocarbon years had elapsed since the first arboreal colonisation of any significance. A remarkable feature of this period is that less than 1m of sediment accumulated in the loch basin, giving an average rate of deposition of 0.019cm per ^{14}C year. This suggests that environmental disturbance in the area was minimal. It might be suggested, therefore, that, if there was a Mesolithic presence in the area, it was very subdued. The oscillations in the *Corylus avellana*-type curve might be construed as showing the effects of human exploitation of that taxon, but if this was so, it clearly had very little effect upon soil disturbance and thus sedimentation rates. This supposition is supported by the lack of microscopic charcoal throughout the Rae Loch profile. Burning, whether for clearance, browse-creation, or domestic purposes, is frequently linked to possible Mesolithic activities (cf Edwards 1996; Simmons 1996; Edwards & Whittington 1997). Additionally, the herbaceous component in pollen zones RAE-2 and 3 is poor. This is demonstrated by the dominance of trees and shrubs in the summary pollen curves (illus 6; 7; 8; 10); the pollen of grasses and sedges manages only a meagre showing.

Furthermore, there is no positive support for woodland management in the form of coppicing or leaf-foddering (Göransson 1986; Edwards 1993); nor is there any indication of possible pioneer farming as may be intimated by pre-elm decline cereal-type pollen (Edwards & Hirons 1984; Edwards & Whittington 1997). Such inferences may be thwarted by the cloaking effect of a strong woodland pollen component which could prevent herbaceous pollen and microscopic charcoal from reaching the sampling site. The probability also exists, however, that dense woodland would have been unfavourable to human activity.

WOODLAND REDUCTION, REGENERATION AND EQUILIBRIUM IN NEOLITHIC AND BRONZE AGE (c 5220-2920 BP)

It was in this period that the Cleaven Dyke was built. The start of zone RAE-5 marked a significant change to the landscape within Rae Loch's pollen catchment area. At 5220 BP (4010 cal BC) is recorded one of the most notable features of Scottish (and European) woodland history - a major and sudden collapse in the representation of elm pollen. This decline in elm at Rae Loch is also closely coincident with those for oak, hazel, pine and, a little later, alder and birch. While the fall in elm is, to all intents and purposes, a permanent phenomenon (it barely rises above 2% TLP for the next five millennia), the fortunes of the other woodland taxa recover and then experience further decreases through the remainder of zone RAE-5.

The widespread elm decline of c 5100 BP (3830 cal BC) has been ascribed to a variety of causes, singly or in combination, including disease, climate change, soil change and clearance for agriculture and leaf-foddering (Ten Hove 1968; Whittington *et al* 1991c; Tipping 1994a). There is no obvious indication that arable agriculture began c 5220 BP around Rae Loch, but the pollen of grasses, ribwort plantain (*Plantago lanceolata*), common sorrel (*Rumex acetosa*), cf buttercup (*Ranunculus acris*-type), heather (*Calluna vulgaris*) and the spores of bracken (*Pteridium aquilinum*) begin to expand from the start of subzone RAE-5a. This pattern strongly suggests that Neolithic pastoral activity was taking place in the vicinity of Rae Loch, but that woodland, bereft of elm, continued to dominate the landscape. The demise of elm and the slight expansion in heather may suggest that the sandy soils of the area were becoming podsolised. Could grazing on soils with thin organic surface horizons have led to the loss of those horizons, exposing mineral horizons to erosion from a combination of animals and sheetwash (LOI values exhibit a fall from this point on)? Sedimentation rates through most of subzone 5a increase to c 0.346cm per ^{14}C year. If animals were also being fed elm leaves and twigs, and if some arable activity was occurring in the catchment area, this may have provided conditions suitable for pathogenic attack brought by the elm bark beetle (cf Girling & Greig 1985). Whatever the cause, once elm had been reduced, the existence of increasingly eroded or podsolised substrates could have prevented its regeneration (cf Sturludottir & Turner 1985). The similar, though more muted, decline in pine might suggest that, if it were local, it had been growing on the sandy soils now being given over to grazing.

Cereal-type pollen appears first at an estimated date of 4420 BP (3040 cal BC). The low and local dispersal of cereal pollen means that its initial presence in the pollen diagram need not be a certain indication of the date of adoption of arable activity. Indeed, many herbaceous taxa frequently found as weed flora in arable and pastoral habitats become consistently present within zone RAE-5a. These include mugwort (*Artemisia*-type), goosefoot family (*Chenopodiaceae*), cabbage family (*Brassicaceae*), carrot family (*Apiaceae*) and the dandelion group (*Cichorium intybus*-type), as well as the previously noted pollen of such taxa as grasses and plantain, and the spores of bracken.

A pattern of woodland dominance, accompanied by a consistent representation of taxa indicating the existence of some open land, continues into subzone RAE-5b. The drop in the percentage of tree pollen from about 80% to 67% TLP near the 5a/b boundary, c 4050 BP (2510 cal BC), suggests that an extension of the cleared land was continuing. It may be the case that subzone 5b is largely reflecting landscape impacts of early and middle Bronze Age peoples–a typical feature in Scottish pollen records (Edwards & Whittington 1997).

Throughout the period to 2920 BP (1120 cal BC), there are only sporadic recordings of cereal pollen and the ribwort plantain profile shows varying but rather low percentages. These features might lead us to question whether the area around Rae Loch was only farmed at low intensity up to 2920 BP (the end of subzone 5b) or, at least, to wonder about the extent to which the farming was of an arable nature. The sedimentation rate in the loch indicates that a period of major soil disturbance was occurring and LOI values continue to fall. The strong presence of trees, along with an apparent paucity of evidence for a well-developed arable, and indeed pastoral, farming system and a high sedimentation rate, cannot be construed as a lack of human activity over this long time-span. Unless there are special pollen dispersal considerations which might be thought to have been occurring at Rae Loch, the pollen evidence might be reflecting a pervasive, though 'hidden' practice of forest farming, in which openings in the woodland are cultivated and then used for pastoral activity (Edwards 1993; Göransson 1986). The generally steady percentage values for the trees may indicate that they have reached an equilibrium within a managed system, untroubled by natural competitive pressures. The demise and lack of recovery in the elm pollen record could also be in accord with this development, as the use of elm foliage as cattle fodder is a well-established feature of European agriculture–did this stop the flowering of elm, or did elm simply not flourish on the increasingly poor sandy soils?

WOODLAND REDUCTION AND THE EXPANSION OF FARMING IN LATE BRONZE AGE, IRON AGE AND ROMAN TIMES (c 2920-1740 BP)

The boundary area between zones RAE-5b and 6 exhibits a decline in sedimentation, a rise in LOI values and an apparent expansion in oak woodland. There may well have been a temporary lull in human activities which enabled the landscape to 'recover'. Most of subzone 6a sees a renewed fall in arboreal pollen taxa which spans the late Bronze Age, Iron Age and early Roman periods (2920-1740 BP [1120 cal BC-cal AD 280]). This does not accord with the increased erosion that occurs until 2000 BP (cal AD 10), or sometime thereafter. After that time, the organic content of the loch deposits falls once again, which could be a function of further impoverishment of the carbon-poor soils. Subzone 6a features expansions in grasses, sedges, plantain, sorrel and bracken, with cereal-type not much in evidence until the closing stages. On the available evidence, it seems that an extension in pastoral activity could be occurring and this may have reduced soil erosion until the recommencement of mixed farming during the Roman/Early Historic period, c 1990 BP (cal AD 20), when cereal pollen is again present. It would be necessary to conclude from this that the Rae Loch area, or at least the area beyond its immediate environs, did not witness the upsurge in arable agriculture that most other areas in Scotland experienced during the Iron Age. That seems unlikely and is perhaps due to the very local, and still heavily extant wooded picture associated with the Rae Loch site.

It would seem, however, that enhanced soil erosion was a feature of the loch's catchment area once arable cultivation again became part of the farming regime from around 1990 BP (covering at least the period 90 cal BC–cal AD 130 at one standard deviation if a precision of 100 ^{14}C years is assumed). This could embrace either the end of the late Iron Age or the start of the Roman period. That this area was one of intense Roman activity is borne out by the legionary fortress at Inchtuthil, the major monument of the Flavian period (c AD 84-7) and located only 5.5km to the SW of Rae Loch. It provides an early example of large-scale, timber-intensive construction of military works, the introduction of which might conceivably have contributed to the continuing decline in the oak tree component of the woodland, well-marked in subzone RAE-6a. The decline in the woodland cover of the area continued until c 1740 BP (cal AD 280).

POST 1740 BP

The largely unvaried nature of the pollen record until the close of the period c 1740-250 BP suggests that population pressure in this part of Strathmore for most of the centuries AD was never excessive and could well have been at a lower level than during the late Iron Age and Roman periods.

Although the site provided environmental evidence up to the present day, it was not felt appropriate to discuss it in any detail here.

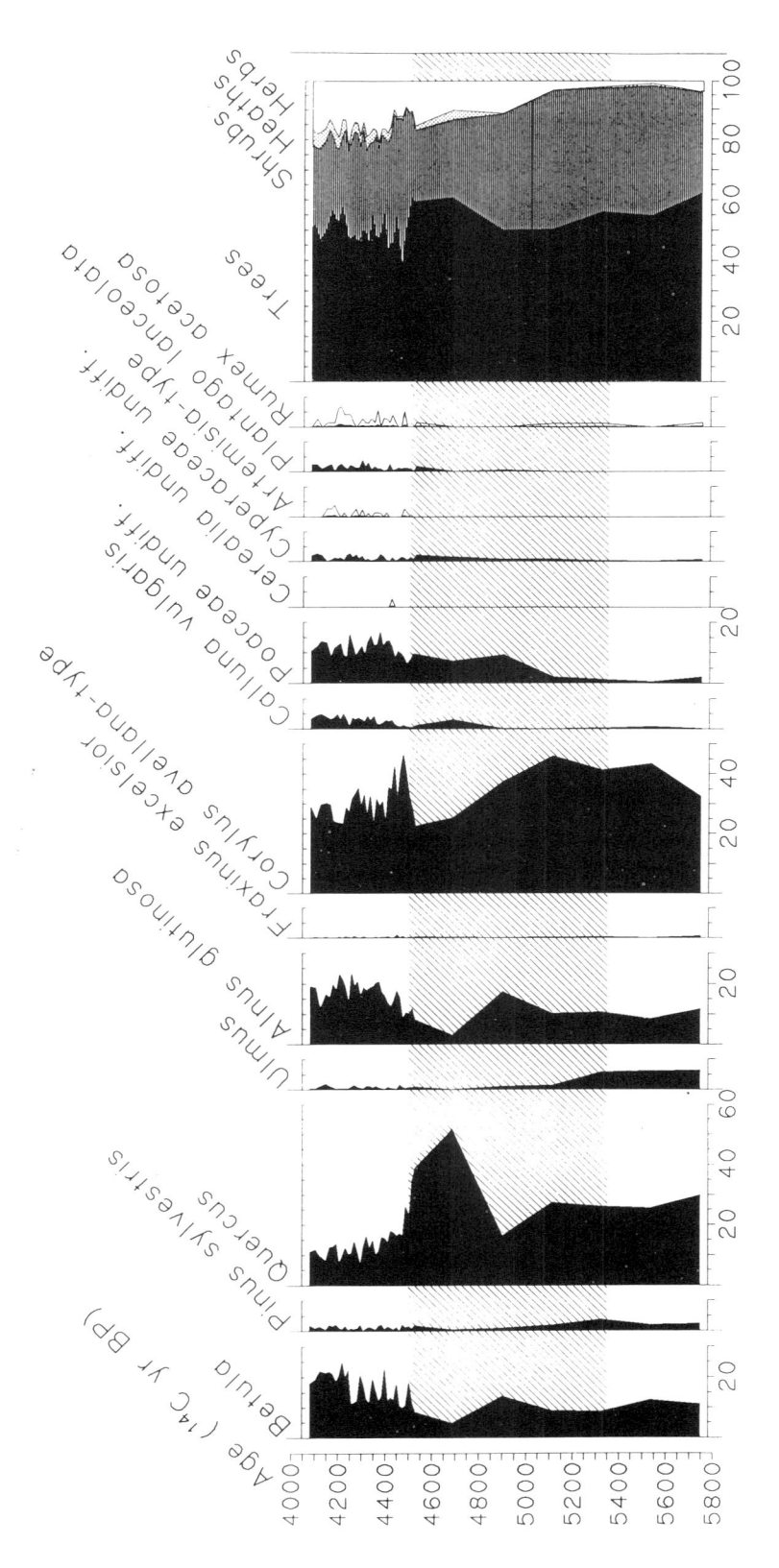

Illus 10
Selected percentage pollen taxa from Rae Loch for the period 5750-4100 BP.

DISCUSSION AND CONCLUSIONS

The palynological record at Rae Loch provides a detailed statement on vegetational development for the complete period of the Holocene. The timing of the arrival of the major woodland components in the area can be established, providing an important corrective to the isopollen maps developed by Huntley and Birks (1983) (the construction of which was severely hampered by the lack of dated pollen diagrams at that time for the central and eastern lowlands of Scotland). According to the maps, hazel arrived at c 9000 BP (8030 cal BC), yet it is clear that hazel was established at Rae Loch by 9650 BP (8950 cal BC). The maps indicated that oak and elm had only achieved values of 2-5% TLP in the west of Strathmore by around 8000 BP (6840 cal BC), but the Rae Loch record shows that both taxa were established by 8620 BP (7580 cal BC). Throughout Britain, the establishment of alder is a very varied chronological event. For example, two sites in Fife, Black Loch and Pickletillem, lying about 50km apart, have dates for this event of 7300 BP (6090 cal BC) and 6605 BP (5520 cal BC) (Whittington *et al* 1991a, 1991b). The date of 7650 BP (6460 cal BC) for Rae Loch not only adds to these variations but also establishes a very early record compared to one of c 6500 BP (5440 cal BC) predicted by the isopollen maps. The sheltered, inland situation of western Strathmore and its sandy substrates lead to rapid soil warming in the spring and the maintenance of high levels of accumulated temperature conducive to the growth of trees which prefer higher temperatures.

That human activities have had a recognisable effect on the vegetation of the Blairgowrie area was indicated by the investigations at Stormont Loch (Caseldine 1980), and the Rae Loch study has not only confirmed this but also put them into a chronological framework. There is little or no sign of any Mesolithic activity in the area. At the time of the major elm decline, after c 5220 BP at Rae Loch, not only are other tree types reduced, but pastoral activity seems to be indicated and an inference of podsolisation is also made. It is not until 800 ^{14}C years later that cereal-type pollen appears in the fossil record. We should not place too much reliance, however, on the sparse incidence of such pollen grains; open land indicators were already frequent and soil erosion was evident from increased sedimentation at, or after, a date of 4530±70 BP (3360-3090 cal BC). Such soil instability could have resulted from the grazing on and damage to thin sandy soils. The lack of elm regeneration could have been due to soil impoverishment, as could the fall in representation of pine pollen.

Evidence to be cited by the excavators (**3.1** below) suggests that one area of the bank of the Cleaven Dyke in the area of burnt context F5 was possibly constructed between the late 5th to mid/late 4th millennium cal BC. This might be taken to approximate the period 5350-4500 radiocarbon years BP, which would correspond to the shaded area in pollen diagram illustration 10. As we have seen, the pollen record for this interval around Rae Loch is indicative of woodland reduction, possible incipient soil podsolisation, and woodland regeneration. Even in a record rendered mute by the dominance of arboreal taxa in the pollen profile, it is apparent that clearance could have been occurring in the Rae Loch area. It may be noted that the soil pollen record from beneath the Cleaven Dyke (**2.5** below) brought forward the suggestion from us that the bank was constructed in post-elm decline times, that birch and hazel formed a regenerated woodland community in the area, and that some podsolisation with a heather cover was evident. Pine pollen was also insignificant in the soil pollen spectra. All of this exhibits a similarity to early to mid Neolithic events at Rae Loch; the only marked difference is that oak was clearly an important taxon around the loch, whereas its pollen was absent in the palaeosols at Cleaven Dyke.

The Rae Loch pollen profile suggests that prehistoric activity was undertaken in an environment which continued to be heavily wooded right up to c 2920 BP (1120 cal BC), but that the late Iron Age and Roman periods witnessed considerable farming activity, including that of an arable nature.

THE SURVEY AND EXCAVATION OF THE CLEAVEN DYKE

'Great part of the information obtained ... is contradictory, a still greater part false, and by far the greatest part is of a doubtful character.' von Clausewitz, *On War*, 1832, chapter vi (tr JJ Graham 1908).

2.1 THE HISTORY OF THE INVESTIGATION OF THE CLEAVEN DYKE

The Cleaven Dyke lies on a plateau (illus 1) which is part of an extensive deposit of fluvio-glacial sands and gravels covering much of the area between Blairgowrie and Cupar Angus, in the broad valley known as Strathmore. The gravels are cut by the rivers Tay and Isla and the Lunan Burn, which define the western, southern and eastern edges of the plateau; the northern boundary is formed by the steep valley of an unnamed burn, running westwards to the Tay. The upstanding portion of the Cleaven Dyke runs from NO 1566 4086 to NO 1725 4000.

THE MONUMENT: AN INTRODUCTORY VIEW

The history of the study of the Dyke will make more sense to the reader if the information available from recent fieldwork is presented in summary now, so that previous observations can be considered in context.

The Cleaven Dyke comprises, first, a pair of ditches between 38m and 50m apart (consistently broader near the NW end). The breadth of the ditches is difficult to assess accurately; in many places tracks (of vehicles and possibly cattle) have been formed within them, causing damage and distortion. Where excavated, the width was between 1.5m and 5m. Roughly centrally between the ditches lies a bank (illus 11), varying between 7m and 15m across, and up to *c* 1.7m high (these dimensions excluding the swollen NW terminal). The bank of the Dyke survives as an upstanding earthwork for almost exactly 1800m, mainly in woodland, now partly cleared. The modern contour survey suggests that it terminates at the NW a few metres beyond the boundary fence of the wood; it is argued below that the NW terminal is formed by an oval mound with an E-W axis, to which are attached, first, a long barrow, and then the long bank of the Dyke.

The northern ditch survives in woodland for 20m more than the southern ditch, at the SE end of the wood. To the SE of the upstanding portion of the Dyke the ditches have been detected on aerial photographs in arable fields for a

Illus 11
View of the area of the Cleaven Dyke cleared of trees in 1996, from segment-boundary A10 looking towards the SE end of Section **A**.

further *c* 380m. A *c* 240m length of the bank was visible in the arable field at the time of the first-edition Ordnance Survey map (surveyed 1864, published 1867); a similar length is now visible as both a cropmark and a soil mark. The ditches are visible for rather longer, rising to the low hill on which we believe the Dyke ends. There is no evidence that the monument continued further to the SE. It has been suggested that the Dyke continued beyond both known terminals, and some evidence has been advanced for the extension to the NW; however, it is argued below that the Dyke **does not** continue further, at either end.

There are now four breaks in the line of the bank, all of which seem to be original, at the points marked **W, X, Y** and **Z** on illustration 23. There is evidence that the ditches are causewayed at **W, X** and **Y**, as well as at other points. For the whole period for which map information is available, the greater part of the length of the Cleaven Dyke is shown as lying within woodland.

THE CLEAVEN DYKE'S MORE RECENT PAST

18TH- AND 19TH-CENTURY REFERENCES

References are given in order of date of publication.

1772

Pennant, who has sometimes rather unfairly been credited with the first mention of the Dyke, in his *Tour of Scotland* 1772 (Pennant 1776), provided the vehicle for an account of the Dyke by a local man, Thomas Marshall, which influenced every interpretation until Abercromby (Marshall 1776, 452). The account, like many since, is short on description and long on interpretation:

> 'The Romans profited of the commodious accident of the two rivers, the Tay and the Illa [Isla], which unite at a certain distance below. These formed two secure fences: the Romans made a third wall of great thickness, defended again by a ditch both on the inside and the outside. These extend three miles in a line from the Tay to the Illa, leaving within a vast space, in form of a delta ... I must note that the wall is styled the Cleaving wall.'

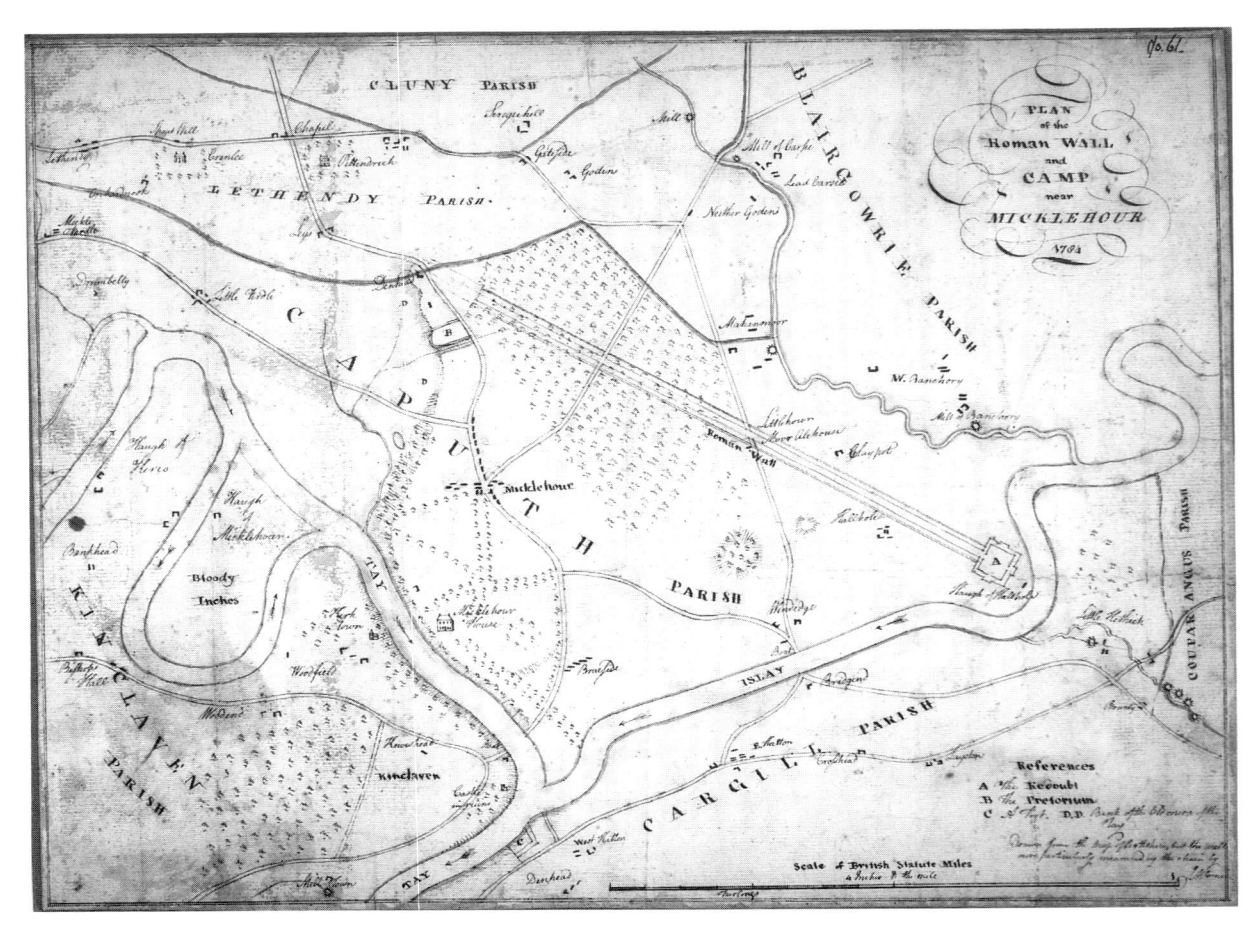

Illus 12
McOmie's map of 1784. (*Crown Copyright: RCAHMS*)

1783

Stobie's relatively small-scale depiction of the Dyke in his map seems surprisingly familiar (Stobie 1783). The size of the wood within which it was preserved 200 years ago has changed little, except at the NW end of the Dyke. The map is, however, at too small a scale for the Dyke to be shown other than as very stylised; in general the representation is similar to McOmie's larger scale mapping.

1784

McOmie's plan of 'the Roman Wall and Camp at Mickleour' (illus 12) (McOmie 1784) is the first reasonably large-scale representation of the Dyke, but even so, it is marked as a ruler-straight feature, connected to the supposedly Roman 'Redoubt' (now interpreted as a burial mound of the Early Historic period (RCAHMS 1994a)). The plan, which is the first to attempt a portrayal of the ditches as well as the bank, should be considered only as a stylised depiction rather than a source of trustworthy archaeological evidence.

1797

The description in the Old Statistical Account of Scotland adds little to that provided by Marshall, apart from some rough dimensions: 'Here the Romans raised a wall of earth, about 24 feet thick, (for it is difficult to ascertain the exact measurement,) defended by a ditch on each side, 60 feet distant from the wall.'

1831

Knox provided a description of the Dyke, taking it, as had Marshall before him, to be one rampart of a vast Roman fortification utilising the Tay and Isla as natural barriers (Knox 1831, 63-4). He suggested that because of the relationship between the Isla and the Tay '... it was only necessary to throw up an intrenchment in front, or on the north side of the camp: accordingly a rampart ... extends from the Isla to the old course of the Tay'. The map is once again at a very small scale and the representation of the Dyke owes much to Stobie and/or McOmie.

1864

The first edition Ordnance Survey 1:10,560 map and 1:2500 plan were surveyed in 1864 by Lt Col Bayly, and published in 1867. Within the woodland the Dyke is once again depicted, at both scales, as a largely rectilinear monument, although minor variations of bulk and alignment are detectable at the larger scale. The Dyke is shown as terminating in the NW at the boundary of the wood, more or less as it does today; the northern ditch is, however, shown as carrying on to the fence, which is not what modern survey indicates (fold-out illus 98). At the SE end, both maps contain important information, surprisingly not referred to by any writer before now (fold-out illus 99). In 1864 the bank survived as a surveyable feature for 240m beyond the end of the wood, into what is now arable land, reflecting almost exactly the evidence provided by modern aerial photography and confirming the minor change of alignment (and possibly a swelling of the bank) in the last 100m. Nor is this the only respect in which the survey materially enhances the interpretation of modern aerial photography; on the south side of the Meikleour to Coupar Angus road, which runs across the low hill where the Dyke probably terminates, an active gravel quarry is depicted. The irregular scar of this feature (which has disappeared by the time of the second edition map) appears as a vegetation mark on modern oblique aerial photographs, and has previously been interpreted as a geological feature (Sharpe 1996) or as a Dyke-related feature. The quarry would effectively have removed any continuation of the Dyke on the south side of the summit of the hill. However, as has been mentioned already, no trace of the monument has been found beyond this hill, despite very intense aerial survey in recent decades (Pitts & St Joseph 1985).

The second edition of the 1:2500 plan (1901) contains less information. On the southern of the two map sheets the northern ditch and bank are not depicted at all, although this is probably the result of a transcription error. The bank extending into the arable field is no longer shown, the boundary of the wood where the Dyke leaves it has changed (to its modern line), new field boundaries have been inserted, and the site of the gravel quarry has been filled in and its site is under the plough.

20TH-CENTURY ACCOUNTS

The first recorded excavations on the Dyke were undertaken by Abercromby during the work, sponsored by the Society of Antiquaries of Scotland, on the Roman fortress at Inchtuthil in 1901 (Abercromby *et al* 1902). His description betrays an assumption that the monument is of Roman date: 'the rampart and ditches run in a perfectly straight line and parallel to each other through the whole length of the Dyke'. Abercromby was the first to note, to the east of the Blairgowrie road, 'the remains of a circular rampart with a ditch outside, about 90 yards in diameter over all' which 'intersects the northern ditch of the Cleven [sic] Dyke'. He also noted the presence here of a deliberately constructed break in the bank of the Dyke (that marked at **Y** on illustration 23). Three cross-sections were cut, at least one (and possibly two) in Section **A** and another probably in Section **C** or **D**. All told the same structural tale: the central bank was composed mainly of sand and gravel revetted externally with a clayey material. Unfortunately, no excavation archive has survived, but although only featureless profiles were published, they are sufficiently clear to indicate that the excavators had recognised the bank's

Illus 13
Photograph showing the location of Richmond's two cross-section and single axial trenches (1939) at the SE end of Section B of the bank of the Cleaven Dyke, looking across the main Perth to Blairgowrie road. (*Crown Copyright: RCAHMS; Ian Richmond Collection*)

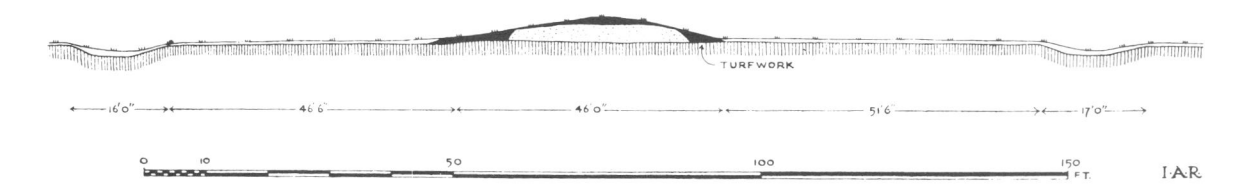

Illus 14
The idealised cross-section drawing of the Cleaven Dyke published by Richmond (1940).

Illus 15
A view of one of the cross-sections through the Cleaven Dyke cut by Richmond. The pattern of deposits closely resembles that recorded in the 1993 cross-section.
(*Crown Copyright: RCAHMS; Ian Richmond Collection*)

varying breadth and profile: in particular the predominant slightness of the SE portion (shown as 7m, compared with at least 10m in the middle portion), and the patently asymmetrical profile in the NW cutting.

Richmond undertook excavations on the Dyke in 1939 (Richmond 1940), once again with the financial support of the Society of Antiquaries of Scotland. He too cut three cross-sections through the bank of the Dyke but provided a written account of the location of only one of them, an axial section cut at the butt of the bank on the west side of the gap at the Perth–Blairgowrie road. The section proved that the turf-toeing of the bank, first noticed by Abercromby, continued round the butt-end, implying the break was deliberately constructed, rather than merely truncated by the building of the road. Unpublished photographs in the National Monuments Record of Scotland (NMRS) show details and general views of this and the other two trenches. From these photographs (particularly PT/6345; illus 13) it can be seen that these two cross-sections of the bank were cut through the bank immediately to the west of the main Perth to Blairgowrie road, just to the west of the axial trench. The approximate locations of the trenches, taken in part from recent observations on the Dyke, are marked on the fold-out plan (illus 99). There is no evidence that any ditch sections were cut. No detailed section drawings were published and no field drawings have been located. Only an idealised interpretation was published (Richmond 1940, fig 2), reproduced here for comparison (illus 14), rather than a record of the stratigraphy recorded in photograph PT/6344 of trench 2, in the NMRS collection (illus 15).

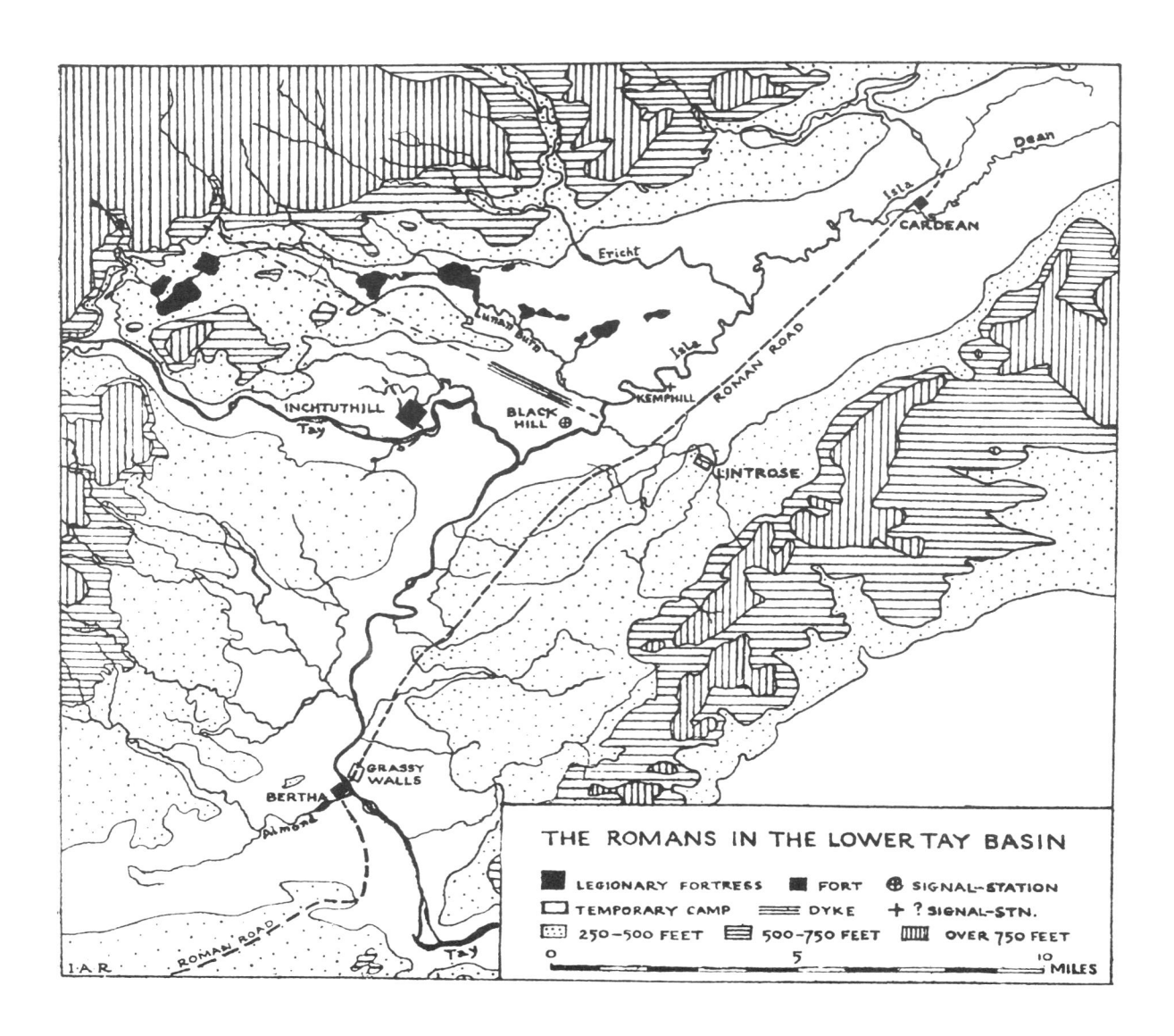

Illus 16
The hypothetical original course and extent of the Cleaven Dyke, as proposed by Richmond (1940).

Although he had explored the possibility of an origin in later or earlier periods, Richmond vigorously promoted the Roman interpretation of the Dyke in his paper, suggesting that it was a *limes* or political boundary related to the fortress at Inchtuthil, running some 14.5km from the Isla to the foothills of the Grampian mountains (Richmond 1940, fig 3; illus 16). The basis of evidence upon which the complex argument rested was, however, mainly circumstantial, depending on an assumed similarity between the Dyke and the Vallum of Hadrian's Wall, and an unsubstantiated claim about its original extent. Crawford (1949, 74-5) accepted the identification, but doubted that it had originally extended much beyond its current limits; for decades the Dyke continued to be seen in this light, Richmond even surmising in a later appreciation (Collingwood & Richmond 1969, 73) that its purpose might have been 'to mark the *prata legionis* or legionary grazing grounds'. This possibility was accepted as late as 1986 (Keppie 1986, 163). Nevertheless, the accumulating weight of aerial photographic material was now making it difficult to persevere with this categorisation, and already Maxwell (1983a), in a review of the results of aerial survey in Scotland, had drawn attention to the irregularity of the Dyke's ditches as they appeared in cropmark form at the SE end; such an appearance, contrasting sharply with the general clear-cut rectilinearity of Roman military ditches, found its clearest analogue in the segmentary alignments and perimeters of Neolithic structures. This view was shared by Pitts and St Joseph; their report on the excavations undertaken between 1952 and 1965 by Richmond and St Joseph on the Roman legionary complex at Inchtuthil (Pitts & St Joseph 1985) included the Cleaven Dyke in their discussion of the context of the Roman fortress. They concluded that the monument was unlikely to be of Roman date, refuting in detail the argument advanced by Richmond; the reasons given for this reinterpretation were: 1) the Dyke did not close the gap between the Isla and the hills (as Richmond - and earlier authors - had asserted); 2) a unit as powerful as the garrison of Inchtuthil would have had nothing to gain from the construction of such a line of demarcation; 3) the ditches of the Dyke are irregular in line, and shallow and flat-bottomed with gently sloping sides, unlike Roman military ditches; and 4) the use of turf in the construction need not imply a Roman date. They drew parallels instead with cursus monuments.

In 1986 there appeared the final report on a limited excavation undertaken in 1975 by Helen Adamson for

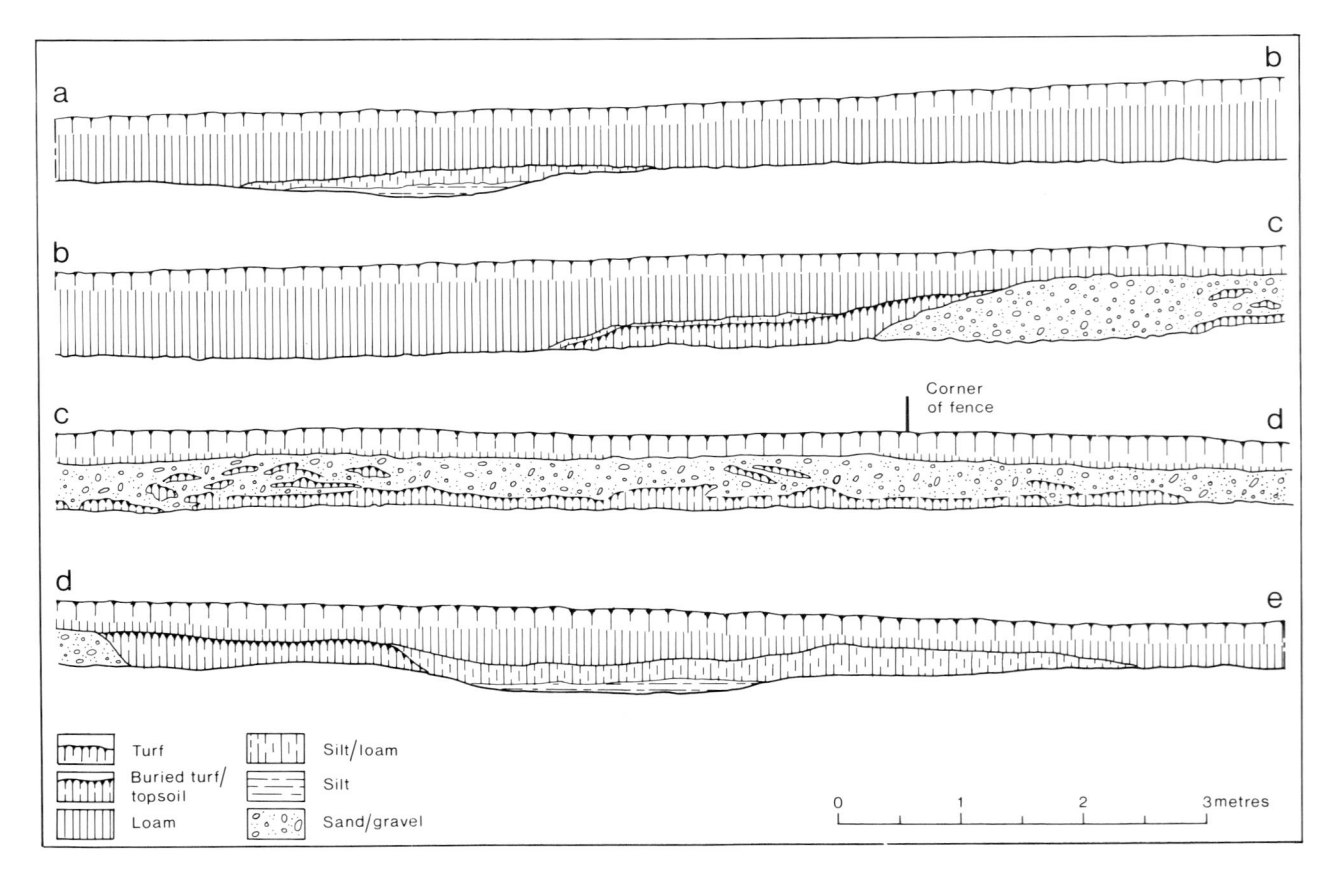

Illus 17
Adamson's section through the Cleaven Dyke, redrawn from the site archive. The soil descriptions, expressed using our conventions, are approximations, based on the authors' own experience on the Dyke.

Historic Scotland's predecessor department. Adamson's work was limited to a long narrow trench cutting NE-SW across the projected line of the Dyke, 3m beyond the boundary fence of the wood at the NW terminal of the Dyke.

She found that the gravel core of the bank was 13.5m across (illus 17). The turf revetment of the gravel had a footprint 2.7m wide on the north side and 2.4m wide on the south side. Adamson also detected to the north of the bank a shallow ditch some 2.5m wide and a maximum of 0.25m deep. Immediately to the south of the bank she recorded a very shallow feature 0.25m deep.

The bank was 18.9m wide in total and survived to a maximum height of 0.5m. What was almost certainly a buried old land surface survived below the bank; it was c 9.5m wide, and Adamson suggested that this had approximated to the original width of the bank at this point; the broadening of the bank within the arable field was interpreted as spread. However, both turf revetments appear to be in their original relationship to the gravel core. We would suggest therefore that the width of the gravel core is relatively unchanged and that the turf revetments may have spread only a little. Adamson interpreted the broadening of the bank within the wood, immediately to the west, as possibly being the result of dumping material during a hypothetical flattening of the mound in the arable field.

Unfortunately, in the illustrations for the final publication, the location of the trench (together with the features it contained) was accidentally transposed c 8.5m to the north, and the width of the trench was given as 3m, rather than 1m (its true dimension over most of its length); the final text seems to have been written with this plan in mind, which had a significant effect on the final published interpretation of the NW terminal of the Dyke. In particular, important (and accurate) observations and interpretations put forward in an interim report (Adamson 1979) were omitted from the final text. Illustrations 18 and 19 are, respectively, figure 3 in Adamson's report, and a plan showing the accurate location of the trench in relation to the recently completed contour plan. The revised trench location is confirmed by the published plan in the interim report, a 1:2500 plan in the site archive and an annotated diagram in the site notebook (NMRS MS/858/6).

In illustration 18 the bank is shown as continuing on the same line as in the adjacent wood. The result is that the northern ditch that Adamson detected appears to be 10m north of the upstanding adjacent bank, and the southern ditch lies immediately to its south. However, the relocation of the trench and the features it contained to their correct location makes the relationship clear: in the interim report Adamson specifically noted that the mound she detected was not on the line of the adjacent upstanding bank, as is shown, erroneously, in illustration 18.

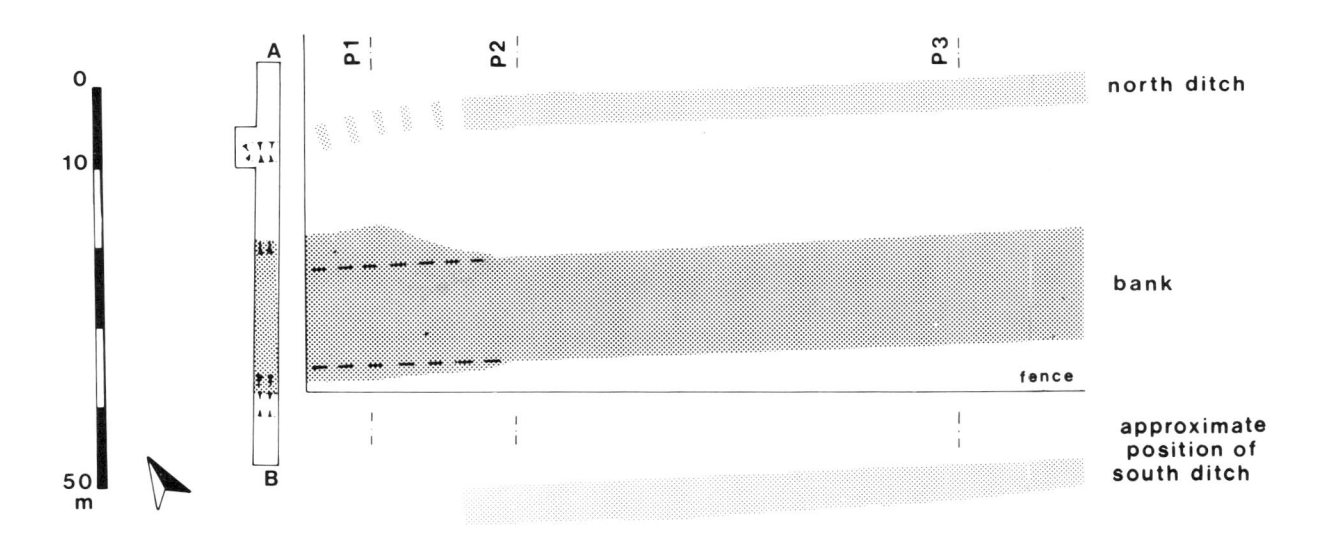

Illus 18
The plan of the Cleaven Dyke published as figure 3 by Adamson & Gallagher (1986). The trench is mislocated c 8.5m to the north and is shown as 3m wide, rather than 1m.

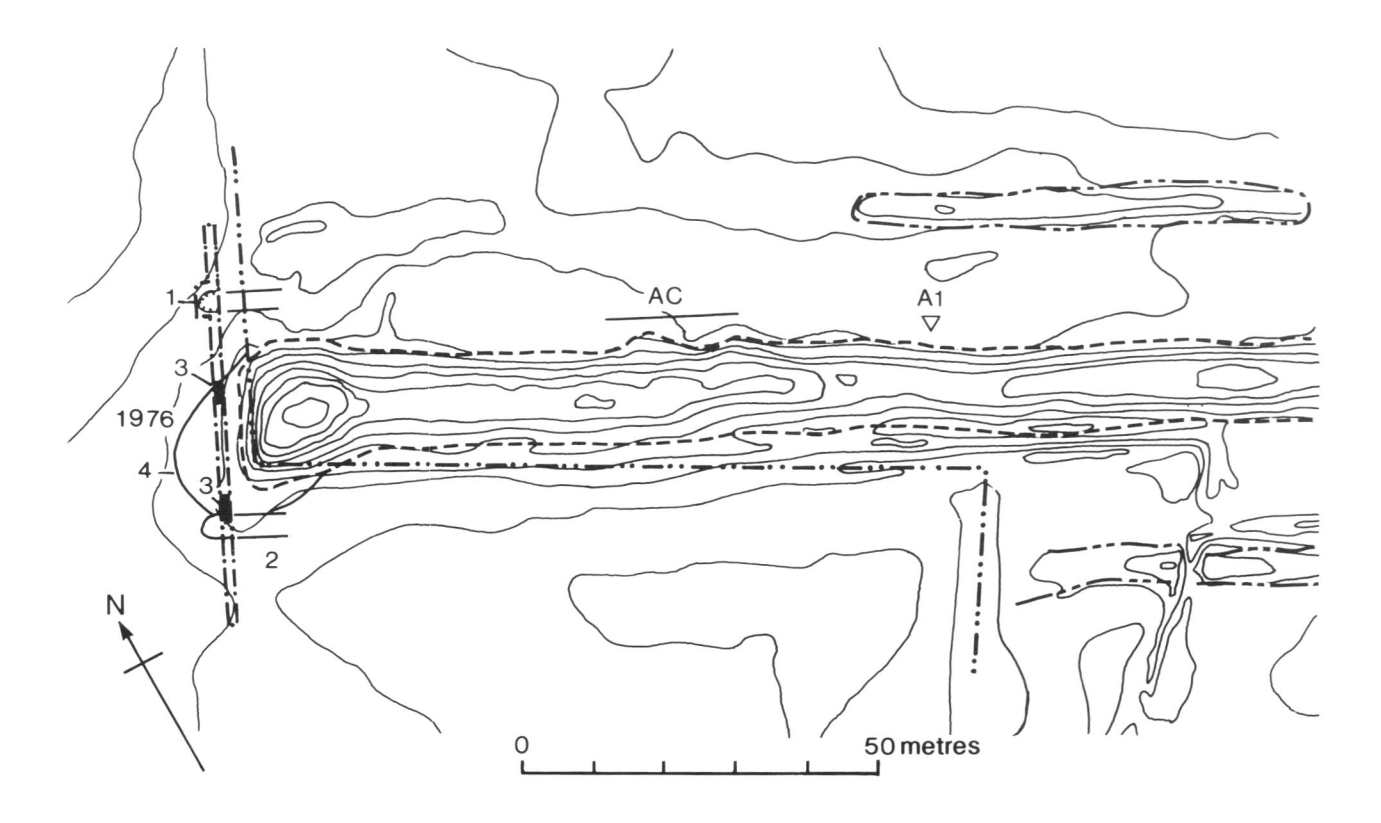

Illus 19
An extract from the new contour survey of the Cleaven Dyke showing Adamson's trench in its correct location. Key: 1 & 2–respectively the northern and southern ditches discovered by Adamson. The butt-end of the northern ditch was found in a small westward extension of the trench; 3–the turf toeing of the mound; 4–suggested edge of the oval barrow forming the NW terminal of the Dyke.

Illustration 18 also makes it appear that the northern ditch of the Cleaven Dyke proper continued beyond the point where it is last visible, and then veered towards the bank, to appear as the ditch located in Adamson's excavation; the recent detailed ground survey contradicts this. On illustration 19 it can be seen that the northern and southern ditches detected by Adamson, instead of being respectively distant and close to the projected line of the Dyke in the wood, are in reality equidistant from the projected line of the bank (3-4m away). In the interim report Adamson noted that the southern ditch cut the turf revetment of the bank (Adamson 1979). In the final report it is noted only that the ditch lay immediately to the south of the turf; we would suggest that the former is the likelier interpretation. Adamson noted that the northern ditch terminated in an extension to the NW of her main trench.

Bradley's observation (pers comm) that the NW terminal of the bank might comprise a round or oval mound is supported by the contour survey. We must consider what it was that Adamson excavated at this point in the field (Adamson & Gallagher 1986). We would suggest that, taking account of the straightening effect of the modern fences at NW and SW, the survey, together with Adamson's evidence, indicates that the NW terminal of the Dyke is formed by an oval mound c 28m E-W by 22m, and now c 2m high at its highest point, falling to c 0.5m where excavated, extending c 10m into the arable field. Adamson's trench seems to have cut across the NW corner of this mound. We would argue that a long mound was attached to the east end of this oval mound; this long mound is not accompanied with the cursus-type ditches of the Dyke, which only start some 60m to the SE, but may be a long barrow. The two ditches located by Adamson seem to parallel the main body of the long mound in the woodland, and we would suggest that, as the southern ditch cuts the revetment of the possible oval mound in Adamson's trench, the ditches she located were the NW ends of the defining ditches of this long mound.

The case for the Dyke being Neolithic was judged 'not proven' by Adamson, who suggested that Richmond's comparison of the Dyke with the Hadrianic *vallum* was strengthened by the fact that cross-dimensions of the Dyke and its structural elements corresponded closely to fractions of a Roman *actus* unit of measurement.

Adamson also noted the existence of three lines showing as cropmarks to the NW of the existing terminal (illus 20). These marks had also been noted by the Ordnance Survey, who used them to suggest an extension to the line of the Dyke on recent 1:2500 and 1:10,000 maps. We would argue that these marks have nothing to do with the Dyke. First, the marks are those of three 'ditches', not two ditches and a bank. Second, they are more closely-spaced than the ditches and bank of the Dyke. Finally, the marks are not on a flat field (the impression given by Adamson's uncontoured fig 2): they run over the edge of the steep drop from the plateau on which the Dyke sits, to the valley of the unnamed burn to the north. It seems more likely, as the character of their cropmark traces indeed suggests, that they are hollow-ways - tracks worn into the edge of the terrace, precursors of the existing metalled but unnumbered road immediately to the west, which is itself a hollow-way, cutting deeply into the scarp (illus 21). There is a local tradition that the Dyke was part of a cattle-droving route, although Haldane does not note it as a major route in his survey of the subject (Haldane 1973); if this was so, then the origin of the hollow-ways is clear: the frequent passage of cattle and other traffic up and down a slope.

In summary, the 1975 excavation revealed more about the Dyke than was appreciated at the time, but it is only in the context of the wider project reported on here, and with the correction of the locational error in the published report, that that significance has, finally, become clear.

Illus 20
Aerial photograph of the NW terminal of the Dyke showing the three hollow ways cutting down the steep drop to the valley in the foreground. The road shown in illustration 21 is immediately to the right of the marks. (*Crown Copyright: Ministry of Defence*)

Illus 21
The modern metalled road immediately to the west of the cropmarks shown in illustration 20. The road is a hollow way, cutting up to 2m into the edge of the escarpment on which the Cleaven Dyke lies.

PREVIOUS SURVEYS OF THE CLEAVEN DYKE

In the past the survey, recording, description and interpretation of the Dyke have been approached as though it was a Roman military earthwork and therefore 'perfectly straight' (Abercromby *et al* 1902) and broadly uniform in dimensions. Some major variations in alignment appear to have been noted by Richmond (although which he means in his description of the monument is impossible to determine, as there is considerable confusion—eg over east and west—in the text) but the many more minor variations were not. Inevitably the survey scale and methodology chosen for a monument perceived as having only gross variations would be capable only of recording gross variations. Until 1996 the only complete surveys of the Dyke were those prepared for various editions of the Ordnance Survey 1:2500 plan. The last published paper edition of the map records only the major changes in direction and some of the more obvious changes in the width of the bank. The current, electronic, version, however, has added a line for the approximate edge of the bank (illus 55). In the early 1990s Historic Scotland asked RCAHMS, as part of its fieldwork in south-east Perthshire, to undertake a survey of part of the Dyke that was about to be clear-felled, as a precaution against possible damage and loss of information during forestry operations. A traditional hachure survey of a length of *c* 300m at the SE end of Section A recorded that the bank was segmented, the boundaries of the segments being marked by dips in the height of the crest (RCAHMS 1994a, 27; illus 22 this volume). In the limited area surveyed the segments appeared to be between 25m and 53m long, some adjacent segments being on slightly different alignments and of different width.

Field observation showed that the features noted in the surveyed area were evident elsewhere in the monument. It was difficult, however, to gain an idea of the overall pattern of variation in the height and alignment of the Dyke, because of the heavy tree-cover over much of its length.

As it appeared that the Dyke displayed both small- and large-scale variation, and was structurally more complex than had been believed, we decided that a complete survey of its upstanding remains was needed to ease definitive observation and interpretation. Consideration of the results of the RCAHMS survey led us to believe that our aims would be better met by a contour survey, rather than traditional hachure drawing, a decision that has proved justified by the results. The contour survey, a daunting task in the dense woodland, was undertaken between 1994 and 1996 by Christopher Burgess (**5.1** below) with a range of assistants, as funding and surveyors' time became available. No comparable survey had been done in Scotland to give any realistic idea of the time or funding needed; in the event, our initial estimates of both were woefully inadequate. The felling of the trees at the NW terminal in 1995, and the likelihood of further forestry work in the near future, forced the pace, and the last *c* 40% of the survey was funded by Historic Scotland.

We should note, before moving on, the other important observations made by the RCAHMS surveyors: between the bank and the southern ditch two phases of later agricultural rigging were noted. In the earlier phase the rigs were almost at right angles to the bank. The later phase of rigging runs parallel with the Dyke.

ARCHAEOLOGY IN THE IMMEDIATE AREA

Apart from the Littleour structure (**4** below), the immediate vicinity of the Dyke is surprisingly poor in archaeological remains that can be assigned confidently to the Neolithic. The cropmark record includes the sites possibly related to Littleour, the 'long mortuary enclosure' and pit-circles at Inchtuthil, and the Milton of Rattray cursus monument, all described below. Two substantial flint scatters have been found in the vicinity: one at Nether Pittendreich, close to the NW terminal of the Dyke (NGR NO 158 411), and the other on the opposite bank of the River Isla from the Herald Hill long barrow (NGR NO 189 393 to 189 393). Elements of the Pittendreich scatter were collected from 1977 to 1983 (Lye 1977, 1983, 1984; Reid 1985), and reports prepared by James Kenworthy were deposited in Perth Museum. The assemblage of 17 pieces included trimming flakes, core preparation flakes, six scrapers and two plano-convex type knives, and was identified by Kenworthy as late Neolithic/early Bronze Age.

Alan Saville has kindly surveyed the material from the banks of the Isla, opposite the Herald Hill.

LITHIC SURFACE FINDS FROM BESIDE THE RIVER ISLA

Alan Saville

A small collection of 46 struck lithic pieces was recovered as a dispersed scatter of surface finds from fields close to the River Isla, near its confluence with the Tay. The main location, from which derive all the implements specified below, is on the eastern bank of the Isla, opposite Herald Hill, approximately centred on

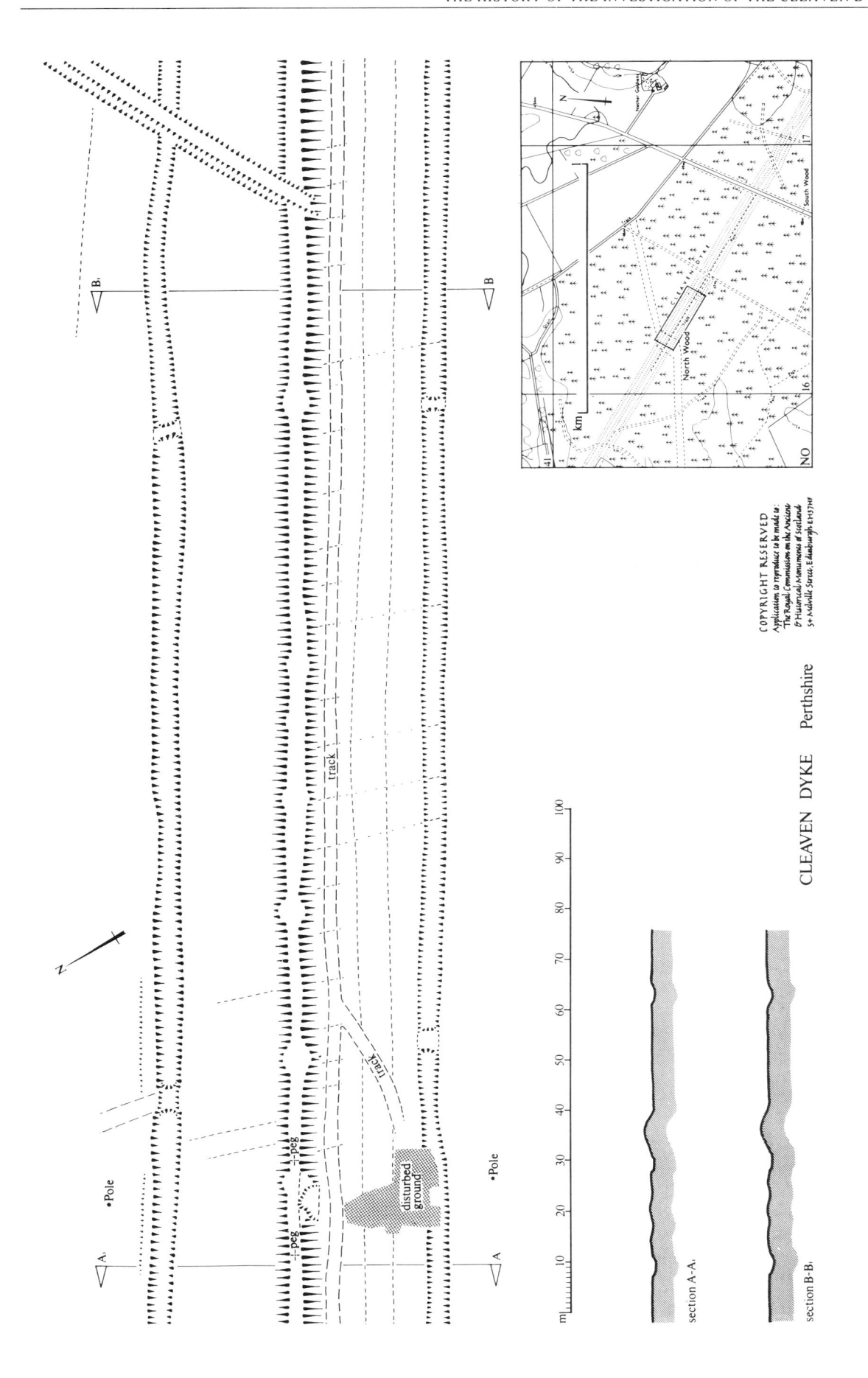

THE HISTORY OF THE INVESTIGATION OF THE CLEAVEN DYKE ♦ 23

CLEAVEN DYKE Perthshire

Illus 22

The plan prepared by RCAHMS of the area between segment-boundary A10 and close to the SE end of Section A of the Dyke. (*Crown Copyright: RCAHMS*)

grid reference NO 189 391. The pieces are of flint of various types and colours, apart from two pieces of flaked opal/agate. From those flints with surviving cortex it is clear that both beach/gravel pebble flint and flint with non-waterworn cortex are involved, and the colours include, red, brown, and yellow as well as various shades of grey.

The classifiable implements among the collection comprise an arrowhead, two knives, three scrapers, and two probable gunflints. The arrowhead is a very large (50mm x 42mm) example of a Late Neolithic chisel type (Green 1984), which can be compared to the larger of the examples from Airhouse, Berwickshire (Callander 1928, fig.7). One of the knives is a classic Late Neolithic/Early Bronze Age plano-convex type (Clark 1932), and the other is a variant of the same type, with bilateral scale-flaking on a blade of triangular cross-section. The latter example is noteworthy for having edge gloss inversely on parts of both lateral edges. The scrapers include one example on a core, but none is a diagnostic example in terms of date. Neither of the two possible gunflints are standard types and no specific date for them can be suggested. A large unretouched blade of grey flint is so substantial (L:71mm x B:36mm x Th:10mm; weight: 24g) that it might also be connected with gunflint manufacture rather than being a prehistoric artefact.

Only one piece, a thick plunging flake from the face of a small bladelet core, is at all suggestive of a Mesolithic date, though it cannot be regarded as wholly diagnostic. Otherwise a blade element among the flakes may suggest some Early to Middle Neolithic activity, but, as far as the prehistoric element is concerned, the only truly diagnostic component is Late Neolithic/Early Bronze Age. The fact that such a small collection should include an exceptional arrowhead and two fine knives is clearly unusual; all sorts of factors could bear on this, but the nearby presence of a site or sites of this period, perhaps of a funerary nature, is probably indicated.

A stone axehead was also found at this location (NO 1894 3960) in 1997. It is a small, squat example (L: 89mm x B: 48mm x Th: 22mm; weight: 172g), polished over the whole surface. The colour is basically light grey-green, with distinctive darker green and brown banding, emphasised by differential weathering. The rock type has not been identified but, superficially, it resembles that of other axeheads made from the hornfels from Creag na Caillich, Killin (Edmonds *et al* 1992). If this were the case, then a later Neolithic date would be appropriate.

The axehead was declared Treasure Trove and allocated to Perth Museum and Art Gallery, which also houses the other lithic finds reported upon here.

2.2 THE 1993-1997 SURVEYS

In the preceding section covering the history and early survey of the Dyke, its general appearance and composition will have become familiar to the reader. In this section the detailed analysis of the form of the monument made possible by the 1993-1997 surveys is described.

GENERAL OBSERVATIONS

As already described, the Cleaven Dyke comprises a pair of ditches and a central bank. The bank of the Dyke survives for almost exactly 1800m as an upstanding earthwork, mainly in woodland. The most sensible way to examine the Dyke seems to us to be to 'walk' the reader along it, using the detailed contour plan as a substitute for the monument itself. Tilley (1994) describes the Dorset cursus in relation to its surrounding landscape, natural features incorporated within the monument, the features of the cursus (where visible) and artificial features (eg long barrows) in and around it. For the Cleaven Dyke the approach must be different. On the one hand, its excellent state of preservation means that we can describe the structure of the monument in greater detail. On the other hand, the heavy tree-cover immediately around the monument restricts direct observation of the surrounding landscape. Tilley founded his approach to the Dorset cursus on the normal assumption that cursus monuments were built in one or two construction events and were designed primarily to operate as unitary monuments in their final state. This is perhaps arguable at the Cleaven Dyke and some other sites (eg Maxey, Pryor 1985). The survey of the Dyke, undertaken by Chris Burgess, is presented below in four parts on the fold-out (illus 98/99). The relationship between the individual plans is shown on the index map, illustration 23. Where the formally identified 'Sections' of the monument are referred to, a capital 'S' is used throughout the report to distinguish them from the archaeologically cut sections.

Illus 23
Map showing the main subdivisions of the Cleaven Dyke (the breaks W, X, Y and Z divide the Dyke into five Sections–A, B, C, D and E). (*Based on the Ordinance Survey 1:10,000 map with the permission of the Controller of Her Majesty's Stationery Office. © Crown Copyright MC/98/172.*)

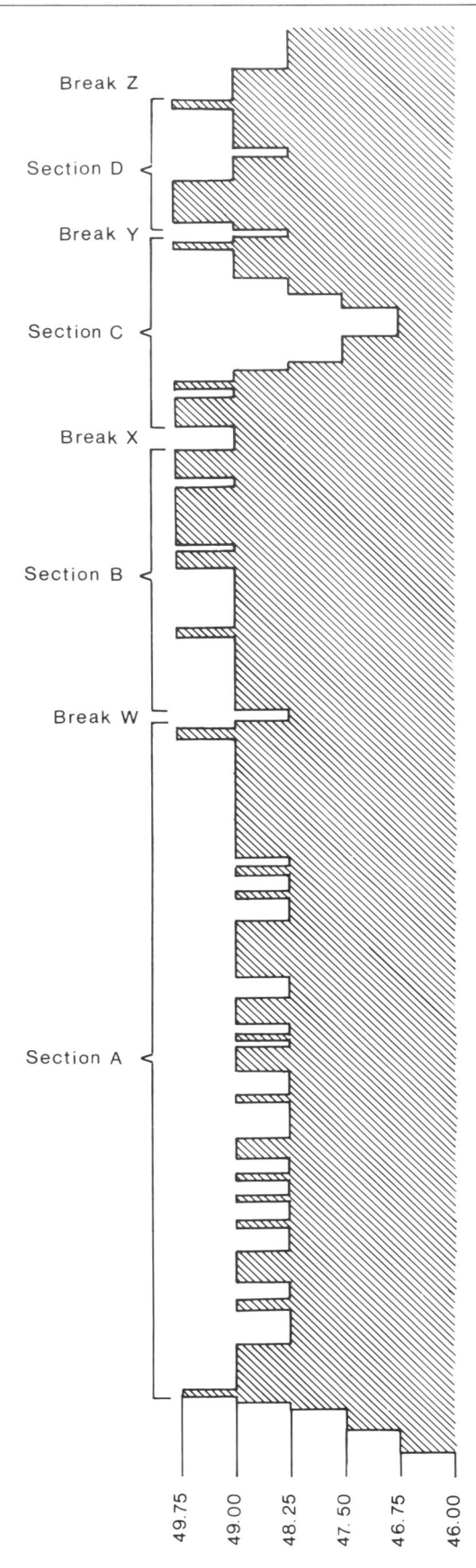

Illus 24
Cleaven Dyke: diagram showing the height of the bank and the ditch bottoms in relation to Ordnance datum, in 0.75m bands.
(*Christopher Burgess and Peter McKeague*)

Some general observations can be made on the form of the monument. There are four breaks in the bank of the Dyke, **W**, **X**, **Y** and **Z**, which are, or appear to be, original and are set at significant intervals. These break the monument into (from the NW) five main Sections: **A**, **B**, **C**, **D** and **E**. In Sections **A** and **B**, the north face of the bank is consistently steeper than the south face. Where the ditch changes angle the changes are not sharp, but are complex (eg that north of segment-boundary A3).

The limited evidence from excavation confirms the impression gained from field-observation that the monument was built from NW to SE, and we describe its elements in that order. Within the Sections clear segments can be identified which can be characterised as relatively broad or narrow, the width changing abruptly at segment boundaries. The segments are further marked by:

- variations (occasionally abrupt) in the height of the bank;
- slight changes in the alignment of bank and ditches;
- changes in the width of the ditch or the platform between bank and ditch on each side;
- variations in the cross-section of the bank.

Some of the segment boundaries appear to be more significant than others: they are marked by a combination of narrowing/broadening of the bank, significant angle-changes in bank or ditch, perturbations in the line of the ditches, or causeways in the ditch. We have observed that where the ditch changes angle, the change is not usually sharp, but complex, and where there is a complex change, it more often takes effect in the northern ditch first, the southern changing later (eg the change north of segment-boundary A3 in the northern ditch is matched 25m to 60m east of A3 in the southern ditch; see fold-out illus 98). Within each segment of the bank it is occasionally possible to identify individual construction dumps.

A diagram (illus 24) representing the height of the bank at intervals in 0.75m bands (above Ordnance Datum) shows the rise and fall of the monument over its upstanding length. It shows clearly that the highest points lie within the same 0.75m band: they are the NW terminal, the SE end of Section **A**, the SE end and terminal of Section **B**, the NW and SE terminals of Section **D**, and the NW and SE terminals of Section **E**. Although it cannot be checked while the tree-cover remains over most of the monument, it seems likely that the only place that someone travelling along the Cleaven Dyke would lose sight of the whole of the earthwork, would be in the distinct dip within Section **C** (discussed further below).

Illus 25
View along the NW part of the bank of the Dyke, looking towards the terminal, in 1997, after the clearing of trees. (*Crown Copyright: Historic Scotland*)

DESCRIPTION AND DETAILED ANALYSIS

SECTION A

The visible remains of the monument begin just to the NW of the boundary fence of the wood. Just inside the wood the bank is at its highest and broadest (illus 23; 25; fold-out 98). As is argued above (2.1), a long mound apparently abuts a pre-existing oval mound; it seems to be some 80m long (ending c 99m from the fence), but may be bipartite, since at a point some 38m from the edge of the oval mound (c 56m from the fence) it displays a slight change of alignment and profile, there is a pronounced bulge on its north side, and there is a perceptible drop in height. No quarry-ditches of the kind that would be expected beside a long barrow are visible within the plantation, but Adamson located, in the arable field, what appear to be the NW ends of two very shallow ditches that lay 3-4m from the base of the long mound on either side; she observed that the southern ditch cut the revetment of the oval mound. As these ditches were no more than 0.25m deep, and seem to act more to define the monument than as quarries, it is hardly surprising that they are not visible in the wood. However, the geophysical survey profiles taken across the arable field to the south of the bank may indicate the possible course of the southern ditch.

Towards the end of the long mound (c 99m from the fence), the top of the bank falls in height at a fairly even rate; at that point it dips in the first of the identifiable segment boundaries (A1). Beyond here, the line of the Dyke 'wobbles' considerably and returns to the alignment of the western part of the long mound. Some 14m back from segment-boundary A1, the northern ditch begins. There is no evidence of the ditch having existed further to the NW; the contour survey shows what may be a further extension to the NW, but on the ground this may be interpreted as a reflection of the local topography. The geophysical survey profiles in the arable field south of the bank seem to indicate that the ditch extends as far as profile 'b' in a straight line from where it was last visible in the wood; that is, to a point corresponding broadly to the terminal of the northern ditch. From that point the geophysical anomaly, the southern edge of which lay outside the area surveyed, begins to veer slightly to the south. The indeterminate end of both the northern and southern ditches may have a prosaic explanation; we know that the Dyke is supposed to have been used as a customary route for cattle droving. If cattle were driven along the ditches, then the ends of the ditches, where the cattle left them to move towards the hollow-ways to the NW, might have been eroded by traffic, subsequently filled with humus, and obscured.

To sum up, therefore, the first c 90m of the monument (the appearance of which may be considered atypical) seems not to be flanked by ditches as widely separated or as deeply cut as the normal Cleaven Dyke ditches; as has been noted above, the ditches located by Adamson appear to be associated with a possibly multi-phase structure resembling a long barrow that incorporated a free-standing oval mound as its NW terminal. How far they extended cannot yet be determined; the significance of aerial photographic and geophysical evidence on this point is still uncertain, both sources hinting at anomalies of one kind or another in the arable field to the south. Our reading of the totality of the evidence, however, is as follows: only at segment-boundary A1, at the end of what may be interpreted as a normal long barrow, does the cursus/bank barrow proper of the Cleaven Dyke begin. From here the rest of the Section is c 840m long and is relatively straight and regular.

The first segment of the Dyke proper, between A1 and A2, is 57m long and may be characterised as narrow. The south side of the bank and a portion of the southern ditch are overlain and obscured by an L-shaped bank of relatively recent date, while segment-boundary A2 has been largely occupied by a modern forestry track, which also crosses the northern and southern ditches.

The next segment-boundary, A3 (190m from the fence at the terminal), is marked, not by a dip in the bank's height, but by an appreciable increase in its breadth, accompanied by a very significant change of alignment - some 3.5° to the south. The northern ditch undergoes a complex angle-change over a length of c 60m to either side of the same point. The southern ditch executes a similar change a little further to the E.

The segment between A3 and A4 measures c 88m. The bank is straight and can be characterised as broad. Between 25m and 60m from segment-boundary A3, the southern ditch undergoes a complex change of direction. Some 35m short of A4, it is crossed diagonally by a modern track and disappears from view for a length of 10m. At segment-boundary A4, the northern ditch undergoes a complex change of direction, which is mirrored in the bank, the terminals of the adjoining segments inclining slightly north to the junction point. This deviation has an additional significance: where it terminates, some 20m beyond A4, the bank adopts an altogether new consistency of alignment, pointing directly at the hill where the Dyke terminates, another c 1850m to the SE.

The segment from A4 to A5 measures c 107m in length. It is of even height and straight, apart from the western portion just described. A few metres to the east of A5, the southern ditch exhibits an undoubted causeway, c 3m wide, east of which it again undergoes one of its complex changes of direction. The northern ditch appears to narrow slightly at a corresponding point.

The segment from A5 to A6 is c 28m long and can be characterised as narrow, the decrease in girth being marked, as elsewhere in the Dyke, by a northward re-alignment of the bank's southern edge.

At A6 the bank once again broadens markedly, maintaining its broad character throughout the c 83m length of the segment, and attaining a maximum just before A7.

East of A7 the bank once again becomes narrow and remains thus throughout the next two segments, each relatively short at 40m and 49m respectively. From A7 to A9 the course of the Dyke appears to be slightly curved, an appearance which is mirrored by the complex-angled re-alignment of the southern ditch in this Section.

At A9 the bank again becomes broad and straight, the segment between A9 and A10 measuring c 73m. A10 is a particularly well-defined boundary: both the height and width of the bank decrease sharply. This is the segment-boundary chosen for excavation in 1995, the westernmost then unencumbered by trees. Two of the shortest segments occur together just after segment-boundary A10.

A single geophysical cross-profile of the mound and northern ditch (near the SE end of segment A9/A10) indicated in this area some sort of anomaly to the north of the bank, a depth of up to 1.5m to 2m being indicated; no feature in a comparable location was found at the immediately adjacent excavation site and no pit or ditch can be detected on the surface (unlike the shallow cursus ditch, which is still visible after over 5000 years). It is suggested therefore that the resistivity-detected feature was of natural origin.

The next segment is only 25m long and is narrow. The northern ditch is interrupted for the first time a few metres west of A11, the southern a metre or two to the east. Immediately to the west of the southern causeway, the ditch undergoes a slight change in angle, while to the east, opposite bank-segment A11-A12, which is narrow and short (30m), the ditch inclines a little to the S.

The segment between A12 and A13 is c 103m long and once again narrow. Both ditches 'wander' a little towards the east end of the segment, near which both ditches are broken by narrow causeways– the northern just before, the southern directly opposite, the segment-boundary.

From the area around the causeway, up to the point where a modern bank crosses the monument from the east (terminating on the crest of the bank), the northern ditch diverges considerably from the straight alignment. The segment-boundary A13 appears to be significant: to the east the bank broadens, while the ditches not only undergo unusual perturbations of course but also narrow.

The last segment of Section **A** (A14 to Section boundary **W**) measures *c* 50m long. It rises higher than the previous segment and, particularly at the east end, has a more massive appearance, while the ditch on both sides is unusually slight.

SECTION BOUNDARY W

The Section-break marking the boundary between Sections **A** and **B** is now some 10m wide, but it seems likely that this represents a widening of the original gap by its accommodation of the old road leading north from Meikleour village and, in modern times, of a forestry track. However, it is only on the eastern edge of the Section-break that road-formation has caused serious damage, for, on the west, the butt-end of the northern ditch of Section **A** can still be seen, and the massive terminal of the bank on that side appears to have been only slightly trimmed. How wide the break was originally cannot now be determined.

SECTION B

Section **B** is *c* 365m long (illus 23; fold-out 98/99). The segment between Section boundary **W** and the first segment-boundary of Section **B** (B1) is narrower than the last of Section **A** (and is in absolute terms a narrow segment as well as being on a slightly different alignment). At B1 the alignment of the bank changes slightly to the south and the gauge changes again from narrow to broad. Segment B1-B2, which is *c* 68m long, incorporates a complex change of alignment *c* 25m from its east end; significantly, this manifests itself most clearly in the north edge of the bank–a departure from the norm observed in Section **A**. Equally significant is the sharply increased width of the ditches in these sectors, compared with the adjacent portions of **A**. It is also worth noting that from break **W** to B3, the berm between the northern ditch and the bank is 2-3m wider than that on the south; for most of Section **A** the berms are roughly equal.

Segment B2-B3 is *c* 80m long and is characterised as broad. At B2 the alignment of the bank once again changes, this time a little to the north, and this is matched by the northern ditch. Segment-boundary B3 has been identified as a significant boundary; the character of the bank changes: it thickens in a pronounced way on the north side, and both ditches are causewayed at this point, the northern ditch just beyond B3, the southern ditch, just before it. Although B3 has been used to accommodate a track at some time in the past, it and the causeways are certainly original, the ditches to either side of the latter confirming this by complex, though slight, angle-changes.

The segment B3-B4 is once again short, only 31m, the bank beginning to encroach on the northern berm.

At segment-boundary B4, the bank again broadens considerably, bulging out to both north and south. Alongside it the northern ditch undergoes a complex angle-change.

At segment-boundary B5 the bank changes alignment abruptly to the south, as does the southern ditch, which now moves onto an alignment parallel to the northern ditch, which had already changed alignment. The southern ditch stops *c* 8m short of the end of Section **B**, at break **X**. The northern ditch stops opposite the terminal of the bank, just short of which the bank reaches a height of just over 2m.

SECTION BOUNDARY X

This break in the Dyke (fold-out illus 99) was investigated in 1939 by Richmond (1940), who cut two cross-sections and one axial section at the terminal of the bank. In the cross-sections he noted, as had Abercromby before him (Abercromby *et al* 1902), that there was a 'toe' of turf at both sides of the bank, apparently holding the gravel of the bank in place. In the axial section at the tip of the bank he noted that this 'toeing' was carried round the end of the section, showing that the end of the segment had been finished off neatly, and therefore that the break had been constructed deliberately. It seems likely that the modern A93 has removed the matching bank-terminal of Section **C**, for, as it reappears on the SE side of the road, the bank appears to have been truncated. The width of break **X** therefore cannot be determined with accuracy, but was probably similar to the gap of *c* 10m in the southern ditch.

It may be significant that at the breaks **X** and **Y** the northern ditch stops slightly further to the SE than in the matching gap in the southern ditch: at **X** the difference is *c* 7m; at **Y** the difference appears to be less. The effect in both cases seems to have been to preclude an access across the monument that was perpendicular to its axis.

SECTION C

This Section lies almost entirely to the east of the A93. The point at which the northern ditch resumes has been lost beneath the road. However, the terminal of the southern ditch, on the SE side of the Section boundary survives *c* 14m to the west of the road. The southern ditch then undergoes a complex angle-change just to the east of the A93 and the bank starts the Section on an alignment considerably different from the last part of Section **B**.

When it resumes in Section **C** the bank follows a different alignment and is not only of narrow character, but is also of almost symmetrical cross-section. This is furthermore the most variable Section of the monument. About 35m from the NW end of the Section, the angle of the bank changes significantly again, to the south (at C1). This change is paralleled by a change in the angle of the northern ditch; the southern ditch undergoes a similar change *c* 20m later, to the east. The bank then runs on its new alignment for *c* 40m before making a further angle-change (at C2), with a complex angle-change in the northern ditch just to the east. At this point the land on which the monument is constructed begins to slope slightly downwards from NE to SW, as the Dyke leaves behind the area of negligible contour variation of Sections **A** and **B**.

The segment from C2 to C3 is *c* 65m long and fairly straight, disrupted only by a track crossing both ditches and the bank. It is constructed for the most part on still falling ground but, at the east end, on the flat. The height of the bank falls evenly from the beginning of Section **C** all the way to segment-boundary C3. All three segments are narrow and continue to be of symmetrical cross-section.

At C3 the angle of the bank changes towards the north. The northern ditch had already made the angle-change at the point where the modern track crossed, *c* 10m to the west. The southern ditch undergoes a similar angle-change.

The next segment (C3-C4) is relatively short, 35m in length, and is, in contrast to the elements to the west, narrow. It is built on the flat at the bottom of a local depression. The southern ditch is still undergoing its complex angle-change and the northern ditch also changes its angle again.

The next segment, from C4 to the end of the Section, is the most unusual part of the monument apart from the NW terminal. From the flat ground of segment C3-C4, it rises, with a slight change of alignment, up a slight slope, the top of which provides to the walker a false horizon. As the ground also slopes up to the bank from the south, the effect of the terrain is also to make the central bank look distinctly higher on the south side than on the north. The bank rises rapidly, at a rate greater than the slope it is climbing and broadens considerably towards its end, which lies over the false horizon. This last segment of Section **C** is *c* 88m long. At its eastern terminal the segment rises to a height of 1.75m above the ground on the south side and broadens into an oval mound measuring *c* 14m in breadth and at least 23m long. The end of this Section thus seems almost to mirror the NW terminal of the monument, with its swollen bank and oval terminal mound.

SECTION BOUNDARY Y

This is the only boundary break not to have been occupied by a more recent roadway. The space between the bank terminals is *c* 15m across.

About the corresponding gaps in the ditches it is less easy to be sure: that on the north is obscured by a later circular earthwork; the southern gap is quite poorly defined, but is probably *c* 13m across. The northern ditch continues beyond the end of the segment, by a metre or two, as does the southern. The southern ditch, however, undergoes the most sudden change at any point in its length; *c* 15m from its end it appears to 'dog-leg' *c* 5m to the north. It is possible that this unique feature reflects the incorporation of a pre-existing ditch related to the oval terminal mound.

SECTION D

The NW terminal of the bank of Section **D** is offset sharply to the north and built on a scale only a little less massive than the opposing terminal of **C**. After 15m, however, it resumes the main alignment (once more with asymmetrical profile).

At segment-boundary D1 the bank narrows dramatically, once again the loss in width being achieved by the southern edge of the bank moving north. The segment from D1 to D2 is *c* 70m long and is narrow. It is very badly disturbed by more recent banks, but the individual dumps of which it is composed can be distinguished clearly.

The segment from D2 to the end of Section **D** is short, only *c* 28m long, and is broad, although its wedge-shaped plan gives it the appearance of a single dump.

SECTION BOUNDARY Z

The boundary between Sections **D** and **E** is, as are three of the four original breaks, colonised by more recent roads-in this case the 18th-century route serving Muiralehouse. From field examination it seems likely that the SE terminal of Section **D** has been disturbed only a little, and that, as at breaks **W** and **X**, it is the east side of the gap that has been slighted to accommodate the road.

SECTION E

In the wood to the north, 25m of the northern ditch of Section **E** survives. The NW terminal of the ditch is preserved, just to the SE of the track. The remainder of this final Section traverses arable land, now appearing either as a cropmark (both bank and ditches) or a soil mark for the bank alone. Geophysical survey just into the field appears to have located the expected features of the bank and ditches. We are fortunate to have the map of the surviving bank by the Ordnance Survey in 1867, but the character and course of the monument are less easy to assess beyond the wood. The Dyke in Section **E** appears to be on a slightly different alignment from Section **D**. There is no evidence of any further major break in the bank, so far as it survives or is visible, and no gap was recorded by the Ordnance Survey. However, aerial survey does reveal what appears to be an original break in the northern ditch not far into the field. There also seems to be an angle-change in the ditches at a point about half way from the edge of the wood to the terminal, and *c* 50m further on the soil mark of the bank abruptly ceases. The end of the soil mark seems to correspond with the end of the earthwork recorded by the Ordnance Survey, and there is no evidence that the bank continued beyond this point. The ditches continue, fading out of sight as they rise on to the summit of the low hill to the SE (an observation confirmed by excavation in 1993).

Excavation was undertaken in the field on a 15m length of the southern ditch and in a number of narrow trenches on the hilltop (**2.3** below).

There is no evidence of the Dyke ever having gone beyond this point. A feature visible to the SE of the Dunkeld to Coupar Angus road, occasionally put forward as evidence of a continuation, seems to represent a gravel quarry depicted on the first Ordnance Survey mapping.

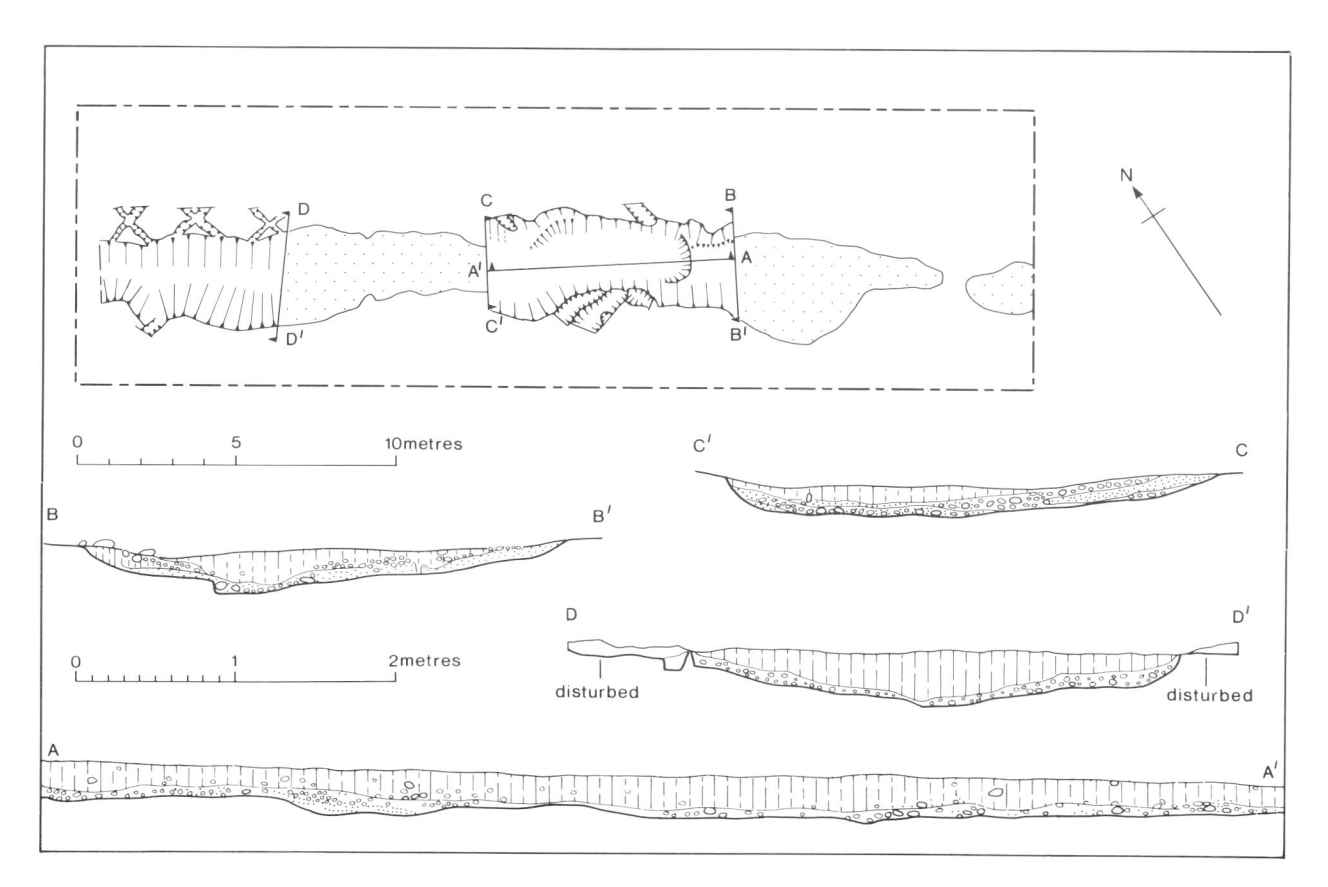

Illus 26
Cleaven Dyke: plan and sections of the ditch in excavation area I/1. The 'crossing' marks on the plan at top left are modern subsoiling tracks.

2.3 EXCAVATIONS ON THE CLEAVEN DYKE: 1993 AND 1995

STRATEGY

The first season's excavation in 1993 had three aims: 1) to examine a length of the ditch in the arable area to check the evidence of aerial photographs, which suggested that the ditch was irregular in line, and possibly segmented; 2) to try to locate the SE terminal and 3) to excavate a cross-section of the bank, the berm and one ditch of the Dyke within the wood, where best preserved, to provide a reliable and well-recorded section, and to look for features below the bank and on the berm.

The second season's excavation in 1995 had two objectives: 1) to investigate the boundary of two of the segments of the bank, particularly to determine the sequence, if any, of their construction and 2) to look for further features below the bank.

Excavation was undertaken in two Sections of the Dyke: in Section E, Area I was excavated across the ditch in the arable field and at the SE terminal; in Section A within the wood, Area III, the cross-section, and Area IV, the axial section were cut. The location of each trench is shown on the fold-out illustration 98/99.

AREA I - THE MAIN TRENCH IN THE ARABLE FIELD

In Area I, two 2m x 10m trial trenches were hand-dug prior to machining of a 9m x 30m trench over the southern ditch of the Dyke at the point shown on fold-out illustration 99; the southern trench lay within the area subsequently machined. Three 'segments' of the ditch were taken down in plan (providing axial and transverse sections) within the machined trench (I/1). The surviving hand-dug cutting (I/2) provided a section of the ditch-fill and ploughsoil. The excavated sections showed sand/gravel inwash of limited depth, the rest of the ditch being filled by silty black loam (probably water-deposited) (illus 26; 27). In the machined trench parts of three ditch segments were investigated, one completely, the others only being exposed. The completely exposed segment was separated by a causeway at the SE end and by a distinct shallowing of the ditch at the NW (illus 28). The ditch was nowhere deeper than 0.35m; in places subsoiling had disturbed the edges and fills of the ditch to a depth of 0.25m. The ditch was a maximum of 2.5m wide.

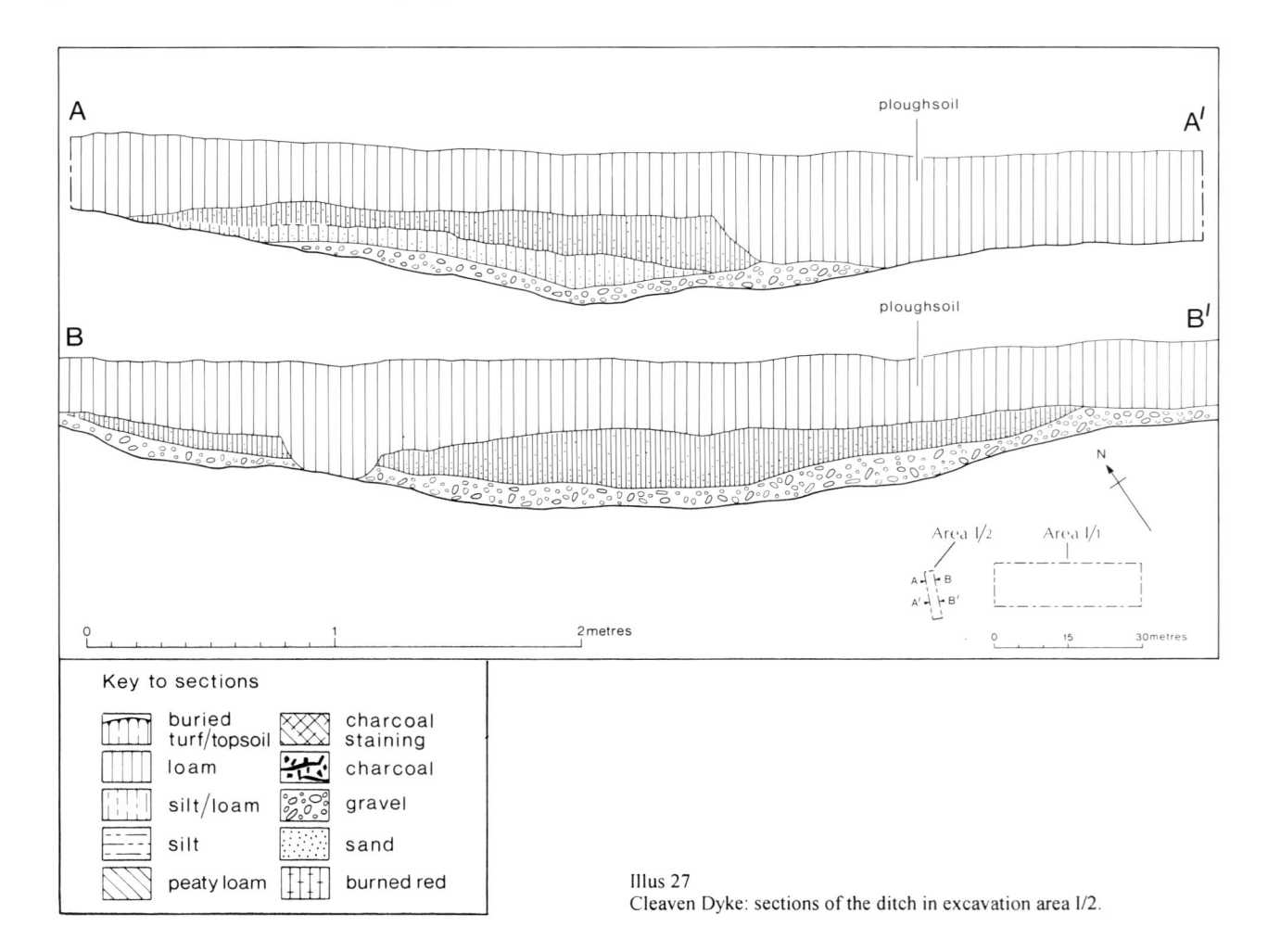

Illus 27
Cleaven Dyke: sections of the ditch in excavation area I/2.

Illus 28
Cleaven Dyke: a view to the SE along the portion of the southern ditch in Section E (excavation area I/1), excavated in the arable field near the SE end of the monument.

AREA II - THE SLOTS EXCAVATED TO LOCATE THE SE TERMINAL

The area in which these narrow trenches were dug lay on the higher ground to the SE of Area I, where the last traces of the ditches of the Dyke were visible as cropmarks (fold-out illus 99). Two trenches were dug to locate the northern ditch (II/1 and II/6). Neither was successful as the cropmark plot now available (fold-out illus 99) reveals that they were in the wrong place. The other cuttings (II/2 to II/5) were designed to locate the southern ditch. Only in II/2 and II/3 did we locate it; in II/3 it was less than 100mm deep. It seems likely that the ditch had been severely eroded by ploughing on the very friable sand subsoil on the hill. In II/4 a dark greasy, stone-free soil was noted, a few centimetres deep. It is possible that this was the last slight remnant of the ditch, but it is not marked as such on the plan (fold-out illus 99).

AREA III - THE CROSS-SECTION CUT IN 1993

Area III lay 1300m to the NW of Area I, in the woodland where the Dyke survives as an upstanding monument (fold-out illus 98). A 3m-wide cross-section was cut by hand through the bank of the Dyke at a point where it had already been damaged by quarrying but had escaped recent afforestation because of the presence of an overhead power line. The Section extended to and across the northern ditch (illus 29).

The bank is composed of redeposited turf, topsoil and subsoil, apparently the spoil of the flanking ditches; at this point it measures c 8.6m in width over the toeing banks of turf which demarcate and partly revet the bank on either side, and it survives to a height of c1.5m above the old ground surface. Interpretation of the section suggests that the bank was probably built in the following sequence:

1   Turf stripped from the site of the northern ditch was placed to form a low bank a little to the north of the axis of the final bank. Apparently at much the same time a low bank of turf was built along what would become the northern edge of the bank, forming the toeing already mentioned.

2   Various tips of the lower ditch-fill—mixed soils and subsoil— were then deposited over the turf and topsoil dump, and against the turf toeing. Care seems to have been taken not to overlap the toeing.

3   The south face of the bank produced so far in the process was then covered on its southern flank, first by turf, probably cut from the top of the southern ditch, and then by mixed soil and subsoil dug from that ditch, this being finally held in place by another toeing of turf, which, however, laps over the edge of the material of the bank.

4   Finally, a root- and animal-disturbed layer can be seen to cover the whole bank, presumably resulting from a combination of turbation of the layers already described and deposition of leaf litter and other organic material. The disturbed area to the left of the area affected by rabbit burrowing appears to be related to the growth of a tree.

This sequence has produced the markedly asymmetrical profile of the bank over much of its length - with a markedly steeper face on the NE side (illus 30). These observations confirm and amplify the results of Richmond's trenches (1940), as illustrated in his unpublished photographs in the NMRS (although not in his schematic published section drawing, which shows little detail, an almost symmetrical cross-section and confuses the turf toeing with the dark humic mixed layer mentioned in (4) above).

There were various features below the bank (illus 31). A small shallow depression in the topsoil buried beneath the bank (F5) had been the site of one or more fires, sufficient to affect the soil structure; it contained quantities of oak charcoal. The soil micromorphology report below casts light on the relationship between the burning and the construction of the bank.

A substantial pit, probably a posthole (F1), was found below the bank near its northern edge (illus 31); it is not clear whether the post was *in situ* when the bank was built round it, or had rotted before construction. However, it was not visible on the cleaned old land surface (OLS); it only became visible after the old land surface was removed. It appears likely, therefore, that the post pre-dated the bank. As no further postholes were found in an equivalent position in the 1995 excavation trench, and no cropmark traces of such features have been observed in Section E, it seems likely that this was an isolated post. The remaining features, F2, F3 and F4, seemed to be of human origin, but their interpretation is unclear. F4 was the only feature visible on the cleaned OLS, where it appeared as a very clear 'dimple', which had filled with the overlying bank material. The published section drawing does not include the OLS.

The trench was continued to and over the northern ditch, which was revealed to have a very shallow profile and to be c 5m wide and 1m deep below the modern topsoil surface. Its fill is interpreted as the result of natural silting.

Calculation of the volume of the ditches and the bank suggest that the material of the bank could be accounted for completely by the contents of the ditches; it is not necessary to suggest the importation of turf from the berm, as has been proposed in the past, to account for a supposition (inaccurate as it turns out) that the bank had a greater bulk than the sum of its two ditches (Richmond 1940, 41).

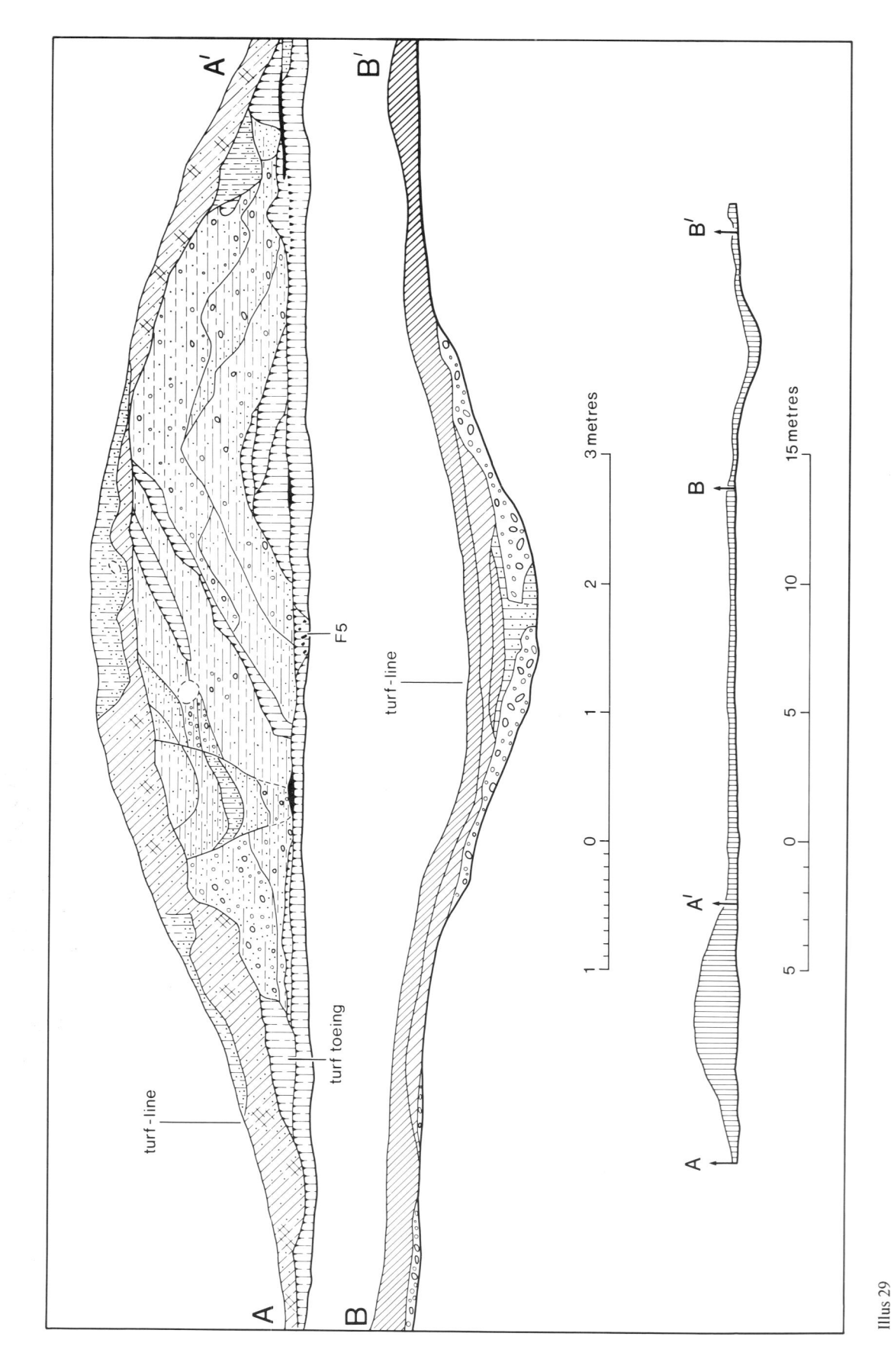

Illus 29 Drawn section of the bank and northern ditch of the Cleaven Dyke in excavation area III.

EXCAVATIONS ON THE CLEAVEN DYKE: 1993 AND 1995 ◆ 33

Illus 30
Cleaven Dyke: view of the NW face of the cross-section trench in excavation area III.

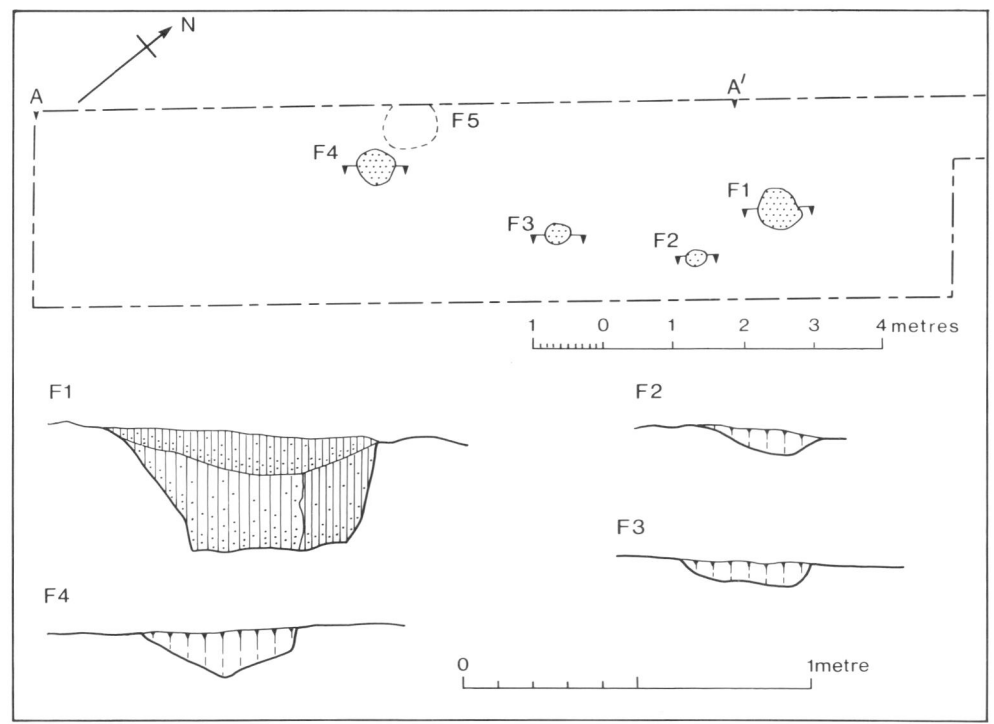

Illus 31
Plan of features below the bank of the Cleaven Dyke in the cross-section cut in excavation area III.

Illus 32
View from the NE of the axial section cut along the length of the bank of the Cleaven Dyke in excavation area IV. The NE side of the bank was removed.

Illus 33 Drawn section of the bank of the Cleaven Dyke revealed by the axial section in excavation area IV.

Illus 34
View from the NW towards the SE along the bank of the Cleaven Dyke during the excavation of the axial section at segment-boundary A10 (excavation area IV). The upper part of the bank has been removed, showing clearly the turf 'toeing' of segment A9-A10 closing off that segment before the construction of segment A10-A11 began.

AREA IV - THE AXIAL SECTION CUT IN 1995

The 1995 excavation lay immediately to the SE of the 1993 cross-section, within a rectangular trench 9.5m by 6m, cutting axially along the NE half of the bank and crossing segment-boundary A10 (illus 32). The pattern of soils within the trench was recorded in plan at five levels: twice during the removal of the bank; at the old land surface (OLS); at a level within the buried topsoil under the OLS; and on the cleaned subsoil surface.

Perhaps Richmond's most significant observation during his excavation was that, at the constructed terminal of the central bank, next to the modern A93 road, the 'toeing' of turf on the sides of the mound, holding the gravel bank in place, continued round the end of the bank, bringing it to a neatly finished stop. In the excavation segment-boundary A10, the NW bank-segment (A9/A10) was found to have a similar 'rounding off' or completion marked by deposited turf at its SE end; the bank-segment to the SE (A10/A11) did not; its toeing ran parallel to the bank edge, up against the NW segment. This implied—and the axial section subsequently demonstrated—that the NW bank-segment was built first and finished off with the toeing of turf, before the next segment to the SE was added (illus 33). This is particularly evident in illustration 34, which shows the trench looking from the NW along the axis of the bank, prior to the removal of the lowest layers of bank material; the lateral turf 'toeing' at the northern edge of the bank shows clearly as a dark line along the left-hand side of the bank; the arc of 'toeing' terminating the segment on which the photographer is standing is also clearly visible, curving round from left to right.

Beneath the bank 11 features were noted on the cleaned old land surface. Of the four which could not be dismissed as of natural origin, two (F6 and F7) were certainly the result of human activity, and the others (F8 and F9) possibly so (illus 35).

F8 and F9 were small shallow features with uniform fills resembling the OLS. It is possible that they represent the remains of two shallow postholes or stakeholes.

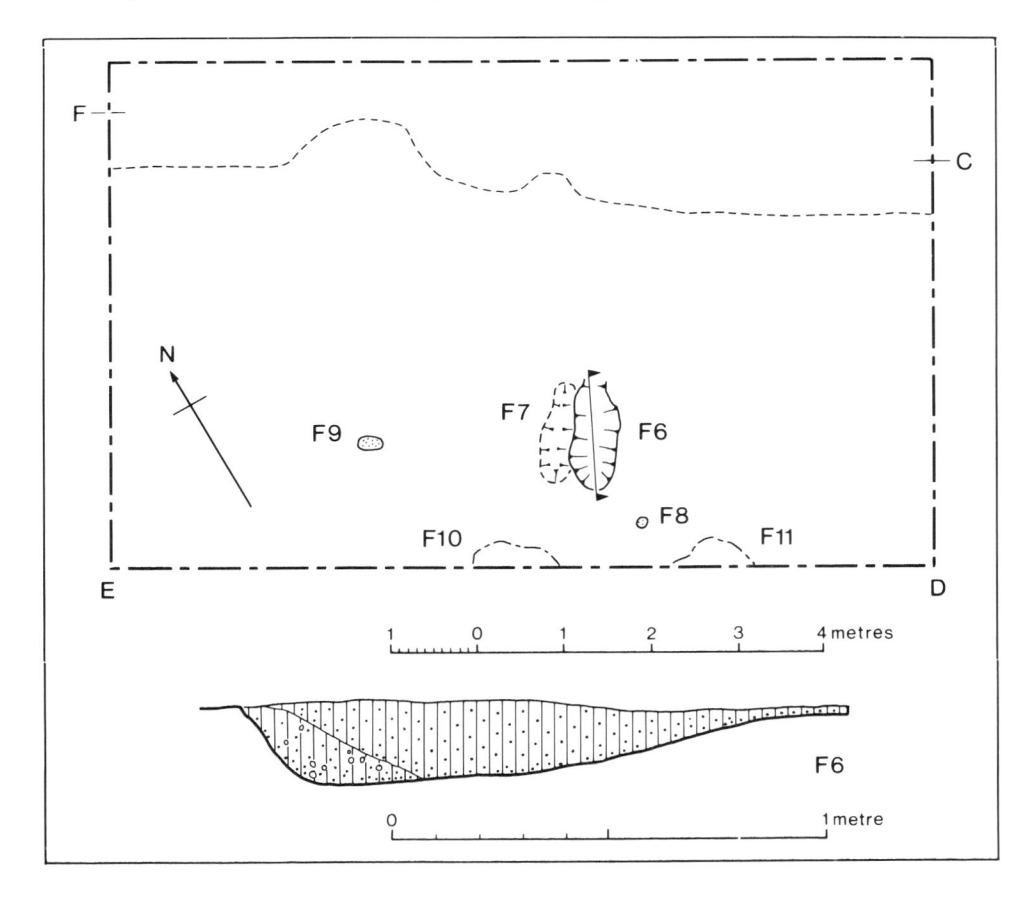

Illus 35
Plan of excavated features below the bank of the Cleaven Dyke in excavation area IV.

F6 and F7 appeared to be the quarry and bank respectively for an unusual feature: during planning of the OLS a small mound of gravel was noted and planned. It was thought to be a rise in the natural subsoil, but on excavation it was shown to be a pile of gravel apparently dumped on the OLS and gradually absorbed (presumably by the accretion of organic matter) into it. F6 appeared on cleaning. The profile of the two features matched exactly–F6 was deeper at the west, and F7 was higher at the same end. We have interpreted this shallow pit and the upcast from it as in some way associated with the construction of the Dyke, perhaps a crude marker for the line on which the Dyke was to be built.

Two areas of charcoal-stained OLS were identified (F10 and F11). On excavation neither proved to be the top of a deeper feature–only darker areas of old land surface. Fragments of charcoal were found in F10. Fragments of charcoal were also recovered from the old land surface to the NW. The soil micromorphology report cast light on their origins.

2.4 PALAEOSOLS OF THE CLEAVEN DYKE

Ian A Simpson & Donald A Davidson

The 1993 and 1995 excavations of the Cleaven Dyke identified an underlying fossil surface soil and other buried surface soils within the monument, while excavation of the ditches established the occurrence of inwashed soil materials. These are 'palaeosols'–literally ancient soils. Soils are dynamic, natural bodies the properties of which reflect the environmental conditions under which they have been formed (Jenny 1980) and so the palaeosols associated with the Cleaven Dyke provide an opportunity to assist in reconstructing the environment immediately preceding and during the formation of the monument. In this study the technique of soil thin section micromorphology is used to describe the natural and human-influenced properties of the Cleaven Dyke palaeosols. From the descriptions simple categories are presented and interpreted within the context of soil formation chronology. These different strands are then synthesised to provide an indication of the environmental conditions associated with construction of the Cleaven Dyke.

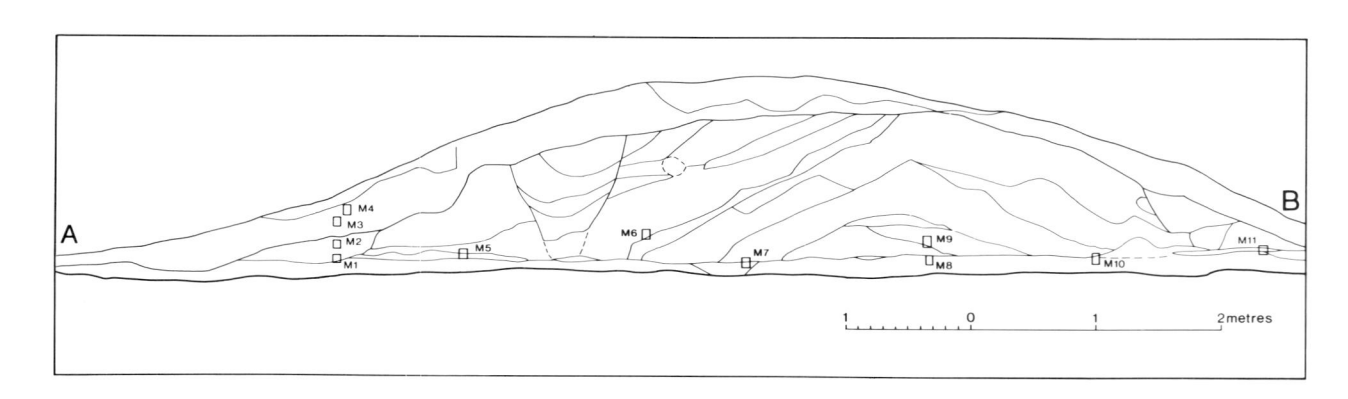

Illus 36
Cleaven Dyke: location of micromorphology thin section and soil pollen samples in excavation area III.

METHODS

Twenty-two undisturbed samples from excavated profile faces of the monument were collected in 75mm x 55mm x 45mm Kubiena tins in 1993 (11 samples from the bank, illus 36; two from the ditch) and 1995 (nine samples; illus 37). Sampling was designed to ensure the maximum range of soil types within and beneath the monument. Thin sections were prepared at the Micromorphology Laboratory, University of Stirling, following the procedures of Murphy (1986). Interpretation of the observed features rests upon the accumulated data of a number of workers, notably Courty *et al* (1989) and Fitzpatrick (1993).

RESULTS AND DISCUSSION: SOIL TYPES

In all the thin sections described, basic mineral materials are broadly similar in both terrigenous type and relative frequency. Descriptions indicate a high proportion of coarse angular and subangular quartz with a range of other, less frequent, minerals resulting in a freely-drained soil (tables 3-6). Rock fragments are usually metamorphic in origin but there are also a very few siltstones present. The mineral and rock fragment suite is typical for this area of Scotland where glacial outwash sediments from the Highlands form the soil parent material. These observations also serve to indicate that the materials used in the formation of the monument were local to the area, as was the material infilling the ditches. No erratics introduced by human occupation were observed.

Despite the similarities in parent material, pedogenic differences are discernible with microstructure, birefringence fabric (the fabric of the fine mass observed between cross polarizers and described by the nature, orientation and distribution of the patterns of interference colours) and related distribution characteristics permitting classification of the thin sections into four types. Type 1 soils are characterised by intergrain microaggregate structures together with

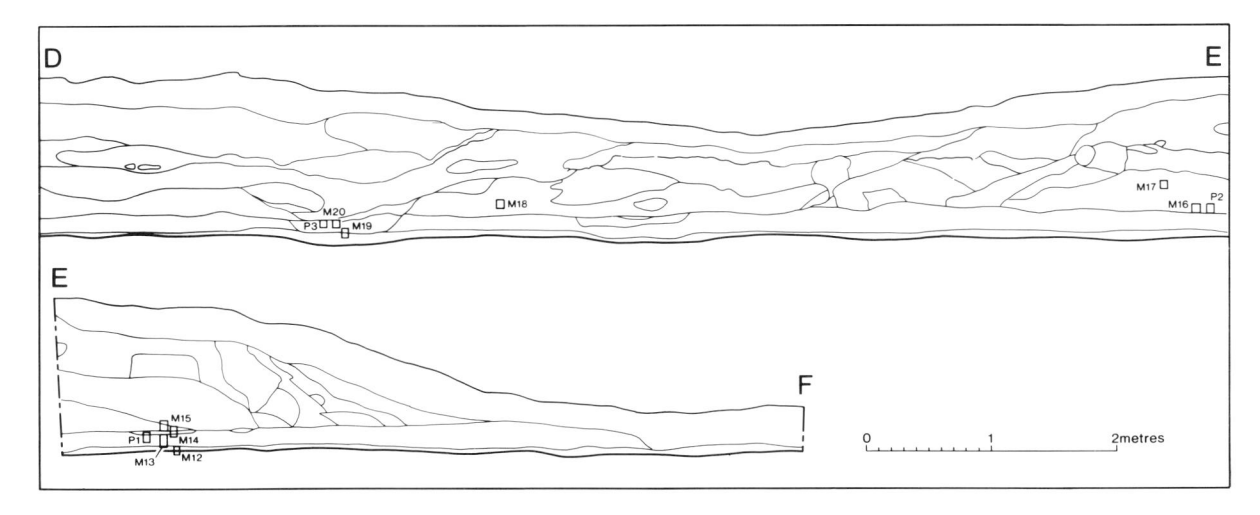

Illus 37
Cleaven Dyke: location of micromorphology thin section and soil pollen samples in excavation area IV.

stipple speckled birefringence fabrics and enaulic related distributions (enaulic distribution patterns refer to a skeleton of larger fabric units with aggregates of smaller units in the interstitial spaces). Such soils represent the land surface buried by the bank, some areas of which have been subject to small-scale anthropogenic disturbance, and the turf lines and dumps within the bank. Type 2 soils have a fine granular microstructure with isotropic birefringence fabrics predominating and enaulic related distributions, and are found on the edge of the bank. Type 3 soils have a range of different microstructures which includes intergrain microaggregate, granular and subangular blocky, together with stipple speckled birefringence fabrics and enaulic to porphyric related distributions. These soils are found infilling the ditches of the monument. Type 4 soils are single grain microstructures with monic related distributions and represent the sands and gravels forming the largest proportion of the bank (monic distribution patterns refer to fabric units of only one size group). These soils are sampled with other soil classes (the upper part of samples M5 and M10) and are not discussed further, as they provide no evidence with which to interpret the palaeoenvironment of the monument, other than that bank is comprised of local sands and gravels (table 6).

TYPE 1 SOILS

Of the Type 1 soils (tables 3 and 4), samples M8, M10, the lower part of M11, M12 and M13 represent the minimally disturbed buried land surface (illus 36; 37). These soils have brown to dark brown organo-mineral fine material with dotted limpidity (limpidity expresses the transparency of the fine mass and is associated with the presence or absence of micro-coated particles). A range of fine organic materials is evident, together with excremental pedofeatures, but, with the exception of very few fungal spores and rare fine organic coatings, coarse organic material and other types of pedofeatures are absent. These characteristics suggest a high degree of biological activity with rapid turnover of organic material and limited loss of nutrients from the soil. Such characteristics and their associated pedogenic processes are indicative of the surface horizons of a brown forest soil that would have supported a deciduous woodland vegetation cover. However, the occurrence of occasional phytoliths suggests that grassland was a significant component of the vegetation cover immediately prior to the formation of the bank, and in the absence of infilled tree root channels within the stratigraphy it is entirely feasible that major woodland cover may have been cleared from at least the line of the monument at some earlier period. Limited evidence of small-scale disturbance is found in these samples, with traces of small stones that are bright orange in oblique incident light and fine charcoals, suggesting a light burning of this early land surface. Dusty clay coatings up to 30µm in thickness are also evident in M11 indicating small-scale anthropogenic disturbance to the soil horizon, but there is no horizon disruption to suggest major woodland clearance activity immediately prior to the formation of the bank.

A greater degree of anthropogenic disturbance is evident in samples M19 and M20, representative of the small areas of charcoal-stained old land surface evident beneath the monument (illus 37). These areas are not part of a deeper feature and are characterised in thin section by very few to few charcoals (not strongly lignified tissue, with which it can easily be confused), the increased frequency of fine organic debris remains, the occurrence of very few heated stones, and the occurrence of a bone fragment in sample M19. Such observations serve to highlight the occurrence of human activity in the pathway of the monument prior to construction, and it may be suggested that this area represents small patches where light brush vegetation cleared from the pathway of the monument was gathered for burning. However, sufficient time must have passed for the main products of these fires to have dispersed before construction of the monument.

Further anthropogenic disturbance is evident in sample M7 beneath the bank (illus 36). Here there is a greater proportion of small burnt stones together with small areas of clay coatings up to 50µm in thickness and light brown fine mineral material, confirming the excavators' observation of a small hearth site at this point in the land surface. The extent of biological activity and microstructure of the hearth site is of the same order as that identified in the other buried land surface soils although red brown organo-mineral fine material remains evident. This means that this locality was regrading back towards a brown forest soil after disruption, although this process was not complete, and implies a limited impact of the hearth on local pedogenesis. The length of time for an A1 horizon to form and reach equilibrium is generally estimated to be between 600 and 1500 years (Douchafour 1982) but in view of the limited disturbance to the soil by the hearth and incomplete regrading, it is evident that the hearth site pre-dates the formation of the monument by a relatively short period of time. This period is likely to be in the order of a few decades to a few centuries.

Samples M5, M6, M9, M14, M15, M16, M17 and M18 represent turf lines and dumps within the bank. They are very similar in their micromorphological characteristics to the soils beneath the bank discussed above, suggesting that the turves were part of a mature brown forest soil surface horizon. One sample, M14, immediately above sample M13 from the old land surface does however contain evidence of rare depletion pedofeatures, and thin (100µm thick) linear accumulations of iron suggest that incipient podsolisation may have commenced immediately prior to the construction, at least in some parts of the landscape in the area around the monument. Because of their mature, rather than skeletal, nature, the position of these turf lines in the bank can be explained as having been stripped from local areas and transported to the bank, rather than having formed *in situ* on top of the deposited sand and gravels. Use of stripped turves in this manner would have provided a ready-made vegetation surface and provided stability to the evolving bank structure.

Cleaven Dyke Type 1 soils, buried land surface

Coarse Mineral Material (>10 μm) and Fine Mineral Material (<10 μm)

	SECTION	QUARTZ	FELDSPAR	BIOTITE	GARNET	MUSCOVITE	HORNBLENDE	COMPOUND QUARTZ GRAINS	SANDSTONES	SILTSTONES	METAMORPHICS	PHYTOLITHS	HEATED STONE	BONE	FINE MINERAL MATERIAL (<10 μm)
BURIED LAND SURFACE	M8	•••	•••	•••	•	•	•	•	•	•	•				ORGANO-MINERAL; BROWN; DOTTED LIMPIDITY
	M10 UPPER	••••	••••	•••	•	•	•	•	•	•	•				ORGANO-MINERAL; BROWN; DOTTED LIMPIDITY
	M10 LOWER	•••	•••	•••	•	•	•	•••	•	•	•	•	t		ORGANO-MINERAL; DARK BROWN TO BROWN; SPECKLED LIMPIDITY
	M11 LOWER	••••	••••	•••	•	•	•	•	•	•	•	•	t		ORGANO-MINERAL; BROWN; SPECKLED LIMPIDITY
	M12	••••	•••	•••	•	•	•	•••	•	•	•				ORGANO-MINERAL; BROWN; DOTTED LIMPIDITY
	M13	•••	•••	•••	•	•	•	•	•	•	•				ORGANO-MINERAL; DARK BROWN; DOTTED LIMPIDITY
DISTURBED BURIED LAND SURFACE	M7	•••	•••	•		•	•	•••	•	•	•		•	•	ORGANO-MINERAL; BROWN TO SPECKLED LIMPIDITY RED BROWN
	M19	•••	•••	•••	•	•	•	•	•	•	•		•	•	ORGANO-MINERAL; DARK BROWN; DOTTED LIMPIDITY
	M20	•••	•••	•••	•	•	•	•	•	•	•		•		ORGANO-MINERAL; DARK BROWN; DOTTED LIMPIDITY

Coarse Organic Material (>5 cells), Fine Organic Material (<5 cells), and Pedofeatures

	SECTION	FUNGAL SPORES	LIGNIFIED TISSUE	PARENCHYMATIC TISSUE	AMORPHOUS (BLACK)	AMORPHOUS (YELLOW/ORANGE)	AMORPHOUS (REDDISH BROWN)	CELL RESIDUE	CHARCOALS	POLLEN	ORGANIC COATINGS	TEXTURAL (SILTY CLAY)	TEXTURAL (CLAY COATINGS)	TEXTURAL (LIMPID CLAY)	AMORPHOUS & CRYPTO CRYSTALLINE NODULE	AMORPHOUS AND CRYPTO CRYSTALLINE INFILLS + COATINGS	EXCREMENTAL (MAMILLATE)	EXCREMENTAL (SPHEROIDAL)	DEPLETION
BURIED LAND SURFACE	M8					•	•											•	
	M10 UPPER				•/••				t										
	M10 LOWER	•							t									•	
	M11 LOWER				•				t				•				•	•	
	M12	•			•				t								•		
	M13	•			•				t		•						•	•	
DISTURBED BURIED LAND SURFACE	M7	•			•				•		•		•						
	M19				••				••								•		•
	M20				•••				•••								•		•

Microstructure, Groundmass, Related Distribution

	SECTION	MICROSTRUCTURE	COARSE MATERIAL ARRANGEMENT	GROUNDMASS B FABRIC	RELATED DISTRIBUTION
BURIED LAND SURFACE	M8	INTERGRAIN MICROAGGREGATE WITH SINGLE GRAIN LENSES	RANDOM	STIPPLE SPECKLED	ENAULIC WITH MONIC & PORPHYRIC LENSES
	M10 UPPER	SINGLE GRAIN	RANDOM	–	MONIC
	M10 LOWER	INTERGRAIN MICROAGGREGATE	RANDOM	STIPPLE SPECKLED	ENAULIC
	M11 LOWER	INTERGRAIN MICROAGGREGATE	RANDOM	STIPPLE SPECKLED	ENAULIC WITH PORPHYRIC LENSES
	M12	INTERGRAIN MICROAGGREGATE	RANDOM	STIPPLE SPECKLED	ENAULIC
	M13	INTERGRAIN MICROAGGREGATE	RANDOM	STIPPLE SPECKLED	ENAULIC
DISTURBED BURIED LAND SURFACE	M7	INTERGRAIN MICROAGGREGATE GRANULAR	RANDOM	STIPPLE SPECKLED	ENAULIC WITH PORPHYRIC LENSES
	M19	INTERGRAIN MICROAGGREGATE	RANDOM	STIPPLE SPECKLED	ENAULIC
	M20	INTERGRAIN MICROAGGREGATE	RANDOM	STIPPLE SPECKLED	ENAULIC

Frequency class refers to the appropriate area of section (Bullock et al 1985)
- t — Trace
- • — Very few
- •• — Few
- ••• — Frequent / Common
- •••• — Dominant / Very Dominant

Frequency class for textural pedofeatures (Bullock et al 1985)
- • — Rare
- •• — Occasional
- ••• — Many

Table 3

Cleaven Dyke Type 1 soils, buried land surface.

Table 4

Cleaven Dyke Type 1 soils, turf lines and dumps.

SECTION		QUARTZ	FELDSPAR	BIOTITE	GARNET	MUSCOVITE	HORNBLENDE	COMPOUND QUARTZ GRAINS	SANDSTONES	SILTSTONES	METAMORPHICS	PHYTOLITHS	HEATED STONE	BONE	FINE MINERAL MATERIAL (<10 μm)	FUNGAL SPORES	LIGNIFIED TISSUE	PARENCHYMATIC TISSUE	AMORPHOUS (BLACK)	AMORPHOUS (YELLOW/ORANGE)	AMORPHOUS (REDDISH BROWN)	CELL RESIDUE	CHARCOALS	POLLEN	ORGANIC COATINGS	TEXTURAL (SILTY CLAY)	TEXTURAL (CLAY COATINGS)	TEXTURAL (LIMPID CLAY)	AMORPHOUS & CRYPTO CRYSTALLINE NODULE	AMORPHOUS AND CRYPTO CRYSTALLINE INFILLS + COATINGS	EXCREMENTAL (MAMILLATE)	EXCREMENTAL (SPHEROIDAL)	DEPLETION
M14		••••	••	••		•	•	•	•	•	•				ORGANO-MINERAL; DARK BROWN & RED BROWN; DOTTED LIMPIDITY				•		•		t		•					•	•	•	•
M15		••••	••	••		•	•	•	•	•	•				ORGANO-MINERAL; DARK BROWN & BROWN; DOTTED LIMPIDITY				•		•		t		•					•	•		
M16		•••	•	••		•	•	•	•	•	•				ORGANO-MINERAL; BROWN; SPECKLED LIMPIDITY				•		•		t								•		
M17		•••	•	••		•	•	•	•	•	•				ORGANO-MINERAL; BROWN; SPECKLED LIMPIDITY				•		•		t								•		
M18		•••	•	••		•	•	•	•	•	•				ORGANO-MINERAL; BROWN; SPECKLED LIMPIDITY				•		•		t								•		
M5	UPPER	•••	•	••		•	•	•	•	•	•				ORGANO-MINERAL; DARK BROWN; SPECKLED LIMPIDITY				•														
M5	LOWER	•••	•	•••		•	•	•	•	•	•		t		ORGANO-MINERAL; DARK BROWN; SPECKLED LIMPIDITY	•			•		•												
M6		•••	•	••		•	•	•	•	•	•		t		MINERAL; LIGHT BROWN; DOTTED LIMPIDITY				•												•		
M9		••••	•	••		•	•	•	•	•	•		t		ORGANO-MINERAL; BROWN; SPECKLED LIMPIDITY				•		•										•		

SECTION		MICROSTRUCTURE	COARSE MATERIAL ARRANGEMENT	GROUNDMASS B FABRIC	RELATED DISTRIBUTION
M14		INTERGRAIN MICROAGGREGATE	RANDOM	STIPPLE SPECKLED	ENAULIC
M15		INTERGRAIN MICROAGGREGATE	RANDOM	STIPPLE SPECKLED	ENAULIC
M16		INTERGRAIN MICROAGGREGATE GRANULAR	RANDOM	STIPPLE SPECKLED	ENAULIC
M17		INTERGRAIN MICROAGGREGATE GRANULAR	RANDOM	STIPPLE SPECKLED	ENAULIC
M18		INTERGRAIN MICROAGGREGATE	RANDOM	STIPPLE SPECKLED	ENAULIC
M5	UPPER	SINGLE GRAIN	RANDOM	—	MONIC
M5	LOWER	INTERGRAIN MICROAGGREGATE	RANDOM	STIPPLE SPECKLED	ENAULIC
M6		INTERGRAIN MICROAGGREGATE GRANULAR	RANDOM	STIPPLE SPECKLED MOZAIC SPECKLED	ENAULIC
M9		INTERGRAIN MICROAGGREGATE GRANULAR	RANDOM	STIPPLE SPECKLED	ENAULIC

Frequency class refers to the appropriate area of section (Bullock et al 1985)

- t Trace
- • Very few
- •• Few
- ••• Frequent / Common
- •••• Dominant / Very Dominant

Frequency class for textural pedofeatures (Bullock et al 1985)

- • Rare
- •• Occasional
- ••• Many

Table 5
Cleaven Dyke Type 2 soils, podsolised soils.

SECTION	COARSE MINERAL MATERIAL (>10 μm)													FINE MINERAL MATERIAL (<10 μm)	COARSE ORGANIC MATERIAL (>5 cells)			FINE ORGANIC MATERIAL (<5 cells)				PEDOFEATURES							
	QUARTZ	FELDSPAR	BIOTITE	GARNET	MUSCOVITE	HORNBLENDE	COMPOUND QUARTZ GRAINS	SANDSTONES	SILTSTONES	METAMORPHICS	PHYTOLITHS	HEATED STONE		FUNGAL SPORES	LIGNIFIED TISSUE	PARENCHYMATIC TISSUE	AMORPHOUS (BLACK)	AMORPHOUS (YELLOW/ORANGE)	AMORPHOUS (REDDISH BROWN)	CELL RESIDUE	CHARCOALS	TEXTURAL (SILTY CLAY)	TEXTURAL (CLAY COATINGS)	TEXTURAL (LIMPID CLAY)	TEXTURAL (SILT COATINGS)	AMORPHOUS & CRYPTO CRYSTALLINE NODULE	AMORPHOUS AND CRYPTO CRYSTALLINE INFILLS + COATINGS	EXCREMENTAL (MAMILLATE)	EXCREMENTAL (SPHEROIDAL)	DEPLETION
M1	•••	••	••	•	•	•	•	•	•	•	t		ORGANO-MINERAL, DARK BROWN; SPECKLED LIMPIDITY					•		•	•				•			•		•
M2	•••	••	••	•	•	•	•	•	•	•			ORGANO-MINERAL, REDDISH BROWN - YELLOW BROWN, SPECKLED LIMPIDITY	•			•	•								•		•		
M3	•••	••	••	•	t	t	•			•		t	ORGANO-MINERAL, DARK BROWN; SPECKLED LIMPIDITY	•	•	•	•	••	•								•••	•••	
M4	•••	••	••	•	t	t	•			t		t	ORGANO-MINERAL, REDDISH BROWN, SPECKLED LIMPIDITY	•	•	•	•	••	••	•							•••	•••	
M11 UPPER	•••	••	•••	•	•	•	••	•	•	•			ORGANO-MINERAL, DARK BROWN; SPECKLED LIMPIDITY		•	•	•	••	•	•							•		

SECTION	MICROSTRUCTURE	COARSE MATERIAL ARRANGEMENT	GROUNDMASS B FABRIC	RELATED DISTRIBUTION
M1	INTERGRAIN MICROAGGREGATE	RANDOM	STIPPLE SPECKLED	ENAULIC
M2	GRANULAR	RANDOM	ISOTROPIC	ENAULIC
	GRANULAR	RANDOM	ISOTROPIC	ENAULIC
M3	INTERGRAIN MICROAGGREGATE	RANDOM	STIPPLE SPECKLED	ENAULIC
M4	GRANULAR	RANDOM	ISOTROPIC	ENAULIC
M11 UPPER	GRANULAR; LOCALLY INTERGRAIN MICROAGGREGATE			
	INTERGRAIN MICROAGGREGATE AND GRANULAR	RANDOM	STIPPLE SPECKLED	ENAULIC WITH PORPHYRIC LENSES

Frequency class refers to the appropriate area of section (Bullock et al 1985)

t   Trace
•   Very few
••   Few
••• Frequent / Common
•••• Dominant / Very Dominant

Frequency class for textural pedofeatures (Bullock et al 1985)

•   Rare
••   Occasional
••• Many

Table 6
Cleaven Dyke Type 3 and 4 soils, ditch-fill and sands/gravels.

DITCH FILL

SECTION		COARSE MINERAL MATERIAL (>10 μm)										FINE MINERAL MATERIAL (<10 μm)	COARSE ORGANIC MATERIAL (>5 cells)			FINE ORGANIC MATERIAL (<5 cells)				PEDOFEATURES							
		QUARTZ	FELDSPAR	BIOTITE	GARNET	MUSCOVITE	HORNBLENDE	COMPOUND QUARTZ GRAINS	SANDSTONES	SILTSTONES	METAMORPHICS	PHYTOLITHS	HEATED STONE		FUNGAL SPORES	LIGNIFIED TISSUE	PARENCHYMATIC TISSUE	AMORPHOUS (BLACK)	AMORPHOUS (YELLOW/ORANGE)	AMORPHOUS (REDDISH BROWN)	CELL RESIDUE	CHARCOALS	TEXTURAL (SILTY CLAY)	TEXTURAL (CLAY COATINGS)	TEXTURAL (LIMPID CLAY)	TEXTURAL (SILT COATINGS)	AMORPHOUS & CRYPTO CRYSTALLINE NODULE	AMORPHOUS AND CRYPTO CRYSTALLINE INFILLS + COATINGS	EXCREMENTAL (MAMILLATE)	EXCREMENTAL (SPHEROIDAL)	DEPLETION
M21	RIGHT	•••	•	•	•	•	•	•	•	•	•			ORGANO-MINERAL, BROWN, SPECKLED LIMPIDITY	•		•											•			
	LEFT	•••	•	•	•	•	•	•	•	•	•			ORGANO-MINERAL, LIGHT BROWN, SPECKLED LIMPIDITY	•		•									•					
M22		•••	•	•	•	•	•	•	•	•	•			ORGANO-MINERAL, BROWN, SPECKLED LIMPIDITY	•	•	•			•	•									

SECTION		MICROSTRUCTURE	COARSE MATERIAL ARRANGEMENT	GROUNDMASS B FABRIC	RELATED DISTRIBUTION
M21	RIGHT	INTERGRAIN MICROAGGREGATE AND GRANULAR	RANDOM	STIPPLE SPECKLED	ENAULIC
	LEFT	SUBANGULAR BLOCKY AND GRANULAR	RANDOM	STIPPLE SPECKLED	ENAULIC TO PORPHYRIC
M22		INTERGRAIN MICROAGGREGATE	RANDOM	STIPPLE SPECKLED	ENAULIC TO PORPHYRIC

Frequency class refers to the appropriate area of section (Bullock et al 1985)
- • Very few
- •• Few
- ••• Frequent / Common
- •••• Dominant / Very Dominant

Frequency class for textural pedofeatures (Bullock et al 1985)
- • Rare
- •• Occasional
- ••• Many

SANDS/GRAVELS

SECTION		COARSE MINERAL MATERIAL (>10 μm)										FINE MINERAL MATERIAL (<10 μm)	COARSE ORGANIC MATERIAL (>5 cells)			FINE ORGANIC MATERIAL (<5 cells)				PEDOFEATURES					
		QUARTZ	FELDSPAR	BIOTITE	GARNET	MUSCOVITE	HORNBLENDE	COMPOUND QUARTZ GRAINS	SANDSTONES	SILTSTONES	METAMORPHICS	PHYTOLITHS	HEATED STONE		FUNGAL SPORES	LIGNIFIED TISSUE	PARENCHYMATIC TISSUE	AMORPHOUS (BLACK)	AMORPHOUS (YELLOW/ORANGE)	AMORPHOUS (REDDISH BROWN)	CELL RESIDUE	CHARCOALS	POLLEN	TEXTURAL (SILTY CLAY)	TEXTURAL (CLAY COATINGS)	TEXTURAL (LIMPID CLAY)	AMORPHOUS & CRYPTO CRYSTALLINE NODULE	AMORPHOUS AND CRYPTO CRYSTALLINE INFILLS + COATINGS	EXCREMENTAL (MAMILLATE)	EXCREMENTAL (SPHEROIDAL)	DEPLETION
M10	UPPER	••••		••				•	•	•	•			ORGANO-MINERAL; BROWN; DOTTED LIMPIDITY																	
M5	UPPER	••••		••				•	•	•	•			ORGANO-MINERAL; BROWN; SPECKLED LIMPIDITY							•									

SECTION		MICROSTRUCTURE	COARSE MATERIAL ARRANGEMENT	GROUNDMASS B FABRIC	RELATED DISTRIBUTION
M10	UPPER	SINGLE GRAIN	RANDOM	–	MONIC
M5	UPPER	SINGLE GRAIN	RANDOM	–	MONIC

TYPE 2 SOILS

Type 2 soils (table 5) are evident flanking the SW and NE edges of the bank (samples M1, M2, M3, M4 and the upper part of M11). Compared to Type 1 soil thin sections, there is less coarse mineral material and more fine isotropic organic material organised in a granular structure, although this latter feature becomes less with depth in the bank, where soils also show characteristics of the brown forest soils discussed above. Other features which characterise these soils are the absence of fine mineral material in parts of the thin sections, and the occurrence of iron depletion and accumulation pedofeatures in the lower samples. Silt cappings are also evident in the lower of these samples (M1), located on the upper surface of coarse mineral material and up to 20μm in thickness, but absent from samples higher in the bank. Taken together, these features are indicative of the surface horizon of podsolic soils where there has been a reduced rate of organic matter decomposition, acidification of the soil profile and associated depletion of soil nutrients. Formation of such soils can arise as a result of ongoing pedogenesis in freely-drained parent materials, and as a result of wetter and cooler climatic conditions with freeze-thaw processes, and heathland vegetation cover.

The juxtaposition of brown forest soil and podsol features lower in the stratigraphy (M1, M2, and the upper part of M11) suggests that podsolisation was superimposed upon existing brown forest soils, demonstrating the direction of pedogenesis from brown forest soil to podsol. More marked podsolisation is evident in samples from higher in the bank (M3 and M4) with isotropic granular organo-mineral material indicative of the upper horizon of a well-established peaty podsol. In both contexts the most plausible interpretation of these features is that podsolisation was an *in situ* process, developing after the construction of the monument.

TYPE 3 SOILS

The two samples from the ditch-fill are sufficient to demonstrate that there have been different episodes of deposition in the ditch that are predominantly the result of alluvial processes (table 6). In sample M21 the greater proportion of fine material suggests a slower rate of deposition in a low energy environment, while the coarser deposits suggest an environment of higher flow energy. Sample M22 is also characterised by coarser deposits but has a greater proportion of organic material. This suggests a period when there was no deposition in the ditch allowing vegetation to develop. Further work is required to correlate depositional phases in the ditch to the soils evidence found in the bank.

CONCLUSIONS

Description and interpretation of palaeosol micromorphological features associated with the Cleaven Dyke has identified a range of environmental conditions and anthropogenic disturbances. Brown forest soil environments were prevalent at the time of monument construction although not necessarily associated with a woodland vegetation cover, at least on the line of the monument. Similar freely-drained brown forest soils beneath Neolithic earthworks in east central Scotland have been identified at Dalladies and North Mains by Romans and his co-workers (Romans *et al* 1973; Romans & Robertson 1975; 1983; Macphail *et al* 1987). Although these excavations are few, and a considerable range of dates is represented by these studies, the similarities are sufficient to support the view that the Type 1 soils of Cleaven Dyke represent a Neolithic fossil landscape. The radiocarbon dates from the hearth confirm this interpretation. The Cleaven Dyke, however, does contain evidence to suggest that localised and incipient podsolisation had commenced at the time of monument construction, with subsequent full-scale podsolisation processes during wetter and/or cooler conditions modifying the brown forest soils on the edges of the constructed bank.

A feature of the palaeosols of this monument is the lack of morphological indicators of major anthropogenic activities such as cultivation, intensive burning and substantial woodland vegetation clearance in the immediate area of the excavated sections of the Dyke. It is apparent that construction of the monument did not require or attract major ground preparation, such as the removal of large timber or ploughing. The absence of substantially disturbed soils and lack of infilled tree root channels supports the view that all that was required was the removal of a light brush vegetation from the line of the construction. It is also apparent that settlement activity prior to the construction of the monument was genuinely at a low level although not entirely absent. These observations are in contrast with the only other excavated earthwork of this date in eastern Scotland at Dalladies where there is associated burning of vegetation and cultivation (Piggott 1971; Romans & Robertson 1983), but are similar to the Dorset cursus, which Bradley (1986) suggests may also have initially lain in an area marginal to contemporary settlement.

2.5 SOIL POLLEN BENEATH THE CLEAVEN DYKE

Kevin J Edwards & Graeme Whittington

In an effort to reconstruct the vegetation history of the area prior to the building of the Dyke, a programme of soil pollen sampling, to be related also to soil micromorphology, was instigated. Such a history is vital in providing an understanding of the landscape in which the Neolithic peoples worked–was it wooded or cleared? If it was the former, what were the floristic components of the woodland? If the latter, were there signs of agriculture or burning? Soil pollen analysis, despite its difficulties, can provide an intimate view of the immediate vegetation which peat or loch deposits rarely allow.

METHODS

Soil monoliths were collected in 75mm x 55mm x 40mm Kubiena tins. Duplicates were obtained for pollen and soil micromorphological analyses. Results from samples from three contexts (illus 37) are considered here: P1 and P3 are from the old land surface (OLS), P3 being from an area of charcoal-stained OLS (F11), possibly a hearth site. P2 comes from the turf 'toeing' on the north side of the bank and from immediately above the OLS. The sandy soils did not preserve old surface organic horizons; the palaeosol surfaces were marked by a very thin silver-coloured, silty horizon. The stratigraphy for each site is ~70% sand (fine, medium and coarse in roughly equal measures) with the remainder being silt. The organic content was about 4.5%.

The monoliths were sub-sampled at contiguous intervals of 5mm and pre-treatment was undertaken with NaOH, HF, HCl and acetolysis (Faegri & Iversen 1989). Volumetric preparations with the addition of *Lycopodium* 'exotics' enabled estimations of palynomorph concentrations. Samples were mounted unstained in silicone oil of viscosity 12 500 cSt.

Pollen type and plant nomenclatures follow Bennett (1994) and Stace (1991) respectively. A pollen count of 300 TLP was attempted at each level. Microscopic charcoal was quantified using the point count estimation method (Clark, RL 1982).

Pollen and spores counts are presented as percentages of TLP in illustrations 38-40. Only taxa found in more than two sample levels in each profile are included. Curves for total pollen concentration closely parallel those for total palynomorph concentration; only the former are included here. Charcoal concentrations and charcoal to pollen ratios are also displayed on the pollen diagrams. Computations and diagram construction were achieved using the computer programs TILIA and TILIA•GRAPH (Grimm 1991).

Pollen diagrams based on lake and peat deposits are typically zoned into 'local pollen assemblage zones' which demarcate areas of the diagram within which there is a recognisable homogeneity. Palynomorphs from within soil profiles experience movement as a result of processes such as leaching, water-table fluctuations and animal activity; consequently the microfossils do not necessarily possess the same stratigraphic integrity as those recovered from mires and lakes. Nevertheless, areas of soil pollen profiles displaying similarities between spectra are often evident and their demarcation can be important for explanations of site history. In the present account, 'phases', analogous to traditional pollen 'zones' have been indicated on the pollen diagrams (cf Keith-Lucas 1986)–these facilitate both discussion and interpretation. The phases of profile P2 are numbered in 'reverse' order from top to bottom, the reasoning for which is discussed below.

THE POLLEN DIAGRAMS

All pollen and spore diagrams have a good representation for the following taxa: birch (*Betula*), alder (*Alnus glutinosa*), hazel (cf *Corylus avellana*-type), heather (*Calluna vulgaris*), grass (*Poaceae*), ribwort plantain (*Plantago lanceolata*), devil's-bit scabious (*Succisa pratensis*), moonwort (*Botrychium lunaria*), polypody (*Polypodium*) and undifferentiated ferns (*Pteropsida* (monolete) indet). Each diagram, however, displays important variations and these are described briefly below.

P1

The pollen and spore taxa maintain fluctuating but fairly constant values throughout the profile (illus 38) except for the uppermost three levels where birch falls, ribwort plantain rises and there is a small expansion of heather. The diagram is dominated by birch, hazel and grass pollen. Total pollen concentrations fall from 35,000 grains cm^{-3} at the top of the profile to 17,000 grains at 32.5mm, before expanding at 42.5mm and declining to 17,000 grains at the base.

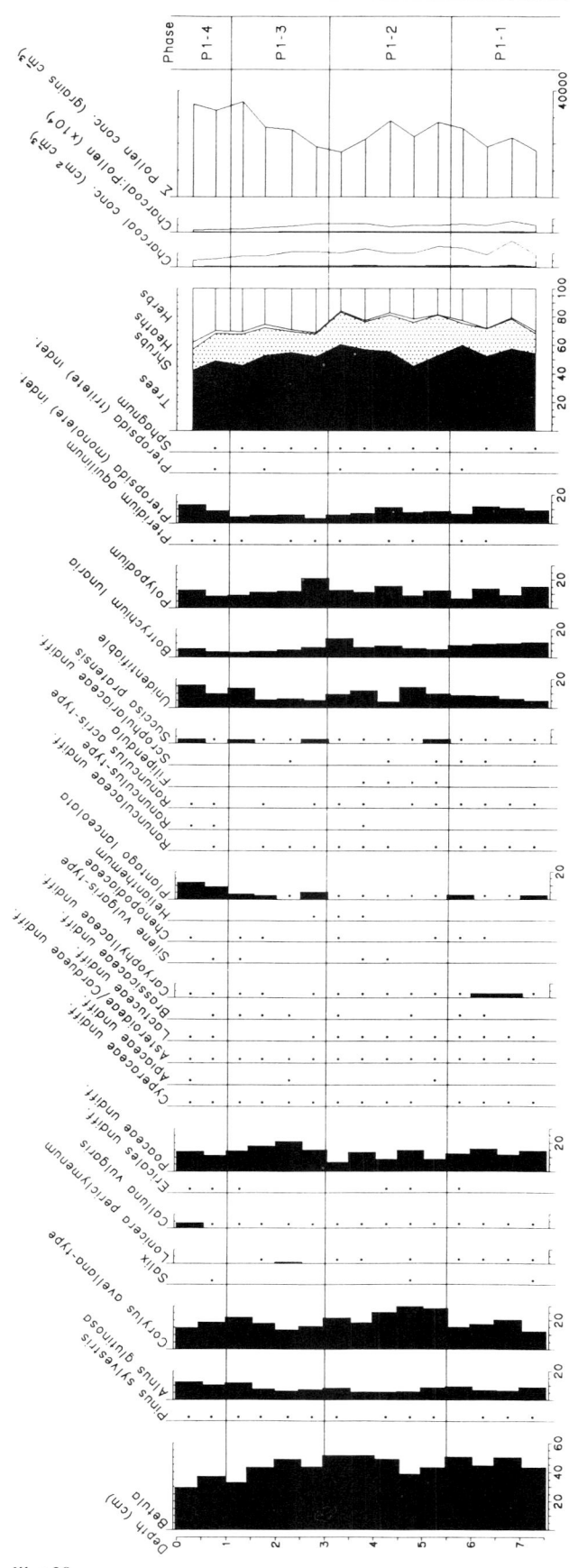

Illus 38
Selected pollen and spore data from Cleaven Dyke soil pollen profile P1 (• indicates <2% TLP; x10 exaggeration curves on charcoal samples).

Illus 39
Selected pollen and spore data from Cleaven Dyke soil pollen profile P2 (• indicates <2% TLP; x10 exaggeration curves on charcoal samples; note the 'reversed' order of the phases).

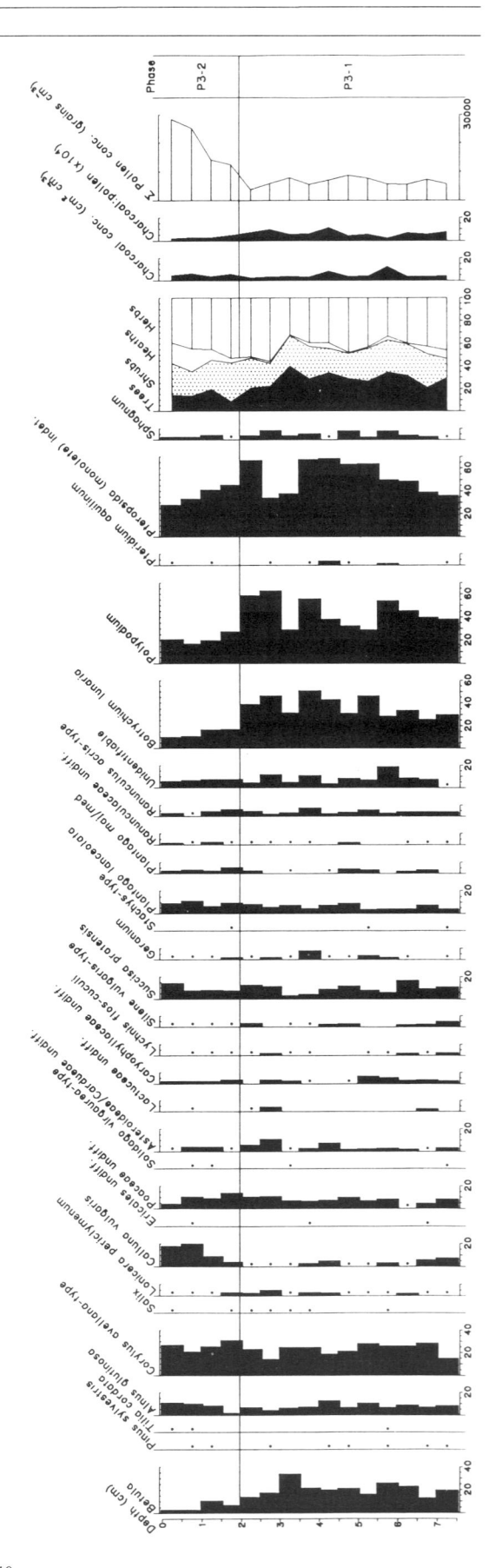

Illus 40
Selected pollen and spore data from Cleaven Dyke soil pollen profile P3 (• indicates <2% TLP).

P2

Alder, hazel and grass pollen values are relatively constant (illus 39). The top part of the profile (phases P2-1 and 2) has a markedly higher representation for birch, moonwort and ferns. The basal section of the profile is dominated by heather (phases P2-3 and 4) and plantain is increased in P2-4. Total pollen concentrations show a continuous increase down-profile with a pronounced bulge in values (maximum 184,000 grains cm^{-3}) in phase P2-3.

P3

Hazel pollen values are fairly constant throughout the profile (illus 40). Birch and the fern taxa are most in evidence in the basal two-thirds of the diagram (phase P3-1). Heather rises in the top three spectra, having been preceded by a rise in grass pollen. Total pollen concentrations fall sharply from 28,000 grains cm^{-3} at the top of the profile, to 4000 grains at 22.5mm; beneath this, values fluctuate at around 7000 grains cm^{-3}.

INTERPRETATION

The three pollen profiles provide both (i) an interpretable general vegetational history of the area covering an undetermined period prior to the construction of the Dyke, and (ii) a statement as to the nature of the vegetation in the landscape at the time of Dyke construction. Profiles P1 and P3, being from the old land surface beneath the bank, make it possible to draw inferences concerning contemporaneous site history. Their differing pollen content is a reflection of the flora of the area and this suggests that a vegetational mosaic existed.

The pre-Dyke vegetation exhibited a wooded aspect in which birch-hazel communities were dominant. Alder was growing in damper areas—presumably along the course of the Lunan Burn as well as more locally. The woodland cover was not complete; the pollen of grasses, daisy/thistle family (*Asteroideae/Cardueae*), pink family (*Caryophyllaceae*), devil's-bit scabious, ribwort plantain, greater/hoary plantain (*Plantago major/media*) and buttercup (*Ranunculus acris*-type), and the spores of moonwort, are indicative of open areas. The polypody and other ferns could well have been represented in both the open land and woodland floras.

By the time that the Dyke was built, this vegetation had undergone a change. Profile P3 in particular shows that the birch was reduced (phase P3-2, and probably contemporaneous with phase P1-3), whereas the hazel presence was maintained, perhaps due to its value as a food resource. The continued presence of birch in P3-2 could reflect the recruitment of birch pollen from the site of profile P1; as the two sites are only 7m apart, it is conceivable that the pollen did not come from P1, but from a birch stand in close proximity to it. The expansion in grass pollen values in P3-2 and P1-3, ribwort plantain in P1-3 especially, and the decline in ferns in P3-2, argue for possible grazing. It is impossible to say whether this would have occurred in deliberately cleared areas or in those where a birch woodland cycle had ended. Within phases P3-2 and P1-4, there are expansions in heather pollen—that at P3 is stronger, suggesting an earlier establishment of heather there. This type of pollen change is frequently taken to indicate increasing soil acidity (Simmons 1996) and a decrease in the value of the pasture. The low abundances of charcoal in P1 (0.5cm^2/cm^{-3} at the surface and with charcoal to pollen ratios decreasing in the upper part of the profile) suggests that burning of the ground flora did not take place there, either as a natural or as an anthropogenic process. The situation at P3 is very different, with quite high surface values for microscopic charcoal of 4.8cm^2/cm^{-3}, though with declining charcoal to pollen ratios in the uppermost five samples. It might be argued that burning of the vegetation had contributed to podsolisation in P3, with the resulting expansion in heather on impoverished soils. The situation is confused, however, in that P3 is located on the charcoal-stained old land surface of feature F11, the site of a fire or fires. It might be noted that a profile maximum for microscopic charcoal in P3 is found at 57.5mm, where charcoal attains a value of 12.7cm^2/cm^{-3}. The section diagram (illus 33) shows that macroscopic charcoal permeates much of feature F11, and it would therefore seem imprudent to argue for fire-related vegetational change on the basis of either the microscopic or macroscopic charcoal records.

The remaining pollen profile, P2, is part of the bank component of the Dyke. It is most probable that the 'toeing' on the north side of the bank was constructed from turves taken from the area of the ditch to the north. Profile P2 shows marked similarities to the other two profiles, with the important difference that it appears to be inverted. The suggestion can be made, therefore, that in this instance the turf had been placed with its vegetated surface facing downwards (it is in recognition of this fact that the phases are numbered in 'reverse' order, that is, from the top to the base). With the inverted nature of the profile in mind, it becomes apparent that it bears a very close resemblance to that of P3. Signs of a decline in birch are intimated in P2-1, and continue, with sporadic expansions (possibly due to off-site inputs) in P2-2. Once again the hazel component remains fairly constant. In P3 the birch decline was accompanied by a rise in the values for heather pollen and that is an even stronger feature at the beginning of P2-3. There is a slight reduction in grass values in phases P2-3, moonwort declines to <2% TLP in P2-3 and ribwort plantain is also much reduced. Thus, an unambiguous 'grazing' phase is not discernible in P2-3 (that is, before heather pollen expands). Indeed, if most of the birch pollen in the profile had originated from beyond this site, it is conceivable that the other components of the pollen spectra in P2-1 and 2 could reflect a grazed habitat. Phase P2-4 witnesses the continued abundance of heather pollen (>30% TLP); it is noticeable that ribwort plantain and moonwort also increase slightly. It is possible that the boundary between P2-3 and P2-4 marks the junction of two turves with adjacent upper surfaces (note the divergence in the pollen concentrations), but this is not explored further here. Nowhere in the profile does microscopic charcoal attain values greater than $1.9 cm^2/cm^{-3}$ and charcoal to pollen ratios are lower than for profile P1.

The pollen assemblages from the three profiles permit the inference that the vegetation of the pre-Dyke land surface was characterised by a dynamic mosaic structure. Areas of woodland and areas of open land coexisted, with the former also giving way to the latter. The open areas also saw a change from grassland to heath. A possible constant in the vegetation was the existence, and perhaps exploitation, of hazel.

CONCLUSIONS

The vegetational landscape which confronted the builders of Cleaven Dyke would have consisted of an intermixture of light birch-hazel woodland, perhaps of a secondary nature, heath and grassland. At face value, this seems to have been achieved through the simple progression from birch-hazel woodland to heath, as might be expected to result from human interference with woodland for pastoral purposes in an area of sandy soils (Dimbleby 1962).

Given the extremely complex nature of soil pollen assemblages, however, the history of vegetation prior to the construction of the Dyke may have been more complicated than suggested above. The pollen obtained from P1, P2 and P3 could have been derived from at least two sources - from plants growing on the site and from those whose pollen has been transported there by the wind. Upon incorporation into the soil, the pollen and spores would have undergone movement within the profiles, such that the final deposition levels of contemporaneous palynomorphs are likely to be mixed with those of other ages, leading to 'blurred' assemblages. Thus, in the case of the Cleaven Dyke pollen profiles, it is feasible that the woodland to heath progression may conceal recurrent instances of such progressions (cf Edwards 1979).

The conjunction of the pollen data and the radiocarbon evidence from oak charcoal in the nearby hearth is of interest. It has been suggested that the pollen indicates possible woodland regeneration. Elm pollen is present in very small amounts (≤0.7% TLP in P1 and P3), while oak is absent–a contrast to the situation found in pollen profiles from the nearby lake sites of Stormont Loch (Caseldine 1980) and Rae Loch (1.2 above). The pollen in the Cleaven Dyke profiles could therefore be of post-elm decline age–a time by which much of the primary elm-oak woodland would have been cleared for agriculture. Any abandonment or reduction in intensity of use of cleared areas would permit colonisation by birch and hazel. This process would be consistent with a date younger than c 5100 BP (3800 cal BC) for the soil pollen assemblages and thus also consistent with the suggestion that the Dyke in this area was possibly constructed within the period of the late 5th to mid/late 4th millennium cal BC (**3.1** below).

THE CLEAVEN DYKE - CONSTRUCTION AND DESIGN

'Not all human constructions are directed at posterity' (Bradley 1993, 98).

3.1 DATING THE CONSTRUCTION OF THE CLEAVEN DYKE

Two samples of wood charcoal from within the small area of burning beneath the Cleaven Dyke excavated in 1993 (F5) were identified by TG Holden and A Duffy. They noted that both samples were 100% oak (*Quercus* sp), the poor state of preservation of the charcoal implying that the wood was rotten before being charred.

The samples were submitted to the Glasgow University radiocarbon dating laboratory at the Scottish Universities Research and Reactor Centre. The determinations were 5500±120 BP (GU-3911) and 5550±130 BP (GU-3912). The calibrated ranges produced are, respectively, 4700-4000 cal BC and 4750-4000 cal BC.

The radiocarbon dates provide only a broad terminus post quem for the construction of the bank: can we tie down the date of construction more closely? There are two variables: the oak wood used for dating was already rotten when turned to charcoal, and some time passed between the fire and the construction of the bank. For the first variable, old oak heartwood, perhaps collected for use as a form of tinder, might have ceased to exchange carbon with the atmosphere (the event the radiocarbon method would age) some very considerable time before it was burned–perhaps up to 400 years (the limit normal for unpollarded English oak) or even more (up to 800 years in modern pollarded oaks) (Rackham 1990, 10-16; Ashmore pers comm). This assessment supersedes that published in the interim account (Barclay *et al* 1995). For the second variable, Simpson and Davidson took and examined a soil micromorphological sample (sample M7, **2.4** above); they suggest that the fire pre-dates the formation of the monument by a few decades to a few centuries. This assessment supersedes the published interim statement that the period was '*c* 60-150 years' (Barclay *et al* 1995). Therefore, it would be reasonable to suggest that the event dated by the radiocarbon method probably occurred somewhere between 200 and 800 years before the bank of the Cleaven Dyke was built at this point. The date range quoted in the interim publication was probably therefore too sanguine. We would be wiser perhaps to suggest a date range tied down no more closely than late 5th to mid/late 4th millennium cal BC. If the Dyke was built in segments over a prolonged period, then the dated bank-segment might also be considerably later than the segments some distance to the NW.

3.2 MENSURATION AND DESIGN

As already observed, for a monument which displays such marked variation of structural detail, the Cleaven Dyke adheres overall to a single alignment with considerable tenacity. This latter characteristic is doubtless what persuaded scholars in the past to believe that its originators could have been none other than the legions of Rome. The 2085m-long line that can be drawn between the Dyke's SE terminal and the point at which it springs from the tail of the original composite long barrow passes very close to the mid-points of each of the breaks that separate the five main Sections of the central bank. Between those breaks, however, the course of the bank and flanking ditches may deviate by as much as 10° from the overall alignment, while the cross-dimension of each structural element may vary by as much as 50%. Clearly, to take account of so much local variation, the builders of the Dyke must surely have had a reliable means of setting out and adhering to a long-term strategy of construction.

Accordingly, any occurrence of a regular dimensional pattern in the surviving remains requires to be investigated carefully, not only as possible evidence of the original design or construction process, but also as an indication of the Dyke's purpose and function.

PATTERNS OF CONSTRUCTION

The most obvious pattern, evident throughout, is the dimensional relationship between the central bank, the ditches, and the intervening berms–a pattern which is modified only by the increasing degree of irregularity in the SE Sections. In general, however, and taking Section **A** as a model, the originally planned width of the bank appears to have been around half that of either berm and twice that of each ditch. Comparable proportional relationships may be seen among early Neolithic structures elsewhere in Britain: for example, the long barrows with widely-spaced ditches in southern England, where the excavated sites of Nutbane, Wayland's Smithy (Atkinson 1965), and West Kennet (Piggott 1962) command particular attention, since they display a maximum between-ditch width close to that of the Cleaven Dyke (45-8m).

With evidence of this kind relating to its cross-section, it would not be unreasonable to expect that a similar care had been taken in the design of the Dyke's longitudinal construction. However, despite our certainty that the monument was built in Sections and segments from NW to SE, the variation in the spacing of segment-boundaries tentatively identified in the upstanding remains of the central bank might lead one to believe that the accumulative growth-pattern was irregular. On the other hand, the spatial relationship between the five major Sections **A-E** displays a clear pattern. Measured between the estimated terminals of the ditched portions of the monument (the Dyke proper), the lengths of the five Sections are: A=848.5m; B=375m; C=289.5m; D=187.5m; E=c 375m (shown divided into segment lengths in table 7).

The measurement of Section **E** is to the last visible appearance of the southern ditch, and is necessarily an approximation. The most immediately obvious elements in the pattern are that **B** and **E** may be the same length, and **B** is, and **E** may be, twice as long as **D**; but it is also true that the combined lengths of **B**, **C** and **D**, and **C**, **D** and **E**, amount to 852m–very close the length of Section **A**. Given the room for error in lineal measurement (in modern as well as ancient times), the close agreement of these fractions and combinations seems significant. While the mathematical relationships of these figures indicate a highest common factor of 94.3, which in structural terms could be taken to imply a design module of around 94m, this does not sit easily with the measured lengths of identified segments.

Scarcity of comparative material makes it difficult to determine if the dimensional patterns which may be observed in the lengths of the Dyke's major Sections are exceptional. However, there is some evidence that analogous structures—specifically pit-defined cursus monuments (see Brophy **6.1** below)—may also occasionally exhibit regular internal subdivision. At Milton of Guthrie, Angus, for example, a total length of c 580m is broken by septal pit-lines into two adjacent pairs of sections, the first each of c 110m, and the second of c 180m; on a much smaller scale, the pit-defined Neolithic enclosure of Douglasmuir is divided by a similar septal line into two equal lengths of c 32m.

Although it is possible that, within each Section of the Dyke, similar regular subdivision may exist, in general the evidence for this is not sufficiently explicit. The exceptions are nevertheless worth noting: for example, segment-boundary A8, very close to the mid-point of Section **A**, marks the place at which the north face of the central bank becomes more rectilinear, conspicuously distinguishing it from the more variably-aligned NW portion. Similarly, segment-boundary B3, situated half way between Section-breaks **W** and **X**, marks the point at which the overall character of Section **B** is significantly changed, not only in the degree of irregularity of the

Segment	Length	Width classification
A1-A2	57 m	Narrow
A2-A3	25 m	Narrow
A3-A4	88 m	Broad
A4-A5	107 m	Narrow
A5-A6	28 m	Narrow
A6-A7	83 m	Broad
A7-A8	40 m	Narrow
A8-A9	49 m	Narrow
A9-A10	73 m	Broad
A10-A11	25 m	Narrow
A11-A12	30 m	Narrow
A12-A13	103 m	Narrow
A14-Gap W	50 m	Broad
Gap W-B1	45 m+	Narrow
B1-B2	68 m	Broad
B2-B3	80 m	Broad
B3-B4	31 m	Narrow?
B4-B5	94 m	Broad
B5-Gap X	45 m	Broad
Gap X-C1	>40 m	Narrow
C1-C2	42 m	Narrow
C2-C3	72 m	Narrow
C3-C4	27 m	Narrow
C4-Gap Y	88 m	Narrow with Broad terminal
Gap Y-D1	77 m	Broad
D1-D2	70 m	Narrow
D2-Gap Z	28 m	Narrow

Table 7
Lengths of Sections and segments of the Cleaven Dyke

bank-line, but also, and more obviously, in the width of the space between the ditches: to the NW the latter measures 43m to 46m, while to the SE it varies between 42m and 43m. That this indicates a significant structural boundary cannot be doubted; coincidentally, B3 also lies very close to what must be reckoned the mid-point of the Dyke proper.

At this point we should remind ourselves that the average between-ditch width of the Dyke varies from Section to Section. It is at a maximum in Section **A**, where it ranges from 46m to 48m; in the two halves of **B**, as we have just noted, the respective measurements are 2m and 4m less; and in Sections **C** and **D**, where a much greater irregularity prevails, the measurement is a uniform minimum of 40-42m. The eroded state of the monument in Section **E** makes assessment difficult, but the width here is unlikely to be much, if at all, greater than that in **D**. It will be observed that the consistent decrease in width as one proceeds eastwards along the Dyke accords well with the evidence that different, perhaps less rigorous, standards of construction were being applied to the project in the SE portion.

QUESTIONS OF ALIGNMENT

It remains to discuss two further design features, the first of which appears to be closely associated with segmental or sectional construction: the occurrence of changes in alignment of the bank at or near structural boundaries. The most obvious example, already described, is provided by the long barrow element of the composite barrow at the NW terminal of the Dyke, which manifests within its structure a perceptible and complex alteration of axis; this, we suggest, is of the nature of architectural features and quite distinct from the adjacent re-alignments of the Dyke as a whole at A1 and A3. The re-alignment of the terminals of Sections **B** and **C** on either side of Section-break **X**, however, invites a different interpretation; the situation, where the two terminals re-align on each other by means of a diversion of the central bank to the south, is replicated in miniature at segment-boundary A4, although the diversion in that case is to the north. At Section-break **Y**, the feature is evident only in the terminal of **D**, which bends sharply north on the SE side of the gap.

Such re-alignments, whether single or paired, might be explained (as in other complex angle-changes of Dyke elements) as local adjustments to accommodate slight differences in alignment between segments being constructed simultaneously; however, the evidence of the single excavated segment-boundary (A10: see **2.3** above) is that one segment was finished off neatly before the next was added onto it. Additionally, the frequent coincidence of this feature with various types of terminal suggests that this might have been a deliberate feature of the design. Changes in alignment at the proximal or distal ends of long cairns or barrows are sufficiently well-attested (see Brophy **6.2** below) to allow us to reject the suggestion that they are the result of either slipshod construction or widely separated phases of building. On the Dyke such terminal re-alignments seem to assume the status of structural colophons–localised devices to indicate the end (or beginning) of a building sector. The comparable angle-change at the terminals of certain Scottish bank barrows is commented on below (Brophy **6.2**). It may be that the oblique angle of the terminal of some ditch- and pit-defined cursus monuments (Loveday's (1985) terminal types Bii and Biii; Brophy **6.1** below) may represent a comparable feature; this arrangement can be seen in three of the pit-defined structures in the same area (Balneaves, Inchbare 2, and Milton of Guthrie) and a similar feature is visible at the SE and SW ends respectively of the ditched cursus sites at Powis and Blairhall. This seems to reflect the familiar Neolithic preoccupation with the proximal or distal ends of long funerary monuments, often involving the construction of façades, portals, and approach-works.

The final design element with which we are concerned is the Dyke's orientation, that is, its overall alignment. The localised divergences, particularly in the long barrow to the NW of A1, before the cursus form was established, seem to us less open to explanation than that of the long, main alignment. We note below that, in terms of local topography, the Dyke aligns on the rounded summit of the unnamed hill (labelled 'Hill of Lethendy' in Pitts and St Joseph's (1985) excavation report on Inchtuthil) forming the skyline above Gourdie on the NW, and to terminate in the SE on the crest of a sinuous hill rising only a few metres above the level of the Meikleour plateau; this orientation maximises the area of the plateau's level ground available for the construction of a linear monument. The same bearing (c 120° south of true North) if prolonged across the wide valley of Strathmore to the distant skyline, would bisect the cloven summit of Northballo Hill. Given that neither the Hill of Lethendy nor Northballo Hill are prominent on their respective horizons, neither alignment seems likely to be significant. We know (Ruggles **3.3** below) that there is no astronomical significance in the alignment.

POSSIBLE BARROWS WITHIN THE BANK

The Dorset cursus, as is well-known, incorporates two long barrows within its fabric (Tilley 1994, 172). At first sight it is possible to suggest that three burial mounds, or features intended to mimic them, may have been built into the Dyke: firstly the oval mound (1) at the NW terminal, and secondly the long mound (2) extending SE from (1) for a length of *c* 83m. In support of this arrangement of features it can be noted that no cursus-type ditch can be seen to accompany the oval mound or most of the length of the long mound. It could be argued that the two founding monuments were classic examples of their kind–a typical Perthshire Neolithic round/oval barrow (cf Pitnacree: Coles & Simpson 1965), with a long barrow attached, the defining ditches probably having lain parallel to the bank at each side (see **2.1** above). In this interpretation, the cursus/bank barrow proper, with its distant flanking ditches, does not commence until the end of the long mound at segment boundary A1. It must be noted that the defining ditches detected by Adamson are not deep enough to have provided all the material necessary for the construction of the long mound, which is unusually massive at the NW terminal.

The third possible barrow incorporated into the Dyke is the SE 88m of Section **C**, which may have been intended to mimic the NW terminal, and may in itself be bipartite, with an 'original' oval mound as its SE terminal. Such an interpretation raises the possibility of the feature also having been, in some form, free-standing, which might explain the mismatch of alignment at segment-boundary C4. The matter is further examined below (**7.1**), but the same degree of separate existence might account for the 18m terminal 'dog-leg' of the southern ditch, which structurally parallels the defining ditches of the long barrow at the NW end.

3.3 THE POSSIBLE ASTRONOMICAL ALIGNMENT OF THE CLEAVEN DYKE

Clive Ruggles

On 21 August, 1997 the Cleaven Dyke was examined in the light of the following hypothesis, which had been supplied by Gordon Maxwell:

'If the Dyke was aligned (to the SE) on the rising sun, Northballo Hill would approximate to the sun's azimuth and altitude in 3500 BC at dawn on either 27 November or 25 May. The former would approximate to the Neolithic equivalent of the quarter day more recently known as All Hallows (1 November). The implications of such a date, with its association for Celtic peoples, if not their predecessors, with the Festival of the Dead and the beginning of the New Year, could be of considerable importance in our attempts to uncover the original purpose of the monument.'

Estimates of horizon azimuths and altitudes were obtained by a combination of two methods: survey using prismatic compass and clinometer (cf Ruggles forthcoming a, Appendix I); and calculation from large-scale maps and plans. [Note: the term 'elevation' is used here to mean the height of a location above sea level, while 'altitude' is used to mean the vertical angle between a viewed point and the horizontal plane through the observer.] The former method is prone to error for determining azimuths because of uncertainties in the magnetic correction; the latter is prone to error for determining altitudes where the elevations of certain locations cannot be determined with sufficient precision. However, comparisons between compass readings and calculations from map data indicate that compass readings consistently gave magnetic North between $5°.5$ and $6°.5$ to the west of true North, while map estimations of altitudes were always within $0°.2$ of the measured reading. Hence it is considered that the quoted azimuths and declinations should certainly be accurate to the nearest degree, and altitudes to the nearest $0°.2$. Declinations are quoted, and should be reliable, to the nearest half-degree.

Although partly obscured by local vegetation, direct observations of the horizon to the SE were possible from the presumed SE terminal and from points to the NW towards Section boundary **Z**; while the NW horizon was generally visible from points in Section **A** of the monument. Part of the latter was also visible from points *c* 200m to the SE of the SE terminal, in line with the monument. Otherwise, these horizons were completely obscured by the woodland in which the central part of the Dyke is located.

In order to demonstrate the range of possibilities, four key points on the Dyke were considered: the junction of the oval and long mounds at the NW terminal;

Location	NGE	NGN	Elev. (m)
Benachally (summit)	^{3}0622	^{7}4916	487
Hill to NW (summit)	^{3}1305	^{7}4247	153
Segment boundary A0 (oval mound/long mound)	^{3}1567	^{7}4087	45 – 50
Segment boundary A3 (marked change in direction)	^{3}1582	^{7}4079	45 – 50
Gap Z, by end of extant bank	^{3}1722	^{7}3998	49
SE end*	^{3}1756	^{7}3978	50 – 55
Northballo Hill (summit)	^{3}254	^{7}354	314

*This position on the ground was determined with the aid of G J Barclay and G S Maxwell

Table 8
Location data for the astronomical analysis. National Grid eastings and northings are given in all-figure form.
(Segment boundary AO = NW terminal; Gap Z = Section boundary Z.)

segment-boundary A3, *c* 80m to the SE, where there is a pronounced change in direction of *c* 3°.5; Section boundary **Z**, *c* 300m from the SE end; and the SE end itself. The relevant location data are presented in table 8 and the relevant alignment data are presented in table 9.

It is evident upon visiting the monument that the Cleaven Dyke is roughly aligned with hilltops in both directions. To the NW is a low rounded hill, *c* 3km from the NW terminal. It is in line with the SE part of segment **A** at an azimuth of roughly 300°, although the part to the NW of segment-boundary A3 is aligned some 3°.5 further to the left. To the SE is Northballo Hill, a rather more distinctive hill, 9km from the SE terminal, as mentioned above. In aligning upon hills, the Cleaven Dyke is similar to many cursus monuments around Britain, including a number in the Upper Thames Valley (Ruggles forthcoming b), and it does not seem unreasonable to suggest that such alignments may have had a symbolic significance (cf Ruggles & Burl 1985, 45-50; Tilley 1996, 169), or, alternatively, hills may simply have been used as sighting devices in laying out the monuments.

The question of symbolic astronomy is important because alignments upon the regular motions of heavenly bodies such as the sun and moon may reflect efforts to 'ally [the monuments] with the workings of nature itself' in an attempt, perhaps, to place their operation beyond challenge (Bradley 1993, 62; Bradley & Chambers 1988, 274). It may even reveal something of world-view (Ruggles forthcoming a, ch. 9). The astronomical potential of, say, a point on the horizon, is determined by combining its azimuth and altitude with the latitude of the observer to obtain the declination (latitude on the celestial sphere), from which it is possible to deduce the heavenly bodies that would have risen or set there at a particular time.

As can be seen from table 9, the declination of the summit of Northballo Hill is about –13°.5 as viewed from the SE end of the monument, decreasing to about –14°.5 when

Alignment	Azimuth	Altitude	Declination	Notes
Hill to NW from A0	300·5	1·8	+17·5	
Hill to NW from A3	300·0	1·6	+17·0	
Hill to NW from Gap Z	299·5	1·2	+16·5	M
Hill to NW from SE end	299·5	1·0	+16·5	M
Benachally from A0	310·0	2·0	+22·5	
Benachally from A3	310·0	1·8	+22·0	
Benachally from Gap Z	308·5	1·6	+21·5	M
Benachally from SE end	308·5	1·6	+21·0	M
Northballo Hill from A0	118·0	1·4	–14·5	M
Northballo Hill from A3	118·0	1·4	–14·5	M
Northballo Hill from Gap Z	118·0	1·6	–14·0	M
Northballo Hill from SE end	118·0	1·8	–13·5	

An 'M' in the final column indicates that the data given were deduced from map data (figures given in table 1) only. In all other cases, survey and map data were cross-checked and combined.

Table 9
Alignment data for the astronomical analysis. Azimuths are quoted to 0.5°, altitudes to 0.2°, and declinations to 0.5°.
(AO = NW terminal; Gap Z = Section boundary **Z**.)

viewed from the further, NW, end. The latter corresponded, in Neolithic times, to sunrise on about 30 October or 10 February in the Gregorian calendar, and the former to sunrise on about 27 October or 13 February (Ruggles forthcoming a, Box Ast 5), so that the centre of the sun would rise behind the summit of the hill on about these days. To the right, Northballo Hill falls steeply away to a junction with another hill; a more distant peak is visible in the gap, forming a prominent double notch. This yields declinations about 1° lower, so that as viewed from the SE end, the sun would have risen in this gap on 1 November.

While the autumn dates are close to 1 November, it is extrapolating far beyond the available evidence to conclude that the monument was deliberately aligned upon the rising sun on a Neolithic precursor to All Hallows. First, around half of the horizon corresponds to sunrise or sunset on some day of the year. Furthermore, there is very little evidence to support the idea that a calendar involving eight-fold divisions of the year was in use during the Neolithic and Bronze Age, mimicking (or perhaps even being a direct precursor of) a later Celtic calendar (Ruggles forthcoming a, Chap 8).

Similarly, the summit of the hill to the NW at $^3131\ ^7425$ yields a declination of +17°.5 from the nearer end of the cursus and +16°.5 from the farther (SE) end, corresponding to sunset on the Gregorian dates of 5 August/10 May and 8 August/7 May respectively.

It is of some relevance to note that from the vicinity of its NW end a prominent hill is clearly visible a mere 10° to the right of the low rounded hill upon which the cursus is apparently aligned. This is Benachally, at a distance of c 12.5km. Interestingly, the summit of Benachally yields a declination of +22°.5 from this terminus (see table 9), a value not far short of the solstitial limit of around +24°, indicating that the sun would have set behind the right-hand slopes of this hill for some three weeks on either side of the solstice. If astronomical orientation really was important it is hard to conceive that such an obvious alignment, with solstitial sunset coinciding with a prominent hill, would have been shunned. Indeed, while the orientation seems to have been constrained by topographic factors (dry gullies within 100m to the NE and SW at different points restrict the width of the plateau on which the Dyke is built), it would certainly have been possible to construct the monument with an orientation a mere 10° different from that used, and keep it on flat ground.

Our conclusion, then, must be that at this cursus at least, there is no obvious astronomical orientation and the possibility of combining a solstitial orientation with an alignment upon a prominent hill was passed over. This perhaps seems curious in view of the arguments–now increasingly commonplace–that those who constructed these monuments did so with regard to their orientation upon specific astronomical events, and in particular sunrise and sunset at the solstices and equinoxes (Ruggles forthcoming a, Chap 8). On the face of it, such arguments seem to be weakened by the wider evidence. Certainly, other factors seem to have been operating at the Cleaven Dyke.

3.4 ESTIMATING THE LABOUR REQUIRED TO BUILD THE CLEAVEN DYKE

Bill Startin

The calculation of labour input is by no means an exact science; the following provides an order of magnitude for the input, no more. The methodology used is that set out for the Neolithic enclosure at Abingdon (Startin 1982).

The bank section has an approximate cross-sectional area of $9m^2$. The excavated ditch section, making allowance for the original contour of the ground, has a cross-sectional area of just over $4m^2$ (an estimate of $4.14m^2$ has been used for the calculations below). Allowing for an expansion factor of 13/12 for excavated material, and for two ditches of roughly the same size, the bank and the ditches appear roughly to match, implying that there is no need to account for material brought in from elsewhere.

Given the distance over which the material has to be carried (a little less than 25m), two people excavating at $0.7m^3$ per hour could be served by one basket-carrier. The labour per linear metre would therefore be (4.14 x 2 x 1) /0.7; multiply by 3 to estimate person-hours = 35.5 person-hours (3 people working for just under 12 hours). The length of segment A10-A11 is about 25m, thus 887 person-hours. Segment A12-A13 is c 103m long, thus 3655 person-hours (ie the equivalent of 4 teams of 3 for 30 days at around 10 hours a day). These figures do not take account of dealing with turf, nor of the variation in the cross-section of the bank of the Cleaven Dyke, but they do give an impression of the scale of the undertaking. Accepting that any figure for the whole of the Dyke can be no more than a gross estimate derived from the calculations of the labour required for individual segments, we can suggest that a monument 2000m long would have taken in the region of 60,000 to 80,000 person-hours to build.

4 EXCAVATION AT LITTLEOUR

4.1 BACKGROUND

The Littleour site was located some 250m to the NE of the Cleaven Dyke at its nearest point (roughly Section boundary **Z**), located on a bench of fluvio-glacial material at the same height as the Dyke, but separated from it by a shallow dry valley.

The feature at Littleour, as recorded by RCAHMS aerial photography (RCAHMS 1994a), appeared before excavation to be a structure comprising two slightly diverging lines of pits, with its east end closed off by two further pits, giving the impression of a curved end (illus 3). Six pairs of posts forming the sides of the structure are visible on the aerial photograph. One axial pit was noted just to the west of the second pair from the east end. We believed we could see on some aerial photographs a possible matching axial pit and matching curved end faintly represented at the west end, and the preliminary results of geophysical survey provided some support for this observation.

Illus 41
A 'Hi-spy' photograph of the Littleour structure close to the end of the excavation in 1996. (*Crown Copyright: RCAHMS*)

The excavation of the site at Littleour (NO 1734 4024) was undertaken in the hope that it might reflect aspects of domestic life broadly contemporary with the construction and use of the Dyke. Specifically, it was hoped that the cropmark might be of a roofed building on the same scale as that at Balbridie, Kincardineshire (Fairweather & Ralston 1993).

In 1995 we undertook a reconnaissance excavation of the cropmark feature at Littleour, exposing the east end of the structure: eight of the boundary postholes and the massive axial pit (L9). At the end of the season we believed we might indeed be dealing with a massive ridged building (Barclay & Maxwell 1995). In 1996 the whole area of the structure was exposed, revealing the shape of the enclosure and that there was no second axial posthole. To distinguish the Littleour excavation from the Cleaven Dyke in the record its features are distinguished below by the prefix 'L'.

4.2 RESULTS OF EXCAVATION

THE MAIN STRUCTURE

The structure as finally revealed consisted of two broadly parallel lines of pits, 22m long and between 7m (at the east end) and 8m (at the west end) apart (illus 41; 42). There are eight postholes on each side. Both ends are formed by a pair of postholes. The distance between all the postholes varies between 2.5m and 3m. The two sides bend slightly north at their mid-point. Of the 20 postholes, seven were fully excavated in the first season, and seven half-sectioned in the second. All were found to be simple single-phase postholes with more or less clear postpipes (illus 43; 44). The timbers in the holes varied between c 0.7m and 1.1m in diameter. The postholes varied between 0.65m x 0.75m and 1.15m x 1.2m across, and between 0.64m and 1.05m deep below the adjacent subsoil (illus 43). However, the contour survey of the subsoil confirmed that the surface from which we were measuring their depth was far from even (illus 45).

Fourteen of the boundary postholes were excavated in the two seasons (see table 10 below and illus 43). All showed the characteristics of postholes where the post, fairly large in each case, had rotted *in situ*. Burnt material in varying quantities was found in all the postpipes, implying the presence of burnt material on the surface during post rotting. The postholes were deep (usually c 1m) and relatively narrow, little larger than the large posts they held. We would suggest that the size of the timbers and the depth and narrowness of the postholes would have given the posts great stability.

Samples from two of the postholes gave dates of 3030-2660 cal BC (feature L3, AA-19620) and 3510-3108 cal BC (feature L11, GU-4827).

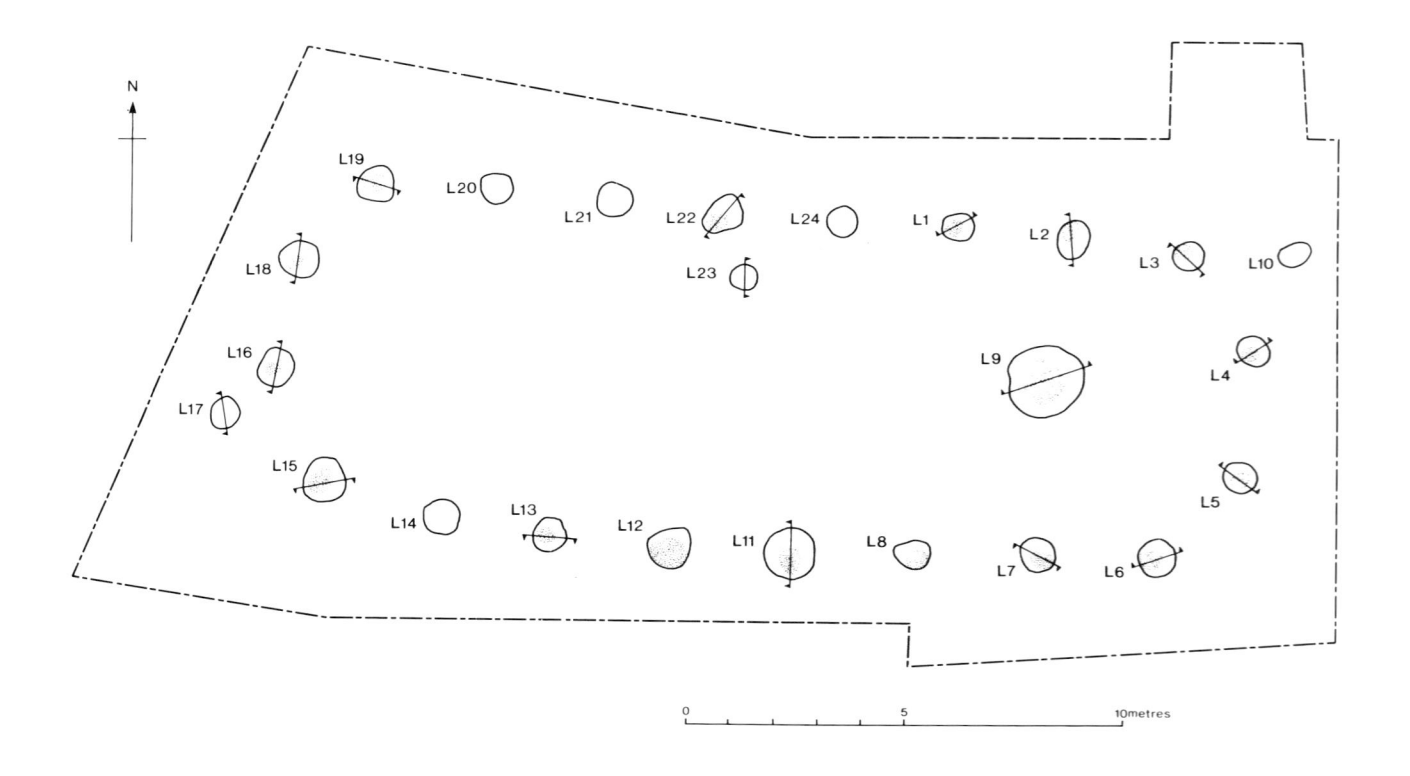

Illus 42
Plan of the identified pits and postholes at Littleour; the toned areas show the locations of probable and (where excavated) certain postpipes.

RESULTS OF EXCAVATION AT LITTLEOUR ◆ 55

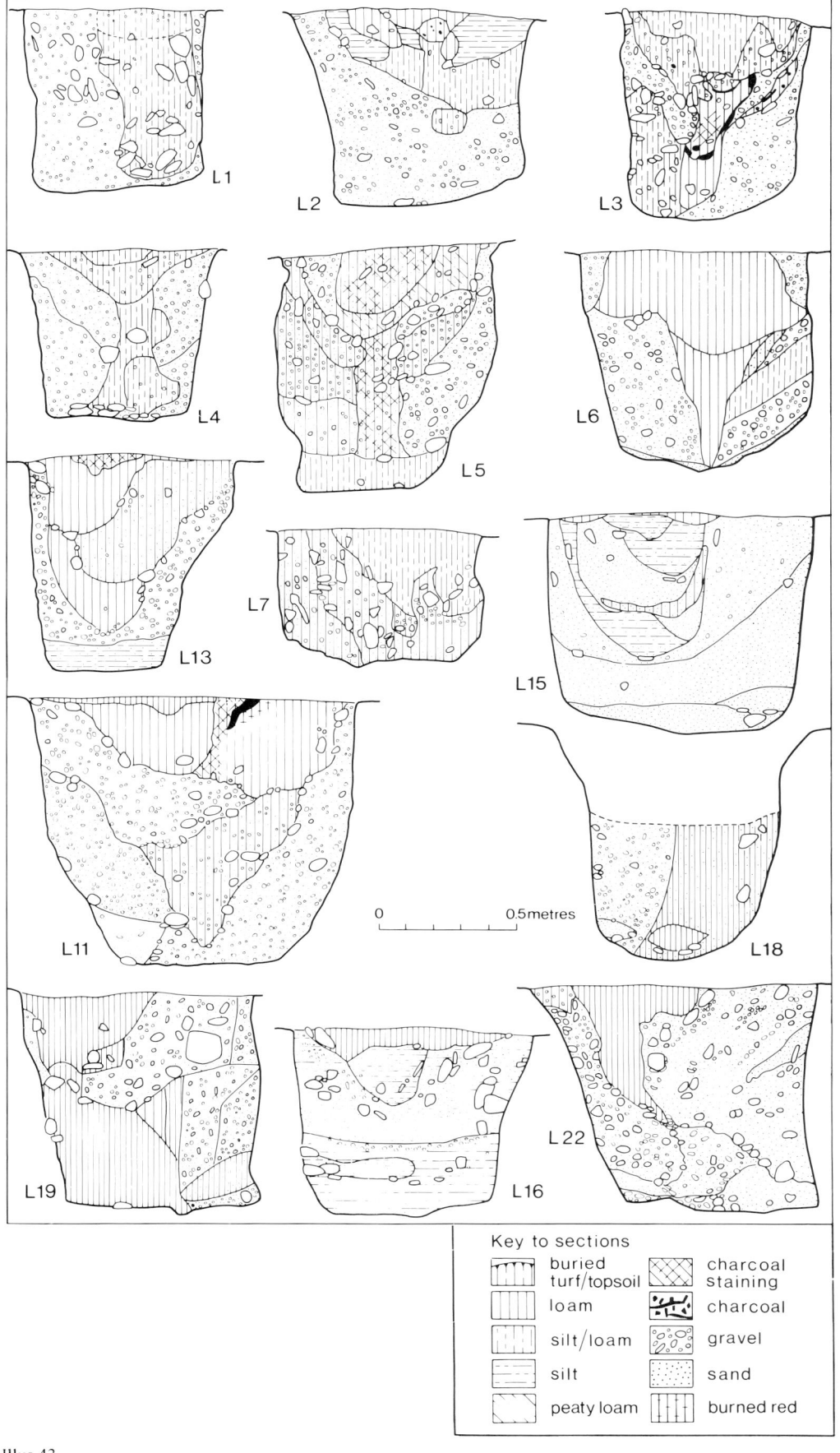

Illus 43
Section drawings of the excavated postholes in the boundary of the Littleour structure.

Key to sections
- buried turf/topsoil
- loam
- silt/loam
- silt
- peaty loam
- charcoal staining
- charcoal
- gravel
- sand
- burned red

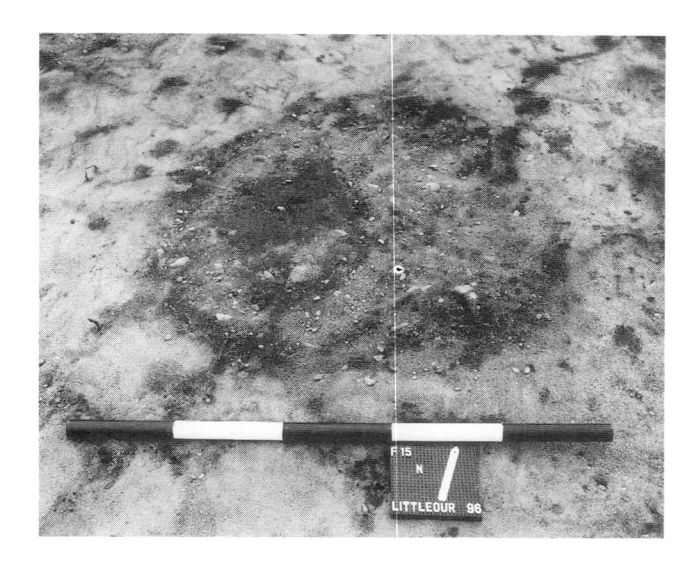

Illus 44
Littleour: posthole L15 before excavation showing the very clearly-defined postpipe.

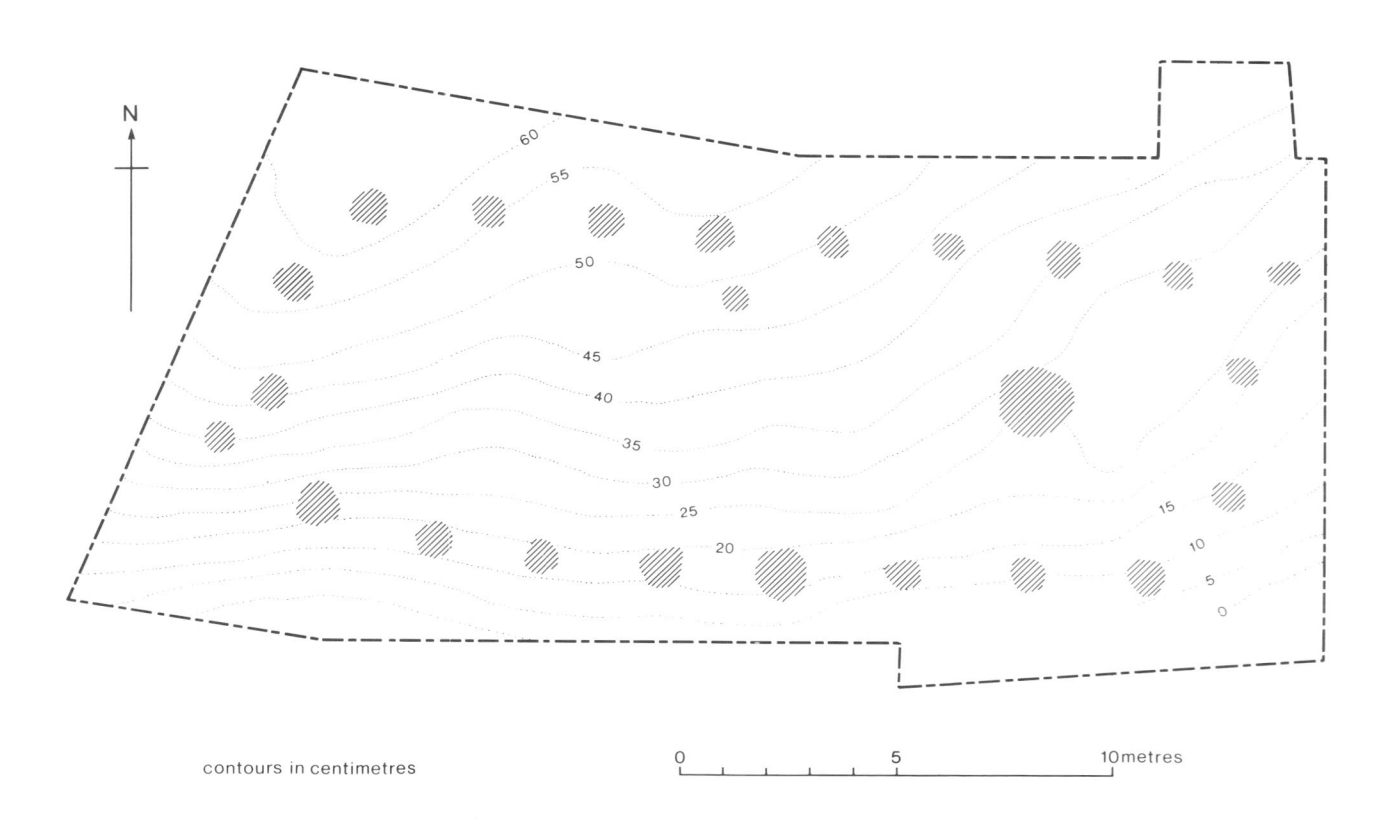

Illus 45
Contour plan of the cleaned subsoil surface at Littleour.

No.	Description	Size	Depth
L1	Posthole of structure. N wall.	75x65cm	66cm
L2	Posthole of structure. N wall.	90x78cm	75cm
L3	Posthole of structure. N wall.	70x75cm	77cm
L4	Posthole of structure. E end.	70x75cm	64cm
L5	Posthole of structure. E end.	80x75cm	91cm
L6	Posthole of structure. S wall.	90x90cm	80cm
L7	Posthole of structure. S wall.	80x80cm	50cm
L8	Posthole of structure. S wall - not excavated.	80x??cm	not exc.
L9	Major pit on axis of structure.	1.75x1.7 m	65cm
L10	Possible pit to NE of structure.		
L11	Posthole of structure. S wall.	1.15x1.2 m	1.05 m
L12	Posthole of structure. S wall.	1.1x1m	not exc.
L13	Posthole of structure. S wall.	80x80cm	80cm
L14	Posthole of structure. S wall.	90x90cm	not exc.
L15	Posthole of structure. S wall.	95x105cm	82cm
L16	Posthole of structure. W end.	90x85cm	70cm
L17	Posthole outside W end.	70x70cm	48cm
L18	Posthole of structure. W end.	85x95cm	88cm
L19	Posthole of structure. N side.	80x85cm	80cm
L20	Posthole of structure. N side.	75x75cm	not exc.
L21	Posthole of structure. N side.	80x85cm	not exc.
L22	Posthole of structure. N side.	105x78cm	84cm
L23	Pit containing pottery and flint.	60x65cm	30cm
L24	Posthole of structure. N side.	75x75cm	not exc.

Table 10
Dimensions of postholes and pits of, and associated with, the Littleour structure.

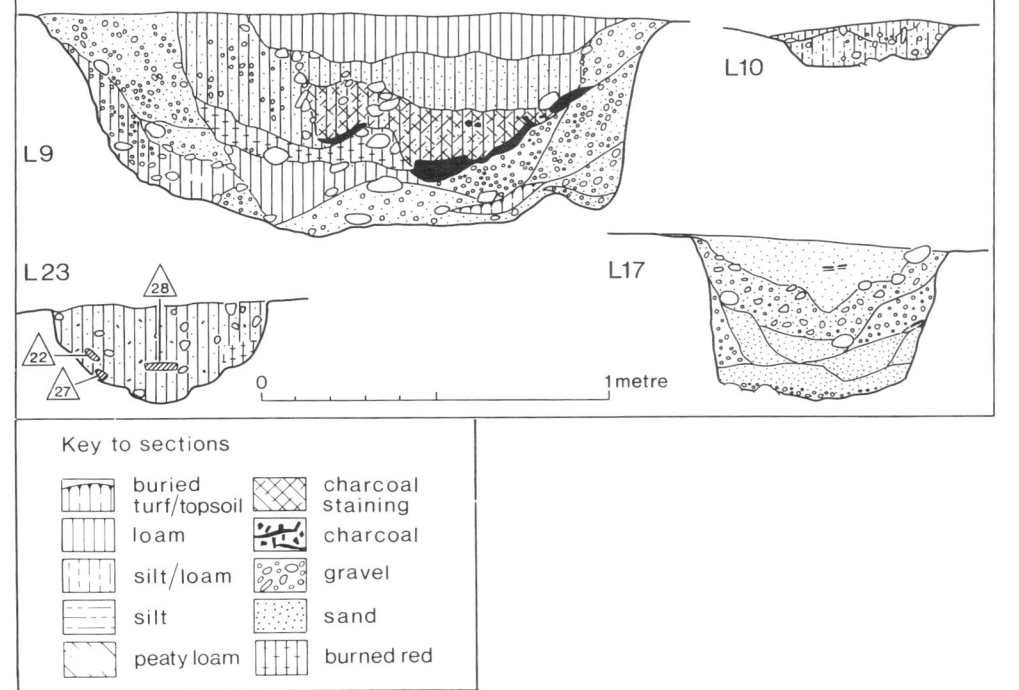

Illus 46
Section drawings of pits and postholes at Littleour: the axial posthole (L9), the pit containing Grooved Ware and flint (L23) and the two pits outside the structure (L10 and L17).

Illus 47
Littleour: cross-section of the axial posthole L9.

ADDITIONAL PITS AND POSTS

PIT L9

Pit L9 was more complex (illus 46; 47); it was massive, measuring 1.75m x 1.7m and 0.65m deep, containing two groups of fills. The first were clean gravel primary fills, surviving at the base and sides, particularly on the east; the edge of these soils was steep at the east and at a much shallower angle to the west. Within and above the primary fills were fills showing varying effects or traces of burning, including charcoal-stained soils, charcoal masses and fire-reddened soils *in situ*.

Excavation of the feature allowed the following interpretation. First, a post, *c* 0.6m in diameter, was set in the pit, packed into place with clean gravels. It is possible that the post fell or was extracted. During this process, or later, burnt or burning material found its way into the pit. This may be interpreted as the result of a major timber being displaced during a fire, or the disturbance of the pit after a fire, or a combination of both. A date of 3650-3100 cal BC (GU-4379) was obtained from charcoal in the pit.

FEATURES L10 AND L17

Immediately outside the west end of the structure, some 2.5m to the south of the axis, was a further posthole (L17), measuring 0.7m x 0.7m x 0.48m deep from which two radiocarbon dates were obtained from charcoal found in the postpipe: 2460-1890 cal BC (GU-4829) for a piece of unabraded oak roundwood, and 2140-1880 cal BC (AA-22907) for a fragment of pine. In a similar location to the NE of the structure a further, but far shallower, feature was located (L10). It measured 0.8m x 0.55m x 0.17m deep. Its fills may be those of a truncated posthole, but it is impossible to tell.

PIT L23

Within the enclosure *c* 1m SSE of posthole L22 was a circular pit, L23 (illus 42; 46; 48). The pit was 0.73m x 0.64m x 0.3m deep. It contained a single homogenous fill of brown loamy soil. Within this fill, but not touching bottom or sides, were found numerous sherds of pottery and ten flints. The pottery comprises the remains of eight or nine Grooved Ware vessels. The flint includes three large retouched pieces in high quality, translucent, dark grey flint. In addition a pebble of micaceous schist, rounded at one end and pointed at the other, was recovered during the flotation of a soil sample. The pebble (find no 54) measured 33m x 23mm x 19mm and the point seemed unlikely to be a natural shape–the pointed end in particular seemed to have been shaped by human action (identification and comment by British Geological Survey). A date of 2350-2030 cal BC (AA-22906) was obtained from a fragment of birch charcoal in the pit.

A programme of wet-sieving and flotation recovered some carbonised seeds, which were identified by Ruth Pelling and Ciara Clarke. The results of their work are summarised in table 11.

Feature	L2	L6	L23
Cerealia indeterminate	1		
cf Fruit indeterminate		3	
Plantago lanceolata		2	1
Corylus avellana L fragments			141
Malus sylvestris Miller			1
cf. *Malus sylvestris* Miller cf. endocarp			1
Avena sp.			1
Weed indet.			2

Table 11
Summary of the nature and location of carbonised macroplant remains from Littleour.

DATING

Six samples were submitted for radiocarbon dating (table 12), after identification of the samples by Michael Cressey. Two were large enough, after cleaning and identification, for conventional radiocarbon dating at the Glasgow University dating laboratory at the Scottish Universities Research and Reactor Centre. The others could only be dated by AMS, at the University of Arizona. Two were samples from postholes of the boundary of the structure (L3, L11), two were from a posthole (L17) just outside the west end of the enclosure, one was from the major axial posthole (L9), and the last from the small pit that contained the Grooved Ware and the exceptional flint.

Illus 48
Littleour: cross-section of pit L23, showing some of the Grooved Ware.

Lab No.	Context No.	Context Description	Material	Condition	Site Sample No.	Uncalibrated Determination	Calibrated Date BC at 2σ
AA-19620	L3	Boundary posthole. From the material that accumulated in the postpipe during the rotting of the post.	*Quercus*	Single substantial piece of charcoal.	95/36	4245±50BP	3030-2660
GU-4827	L11	Boundary posthole. Part of the burnt outer crust of the post or a large burnt mass on the edge of the posthole which had found its way into the upper part of the posthole during rotting.	*Quercus*	Unabraded non-roundwood fragments.	96/2	4600±50BP	3510-3108
GU-4829	L17	Posthole to the west of the main setting. From the material (?destruction debris) that had accumulated in the postpipe during the rotting of the post.	*Quercus*	An unabraded roundwood fragment.	96/8A	3730±90BP	2460-1890
AA-22907	L17	Boundary posthole. Sub-sample (pine) of the same sample as GU-4829 above.	*Pinus*	An unabraded roundwood fragment.	96/8 SS	3620±50BP	2140-1880
GU-4379	L9	Large posthole on the axis of the structure. Carbonised 'crust' of post partially burnt *in situ*, or material on surface when post collapsed/removed.	*Quercus*	Extreme radial splitting reflecting condition of burning rather than post-depositional changes. Sample did not appear to be abraded to any great degree.	95/33	4640±60BP	3650-3100
AA-22906	L23	Small pit containing Grooved Ware. Sample found within dense concentration of sherds. Deposited simultaneously with pottery.	*Betula*	Unabraded non-roundwood fragment.	96/7	3750±50BP	2350-2030

Table 12
Radiocarbon determinations from Littleour.

4.3 THE NATURE AND DATE OF THE LITTLEOUR MONUMENT

A ROOFED STRUCTURE?

When the authors first considered excavating the Littleour structure, we thought that it might represent a building comparable in scale, if not in structural detail, with Balbridie (illus 96 below); if it were also broadly contemporary, then it might represent a building of the period of the Dyke, perhaps even part of a domestic site. At the end of the first season this possibility seemed quite strong, as the vague indications on aerial photographs and geophysical surveys hinted at the presence of a second axial posthole near the west end. That second posthole, however, did not exist.

It seems unlikely to us that the Littleour structure, even if all its surviving different elements were contemporary, could be roofed, unless there are significant elements that have not survived. We would suggest that this is improbable–the structural elements that do survive are on a massive scale. It might be more likely that any internal settings would be on the same scale. The plans of roofed structures of the Neolithic are discussed below (**7.5**).

David Hogg, who analysed the Balfarg Riding School structures (Barclay & Russell-White 1983), was invited to comment on the likelihood of the Littleour structure being a roofed building. His observations are as follows:

> '[Almost] anything could be a roofed building. This pattern of postholes could represent a building, where the rafters would rest on the opposed pairs of wall; the span for a pitched roof is reasonable and member sizes would not be great. My objections, however, are as follows:
>
> 1 The alignment of post group L6 to L15: if this is a building, either the ridge line would not be straight, the roof pitch would vary or the wallhead height would vary. This could be accommodated but would not be desirable for ease and efficiency of construction.
>
> 2 Spacing of 3m between posts: if this reflects the rafter spacing, the span carrying wet thatch and wind load gets rather large. There could be a massive wallhead beam supporting rafters at closer centres, but this would require three member jointing and four member jointing at one point; the curve on line L6-L15 would make the joinery unnecessarily difficult.
>
> 3 Misalignment of pairs of posts across the axis of the building, carrying assumed roof timbers: once again not a serious objection but an easily avoidable source of awkwardness.
>
> 4 Presence of L9: this is patently not necessary to the structure of a building, or there would be one at the other end. It is conceivable that it could have been used to provide E-W stability for the first pair of rafters but this would be getting quite clever for builders who cannot set out a straight line.
>
> All that this body of data shows is a set of vertical or near-vertical posts of indeterminate height; any speculation on further members is based on modern cultural assumptions or other bodies of data. If one looks for buildings, one will find them; the only evidence here shows a real or symbolic enclosure; therefore, while the eye, with its enthusiasms for pattern recognition sees this as a round-ended figure, it is just as valid as an E-W avenue with a pair of posts at either end.'

Given our own and Hogg's doubts we will leave reconstruction of a roofed building to more sanguine interpreters.

In considering the structure as unroofed, we must first consider whether the elements of the structure were contemporary. There are five distinct elements to be considered (the terminology used inevitably includes assumptions about function, which should be set on one side if possible):

1 The main setting: two lines, both of seven or eight posts, run broadly parallel for a distance of up to 19m. Both lines bend somewhat near their mid-point, the southern line in a much more pronounced way. The area defined by these two lines of posts (if contemporary) is closed by a setting of posts at both ends.

2 The large posthole L9: if the posts of (1) do form a setting, then the post in the posthole would have lain very close to the axis of the setting.

3 The small pit (L23) containing the pottery and flint.

4 The posthole (L17) near the west end of (1), and on the same sort of scale.

5 The small pit (L10) to the east of (1) but much shallower.

We can see that the radiocarbon determinations (table 12 above), at first sight, do not suggest that the various elements are contemporary. The oldest dates are for (2) L9 (GU-4379) and for one of the boundary postholes of

(1) the main setting (L11: GU-4827)–the ranges are 3650-3100 and 3510-3110 cal BC; the other boundary posthole produced a date of 3030-2660 cal BC (L3: AA-19620).

There then appears to be a gap, to the two determinations from L17 (2460-1890 (GU-4829); 2140-1880 (AA-22907) cal BC), and the determination from the Grooved Ware pit L23 (2350-2030 cal BC (AA-22906)). Of these, the two dates from the samples from shorter-lived wood (pine and birch), the later pair, seem more likely to represent the date of the event. The close correspondance of the determinations from L17 (4) and L23 (3) seem to confirm that they date a real event; without the dates from L17, the L23 date (from a small sample of birch charcoal) might easily have been dismissed as anomalous.

The nature of the main setting (1) suggests to us the erection of the posts over a relatively short time, the product, if not the intention, being a single coherent setting of posts. There is no evidence as to whether or not these posts were used to support a fence or were free-standing.

There is no evidence for the relationship of the axial post (2) to the main setting (1). The location of the post close to the main axis implies a considerable coincidence in the location of features of different dates, or that one element was erected in a clearly understood relationship to the other, at the same time, or one after the other, while the pre-existing element was still visible or marked in some way. The radiocarbon-dating of charcoal from the two elements does not actually help very much. The single determination from the axial pit L9 (GU-4379), which may date quite old wood (part of the massive post in the hole) provides a calibrated range of 3650-3100 BC. The range of determinations from charcoal from postholes from the main setting is 3510-3108 (L11) and 3030-2660 (L3). The latter seems likely to be material finding its way into the postpipe; the former, from observations on site, has a greater chance of being the charred crust of the post burning *in situ*.

In this context the result of radiocarbon dating of elements of the mortuary structure at Street House, Cleveland (Vyner 1984, 184-5) is instructive. The dating of the central post of the façade (the largest timber on the site) produced radiocarbon determinations over 400 years earlier than other elements of the façade, which is certainly a single-phase structure; the calibrated ranges were 3990-3780 cal BC (BM-2061) for the central post, and a weighted calibrated mean of 3505-3100 cal BC for the other portions of the façade. The mortuary structure, taken to be part of same phase, has a weighted calibrated mean of 3610-3370 cal BC (all new calibrations). At Street House the older date was put down to the dating of older wood from the more massive post. If the situation at Littleour was analogous, then the latest date might provide the more accurate estimate for the date of construction.

Depending on how the charcoal from which the determinations were taken relates to events on site, a number of possibilities emerge:

1   The axial post was erected in the late 4th millennium cal BC; at around the same time the 'enclosure' was erected around it; or vice versa. Charcoal from a later episode of activity found its way into the postpipe of L3 (see Barber 1997, 139 for processes). The enclosure and posts pre-date the posthole L17 and the Grooved Ware pit L23 by around 1000 years. The relationship between the enclosure/axial post and the Grooved Ware is unclear; L23 may have been dug on a known site where little was visible.

2   The enclosure and post were erected in the early to mid 3rd millennium (taking the L3 date as the representative one, and taking the L1 and L9 determinations to be the product of dating pieces of heartwood; that is, the part of the trees that had stopped exchanging carbon with the atmosphere (the event the radiocarbon method would date) long before the trees were felled and used on the site. The enclosure and axial post are therefore less than 1000 years earlier than the deposition of the Grooved Ware in L23 and the episode dated by the charcoal in posthole L17.

3   All the features are broadly contemporary, but there is more than one period of burning on site. By a range of mechanisms (animal burrowing, worms) charcoal from these various episodes found its way into the postholes and pits, giving the impression of a diachronic construction of the enclosure and the other features. Accepting this explanation would require special pleading of a remarkable degree.

Of the three options the second seems to us the most probable.

The relationships of the posthole L17 and the pit L10 outside the main setting are not clear. The posthole is of the same order of magnitude, and had the same appearance, as those of the main setting. At first it seemed likely to be contemporary with the enclosure, acting as a free-standing post or even part of a complex offset entrance, designed to prevent direct visual access into the enclosed area. However, the radiocarbon determinations suggest that the charcoal, if not the feature that contained it, was considerably later than the enclosure.

The function, let alone the purpose, of the axial pit is unclear. The crest-line position of Littleour would have ensured the prominence in the landscape of any monument erected there, whether composed of one element or many.

THE ANALYSIS OF THE STRUCTURE

If, for a moment, we can accept that the Littleour timber enclosure and the axial post are of one phase, we can attempt an analysis. An early report (Barclay & Maxwell 1996) described the Littleour structure as having eight postholes in each side-wall, with two more at each end, the side-walls bending slightly north at their mid-point. However, as illustration 42 shows, the plan is more subtly complex: the easternmost post of the northern side-wall (L3) and the westernmost of the southern wall (L15) lie noticeably closer to the interior than the alignment of their adjacent wall-sector would demand; on the other hand, the opposite end-posts of each side-wall are not similarly displaced. The effect is to give the ends of the structure an offset, rounded appearance, and indeed the five postholes (L2-L6) at the east end, and their mirror-images (L14-L19) at the west, lie on or close to the arc of a circle marginally greater than the width of the building itself. This picture of reversed symmetry is also illustrated by the staggered positions of the flexing-points in each side-wall: at posthole L22 in the north side, but obliquely opposite at L11 in the south. The structure at Littleour thus may be more appropriately described as round-ended parallelogram.

Such a distortion, which is unlikely to have resulted from negligent laying-out, brings the axial pit L9 to occupy a more central position in the easternmost 'bay' of the enclosure. The Grooved Ware pit (L23) seems to straddle a line joining the centre posts of each side (L11, L22), but if this was achieved over a gap of 1000 years, it may merely be a coincidence, unless the elements of the earlier structure were clearly marked. The uniformly skewed geometry of the structure (which comprises four separate building modules–two equilateral parallelograms and two near-semicircular arcs) suggests that this was a building in which form took precedence over practicality, a possibility that is enhanced by the strict regularity of its post-spacing; perhaps the subtleties of the plan strengthen a non-domestic interpretation already suggested by the character of the items deposited, such a long time after, in pit L23. In this context, the nature of the massive timber erected in the axial pit may become clearer; its position and girth make it seem possible that it was a, or the, focus of significance on the site, recalling, at least in scale, the colossal split-trunk end-timbers of the 'linear zone' mortuary enclosures of the earlier Neolithic (Scott 1992). Comparable single uprights may be represented by the single central posthole in the Douglasmuir pit-cursus or the axial feature in Balfarg Riding School Structure 2 (**7.4** below).

4.4 THE POTTERY FROM LITTLEOUR

Alison Sheridan

The ceramic assemblage from the small pit L23 comprised some 71 sherds (now reduced to 51 by refitting conjoining pieces) plus a few fragments, together with two lumps of probable daub, the whole weighing just over 1.6kg. An estimated eight, possibly nine, vessels are represented; all had been broken, and deposited incomplete in the pit. The relatively lightly weathered nature of the sherds' ancient fracture surfaces suggests that the pots had been broken shortly before deposition.

Most of the conjoins resulted from the inevitable fragmentation of the pottery during and after the recovery process, when it was still damp. However, a significant number of joins are between sherds found in different areas of and at different levels within the homogenous fill of L23.

THE POTS

Pot *1* (illus 49)
Pot *1* is represented by 18 (originally 23) pieces, constituting most of the base, around a third of the rim, and various parts of the body of a medium-coarse, flat-based, bucket-shaped pot, decorated over its exterior with a comb-impressed design. The estimated rim diameter is 200-210mm, and the base diameter is *c* 105mm; assuming a gently tapering body, the estimated height is *c* 225mm. Wall thickness varies from 9.3 to 13.4mm, and the maximum base thickness is 21mm.

The rim is slightly pointed and inturned, and has a low moulded bevel on its interior, the purpose of which may have been to aid the seating of a lid. Around 20mm below the rim is a single perforation, bored from the exterior of the fired pot inwards, and there are traces of a possible second hole on another rimsherd (with at least 60mm separating the two). Assuming that these were repair holes, this indicates that the pot was not new when deposited. The base is pedestalled, and its interior surface is slightly domed. Decoration extends over most of the exterior, and consists of impressions of one or more rectangular-toothed comb, of maximum length 27.5mm. No overall scheme can be reconstructed, although on the upper body at least 12 roughly horizontal lines extend down from the rim, crossed in some areas by diagonal lines rising from L to R. The body sherds have decoration varying from horizontal lines (continuous and discontinuous) to diagonal lines and mixtures of the two, and towards the base there is one plain area, one area with discontinuous horizontal lines and another with L to R-falling diagonal lines. The exterior surface had been carefully smoothed prior to decoration, but probably not slipped.

The exterior is a mottled reddish-brown and orange-brown and the core is mid to dark grey. The interior is covered from base to rim with a blackish encrustation up to *c* 1.5mm thick in places, presumably representing the burnt residue of the pot's former contents. The clay is slightly micaceous, and inclusions comprise sand-sized grains and

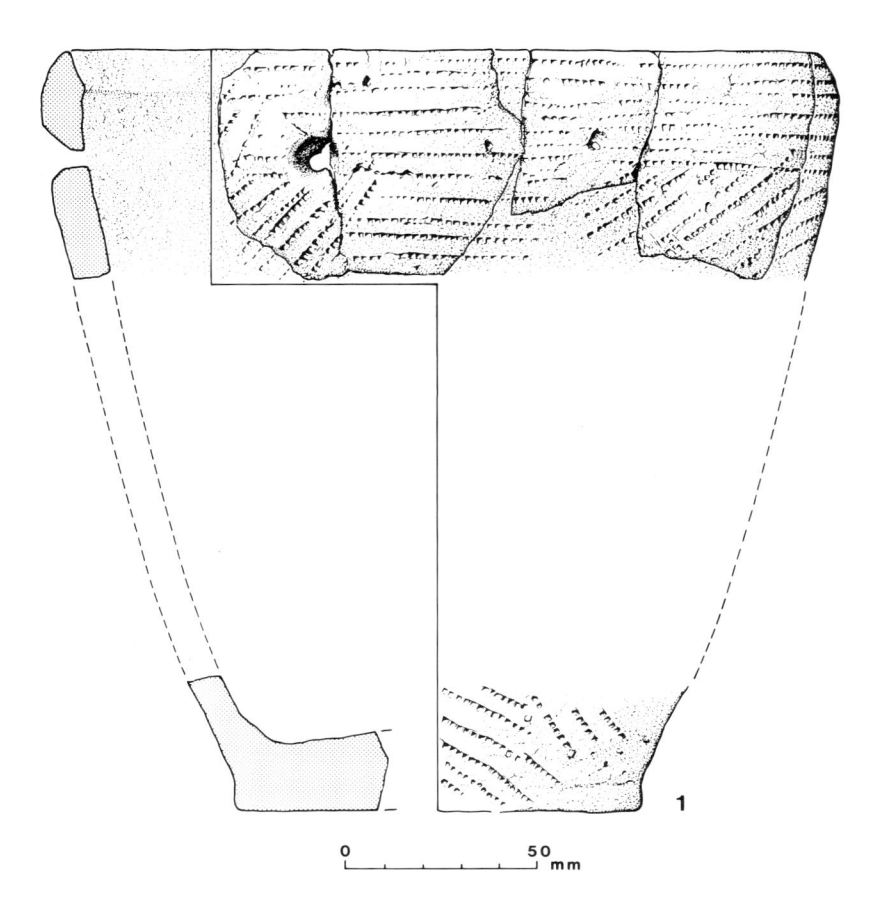

Illus 49
Littleour: Grooved Ware Pot *1*, from pit L23.

sparse angular grits up to 3mm x 2.5mm in size, the latter (if not also the former) almost certainly added deliberately as temper. The grits include a white, quartzitic mineral.

Pot 2 (illus 50)
This vessel is represented by 16 (originally 25) pieces of a large, coarse pot. Unfortunately, the rim and base are represented by only two sherds (illus 50: 2a, 2b), the latter relatively small. The estimated rim diameter is around 240mm, and judging from the size and curvature of the body sherds, this would have been a large, probably bucket-shaped, pot taller than Pot *1*, and with flaring walls. Wall thickness ranges from 11.8 to 17.3mm; maximum base thickness is 19mm.

The rim, which was probably slightly inturned, has an internal moulded bevel, and its rounded top has diagonal slashed decoration. On its exterior is a band of shallow incised diagonal lines rising L to R, and further down the body there are applied ribs, decorated with rough alternating indentations (illus 50: 2c). The ribs appear to run roughly vertically, but are not regularly spaced, and the area between the ribs appears to be undecorated, except on one sherd, where a line of diagonal 'pinpricks' may be decorative (illus 50: 2d. The alternative possibility that these may be a housing for a now-detached rib seems less likely, there being no other surface indications.) One of the body sherds appears to have a post-firing perforation, drilled into a barely perceptible rib (illus 50: 2e); if this was intended to repair a crack, then it implies that this pot, like Pot *1*, was not new when deposited.

The exterior and interior surfaces had been covered with a micaceous self-slip prior to the pot's decoration; subsequent finger smoothing marks are visible on the exterior. The exterior surface and outer part of the core is a rich, mottled red-brown colour, and the rest of the core and interior is a blackish-grey. Some of the body sherds have small patches of blackish encrustation on their interior surface. Inclusions consist mainly of fairly angular, sand-sized grains, but also include larger subangular and angular grits of several rock types (including the white mineral noted in Pot *1*) up to 6mm x 6mm, some protruding from the surfaces; together they constitute around 5-10% of the body of the pot. There is also one impression of straw, and on the inside of the rim there is a globular depression, 6mm in diameter, which does not appear to be a grain impression.

Pot 3 (illus 51: 3)
This apparently consists of a single large rim-and-upper body sherd; there are other sherds in the Littleour assemblage which share the same 'rusticated' decorative motif, but these are insufficiently similar in thickness, colour and fabric to be attributable to this pot, and have therefore been allocated to Pots *4* and *5* (see below).

A large, medium-coarse pot is represented. The rim is inturned, as in Pot *1*, but is less pointed and lacks the internal bevel; its estimated diameter lies between 230mm and 270mm, and is probably around 240mm. The maximum wall thickness is 13.7mm; once more, a bucket-shaped pot may be represented.

Decoration is by loosely-twisted cord and by paired, scooped, thumbnail impressions ('rustication'). The former occurs as four roughly horizontal lines on the outside of the rim, and a corresponding set inside the rim; the latter extends over the outside surface in an irregular 'polka-dot' arrangement. The surfaces had been smoothed carefully before decoration, but show no obvious signs of having been slipped. The exterior is a dark reddish-brown, grey towards the rim, and the core is blackish-grey. All of the interior surface is covered by a 1-2mm thick blackish encrustation.

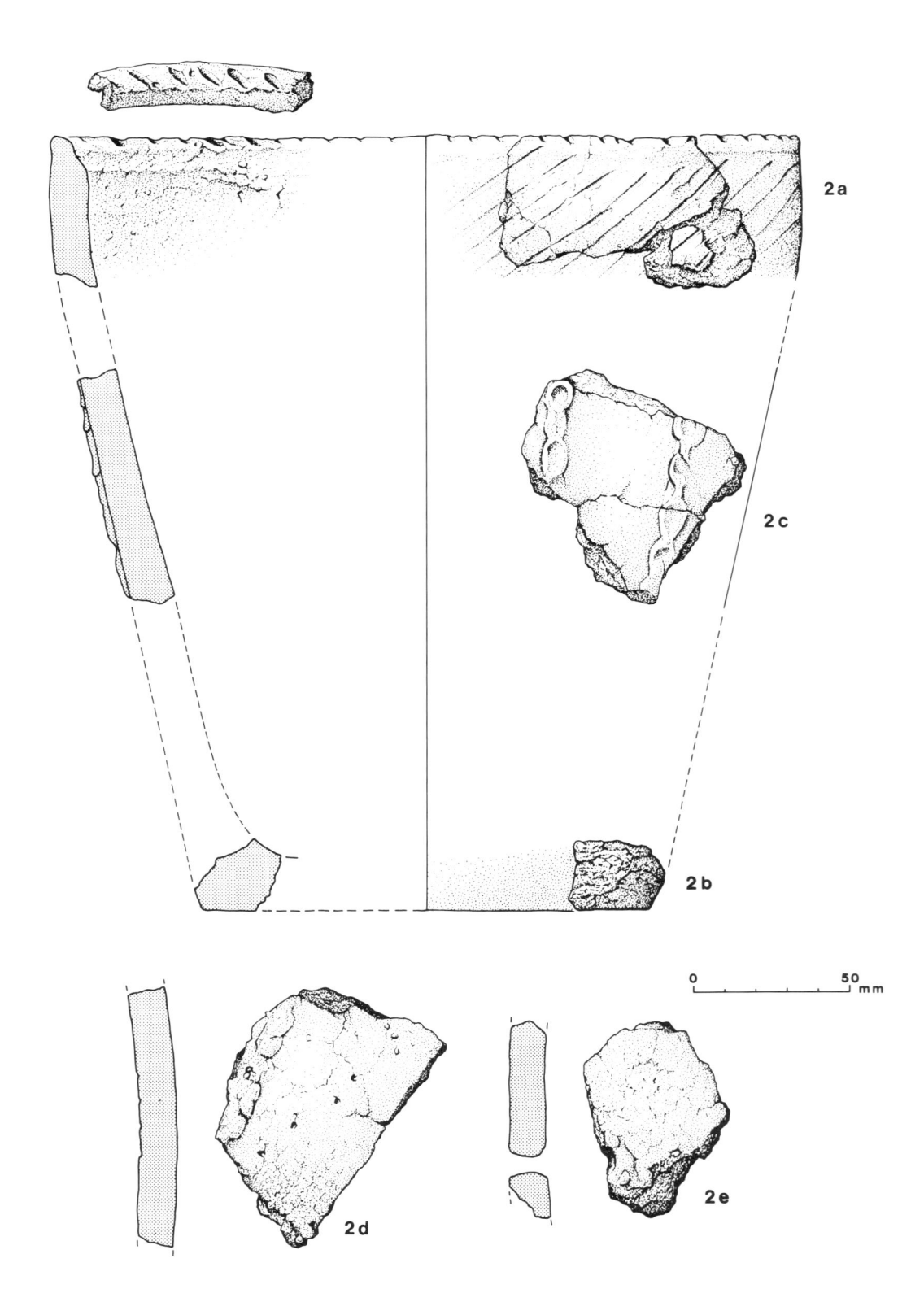

Illus 50
Littleour: Grooved Ware Pot 2, from pit L23.

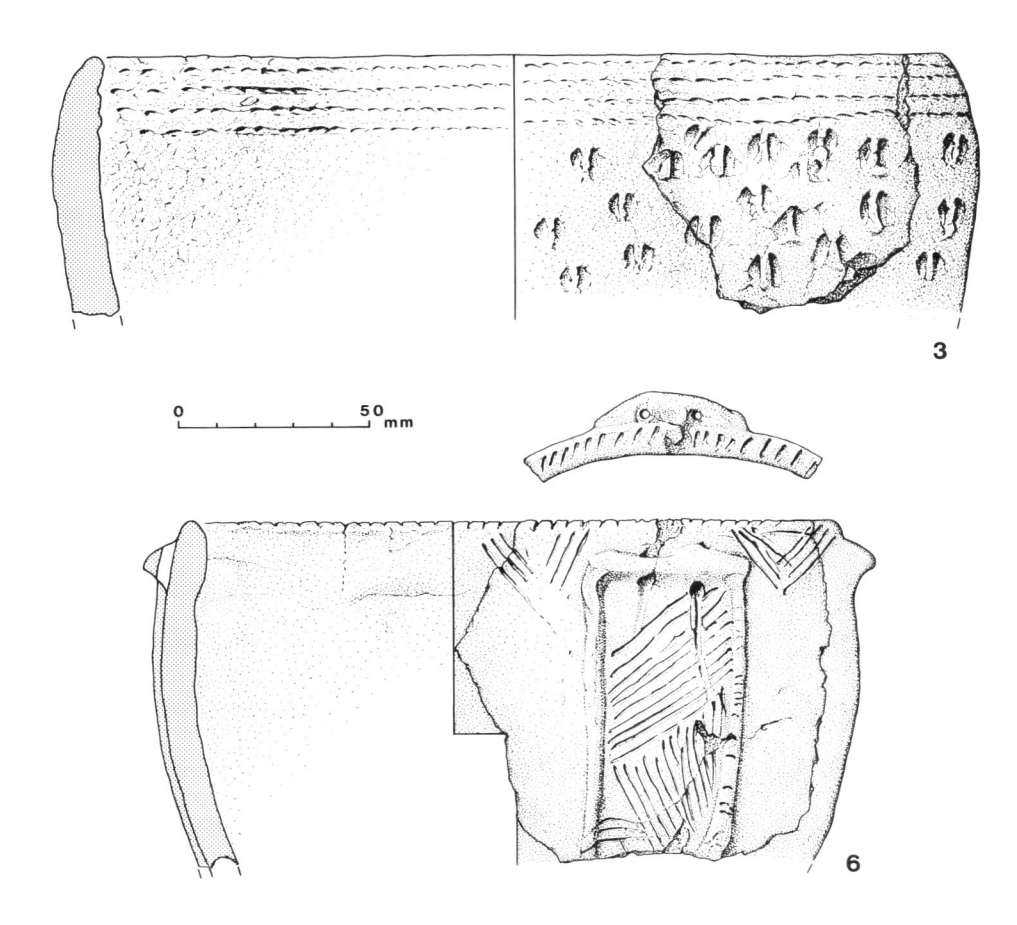

Illus 51
Littleour: Grooved Ware Pots *3* and *6*, from pit L23

The clay is slightly micaceous, and inclusions comprise rounded and subangular sand-sized grains, plus sparse subangular grits up to 4.5mm x 1.5mm.

Pot *4* (illus 52: 4a, 4b)
This is represented solely by seven (originally eight) body sherds; enough survives to indicate that this was a large, fairly coarse vessel, with a body diameter of *c* 300mm at one point. Wall thickness varies from 12.5mm to 15.5mm. The largest sherd (illus 52: 4a) is decorated with an applied, slightly sloping rib, with scooped paired thumbnail impressions on either side and extending onto it. Another sherd (illus 52: 4b) bears further nail impressions, this time single and simply stabbed into the clay. This sherd also has a hint of a horizontal rib; and the sherd's thickness and curvature suggest that it may have belonged to the upper part of the body. The other body sherds are undecorated. A tentative overall scheme may therefore be proposed, featuring a band of simple nail decoration extending from the rim; a zone of ribbed and nail-impressed decoration covering much of the body, perhaps framed by a continuous or discontinuous horizontal rib at the top; and then perhaps a plain zone towards the base.

The vessel had been smoothed and covered in a micaceous self-slip after the addition of the ribs but before the nail decoration. Post-slip (finger-)smoothing marks are visible. The exterior and interior surfaces are a purplish-brown, and the core is a rich reddish-brown. Only the smallest sherd has any traces of black encrusted material. Inclusions consist mainly of rounded to angular sand-sized grains, together with occasional angular and subangular grits up to 5.5mm x 1.5mm. The latter mostly consist of the white, quartzitic rock noted in Pots *1* and *2*, and some of these grits contain mica, making it the likely parent material for the sand-sized grains. The maximum inclusion density is around 10%.

Pot *5* (illus 52: 5)
This vessel is represented by one intact body sherd (formerly two), plus a sherd the external surface of which has spalled off, and a fragment. The two base-and-wall sherds described under Pot *8* could conceivably belong to this pot.

The intact body sherd (illustrated) is from a large, medium-coarse pot, *c* 14mm thick and with a body diameter of at least 240 mm; the wall appears to flare slightly. Its exterior is decorated with a haphazard design of single and paired (thumb?)nail impressions, some scooped. Its exterior is orange-buff; the core varies from reddish-buff to dark grey; and the interior surface is covered with a blackish encrustation up to 1mm thick. There are no obvious traces of a slip. Inclusions are similar to those seen in Pot *4*—including mica particles—but are less numerous.

Pot *6* (illus 51: 6)
This is represented by two small body sherds and one substantial rim-and-body sherd (97.5mm x 95mm, reconstituted from five pieces), forming *c* 15% of the circumference of a thin, fine, decorated, probably tub-shaped pot. The rim is 170mm in diameter and is slightly inturned; its top is rounded, and its interior is thickened by having been rolled over and smoothed down. The vessel's height cannot be estimated exactly, but is unlikely to exceed 150mm and may be between 130mm and 140mm. Wall thickness is 6.5mm to 9.5mm; along its lower edge, the large sherd had broken along a coil joint line.

The pot is decorated with an incised design and with an applied rib, arranged as an inverted, squared U. The top of the U has two vertical perforations, 3-4mm in diameter and 10mm apart, probably made by jabbing a piece of straw through the rib whilst the clay was still wet. Their function may have been to suspend the pot, or perhaps to secure

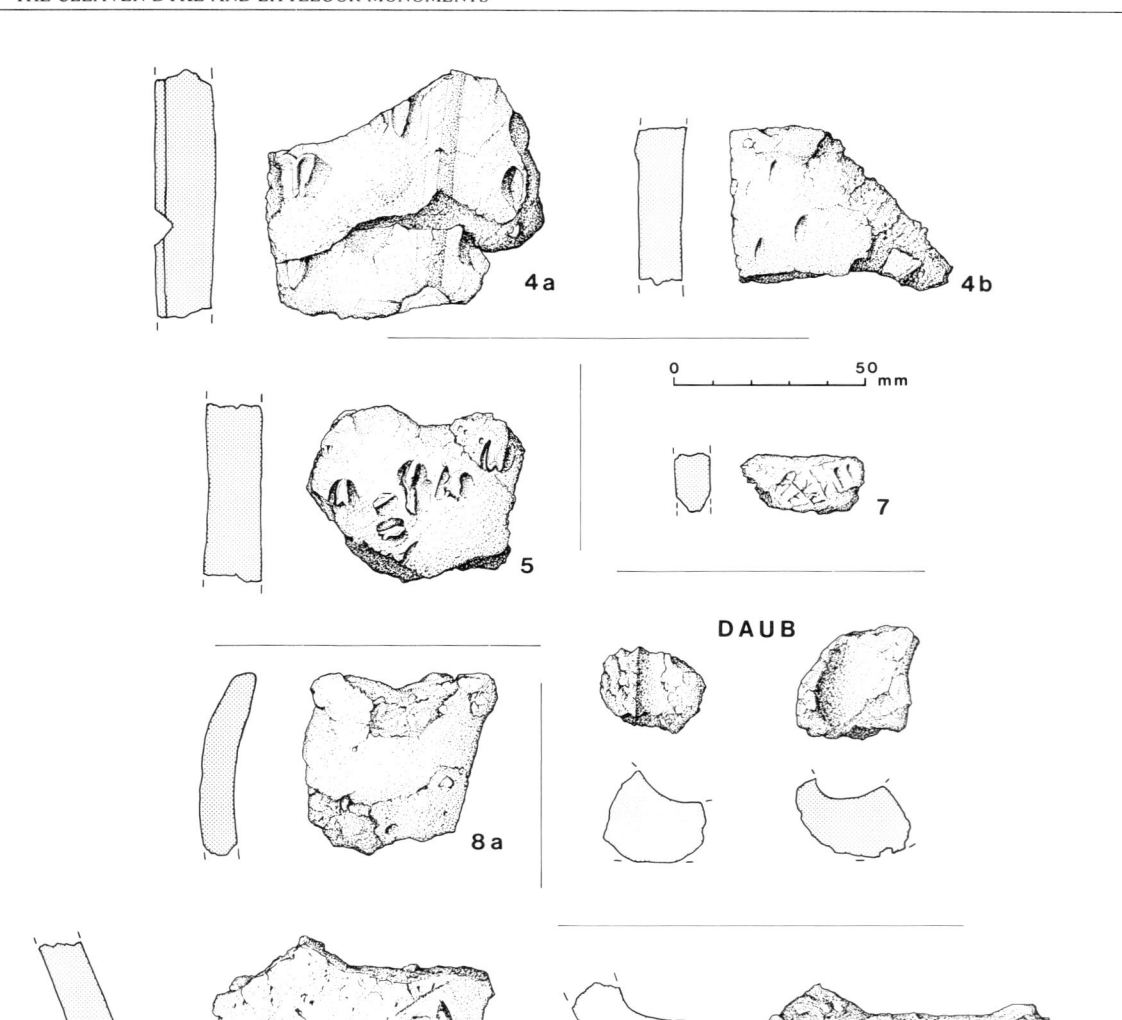

Illus 52
Littleour: Grooved Ware Pots *4*, *5*, *7* and *8*, and fragments of daub, from pit L23.

a lid; but there is no cord wear, either within the perforations or lower down the pot, to indicate heavy use.

The incised decoration consists of closely-spaced slashes across the rim; nested pendant chevrons below the rim, one on either side of the U-rib; and a panel of alternating L to R-sloping and R to L-sloping lines within the U, resembling basketwork. The pot had been carefully smoothed and covered with a micaceous self-slip prior to the decoration. The exterior is a mottled reddish-brown/grey-brown, with a thin and discontinuous black encrustation, suggesting spillage of the vessel's contents. The core is dark brown, and most of the interior (excluding a peculiar medium-brown patch) is covered with a blackish encrustation, up to *c* 1mm thick in places.

Inclusions comprise the sand-sized grains as seen in the other pots, plus sparse, angular grits of the white mineral noted in Pots *1*, *2*, *4* and *5*, up to 2mm x 1mm.

Pot *7* (illus 52: 7)
This is represented by a single small sherd and fragment, of distinctive vesicular texture, from a relatively fine vessel. Most of the external surface has spalled away, and it is hard to tell whether the remaining irregularities represent decoration. The sherd is 9.4mm thick; its exterior and core are greyish-brown and the interior is purplish-brown. The surviving interior surface has been carefully smoothed but probably not slipped. The vesicular texture is caused either by the burning-out of a finely-chopped organic temper, or by the leaching out of an unstable grit; no remaining traces of such a grit are visible, however, and the former interpretation seems most likely. There are also sand-sized inclusions of mica and the quartzitic mineral, plus two small, subangular pieces of the latter.

Pot *8* (illus 52: 8a, 8b, 8c)
This is represented by a single curving undecorated sherd, 52mm x 48mm and up to *c* 10mm thick, which may be part of an inturned rim. Two base-and-wall sherds (illus 52: 8b, 8c) may belong with this pot, or alternatively with Pot *5*, or they could represent a ninth vessel.

The interior surface of the ?rimsherd has a moulding as seen in Pots *1* and *2*; if this is from the rim area, then a diameter of *c* 160-200mm can be estimated. The fabric is slightly coarse. The surfaces have been smoothed, and the interior (but not the exterior) has a slipped appearance, possibly caused by wet-smoothing. The exterior, core, and part of the interior are a light reddish-brown; the rest of the interior is grey-brown. There is no encrusted material. The clay is slightly micaceous, and the inclusions comprise the usual sand-sized grains, plus sparse larger angular grits up to 5mm x 4.5mm, including the white quartzitic mineral noted in the other pots.

The two base sherds are undecorated; they make up around 30% of the circumference of a base c 150mm to 160mm in diameter. Maximum base thickness is 16.5mm; the wall thins to c 11mm. The base sags slightly, and just above the base-wall junction the wall splays at an angle of 105° to 110°. The exterior, probably unslipped, surface is orange-brown; the core dark grey; and most of the interior (down to a 'tide line' at the wall-base junction) is covered with a blackish encrustation. Inclusions are similar to those in the Pot 8 ?rimsherd and in Pot 5.

THE DAUB-LIKE PIECES

Two fragments, the largest c 40mm x 30mm, each with a hollow indentation c 17mm wide, presumably made by a withy (illus 52). One fragment has a narrower indentation (of straw or a stick) on its irregular 'back' surface. This fragment is buff-coloured and relatively soft, as if only partly heated; the other is reddish on its surfaces, has a dark grey 'core', and is harder, as if more thoroughly heated. Like the pots, these fragments contain mica flecks; the more burnt fragment also has sand-sized grains of the quartzitic mineral, and the other contains a soft, reddish material which could be an impurity in the clay.

DISCUSSION

Represented here is a group of bucket- and tub-shaped vessels, of varying size and fabric, but all, except one, attributable to the family of pottery known as Grooved Ware; the fragment of vesicular Pot 7 is too small and undiagnostic to be given any plausible attribution. Most of the pots have clearly been used to contain—possibly to heat—a substance(s) the residue of which remains as a blackish encrustation; at least two were probably not new when used. All seem to have been broken deliberately and deposited incomplete, the sherds of any one vessel finding their way into different parts of the fill of the pit. The similarities in inclusions among most of the pots suggest that they could derive from a single provenance. The find context is suggestive of deliberate burial following a single event (eg a ceremony). The significance of the two daub-like pieces is unclear: lining of the pit with wattle and daub seems unlikely, and would not explain the signs of burning, whereas the use of a partly-covered cooking structure during the hypothetical ceremony might explain their presence.

Parallels for specific aspects of shape and decoration can be cited from various Grooved Ware assemblages throughout Britain: for example, bucket-shaped pots with inturned rims are present in abundance at Durrington Walls (Longworth 1971), and are known from Yorkshire assemblages such as the North Carnaby Temple sites and Low Caythorpe (Manby 1974). However, as MacSween has convincingly argued (1995a), it would be inappropriate to apply Longworth's 'Clacton - Woodlands - Durrington Walls - Rinyo style' classification system to north British Grooved Ware since the material does not fall into such neat stylistic pigeonholes. A better way to understand Grooved Ware in north Britain is to regard it as a long-lived ceramic tradition with a basic 'vocabulary' of design elements, with chronological, regional, local, and site-specific variations on a few basic themes (*ibid*). Unfortunately, despite progress with the Orcadian material (MacSween 1992; Richards 1994), it has not yet been possible to disentangle chronological variation from other aspects of variation for north Britain as a whole.

The Scottish assemblages most similar to the Littleour material are not those nearest to the site; that is, Beech Hill House (MacSween 1995b), Tentsmuir (Longworth 1967) and the Balfarg sites (Henshall & Mercer 1981; Henshall 1993), but rather those from Hillend (Armit *et al* 1994) and Wellbrae (Cowie pers comm), both in Clydesdale. The Hillend material, for example, includes bucket-shaped vessels with inturned rims, applied vertical ribs, differentiated rim vs. body decoration and scooped nail impressions (Armit *et al* 1994, illus 5). It also includes the use of comb-impressed decoration (*ibid*, illus 6), a rare feature on Grooved Ware, which Longworth, in his discussion of the Durrington Walls Grooved Ware, attributed to Beaker influence (Wainwright & Longworth 1971, 244). Like the Littleour material, the Hillend vessels had been broken and then deposited deliberately in three pits, probably following a single event. The more fragmentary Wellbrae material includes plain vessels, a large bucket-shaped pot with irregularly-spaced vertical/diagonal ribs, and two pots with twisted cord impressions. As Trevor Cowie has pointed out in his Hillend report (Armit *et al* 1994), decorative and formal affinities can be drawn with the aforementioned Grooved Ware from Yorkshire and Durrington Walls. Further parallels for specific aspects of decoration can be cited from within Scotland: the use of paired nail impressions, for example, features on a large pot from Beckton, Dumfriesshire (Cormack 1963).

If accepted at face value, the date of 2350–2030 cal BC for the Littleour pottery places it within the later period of currency of Grooved Ware in Britain as a whole (Armit *et al* 1994), and makes it the latest dated Grooved Ware from Scotland. Comparability with some of the Durrington Walls pottery is thus partially accounted for, although the mechanism for shared design ideas still demands clarification. Problems arise, however, in accounting for the comparability of the Littleour pottery with some of the Hillend material, the assemblage from which is dated (once more, regrettably, by a single determination) to the significantly earlier date of 3340–2910 cal BC (4410 ± 70 BP, Beta-73955).

One is forced to conclude, as noted above, that there are simply too few dates available for Grooved Ware from northern Britain to produce a coherent typo-chronological framework. It may be that certain design elements enjoyed a long currency: if the Hillend and Littleour dates are accurate, then this is indeed implied.

Furthermore, if the overall set of radiocarbon dates for British Grooved Ware is accepted, it appears that the idea of using Grooved Ware had spread southwards from Scotland long before the Littleour pottery was in use. However, meaningful discussion will have to await a larger corpus of dates.

4.5 THE CHARRED RESIDUES ON THE LITTLEOUR GROOVED WARE VESSELS

Deborah J Long

Organic residues from four Grooved Ware vessels excavated at Littleour have been analysed for their possible pollen content at time of use or burial, and in particular, to investigate the hypothesis that the vessels had been used in a ritual context (Bohncke 1983; Dickson 1978; Tipping 1994b; Whittington 1993). This hypothesis is based on the excavation of apparently deliberately broken vessels occurring with several flints from a rectangular pit structure at the site, and from the similarities of the structure to one excavated at Balfarg (Barclay & Russell-White 1993), also interpreted as having a ritual context.

METHODS

Residues in the form of hard, organic and charcoal-rich crusts from the apparent interiors of the vessels were sampled by careful scraping with a clean scalpel into clean and sealable glass vials. The precise location of the sampling sites was recorded, and this information is available in the site archive and from the author. Samples were prepared using standard but highly rigorous chemical techniques (Moore et al 1991).

Exotic marker pollen was added in tablet form to estimate pollen concentrations and to check for laboratory error and sampling biases.

Microscope slides were examined routinely at magnification x400 on an Olympus BX40 microscope, and at magnification x1000 for problematic grains. Pollen preservation (Cushing 1967; Tipping et al 1994) was recorded (table 13), and measures of 'reliability' (Tipping et al 1994) used to assess the feasibility of palaeoecological interpretation of the data.

Preservation category	Pot 1	Pot 1b	Pot 2	Pot 3	Pot 6
Well-preserved	3	5	45	2	3
Lightly crumpled	6	9	56	16	7
Highly crumpled	6	11	28	39	5
Broken	4	7	28	20	9
Lightly corroded	1	0	37	11	0
Highly corroded	6	4	42	32	10
Total grains	26	36	236	120	34

Table 13
Summary of pollen preservation.

RESULTS

All four residues contained pollen (table 14), although pollen concentrations were very low in all samples. The most pollen-rich samples, from Pots 2 and 3, had estimated pollen concentrations of 2977 and 2518 pollen grains per ml respectively. Samples from Pots 2 and 3 generated pollen counts of 200 and 100 grains respectively. The pollen concentrations and counts from Pots 1 and 6 were too low to be statistically valid, probably reflecting biases in residue quantity, type and pollen preservation.

Pollen preservation was dominated by some form of mechanical damage, either crumpling or breakage (Havinga 1984). However, there was little evidence for microbiological attack in the form of corrosion or degradation (table 13). This would be in keeping with the

Pollen / spore type	Pot 1	Pot 1b	Pot 2	Pot 3	Pot 6
Alder	2			4	
Birch		2	25	6	1
Hazel	10	3	25	9	6
Pine		1		2	
Oak			3	1	
Willow			1		
Rowan type			1		
Heather type				1	
Ling	6	9	12	29	5
Grasses	4	7	16	17	4
Sedges			1	1	
Buttercup type				1	1
Dandelion type			1		1
Daisy type				2	
Common vetch type			1		
Crucifer type			1		
Meadowsweet			3		
Nettle	1				
Ribwort plantain		1	3	4	1
Ferns undif.		4	39	13	1
Common polypody		2	3	5	1
Bracken	2	4	49	6	1
Sphagnum			20		1
Indeterminable	1	2	29	19	9
Concealed	0	10	26	5	0
Total identifiable grains	25	34	206	100	24

Table 14
Palynological results of residues

archaeological evidence for rapid burial of the pots by infilling sediment, and thus limited opportunity for microbiological attack. Poor pollen preservation is also reflected in the relatively high values of grains rendered indeterminable to taxonomic identification. Up to 30% of pollen grains were concealed by charcoal or plant debris that could not be separated from the matrix; this may bias the identifications in favour of those grains easily recognised, although the vast majority of concealed grains were made indeterminable through other processes.

Measures of 'reliability' were calculated for the pollen spectra from each vessel (Tipping *et al* 1994). Three measures were used: Polypodiaceae undiff as a percentage of total pollen, the ratio of fern and moss spore concentration to total pollen concentration (concentration ratio) and the ratio of numbers of spore-producing taxa to numbers of pollen-producing taxa (taxonomic ratio). Using all three measures, Pot *3* was shown to have a 'reliable' pollen assemblage, apparently unaffected by differential pollen preservation. Pot *2* had high reliability scores in two of the three measures. Pots *1* and *6* have already been disregarded for palynological interpretation, owing to the low initial pollen counts.

Pot *1*: Rimsherds

Low pollen counts were achieved. The assemblage was dominated by hazel, with alder, ling, bracken, grasses and nettle (*Urtica*-type). The residue contained comparatively few charcoal fragments, and was principally composed of unidentifiable plant remains. Base sherd No. *46* also had a low pollen count, from a charcoal-rich residue, and was dominated by ling and grasses with evidence of undifferentiated ferns, bracken, birch and hazel.

Pot *2*

This vessel produced a count reaching 200 pollen grains. The assemblage was dominated by hazel and birch, with bracken and fern spores, oak, willow, rowan-type, ling, dandelion-type, ribwort plantain, meadowsweet and crucifer-type present. Sphagnum spores were also recorded. The matrix was charcoal-rich.

Pot *3*

A count of 100 pollen grains was achieved and was dominated by ling and grasses with undifferentiated fern spores, with alder, birch, hazel, pine, oak, heather type, sedge, daisy type and ribwort plantain, buttercup, bracken and common polypody. 'Reliability' measures showed that there has been no apparent differential decay within the pollen assemblage and that the assemblage may therefore be interpreted.

Pot *6*

Very low pollen counts were achieved from the matrix of unidentified plant remains with low amounts of charcoal. The pollen assemblage is characterised by hazel, ling and grasses with evidence of birch, dandelion type, ribwort plantain and buttercup with undifferentiated fern and bracken spores.

DISCUSSION

Pollen in the residues from the vessels at Littleour is heavily damaged, by either crumpling or breakage. Crumpling of pollen grains from soils and archaeological deposits is common and may relate to relatively dry micro-environmental conditions.

Estimates of 'reliability' have suggested that the pollen assemblage from Pot *3* does not appear to have been affected by preservational biases. The 'reliability' measures have also suggested that Pot *2* has a pollen assemblage that may be interpreted with caution. The assemblage does contain a high proportion of fern and moss spores and this may reflect some differential decay. However, the pollen preservation analyses do not indicate high rates of decay in any of the pollen or spore types recorded. The remaining two measures suggest a relatively robust pollen assemblage. Pots *1* and *6*, with low total pollen counts, are not considered to be interpretable for this reason, although the pollen and spore types recorded and their relative counts, are in line with those from Pots *2* and *3*.

The high proportion of concealed grains, contained and enmeshed within residue of unidentified plant tissues, may suggest that this pollen is contemporary with the residue, and is not a post-depositional contaminant. There is no obvious enhancement of particular pollen types in these residues. There are also no distinctive ingredients for either food, drink or hallucinogenic preparations. The main pollen constituents of the residues and known uses of these plant types in edible preparations (Darwin 1996) can be summarised:

Main pollen constituents of residues: ling, birch, hazel, grasses, fern spores, bracken.

Possible edible constituents: hazel, ling, nettle, ribwort plantain, dandelion, meadowsweet, crucifers.

Possible weeds from gathering: sedges, buttercup, common vetch.

Unexpected constituents: Sphagnum moss.

However, it is stressed that none of these pollen taxa are present in the vessel residues at proportions high enough to warrant discussion.

The pollen and spore types identified within the organic residues are all likely to have originated from an open woodland environment and may represent plants gathered from such an environment. The pollen evidence from the vessel residues does not suggest any enhancement by selected plant materials.

CONCLUSION

The pollen types identified in the residues from the pots at Littleour suggest their origin within the 'background' pollen 'rain' inherent in any environment. The probability exists, from the way pollen is embedded within the organic residue, that the pollen is contemporaneous with use or burial of the pot. Pollen may have been incorporated into the residue when it was viscous, and probably before it had congealed into the crust that was then preserved. The pollen taxa, however, do not provide any indication that the organic residue contained plants that were gathered for a particular purpose and placed in the vessels.

The pollen taxa indicate an open woodland environment. This need not necessarily represent woodland around the pit structure if the vessels were used elsewhere and transported to Littleour. There is no enhancement of pollen types that would suggest preferential selection or cultivation of certain plants. There are thought to be two possible sources for the pollen spectra present in the pot residues at Littleour: the contemporaneous local environment at the time and place of use of the pots, or at the time and place of burial.

4.6 THE FLINT FROM LITTLEOUR

Alan Saville

with microwear report by Bill Finlayson

THE PIECES (illus 53)

Only ten pieces of flint were found during excavation. They are referred to below by their site small-find (SF) numbers. Three of these were from the topsoil or otherwise unstratified; the remainder were from the fill of pit L23, the same context as the Grooved Ware pottery (Sheridan **4.4** above). The assemblage, for reasons set out below, is odd; there is a preponderance of 'special' pieces and the flint used is of unusually high quality.

The three unstratified pieces comprise an unlocated, unclassifiable burnt fragment (*53*), an unretouched flake (*2*) from the NW edge of the excavation area, and a small, broad flake with some irregular edge-trimming (*1*) from the topsoil surface to the SE of the site.

DETAILED DESCRIPTION

SF *2*
This piece, which is in a fresh condition and must have come from a previously protected context, is a hinged-out flake from the face of a bidirectionally-flaked parent object. It is of some interest because its raw material correlates with that of the larger pieces from pit L23, but unlike them it has a ridged, crushed platform of the kind found on flakes from scalar, anvil-struck cores.

Dimensions–L: 31.7mm; B: 20.1mm; Th 6.7mm. Weight: 4.3g.

The seven pieces from pit L23 include two instances of broken segments which refit, making a total of five separate items. These are described individually below.

SF *4* and *7*
A substantial, thick-butted flake with faceted platform, comprising two segments, conjoinable at the snap break near the distal end. The proximal segment (*7*) is also incomplete on the right-hand side, from which a further snapped segment is missing, and this somewhat hampers reconstruction of the history of the artefact.

The larger proximal segment has shallow, scraper-like retouch along the upper part of the left-hand edge, continuing beyond the overhanging lower left-hand corner of the distal segment. The retouch on this edge is uniform and continuous, however, and is most likely to post-date the break entirely.

The retouch on the smaller, distal segment (*4*) is also best explained as post-dating the break. This is obviously the case with the modification effected from the break-edge itself, but it is also difficult to relate any of the other retouch to the overall form and potential typology of the proximal segment. The most substantial retouch, on the top left-hand edge, firstly dorsally then subsequently inversely, could just conceivably pre-date the break, but it is unlikely in view of the bifacial thinning retouch at the top right-hand side.

Without knowing at what stage the snap break on the right-hand side of the proximal segment occurred, it is difficult to speculate on its history, but it can be suggested that the intention may have been to create a scraper, abandoned either because of the right-hand side break or because the thickness and steepness of the distal break-edge hindered further retouch.

The distal segment appears to have been in the process of modification into an implement in its own right, presumably an arrowhead. Although potentially complete in its present form it appears unused and may have been rejected because of dissatisfaction with the thickness of the piece at the remaining break-edge.

Dimensions–L (total on bulbar axis after refitting): 74.9mm; B: 42mm; Th: 12.1mm. Weight: 19.6g. Maximum dimension of the distal segment is 37.3mm; Th: 3.2mm. Weight 2.5g.

SF *6* and *9*
An elongated blade with plain platform, pronounced bulb, and lipped platform-edge on the ventral surface. The pointed distal tip of the blade (*6*) refits to the main segment (*9*) at a simple snap break. The size of the blade, the nature of the dorsal flake-scars, and the absence of cortex, indicate it has been struck from a very substantial core. Despite the blade-character of this piece, however, the flake-scar pattern shows the core need not have been a specialised blade type.

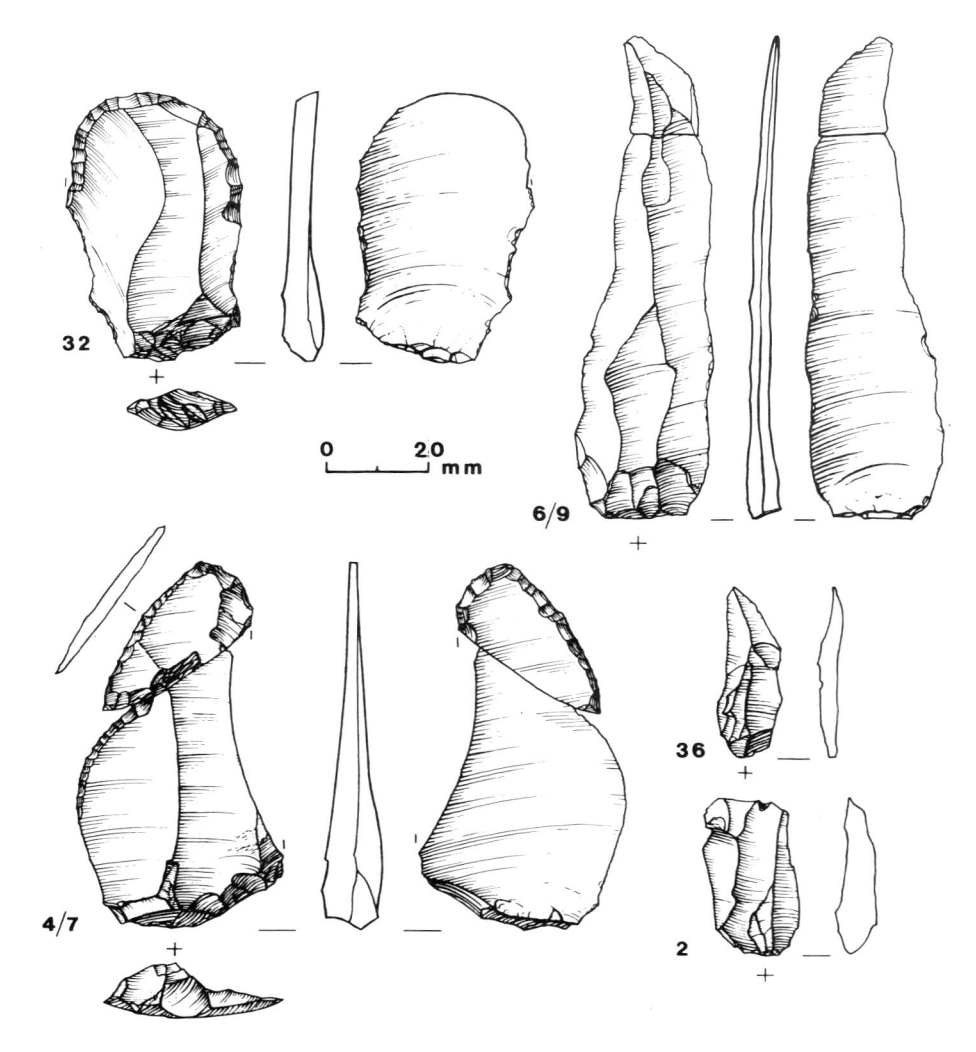

Illus 53
Littleour: flint from pit L23 and (2) unstratified piece.

The distal tip is unmodified, but the blade has trimming inversely along both edges. It is clear from the way the trimming stops at the snap edge that it either post-dates the loss of the tip, or that the break and the trimming were essentially contemporary, the break occurring as part of the same process which produced the trimming. The snap edge is fresh and unmodified and both segments of the blade appear to have been abandoned at the time of the break.

Dimensions - total L: 98.4mm; B: 27mm; Th: 7mm. Combined weight: 11.5g (the tip on its own weighs 0.7g).

SF 32
End scraper on a flake with faceted platform, pronounced bulb, and lipped ventral platform-edge; the retouch forming the convex scraping edge is extended slightly further down the right-hand edge than the left. Ancillary retouch both dorsally and inversely has modified the lower edges on both sides, presumably to facilitate hafting/handling. The lowermost edges on both sides exhibit abrasion consistent with the scraper having been hafted or used with some sort of wrapping or binding, and the scraping edge itself has signs of use.

Dimensions - L: 54.6mm; B: 34.8mm; Th: 8mm. Weight: 14.8g.

SF 36
Unretouched bladelet with plain, punctiform platform.

Dimensions - L: 34mm; B: 12.6mm; Th: 4mm. Weight: 1.3g.

SF 39 (not illustrated)
Unretouched, distal-tip snapped flake fragment.

Max dimension - 20.6mm; Th: 1.4mm. Weight: 0.3g.

RAW MATERIAL

The three large pieces from pit L23 are of high-quality, translucent dark grey flint, undiscoloured by any post-production, post-depositional modification of the flint surfaces. The flint is not entirely uniform in colour, but has variegation between patches of dark and less dark grey. Pieces *4/7* and *32* could have been struck from close by on the same core, and *6/9* could also have derived from the same core. Pieces *1*, *36*, and *39* are all of lighter grey flint and are certainly not from the same core as the previous pieces, though they need not be from a different flint source. On the other hand, piece *2* is identical in flint type to pieces *4/7* and *32* and definitely from the same source. Both pieces *2* and *6* have small areas of light grey variegation.

Consideration of the raw material origin is hampered by the complete absence of cortex on any of the pieces. In itself, however, this points to the relatively large size of the parent material and, combined with the obvious quality, suggests the flint was obtained from a primary geological context outwith Scotland. In colour and texture this flint does not match that from Northern Ireland, and a source from somewhere within the chalk zone of England seems probable.

MICROWEAR EXAMINATION

Bill Finlayson

In summary the following observations were made as a result of examination using the combined low and high power microscopy methods detailed elsewhere (Finlayson 1989):

SF *1*
Unused

SF *2*
Unused; some manufacture traces

SF *4*
The break edge has a narrow band of polish, which does not appear to be the result of the break. It might be the result of a brief use-episode, but it appears more like a general rubbing of this area, possibly as the result of holding or hafting. Given the unfinished nature of the piece, perhaps the most likely explanation is that the polish arises from holding the piece during retouching.

SF *6*
Unused

SF *7*
Unused

SF *9*
Unused, with traces probably related to the break. The suggestion by Saville (above) that both pieces were abandoned at the time of the break is supported by the absence of subsequent trace development.

SF *32*
The ventral surface along the scraper edge has a narrow band of polish along the extreme edge. In addition there are some linear polish features perpendicular to the scraper edge. In combination they suggest that the scraper has been used, but as both are poorly developed, the use was probably not intensive. The abrasion on both lateral margins is matched by a very bright polish, both in the abrasion scars and on the surrounding ridges. This type of wear is most typically produced by a very hard contact material, such as stone. The location of the wear, however, does not indicate edge contact. Given that the matching abrasion on both sides suggests some form of hafting, it may be that this polish has developed as a result of the flakes from the abrasion scars rubbing under pressure between haft/binding and the tool.

SF *39*
Unused

In general the flint surfaces are all fresh and show few signs of post-depositional damage or polishing. This would accord with the suggestion (see below) that the flints are contemporaneous with the filling of the pit, and have not been left lying in an exposed depositional context; equally, they could not be residual. The slight use of the scraper (*32*) might be seen as supporting the notion that the flint has representational value, as it has clearly not been worn out by its use before deposition.

SIEVED RESIDUES

In addition to those flints recovered during the actual excavation, post-excavation fine sieving of two samples from the fill of pit L23 produced numerous very small pieces of struck flint.

Only one of these pieces, from sample 3, is larger than 10mm. This is an unclassifiable flake fragment (max dimension 18.8mm; Th: 2mm; weight: 0.5g) with slight traces of edge modification on the only intact edge. It is of translucent, non-cortical, grey flint of similar quality to that of which blade *6/9* is made, but does not refit to this or to any other artefact from the feature.

Sample 3 also contained 12 pieces of flint in the size range 5-10mm, including one burnt fragment, together weighing 0.3g; and 51 pieces in the size range 0-5mm, including 3 burnt fragments, together weighing only 0.1g.

Sample 4 contained one burnt piece of flint in the size range 5-10mm, and 11 pieces of flint in the range 0-5mm. All 12 pieces together weighed only 0.1g.

Apart from the flake fragment, which could possibly have been part of an implement, these pieces of flint are all spalls and chips, most of which are likely to be retouch spalls or the incidental product of general flint-knapping activity or flint tool use. No flint of any kind was recovered by excavation or in the sieving of soil samples from any other feature on site.

DISCUSSION

Most of the flints come from the pit L23. Pieces *4/7* and *6/9* were in the top 50mm of the east half of the pit fill; piece *32* was 100mm down in the western half. Piece *36* was 50mm down in the western half and piece *39* was also in the western half. The fresh condition of the flints suggests contemporaneity with the infilling of the pit; there is certainly no way in which the larger pieces could have been residual, unless one imagines they had been disinterred from another protected context and re-interred in this pit. Piece *2* is also fresh and clearly has been disturbed from its context, which conceivably could have been the top of pit L23. Although all together in the same pit fill, the flints were dispersed rather than appearing to represent a cache or the contents of a decayed container of any kind.

The virtual absence of any other flints from the Littleour site is problematic. Evaluation of the composition of the recovered assemblage is not helped by the fact that the mechanical stripping of topsoil during excavation leaves the question of background flint presence unanswered. While 76 tiny pieces of struck flint were recovered from the sieving of part of the fill of pit L23, as noted above, the sieving of other pit fills did not produce similar results. This raises the issue of whether sieving of topsoil would have produced similar results.

Whatever the case, the assemblage available is clearly, as it stands, odd; there are no cortical pieces or cores, and an unusual predominance of 'special' pieces. Both *4/7* and *6/9* appear to derive from an actual event; in the case of *4/7* an event with separate episodes, both of which resulted in discard in the same place. A degree of intentional curation of these two segments at least is implied. One might speculate that this circumstance could have arisen within a social context in which flint of this quality had some intrinsic representational value beyond the mundane.

However, while the temptation to suggest some kind of structured deposition of a 'ritual' nature is strong, there can be no substantive justification for such an interpretation without knowing what evidence may originally have been present on the contemporary ground surface surrounding the pit. The presence of spalls, which could derive from the same flint from which *4/7*, *6/9*, and *32* were made, or from the actual manufacture of those pieces, raises the possibility that they were knapped over the pit or over the material with which the pit was infilled. On the other hand, the absence of any cores or cortical flakes suggests the artefacts themselves may have arrived on site already roughly shaped.

The inclusion of burnt flints among the spalls and chips from pit L23 is also of some interest. These could not have become burnt within the feature, so, assuming they are contemporaneous with the other spalls and not in some way subsequently intrusive, they suggest the fill is derived from a deposit containing debris derived from more than one activity, that is, not just flint-working. Such a mixture of burnt and unburnt spalls might be anticipated in a context of domestic debris, and points to the fill relating to deposits which are otherwise now completely unrepresented amongst the excavated remains.

Of note is the quality of the imported flint available to these users of Grooved Ware. Reference has been made in the literature to the prevalence of dark grey flint used for oblique and chisel arrowheads in Scotland, types usually considered as linked to Grooved Ware use (Saville 1994, 66, n.5), but it is difficult to find published parallels from Scotland for flints of the size represented here. There are examples of large flakes and implements of good-quality dark grey flint among the surface-collected pieces amassed by early collectors and now in the National Museums of Scotland collections. These, however, are isolated examples with no context.

Typologically there is little that can be said about the present assemblage. The scraper is a classic Neolithic type and this association with Grooved Ware in Scotland is useful. The preliminary classification of piece *4*, before the realisation that it refitted with piece *7*, was as a broken transverse arrowhead. The refitting made it clear that it was not a broken implement but one being modified, presumably into an arrowhead, in its present form. This insight into a manufacturing strategy capitalising on a presumably fortuitous break is a cautionary tale, as is the revision of the preliminary classification.

SURVEY METHODOLOGY AT THE CLEAVEN DYKE AND LITTLEOUR

5.1 CONTOUR MODELS AND DIGITAL TERRAIN MODELLING IN ARCHAEOLOGICAL SURVEY: THE DEVELOPMENT OF APPROACHES TO THE CLEAVEN DYKE

Christopher Burgess

The survey of the Cleaven Dyke was carried out over five seasons between 1994 and 1997. The aim of the exercise was to provide a survey that clearly showed all of the features, details and complexity of a monument that had in the past been assumed (wrongly) to be reasonably uniform. The monument presents a unique set of challenges to the surveyor; it consists of an asymmetric bank located between two ditches traversing over c 1800m of occasionally undulating terrain. The problem was further complicated by the fact that 80% of the monument's length was under a maturing crop of spruce, which in places reduced visibility to a few metres. Considerable care therefore had to be taken to ensure that the separate segments of the survey were married together accurately and tied in to the real and mapped landscape.

The digital terrain model (DTM) approach to the site was decided upon to allow the complex nature of the monument to be depicted consistently and objectively over its whole length. The initial survey was carried out over a 300m length of the Dyke that had previously been cleared of trees. At that time constraints of hardware and software led to a gridded survey approach being used. Points were recorded at 0.3m intervals over the bank and ditches and at 5m intervals in the area between the features. The completed model from this first season consisted of 10,000 spot heights collected over five days.

Upon returning to the site in the autumn of 1995 new software and hardware allowed the site to be surveyed as a series of strings and spot heights. The use of strings (groups of points taken along a feature) allowed for subjective archaeological input into the survey. It was also decided to re-survey the 300m covered during the first season, to make the whole survey consistent. The resultant DTM prepared over four one-week seasons consists of some 12,000 points in total (for the whole upstanding length of the Dyke), with the key topographic features (top of bank, bottom of bank etc.) defined as strings (and consequently breaklines–lines marking a break in slope). These subjective strings were supplemented with three sets of spot heights: one on the monument features themselves (crest of the bank and base of the ditch) at c 5m intervals, one set between the ditches and the bank at c 10m intervals, and one outwith the ditches to define the surrounding terrain at 50m intervals.

The data collection was hampered by the dense tree-cover on and around the site. Lines of sight on the monument were reduced in places to less than 10m, were never more than 300m, and averaged c 50m. This led to problems in establishing reliable reference objects and relating the stations along the monument accurately. The acquisition of control also proved difficult (though not impossible), the final survey being tied in using fence-lines at either terminal and the A93 road that crosses the monument c 400m from the SE terminal. Considerable time was spent checking the accuracy of the survey by re-surveying stations, establishing control and re-checking prominent features on the monument. The final survey was overlaid on vector-based Ordnance Survey data which confirmed that the results of the survey were accurate to within c 2m over the length of the Dyke (the equivalent of 0.11% of the overall length).

PURPOSE & METHODOLOGY

Traditionally, earthwork sites have been depicted using hachures. To do this the surveyor must record the tops and bottoms of slope features; the draughtsperson then pens hachures between these lines to mark the slope, the broad end of the hachure marking the top break of slope and the hachure tail marking the bottom. Hachures generally imply a high degree of subjectivity, involving the pre-selection of significant features, thus rendering the survey more opaque to subsequent re-assessment, should that be required. What follows is an appreciation of the considerable advantages of survey by contour terrain modelling, especially in the light of the experience on the Cleaven Dyke. That is not to say that the representation of earthworks by hachure is completely superseded. It is shown below that an archaeological survey collects the same information for both forms of presentation, leaving the choice of style or approach to the needs of a particular monument and the way the information is to be published.

An alternative approach to the depiction of such sites is to produce a digital terrain model (DTM) or contour plan of the features. It has been asserted in the past that the production of such surveys is both time-consuming and unnecessary–merely a distraction or a waste of time. It may be that this attitude originated in a time (not too many years ago) when the recording of each individual survey point was time-consuming and the recognised method of producing a DTM would involve the collection of a much greater number of points than necessary for a hachure survey. Relating the feature or site to the surrounding terrain would require an even greater investment of time.

The vast majority of earthwork surveys follow a very similar pattern, with individual features being surveyed in strings such as 'top of bank', 'top of ditch' and 'bottom of break of slope'. This survey method gives us a linear computer illustration that is usually interpreted by hand to produce a hachure drawing. This is no different from the methods employed in surveying with instruments such as plane table/alidade combinations, where the tops and bottoms of features are recorded and the hachures are added between the lines.

However, if these lines are recorded electronically in three dimensions, they can be designated as breaklines within the software used. This designation allows the computer to interpolate a contour model around the strings treating the gradient as constant between them (of course, where the gradient changes, a new string should be surveyed, even for a hachure survey). Therefore, the collection of the same amount of information allows for the option of the contour display while additional time has been spent on site.

This author tends to illustrate only one key part of the feature, eg the bottom of a bank or the top of the ditch, as these are the parts of the feature which define its extent. This can be seen clearly in the example of the Cleaven Dyke. The monument stretches for over 1800 metres, but the c 300 m shown here has been surveyed once by RCAHMS (illus 22) and twice by this author. RCAHMS undertook a standard earthwork survey with the results displayed as hachures. While of the highest pictorial and metrical standard, the hachure presentation is, in the opinion of this author, an inadequate depiction of the complexity of the monument.

Indeed, the scale and underlying complexity of the monument challenged all the existing archaeological survey techniques, leading to experimentation with two different methods to find the best approach to produce a DTM. The contour plans clearly show the segmented nature of the monument that RCAHMS has attempted to illustrate in the hachure drawing. It is interesting to note that the two surveys, RCAHMS's (illus 22) and the authors' (fold-out illus 98/99) are constructed from basically the same information. Little or no additional site time was required to produce the contour plan, yet at the same time it provides us with much more information about important aspects of the site in question.

The first DTM of this area was prepared on a grid basis. It is ironic that the 10,000 points recorded over five days to form this DTM provide us with less information than the survey for the same area (which took 1.5 days) within the second contour model (fold-out illus 98/99). The first DTM survey carried out on a grid at c 0.3m over the Dyke itself tended to produce more 'bubbled' results with individual points becoming 'contour islands' in the drawing. Also, this survey of this DTM had little or no element of interpretation, resulting in any feature more subtle than the resolution of the grid being lost. The second DTM carried out by means of recording breaklines allowed for this interpretation, and produced results with fewer 'bubbles' and 'islands' that gives a better indication of the nature of the monument. Illustration 54 is a key to line types used by the author in such plans.

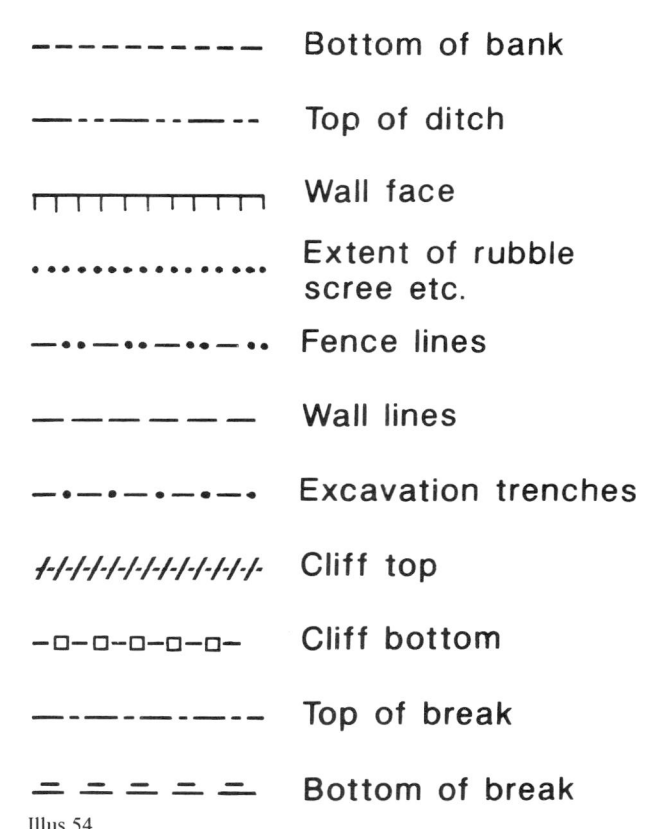

Illus 54
Suggested key line conventions for use in labelling contour surveys.

The Cleaven Dyke is a case in point; the monument itself consists of a bank and two parallel ditches with a surviving length of c 1800m in length. Over that distance the terrain undulates to some extent, and the elements of the monument change in size to deal with this. While most of the site is situated on level ground, at one point, c 500m from the SE end, the monument runs across sloping terrain. The only previously existing survey of this part of the monument was that at 1:2500 carried out by the Ordnance Survey in the 1970s. As the 1:2500 survey does not have an associated DTM (unlike the 1:10,000 or 1:25,000 surveys), it is impossible to appreciate the complex relationship between the monument and the terrain, and the effect one has had on the other (illus 55, upper). In the most recent 1:2500 plan, produced from digital data in 1996, a line marking the approximate bottom of the bank of the Cleaven Dyke has been added (illus 55, lower).

To survey this stretch of the monument in the traditional manner (previously employed by RCAHMS) would allow us to study only in the most general way the nature, size and disposition of the earthwork. The survey carried out during April 1996 to create a DTM survey allows the user of the survey results to visualise the form of the monument and of the terrain in which it sits (fold-out illus 98/99), and thus better to understand their relationship.

The advantages of this kind of DTM production are clear:

1 It is just as quick, if not quicker, than traditional methods employed at comparable degrees of resolution.

2 The final product is more objective and provides more information

3 These surveys are three-dimensional; in the simplest terms this means that we can take accurate measurements from them not only in the horizontal plane, as one might from a standard hachure illustration, but also in the third (vertical) dimension.

It might be said that no modern survey should record less information than that required to produce a terrain model. Frequently with

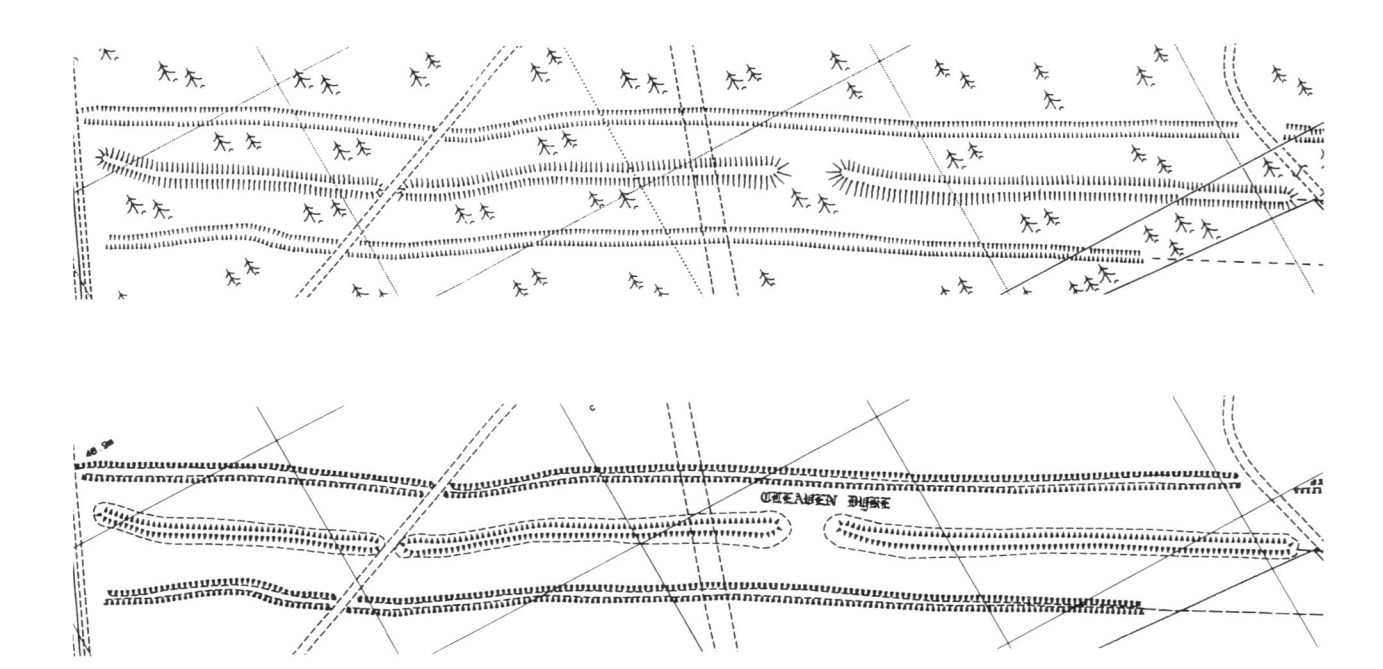

Illus 55
The portion of the Cleaven Dyke to the east of the A96, as depicted on the 1:2500 Ordnance Survey map. (a) the most recent published paper edition of 1977; (b) the current electronic Ordnance Survey data. (*Reproduced from the Ordnance Survey map with the permission of the Controller of Her Majesty's Stationery Office © Crown Copyright MC/98/172.*)

traditional surveys where the final drawing is hachured, it is the case that enough information has been gathered to form a DTM. Much of the archaeological survey work carried out in the past five years using electronic data-logging that has been illustrated with hachures, could, with advantage, be re-presented in contours for a limited investment.

Nor are the advantages restricted to terrestrial sites, for as shown in the work carried out by the author at Lake of Menteith (Burgess & Henderson 1996), contour models have allowed detailed morphological studies to be made of sites where visibility in an underwater environment is limited. Other studies of crannogs (or man-made islands) presently underway in Scotland would benefit from similar treatment of the data.

At the end of the day, the information required by the draughtsman to produce a traditional hachure drawing will still be available. If it is felt that the contour survey is misleading or difficult to interpret, the traditional option still remains. It is not suggested that creating a DTM is the solution for all sites, or all surveyors. Hachures remain particularly useful when a site has to be viewed at a glance, or by people who would find a contour plan difficult to interpret.

In summary, it should be clear that the extra time taken to gather the additional information needed to produce a DTM is worthwhile in enabling the production of plans displaying the third (height) dimension: the addition of the third dimension allows the presentation of 33% more useful information about a site and its landscape.

CONCLUSION

The results of the DTM survey of the Cleaven Dyke (discussed in **3.1** above) have clearly shown that the monument is constructed of a series of shorter mounds, with at least four deliberately constructed breaks. The bank can be seen to change in size in direct relationship to the terrain that it crosses, and the larger the bank gets, the larger the ditches get. Calculations have been undertaken to compare the volume of material in the bank with the apparent volume of the ditches. The DTM has also been used to allow modelling of inter-visibility between parts of the monument. Ordnance Survey data has been used to provide details of the terrain beyond the extents of the monument. These data are supplied at 50m intervals and complements the 50m spot heights collected during the survey.

Future uses of the DTM may include more detailed GIS work and reconstruction of the features recorded from such sources as aerial photographs, geophysics and excavation. One of the major problems in the interpretation of so large a monument is one of conception, or visualisation. In the case of Cleaven Dyke this is clearly made worse by the tree-cover. In the future, the existing DTM could be used to prepare animated sequences that display the monument in its environment, as it is today and as it was at the time of its completion. This animation could be presented as a video, on CD ROM or on any similar media, making the monument accessible to a much wider audience.

5.2 GEOPHYSICAL SURVEY ON THE CLEAVEN DYKE AND LITTLEOUR

Lorna Sharpe & Paul Johnson

Our involvement with the work at the Cleaven Dyke began with a geophysical survey at the Littleour enclosure. An area of 900m² was surveyed in advance of the first season of excavation. Survey at the two sites was undertaken during 1995 and 1996. At the Cleaven Dyke electrical resistivity profile surveys were carried out at the NW terminal, over the SE cropmark portion of the monument, and at an upstanding portion of the Dyke adjacent to the area excavated in 1995. At Littleour resistivity and geomagnetic surveys were undertaken. Soil samples were taken from the enclosure features and surrounding area as they were excavated, to determine their magnetic susceptibilities.

IMPLICATIONS OF THE AREA'S GEOLOGY FOR GEOPHYSICAL SURVEY

The surveys at Littleour illustrate the widespread problems encountered in Scotland in conducting geophysical surveys in areas of glacial drift. The major problem, particularly in relation to resistivity survey, is the non-uniform nature of deposits over small areas. These deposits consist of boulders, through gravels and sands, down to silt- and clay-sized particles. Random distributions of lenses of material of different sizes occur as a result of local variations in transport and depositional environments which cause abrupt changes in drift materials over relatively short distances. This can create considerable difficulties for archaeologists (eg Mercer 1981), not least when attempting geophysical survey. The effect can often be seen clearly in aerial photographs as geological cropmarks (Wilson 1982) which occasionally can be confused with archaeological marks.

Electrical resistivity surveys measure changes in resistance as electrical current travels through different subsurface media, reflecting differences in composition, particle surface area, porosity, permeability and structure (Scollar *et al* 1990,12). It is often difficult to obtain coherent survey results over the constantly changing compositions of a typical glacial drift: the larger scale bulk differences that are the result of geological processes are prone to mask the much more subtle anomalies that archaeological features produce. If there are lateral changes in the make-up of the deposit, the resistive properties of any features present will themselves be affected by the change in substrata. So, for example, if there are two 'postholes' with similar dimensions and a humic, water-retentive fill, but one posthole is cut into a lens of sand and gravel, and the other into boulder clay, the anomalies they are likely to produce could be very different.

Geomagnetic survey is often hindered by the presence in the drift of iron-rich minerals eroded from the higher volcanic, igneous and metamorphic areas ubiquitous in the north of Scotland, over which many of the ice sheets advanced (Bluck pers comm). Presence of these minerals makes possible their conversion to highly magnetically susceptible iron minerals, maghemite and magnetite. The main mechanisms of conversion are combustion and fermentation. These processes allow the detection of past human activity below the ground, and are the basis for magnetic survey in archaeology (Aitken 1972). However, as can be seen at Littleour, these processes also occur through more recent activities such as stubble burning, and can cause more subtle archaeological signals to be obscured.

There are several implications for geophysics in Scotland to be addressed from the work at Littleour and the Cleaven Dyke. Most importantly, we must realise that a negative survey result does not necessarily mean that an area does not contain any archaeology. This is most important when considering developer-led rescue archaeology. Geophysical survey is seen as a good, rapid method of assessing large areas of ground, which is necessary in this area of archaeology. However, it is easy to see how many sites producing similar responses to Littleour could be overlooked and destroyed; not every site has the luxury of producing such obvious cropmarks.

The initial survey results presented us with a practically irresistible challenge: to design a sampling regime that might work at Littleour, and to find out whether the Cleaven Dyke and its surroundings would prove equally elusive were we to attempt to gather more information about that monument.

Sandstones tend to provide 'quiet' backgrounds to geophysical survey, as has been proven from results obtained in Mainland, Orkney (Dockrill & Gater 1992). The area around the Cleaven Dyke is underlain by Old Red Sandstone (ORS). However, the overlying fluvio-glacial drift revealed during excavations at Littleour proved troublesome for both survey techniques employed in this study, particularly at Littleour. Both the Cleaven Dyke and Littleour produce good, well-defined cropmarks, suggesting that clearly-defined changes exist in the subsurface media, which is necessary for successful survey. Because of this we believed that we should be able to detect with reasonable ease at least the features producing the cropmarks.

SURVEYS AT LITTLEOUR

All surveys were carried out using Geoscan Research Ltd instruments: an FM36 Fluxgate Gradiometer and an RM15 Resistivity Meter. Data was processed from the area surveys at Littleour using Geoscan's Geoplot 2.00. The 1995 surveys covered a 30m square grid (900m^2), using a 0.5m sampling interval. The resistivity survey employed a twin electrode configuration with the mobile electrodes set at a 0.5m inter-electrode spacing.

It was only with hindsight that any anomalies representing the postholes could be identified. The most obvious features on the gradiometer plot were linear, running N-S; these were traces of ploughing, still visible on the ground today as narrow furrows defining low ridges c 2m wide and of negligible height. Disturbance to the cultivation lines in the middle of the plot, although these are of later date than the enclosure, marked its position.

The central area of the resistivity plot also displayed evidence of disturbance. It is less obvious that the enclosure is the cause, however, because of the effect of the drift geology on the survey. The plot illustrates perfectly the problems involved in surveying over fluvio-glacial drift deposits discussed above. An area of low-resistance material in the NW corner of the grid terminates in a sharp boundary (illus 56; D, R1). This is a response to the increased depth of topsoil, or plough headland, which has accumulated against the field boundary. From here, south-eastwards across the site, materials of increasingly high resistance were recorded.

Unfortunately, the high-resistance material blankets most of the area of the enclosure. This could be explained as a change in resistance in response to the construction of the enclosure, but, as illustration 56 shows, the high resistance marks an area of gravel. This tends to give high resistivity readings and is the more likely explanation for the results. In short, the resistivity survey successfully sampled the underlying drift at the expense of the archaeology!

In the 1995 excavation, the postholes that defined the enclosure were immediately obvious, their dark fill contrasting dramatically with the surrounding subsoil. As the excavation proceeded, it became clear that they were substantial features. At this stage, before the survey results became available, it was thought that the geophysical survey should have located most, if not all, of these postholes.

When this proved not to be the case we decided to return to Littleour to re-survey the unexcavated, western portion of the enclosure to try to identify the factors preventing detection of these relatively large features. We were curious to find out whether a modification to the survey methodology, specifically an increase in sampling density, would allow the postholes and any other features of the enclosure to be detected. These ideas had been explored in some depth by Sharpe (1996). Alternatively, could failure to detect the postholes have been due to some feature associated with the site, such as the solid or drift geology, the soils present, or the posthole fills?

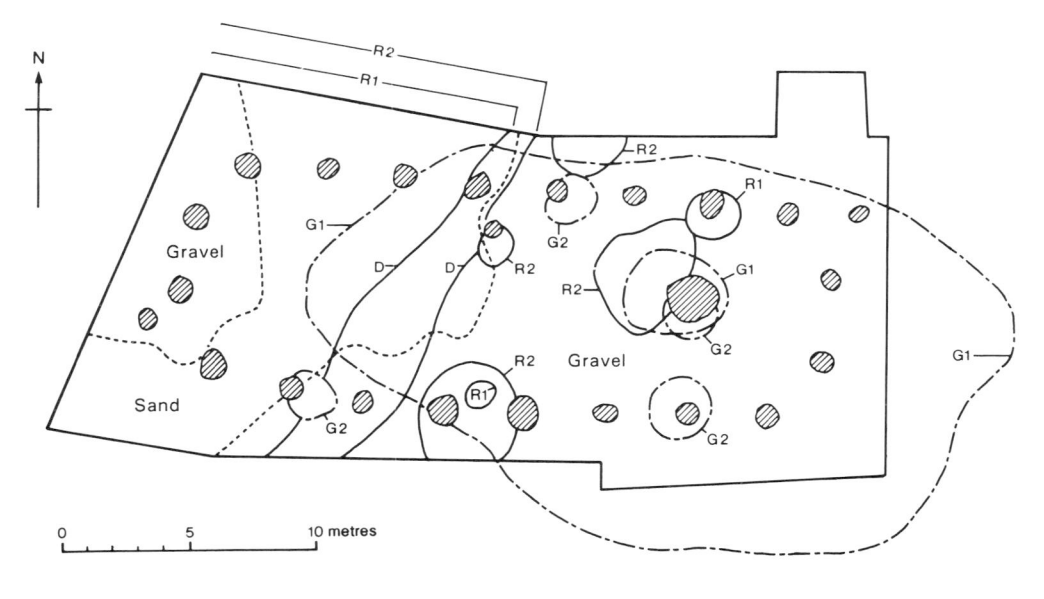

Illus 56
A final interpretation of the results of both seasons of geophysical survey at Littleour. The unlabelled dashed lines mark the boundaries between sand and gravel.
R = anomaly detected by resistivity survey
G = anomaly detected by gradiometer survey

THE MAGNETIC SUSCEPTIBILITY MEASUREMENTS

Measurement of the soil samples from Littleour (using a Bartington MS2D Magnetic Susceptibility Meter) showed that the topsoil on the site possessed a high magnetic susceptibility. These measurements also revealed that the pit fills and the surrounding subsoils have similar magnetic susceptibility values, which means that there was very little magnetic contrast between the features and surrounding subsoil. Without such a contrast, there is little scope for detecting archaeological features by means of geomagnetic techniques. This, together with the high susceptibility topsoil, meant that the much weaker contributions of the pit fills to the total vertical field strength could easily have gone undetected.

The anomalous values recorded along the cultivation lines in the field during the gradiometer survey indicate magnetic enhancement and suggest that stubble may have been burnt in the field over some time. This is likely to be responsible for the high topsoil susceptibility values.

In direct contrast to this, we are also considering the possibility that at Littleour iron is present in a different form, such as limonite (Hall pers comm), which is non-magnetic, but like all substances will have magnetic susceptibility. We hope to examine the samples taken from Littleour, in particular those from the postholes, using X-ray diffraction and fluorescence to determine in what form, and in what quantities, the iron minerals exist.

We also wanted to explore the possibility that the first survey strategy might have prevented us from detecting the features. The 1995 excavation revealed the postholes of the main setting to be between 0.75m x 0.65m (L) and 1.15 by 1.2m (L11) across. The sampling interval chosen for the first survey was 0.5m. This suggested that there was a real possibility that the sampling points lay between the pits, thus missing any maximum anomaly being produce by them. This situation is known as 'aliasing', and should be considered very seriously when planning a survey. Therefore, during the 1996 survey of the unexcavated, western portion of the enclosure, the sampling density was increased to 0.25m over a maximum area of $400m^2$, once again using magnetic and electrical prospecting techniques. To exclude the effects of shallow resistivity changes, and with the knowledge that the topsoil was c 0.3m deep, a twin electrode resistivity frame with an inter-electrode separation of 1m instead of 0.5m was employed, biasing the measured apparent resistance to a depth of 0.5-1m, rather than to the 1995 0.25-0.5m depth, to equate with the depth at which the archaeological remains were thought to occur. Illustration 56 summarises the results of the surveys.

THE 1996 RESULTS

The gradiometer once again revealed the plough marks that were visible in 1995. There were certain other features in this plot including the disturbance caused by the 1995 excavation trench. Based on the results of this survey, and on slight indications on the aerial photographs, it was originally thought that there was a second axial pit in the west end of the enclosure. However, no such feature was discovered when the whole enclosure was excavated in 1996.

The resistivity plot was less affected by the drift deposits, producing a much more consistent background resistance. However, despite the increase in the measuring depth of the survey, the cultivation remains could also be seen to affect the resistance on this plot. A linear feature (illus 56: D, R2) present was once again caused by the plough headland. Despite the lessened effects of the drift deposits, the resistivity plot still failed to produce a clear picture of the enclosure. The final resistivity grid could not be completed due to instrument failure.

Individually, the four plots do not provide much information about the enclosure. In comparison with the cropmark of the site the geophysics results were disappointing. Illustration 42 shows the plan of the enclosure after full excavation in 1996. As the final plan of the site was made, changes in drift geology over the site were also noted (illus 45). These ranged from patches of quite coarse gravel through to an area of very fine sand in the western half. The final retrospective interpretation of the surveys, together with the actual features and drift geology is presented as illustration 56 which shows the areas of anomalous resistance (R1 and R2) and magnetic values (G1 and G2); those detected by both instruments, indicated by dashed lines, can most confidently be said to indicate postholes, since there is an increased likelihood of the existence of a tangible feature if both instruments detect a change in ground properties.

Generally the features present at Littleour have produced very subtle, weak anomalies, if any at all. This poor response is assumed to be due in part to the high magnetic susceptibility values measured in the topsoil, but mainly to the lack of magnetic susceptibility contrast between the feature fills and the surrounding drift deposits. The survey results were improved slightly by sampling at a smaller interval, and by measuring resistance values at a deeper level, as witnessed by the cleaner responses seen in the 1996 survey plots.

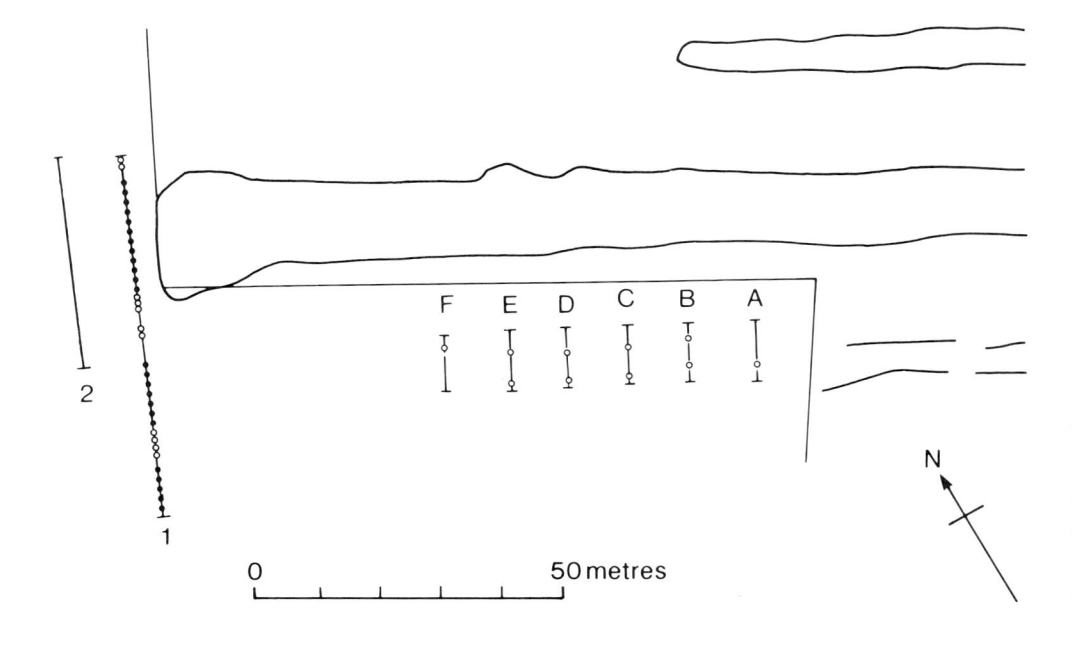

Illus 57
The location of the resistivity profile lines and an interpretation of the results at the NW end of the Cleaven Dyke. The open circles represent low resistivity, the closed circles, high.

SURVEYS AT THE CLEAVEN DYKE.

We performed a series of vertical electrical resistivity profiles at the NW terminal of the Dyke (illus 58), commencing at the boundary between the wood and the arable field where the extant portion of the southern cursus ditch terminates. These profiles appeared to be successful, therefore the investigation was continued across the NW end of the Dyke in an attempt to ascertain whether the cropmarks seen further to the NW in the field adjacent to the Dyke might be linked to the monument, or, as is now thought, whether the terminal in the wood was the original end of the earthwork.

We also examined a section of the extant earthwork close to the position of the cross section dug in 1993 to try to correlate resistivity figures with excavation information concerning the Dyke's construction.

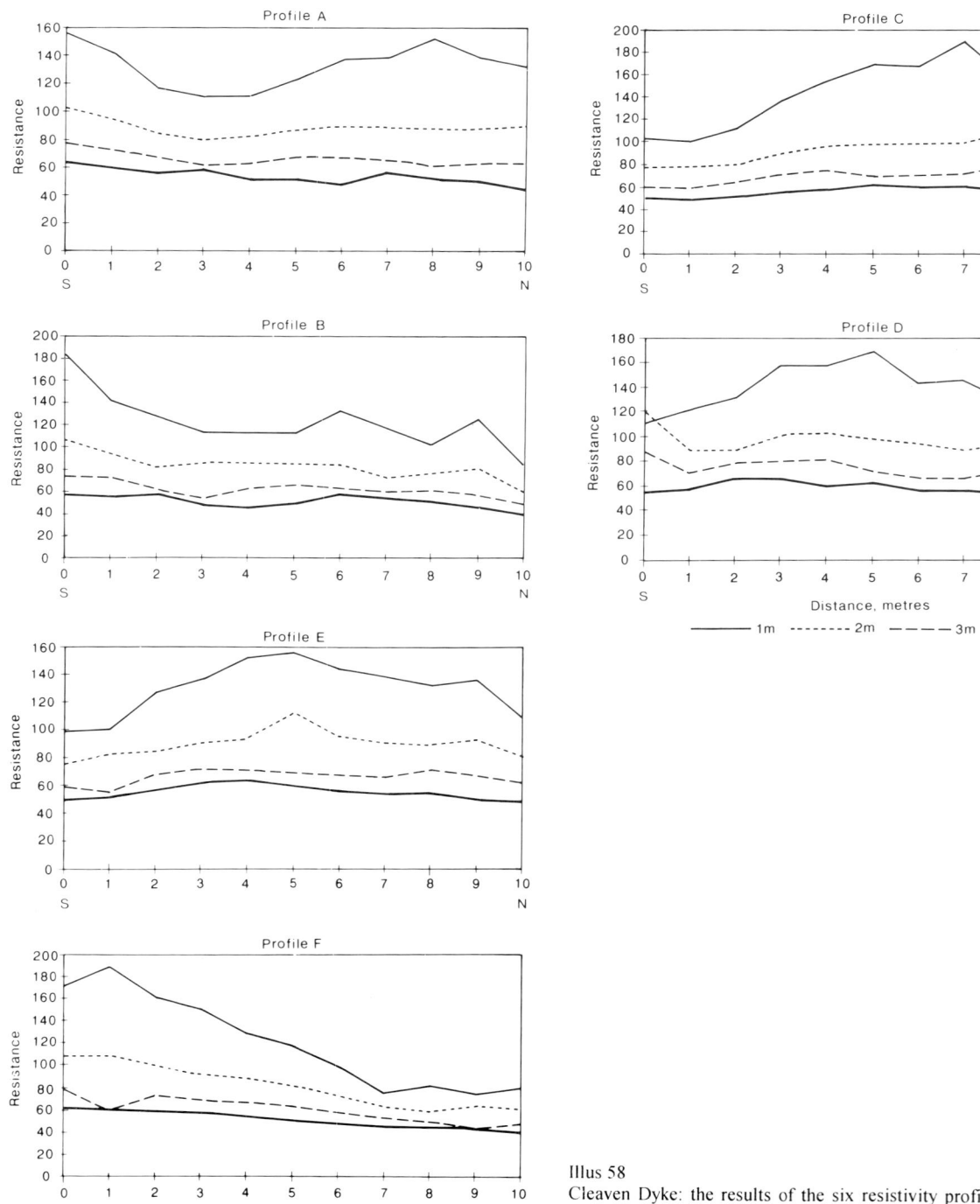

Illus 58
Cleaven Dyke: the results of the six resistivity profiles across the southern ditch. Resistance is measured in ohms.

METHODS

The profiles were made using a configuration of electrodes known as the Wenner array (Clark 1990; Keary & Brooks 1984). For each point at 1m intervals along each profile line, the electrode configuration is expanded so that the inter-electrode spacing is increased progressively from 1m to 4m. This biases the current increasingly deeper into the ground so that resistance for each point along the profile line is measured at a depth of around 0.5m, 1m, 1.5m and 2m. The results of these measurements are reproduced in illustration 57.

THE 1995 VERTICAL ELECTRICAL PROFILES

The evidence for the southern ditch of the Cleaven Dyke proper extending into the arable field from the wood near the NW terminal is limited to a few records of cropmarks. It was therefore important to gather as much information as possible about any further continuation. Six profile lines were set out over the expected line of the southern ditch (illus 57).

As the results of the profiles reveal (illus 58), there are features in the field causing variations in the resistive properties of the ground along the profile lines.

Generally, the irregularity in the resistance readings along each profile line decreases when a larger electrode separation is used. This irregularity is due to the weathered topsoil layer, resulting in part from cultivation. The 2m and 3m profile lines are considered to be most important in this survey. Representing average measurement depths of 1m and 1.5m respectively, these profile lines are most likely to contain anomalies relating to the ditch. The ditch in the upstanding portion of the Dyke today is between 0.5 and 1m deep. The profiles depict low resistance values on their south sides, at between 1m and 3m along profiles A-E, at approximately these depths, which is consistent with the continuation of the ditch.

When the inter-electrode separation reaches 4m, the profile lines can be seen to flatten out. This would indicate that the depth to which the current is biased exceeds the depth of the presumed archaeological feature.

A narrow band of lower resistivity can be seen in the northern side of the profiles, from profiles B to F at between 6m and 8m along the profiles. The strength of the anomalies is comparable to those produced by the presumed continuation of the ditch along the south of the profiles. It is possible that these anomalies may represent a second ditch closer to the cursus bank in this area, but this interpretation is uncertain. An interpretation of the profile results is given in illustration 57.

THE 1996 RESISTIVITY PROFILES

In 1996 the profiles across the NW terminal of the Dyke were completed, along with a profile at the SE end of the monument, and one over the extant portion of the Dyke. The 1996 profiles across the NW terminal are marked 1 and 2 on illustration 57.

Illustration 57 presents the results of the 1995 and 1996 resistivity profiles to give an interpretation of the features present at the NW terminal. One interpretation of the survey results is that there may be two ditches running along the south side of the cursus bank in this area. Across the terminal, the first profile detected three resistivity lows in the immediate area of the Cleaven Dyke bank-terminal. Two may be interpreted as the two ditches found by Adamson in 1975, or a reflection of the complex turf revetment of the mound. The high-resistance feature may represent the ploughed-out bank. The continuation of the postulated inner ditch appears to align with both the excavated ditch feature and one of the southern low-resistance areas detected in 1996, although it is perhaps unwise to extrapolate this feature over such a large area of unsurveyed ground.

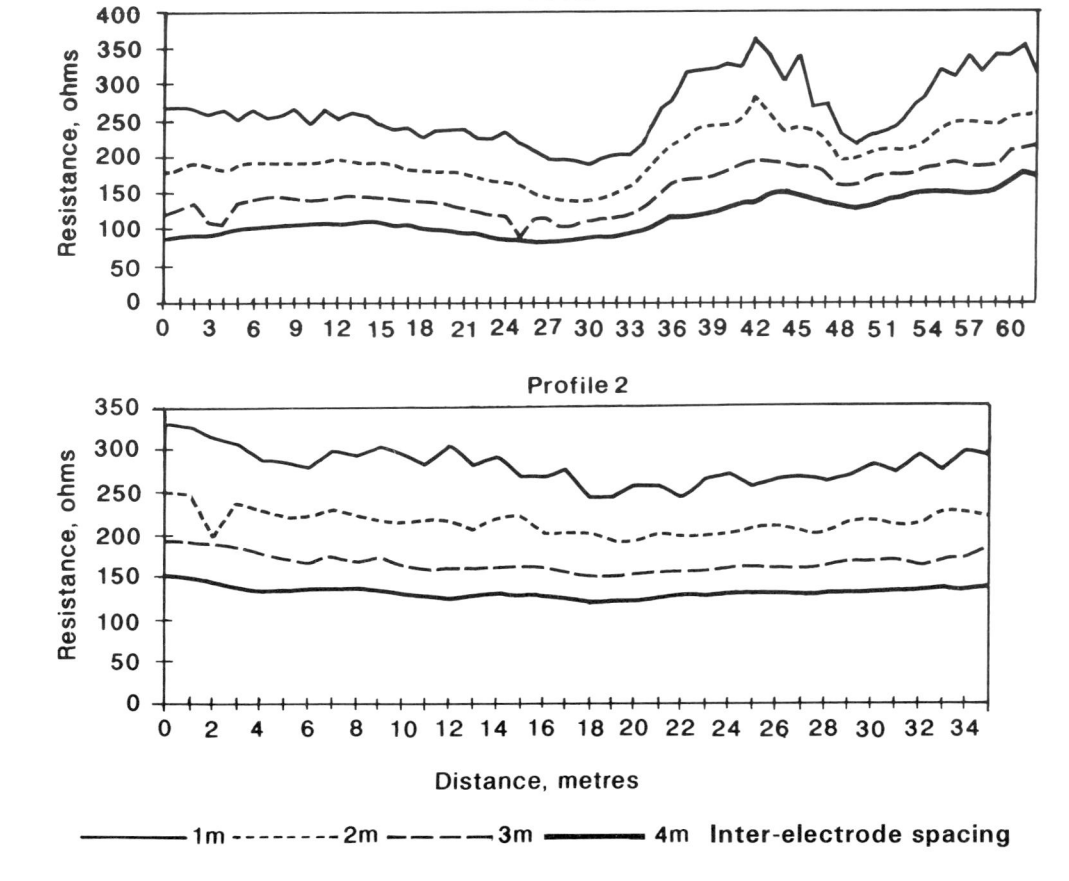

Illus 59
Resistivity profiles at the NW end of the Cleaven Dyke (see illus 57 for location).

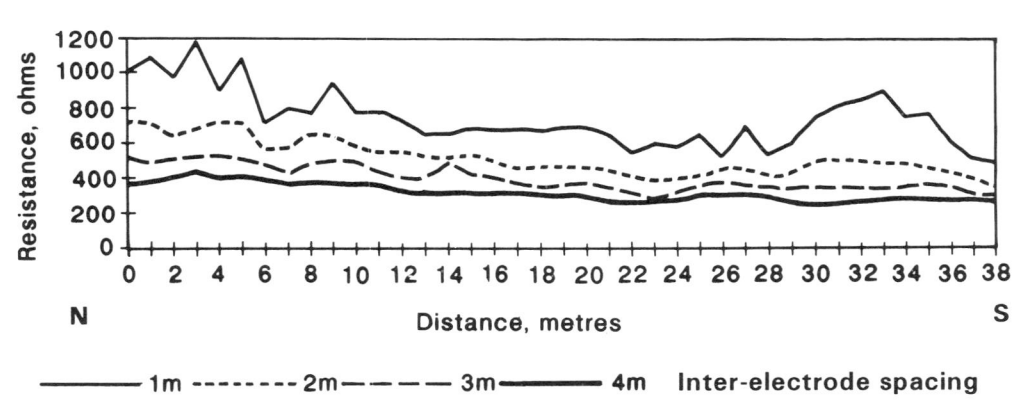

Illus 60 Resistivity profile across the extant section of the Cleaven Dyke.

The higher resistance seen at the southern end of profile 1 may be associated with the beginning of the hollow-ways caused by cattle droving along the Dyke; it is suggested below that the southernmost low-resistance area could also be associated with this activity, rather than the continuation of the outer ditch.

The second 1996 profile indicates that the monument did not reach as far as 15m out from the surviving bank-terminal. This confirms the view of Pitts and St Joseph (1985) and Barclay and Maxwell (this volume) that the Cleaven Dyke does not extend any further to the NW.

THE PROFILE ACROSS THE EXTANT PORTION OF THE DYKE

This profile was located parallel to the cross-section dug in 1993, c 5m NW of it. It was expected that the results from this profile would show the cursus ditch producing a low resistance because of the water-retentive silts in its fill, and that the central bank would produce a higher resistance feature. The results actually provided a much more subtle indication of the Dyke's subsurface composition. This could only be fully appreciated with the benefit of excavation. However, it does suggest that if results such as these could be quantified and examined with regard to the features and materials that could be causing the anomalies, we would have a much more powerful predictive tool in geophysics.

For the first 5m of the 1m profile line, and possibly up to the first 10m, there is disruption from nearby trees (illus 60). The small decrease in ground resistance around the 6m mark may be associated with the bottom of the cursus ditch, where natural silting at the lowest point of the depression would cause a lower resistivity due to the large total surface area of the silt-sized particles (Scollar et al 1990,12). At c 12m the resistance decreases again. This decrease is also seen in the 2m and 3m profile lines. It is possible that the lower resistance may indicate the presence of a second ditch, similar to that postulated from the 1995 profiles, at the NW terminal. However, it is difficult to judge this from one measurement; this low could be caused by a hole, or be related to the agricultural ridging parallel to the Dyke, detected by the RCAHMS survey (illus 22). The feature appears on the 2m profile as a slight rise in resistance. If this feature represents a second ditch, agricultural ridge or erosion hollow, it could indicate a water-retentive upper layer, sampled at the 1m inter-electrode spacing, covering a deeper, less conductive medium such as the sands and gravels that constitute the inner layers of the cursus bank or indeed a layer of compacted soil such as that which would be produced along a trackway. It should be noted that the detailed RCAHMS survey of this area, and two episodes of contour survey and excavation immediately adjacent, located no trace of a ditch in this area; given the clear survival of the Cleaven Dyke ditch, the presence of a second ditch here must be considered unlikely.

From the 21m point along the profile the resistance values become more erratic, and represent the influence of the cursus bank on the resistance measurements. The effect can be seen to a lesser extent in the three deeper profile lines. The exaggerated peaks and troughs in the profile are likely to result from rabbit burrows or stones; the former become more concentrated towards the cursus bank. Although the 1m profile line is most likely to have sampled the uppermost peaty and loamy layers of the cursus, the resistance values recorded would also be expected to be affected, in part, by the underlying soil layers. For example, the high resistance over the cursus bank is probably due to the increased drainage in the underlying sands and gravels causing the uppermost layers also to be drier.

The cursus bank is marked on all four profiles by a drop in resistance at the northern edge, before the rise of the bank. This decreased resistance may be a response to the turf revetments, or to soil slumping along the base of the bank. As expected, a similar low-resistance feature is seen at the S-facing bank base.

The 2m profile line shows a higher resistance at the crest of the bank with a flattening out over the top. This is thought to be in response to an underlying area of sandy material on the flanks with a return to an increased depth of loamy material towards the centre of the bank. This is seen to be a common feature of the bank construction (Barclay et al 1995; 2.3 this volume).

The 2m profile line, which measures to a depth of c 1m, defined the position of the ditch well at between 5m and 8m along the profile. The 3m and 4m profile lines, which measure at a depth of c 1.5 and 2m respectively also indicate the position of the extant ditch between 6m and 8m. Although these measurement depths are deeper than the ditch, again, the resistivity of the material below the cut feature will be affected by changes in drainage and moisture content caused by the ditch.

As the 1995 surveys suggested, the 2m and 3m inter-electrode spacing measurements again appear to be the most responsive to the features known from the excavations to be present. Resistivity rises at either side of the ditch in the 2m profile line could be in response to the gravel patches at the outer edges of the ditch bottom.

PROFILE ACROSS THE CROPMARK SECTION OF THE DYKE

The 1996 profile at the SE end of the Cleaven Dyke lay across both ditches and the bank of the Dyke, in the arable field just west of the wood, and c 30m out from the corner of the field (illus 61). The ditches, and to a lesser extent, the bank can be seen to affect the resistivity measurements, even though the monument is ploughed-out here. The southern ditch appears in the profile from 0 to 3m. The following resistivity rise is in response to the bank material. The profiles show a disturbance from c 3m to 33m, in the form of increasing resistance at the start of the profile line, changing to a decreased resistance approaching the 33m measuring point. This may represent the spread of the bank material under the plough, with its combination of sands and gravels, and more humic turf edges producing local variations in the resistive qualities of the cultivated soils. The sharp drop in resistance at 25m on the 4m profile line on the northern edge of the bank area probably represents the turf revetment used in the bank's construction, although, less likely, it may relate to a ditch at the base of the bank. Several of the aerial photographs of the SE cropmark show the edges of the bank to be defined by two darker, presumably more water-retentive, lines (eg CUCAP print DD 58); on

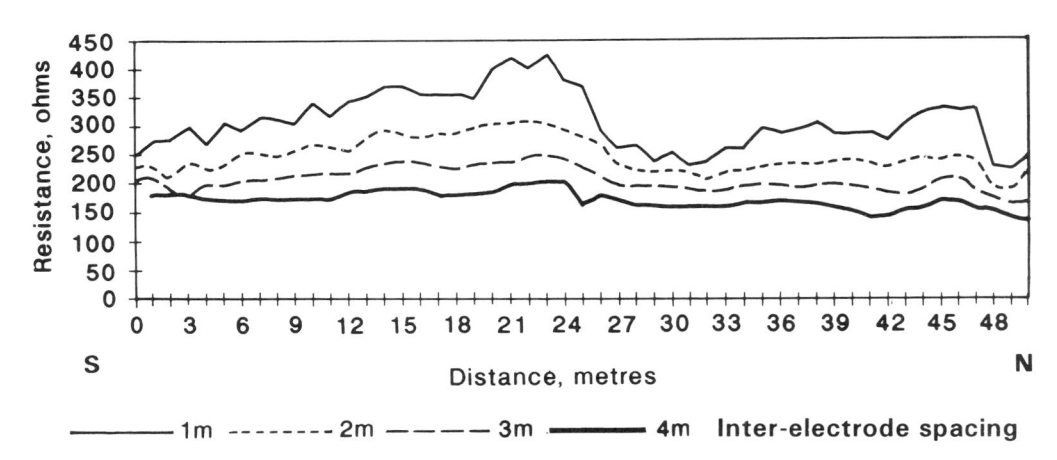

Illus 61
Resistivity section across the cropmark portion of the Cleaven Dyke in the arable field, just to the SE of the wood.

RCAHMS print C06901 soil marks suggest that this feature is the spread turf revetment of the bank. These low-resistance features also appear on the first profile across the NW terminal of the Dyke, where they are known from excavation to correspond to either ditches or turf revetments. A slightly increased, but relatively stable resistance from c 33m to 42m implies the presence of the berm, and the rise and sudden fall in values from here to the end of the profile indicates the northern ditch. The anomaly relating to this ditch again displays the shoulder effect that the Wenner array produces at the edge of some cut features, as was discussed for the extant northern ditch above.

SUMMARY

The results of the geophysical investigations at the Cleaven Dyke suggest the following:

1 At the NW end what may be the southern ditch of the cursus can be detected in the arable field up to profile E.

2 There is evidence for what may be an inner ditch from profiles B to F, which may be a continuation of the southern ditch next to the mound, as located by Adamson (in its correct location).

3 The NW end of the Dyke does not affect the resistivity profile 15m from the terminal bank. At this distance from the bank, the resistance values indicate an undisturbed profile to a maximum depth of 2m.

4 The profile across the cropmark portion of the Dyke, at the SE, indicates low-resistance features flanking the bank on either side. These may be caused by a depth of water-retentive material, probably the turf revetments that have been found to flank the bank, or, less likely, could indicate the presence of two small ditches defining the extent of the cursus bank.

We await the results of the soil analyses for Littleour. If, as is suspected, the iron takes a form other than magnetite or maghemite, even though there has obviously been burning or at least decay of organic matter in some of the postholes at Littleour, we hope to take this study further. We feel that it is important to determine the form of the iron present at Littleour, and whether it is being converted into a form that cannot be detected by magnetometers. This is obviously an important question, specially given the difficulties often associated with producing coherent survey results in Scotland.

On a brighter note, we appear to be achieving consistently good and informative results using resistivity profiling. Apart from the results at the Cleaven Dyke, we have experienced successes at Ardoch Roman Fort (Johnson, in press), and the Lamington Roman Temporary Camp and Iron Age Fort in the Clyde Valley (Bertok 1997).

5.3 ESTIMATING SOIL LOSS FROM CROPMARK SITES: USING THE CAESIUM 137 METHODOLOGY AT LITTLEOUR

Andrew N Tyler, Donald A Davidson & Ian C Grieve

The implementation of policies for the protection of archaeological sites necessitates both evaluation of their archaeological importance and assessment of the risk of partial or total damage by natural or human agencies. One major process affecting archaeological features such as cropmark sites in the rural environment is soil erosion and there is thus a need to develop methods for assessing erosion rates and potential risk to such sites.

This need for erosion risk assessment is predicated upon evidence for recent increases in soil erosion. Several recent reports have highlighted the areal incidence of soil erosion in England and Wales (eg Skinner & Chambers 1996). Although the significance of soil erosion in Scotland has been questioned (Frost & Speirs 1996), there is significant evidence for severity of soil erosion in both the lowlands (Kirkbride & Reeves 1993; Davidson, DA & Harrison 1995) and the uplands (Grieve *et al* 1995). A range of factors is thought to have contributed to an increased incidence of erosion in recent decades, including changes in cropping patterns towards more autumn-sown cereals, increases in livestock pressure, increases in rainfall during the autumn and winter when soils are generally bare, deterioration of field drainage systems and degradation of soil properties such as content of organic matter. Erosion is certainly more prevalent in fields under autumn-sown cereals (Skinner & Chambers 1996) and where cultivation is up and down the slope of the field.

A major difficulty in the assessment of soil erosion risk has been the problem of acquiring reliable data on erosion rates over several decades. Soil erosion events are episodic and risk cannot be assessed from measurements based on individual erosion events or over

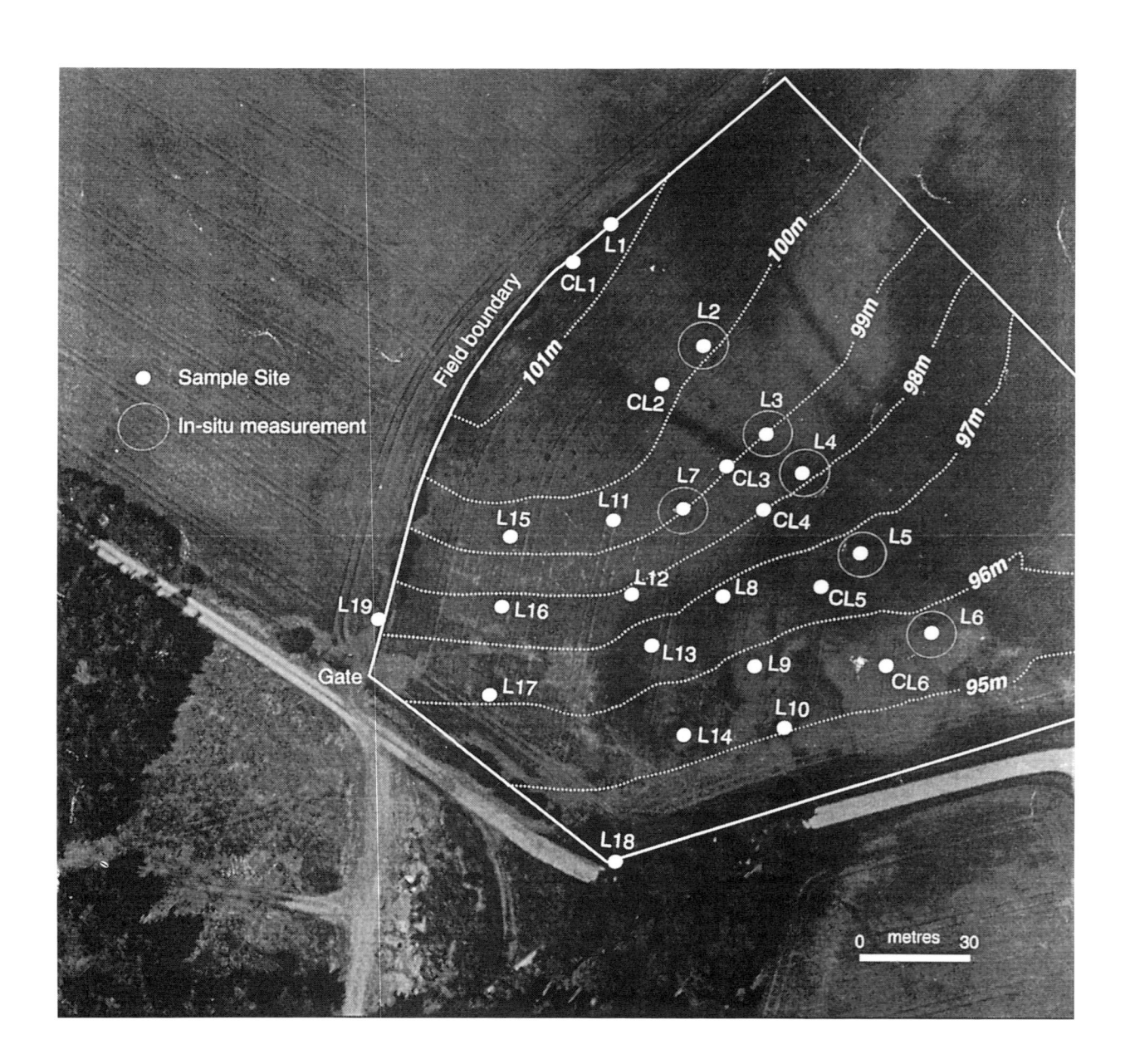

Illus 62
Sample locations at Littleour.

a typical two-three year research project. Knowledge of rates of soil loss measured over the medium term of a few decades is essential if meaningful assessments of the risk from soil erosion to features such as cropmark sites are to be made. The development of techniques of estimating erosion rates from Caesium 137 (^{137}Cs) determinations (Walling & Quine 1991) is applicable at this time-scale but suffers the considerable drawback for use on archaeological sites since it necessitates excavation of soil cores and thus considerable site disturbance. However, recent research has led to the development of *in situ* methods of measuring total ^{137}Cs activity and its vertical distribution using a detector sited on a tripod above the ground (Tyler *et al* 1996a, 1996b). Such methods offer exciting possibilities for estimating medium-term erosion rates directly in the field without site disturbance.

^{137}Cs, which has a relatively long half life of 30.2 years, was released into the atmosphere during atomic weapon testing in the 1950s and 1960s. Following deposition on the soil, the positively charged Cs$^+$ ion is irreversibly adsorbed on illite clays in a similar manner to potassium ions (Walling & Quine 1991). In an undisturbed site the vertical distribution of ^{137}Cs activity in the soil approximates an exponential decline with depth, but in cultivated soils the added ^{137}Cs is mixed uniformly through the plough layer. ^{137}Cs activity within a soil core can be lost when the fine clay particles to which the ^{137}Cs ions are adsorbed are eroded by water or wind. Increases in ^{137}Cs activity result from deposition of eroded particles. The mean net erosion or deposition over the period since weapon testing began can then be estimated from the total ^{137}Cs activity, provided the initial ^{137}Cs added to the site by atmospheric deposition is known. The initial Cs can be estimated from measurements of ^{137}Cs activity at nearby undisturbed control sites.

We have measured ^{137}Cs activity on core samples and by *in situ* methods along a number of transects across a field at the Littleour site. Our aims were:

1. to compare soil erosion rates estimated from ^{137}Cs activity measurements from soil core samples and directly from *in situ* measurements;

2. to examine the spatial pattern of erosion rates at the Littleour site;

3. to assess the significance of soil erosion for archaeological conservation both at the Littleour site and for Scottish cropmark sites more generally.

We used two sites in uncultivated grassland at the edge of the field to determine total ^{137}Cs activity at undisturbed sites. Measurements at these sites provided the control data against which gains and losses of the ^{137}Cs activity, and hence soil, were estimated.

MATERIALS AND METHODS

The Littleour structure is located within a field *c* 6ha in area (illus 62). The structure is sited on a gently sloping bench towards the upper boundary of the field, and from this area there is a convexo-concave slope down to the lower boundary. Soils are humus-iron podsols of the Corby series derived from fluvio-glacial sands and gravels. Textures are loamy sand or sand and the cultivated Ap horizon varies in thickness down the slope of the field from *c* 0.2m to more than 0.5m. At the time of sampling the field was uncultivated and in set-aside.

Soil sampling points were spaced according to slope characteristics and located along transect lines from the bench down the convexo-concave slope along the line of maximum slope angle (illus 62). The field boundaries and sampling points were accurately surveyed in May 1996 using an EDM to locate points relative to known bench marks and differential GPS to provide absolute co-ordinates for the survey points. Illustration 62 shows the locations of the sampling points within the field. One transect was sampled during 1995 and core samples at 50mm or 25mm vertical intervals were obtained from six points for laboratory determination of ^{137}Cs activity. This provided preliminary estimates of soil erosion rates for six points reported previously (Tyler *et al* 1995).

In situ measurements of ^{137}Cs activity were made in May 1996 at sites L1-L6 (illus 62). At each site an n-type 35% relative efficiency HPGe detector was used to collect γ ray emission spectra for periods of up to 8000s. The detector was sited on a tripod at a height of 1m above the ground, giving a field of view of approximately 10m radius.

Core samples were obtained from five points at each of sites L2-L6, located according to a systematic sampling scheme within the theoretical field of view of the spectrometer. Depending on the stone content of the soil, either a cylindrical core 105mm in diameter was extracted or a small pit was dug and a column with surface area 25cm^2 excavated. The core or column was sectioned at pre-determined depth intervals to provide samples of known volume. A detailed analysis of the vertical distribution of ^{137}Cs activity was obtained by subdividing at 50mm intervals from 0 to 0.15m, 25mm intervals from 0.15m to 0.25m, and at 50mm intervals to 0.3m. The 25mm samples between 0.15m and 0.25m permitted more accurate definition of the base of the ploughed layer.

At sites L1 and L7, samples were obtained from a single pit subdivided at the same depth intervals to measure total and vertical distribution of ^{137}Cs activity in the laboratory. At sites L8-L19, samples were obtained from the 0-0.15m and 0.15-0.3m layers in a single pit to measure total ^{137}Cs activity.

Mass of all samples was determined on return to Stirling and used with field volume to calculate field-moist bulk density. Samples were then oven-dried and re-weighed. Moisture content and dry bulk density were calculated from the oven-dry mass. The samples were then ground and packed into sample chambers. The n-type 35% relative efficiency HPGe detector was used to collect γ ray emission spectra in the laboratory. Counting times varied from 20,000 to 40,000s depending on the activity of the sample.

Illus 63
^{137}Cs activity distributions observed in the samples collected along the 1995 pilot Transect: CL 1= 2.4 Bq m^{-2}; CL2 = 1.42 Bq m^{-2}; CL 3 = 1.70 Bq m^{-2}; CL 4 = 1.84 Bq m^{-2}; CL5=1.38 Bq m^{-2}; CL 6 = 2.27 Bq m^{-2}.

EROSION RATE ESTIMATION

Simple conversion of ^{137}Cs activity estimates (Bq m^{-2}) to erosion rates as mm a^{-1} were made by:

1. the directly proportional technique to estimate soil lost from the ploughed layer (assumed to be 0.2m), where the erosion rate E (mm a^{-1}) is estimated from:

$$E = M\left(\frac{C_i - C_r}{C_r}\right)\frac{1}{n}$$

2. Kachanoski's (1993) power function model, where E is estimated from:

$$E = MR^{-1}\left[1 - \left(\frac{C_i}{C_r}\right)^{\frac{1}{n}}\right]$$

where M is the depth of the ploughed layer, Ci is the ^{137}Cs activity (Bq m^{-2}) at any one point, Cr is the reference site ^{137}Cs activity, n is the number of years since ^{137}Cs deposition, and R is the ratio of the concentration of ^{137}Cs in the eroding sediment to that in the ploughed layer (here assumed to be 1).

RESULTS

SOIL CORE DERIVED EROSION RATES ESTIMATES

Illustration 62 shows the sample locations at the Littleour site in relation to the cropmark site. Illustration 63 shows the vertical activity distributions across the area of marked topographic change, CL1 to CL6, sampled in 1995. The results show a relatively uniform activity distribution with depth to about 0.2m. Illustration 64, shows an example of the spatial variability of the ^{137}Cs depth distribution

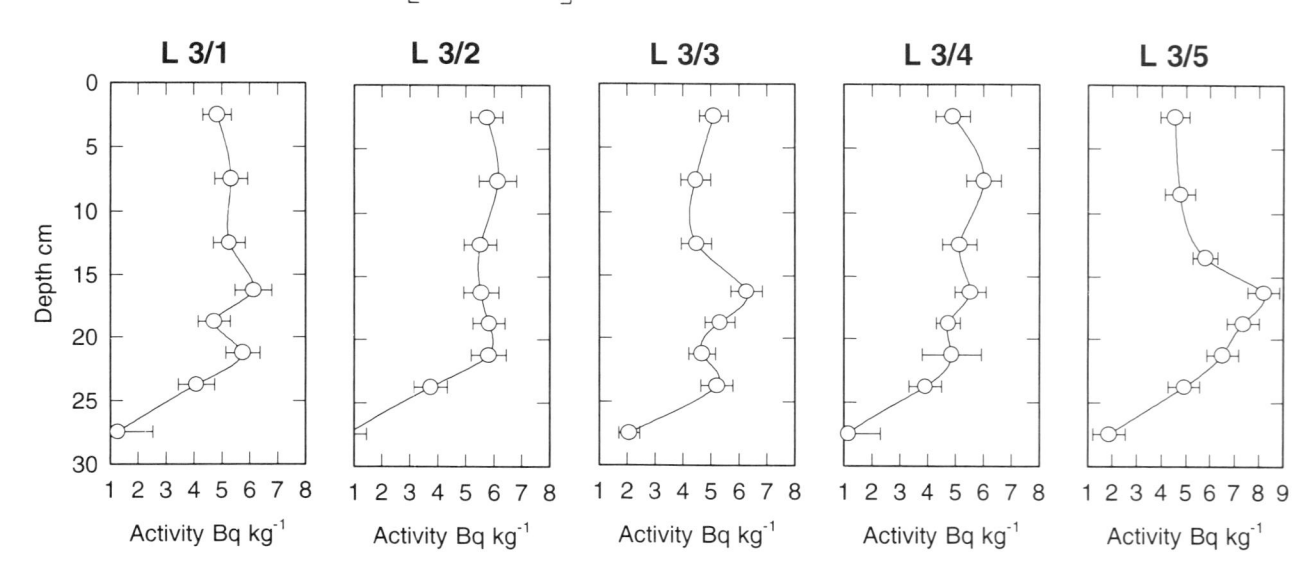

Illus 64
Variation in the vertical distribution of ^{137}Cs activity. Total activities for each site are: L3/1 = 2.04 kBq m^{-2}, L3/2 = 1.91 kBq m^{-2}, L3/3 = 1.82 kBq m^{-2}, L3/4 = 1.71 kBq m^{-2}, L3/5=1.69 kBq m^{-2}.

sampled at site L3 in 1996. Here more detail is observed in the soil profile and the depth of the ploughed layer is observed to be about 0.22m, although this does vary slightly. Both legends of illustrations 63 and 64 show the variation in the total ^{137}Cs activity loading at each site.

Total ^{137}Cs activity and calculated erosion (negative) and deposition (positive) rates are shown in table 15. When comparing time-scales, and differences in the ploughed layer depth, estimates shown in table 15 are directly comparable to Kachanoski's erosion rate estimates derived from erosion plots and his regression model (Kachanoski 1987).

It should be noted that it is standard practice to assume that the ploughed layer depth is 0.2m. Evidence shown here suggests that this assumption may lead to 10% or more underestimation in the erosion rate estimate. However, we recognise that the directly proportional methodology may lead to an overestimate in the erosion rate as a result of, for example, particle selectivity in the erosion process (Quine 1995). These opposing systematic influences may cancel each other out to some degree.

Illustration 65 shows a simple contour map of the erosion rates estimated by the directly proportional technique, superimposed on the aerial photograph of the Littleour site. The erosion rate over the cropmark site was estimated through spatial interpolation and is likely to be of the order of 0.5mm a^{-1}.

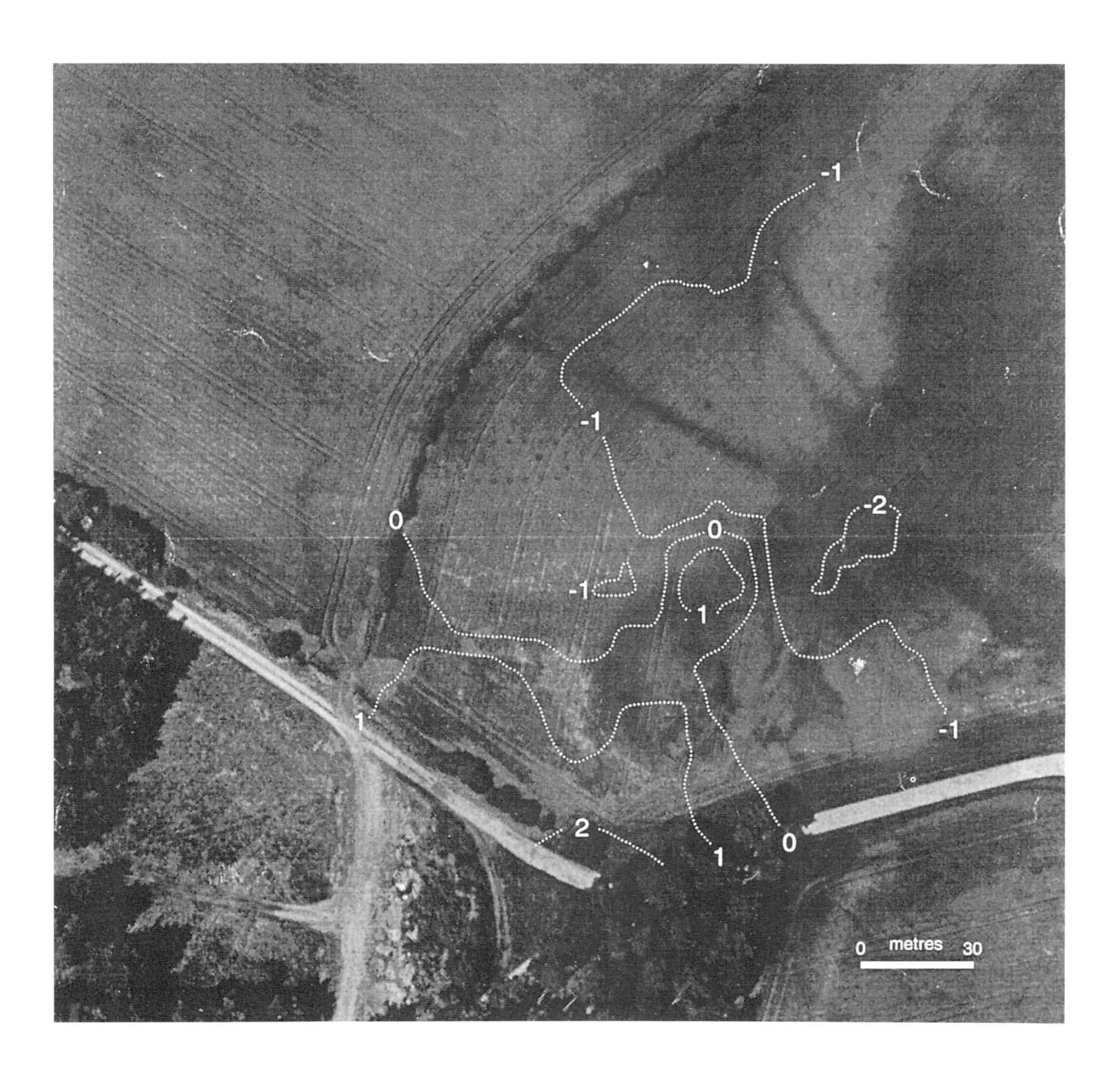

Illus 65
Soil erosion rates in mm a^{-1}.

	Soil Sample Results		Directly Proportional Model		Kachanoski Power Function	
Site No.	Activity kBq m^{-2}	error	mm a^{-1}	error	mm a^{-1}	error
October 1995 Results						
Cl 1^R	2.40	0.30	**0.00**	**0.00**	**0.00**	**0.18**
Cl 2	1.42	0.18	**-1.94**	**0.29**	**-2.48**	**0.18**
Cl 3	1.70	0.24	**-1.39**	**0.22**	**-1.64**	**0.19**
Cl 4	1.84	0.14	**-1.11**	**0.15**	**-1.26**	**0.15**
Cl 5	1.38	0.20	**-2.02**	**0.31**	**-2.62**	**0.19**
Cl 6	2.27	0.15	**-0.26**	**0.04**	**-0.27**	**0.14**
May 1996 Results						
L 1^R	2.37	0.40	**-0.06**	**0.01**	**-0.06**	**0.21**
L 2	1.93	0.40	**-0.93**	**0.19**	**-1.04**	**0.24**
L 3	1.90	0.13	**-0.99**	**0.14**	**-1.11**	**0.14**
L 4	1.64	0.15	**-1.51**	**0.21**	**-1.81**	**0.16**
L 5	1.37	0.18	**-2.04**	**0.30**	**-2.65**	**0.18**
L 6	1.48	0.20	**-1.83**	**0.28**	**-2.29**	**0.18**
L 7	1.44	0.13	**-1.90**	**0.26**	**-2.42**	**0.15**
L 8	3.13	0.20	**1.45**	**0.22**	**1.27**	**0.14**
L 9	2.06	0.17	**-0.67**	**0.10**	**-0.73**	**0.15**
L 11	2.42	0.17	**0.04**	**0.01**	**0.04**	**0.14**
L 12	1.82	0.12	**-1.15**	**0.16**	**-1.31**	**0.14**
L 13	2.47	0.18	**0.14**	**0.02**	**0.14**	**0.14**
L 14	3.00	0.20	**1.19**	**0.18**	**1.07**	**0.14**
L 15	2.26	0.18	**-0.28**	**0.04**	**-0.29**	**0.15**
L 16	2.17	0.17	**-0.46**	**0.07**	**-0.48**	**0.15**
L 17	3.39	0.20	**1.96**	**0.30**	**1.65**	**0.14**
L 18	3.60	0.21	**2.38**	**0.37**	**1.94**	**0.14**
L 19	2.82	0.19	**0.83**	**0.12**	**0.77**	**0.14**
-ve indicates erosion rate +ve indicates accumulation rate ^{R} Samples collected on assumed uneroded sites (control sites)						

Table 15
^{137}Cs activity estimates and erosion estimates using the directly proportional and Kachanoski's power function models.

IN SITU DERIVED EROSION RATES ESTIMATES

Illustration 66 shows the vertical distribution of ^{137}Cs activity in terms of mass depth (g cm^{-2}) at site 3. Variations in soil density play an important part in changing the observed linear vertical distribution. These changes must be accounted and corrected for when calibrating *in situ* gamma spectrometers.

Tyler *et al* (1996a) showed how calibration corrections can be made for variations in the vertical activity concentration which can influence the detector response. The ratio of the full energy peak area to forward scattered step in the spectrum was shown to be sensitive to small changes in the vertical activity distribution and can be used to derive an *in situ* calibration correction. Illustration 67 shows an example of an *in situ* spectrum collected at Littleour. Whilst the

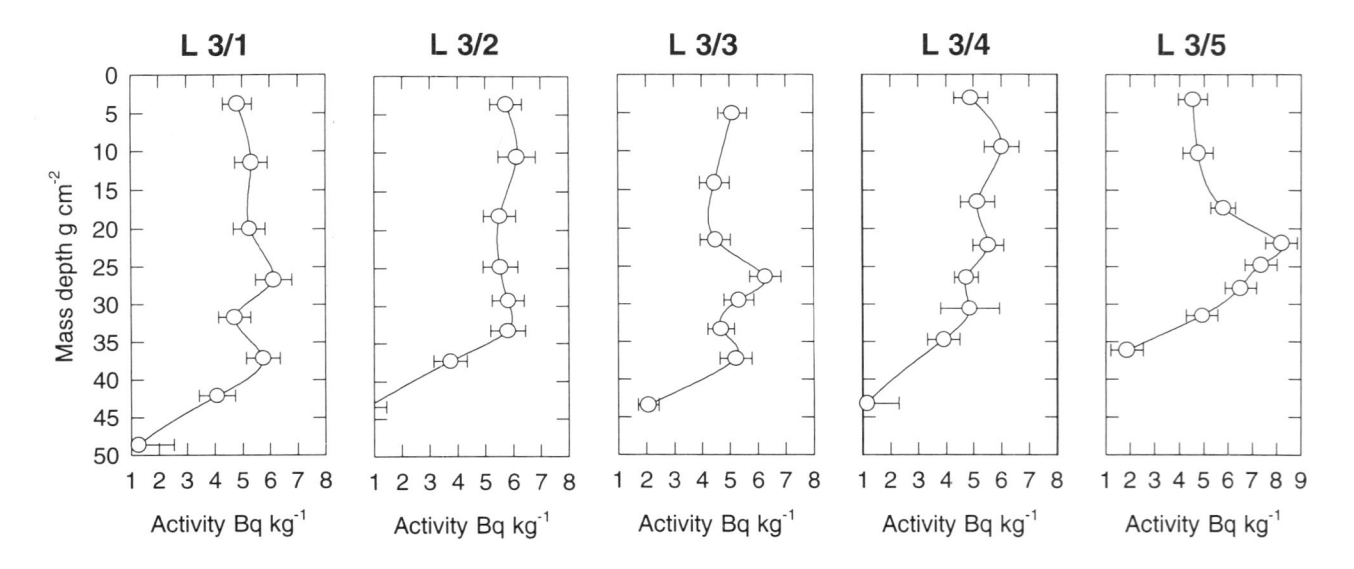

Illus 66
Mass depth distribution profiles of ^{137}Cs activity.

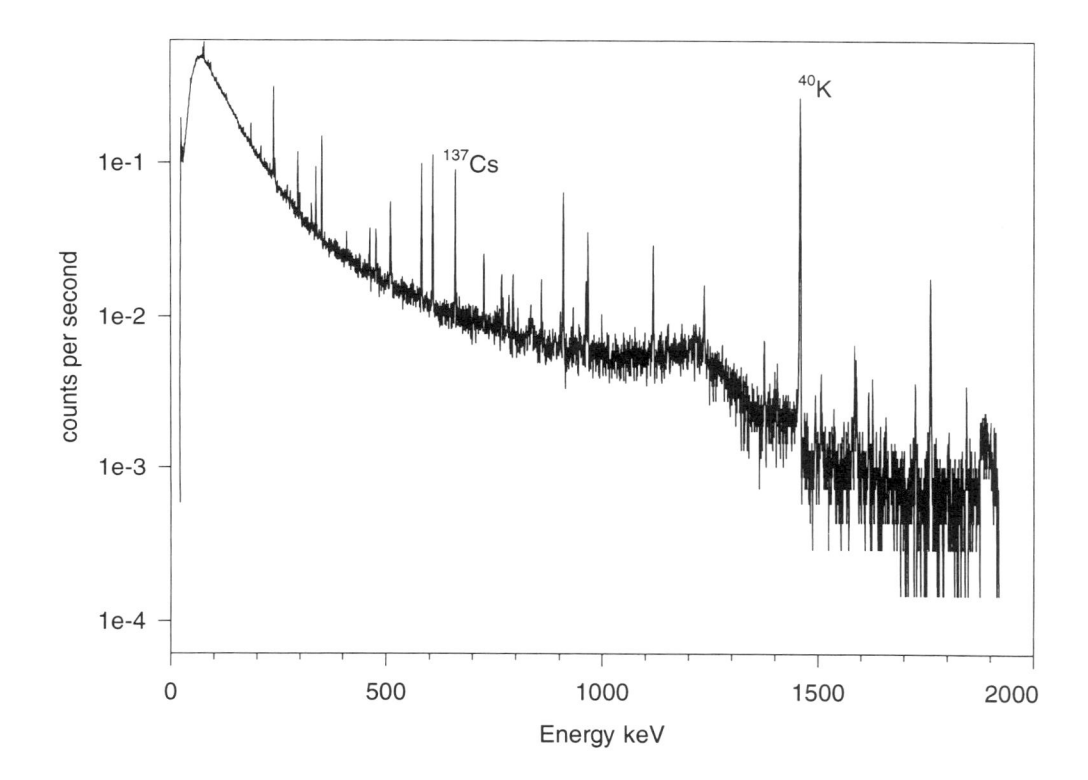

Illus 67
An example of an *in situ* spectrum collected at Littleour (L 4).

enhanced forward scattering can be observed around the 40K peak resulting in the observed step (itself proportional to soil wet bulk density), the ^{137}Cs step is less easily observed, but its presence and magnitude are statistically easy to define given relatively large windows on either side of the ^{137}Cs full energy peak.

Table 16 and illustration 68 show a comparison between *in situ* derived ^{137}Cs activity estimates and soil core/pit derived estimates. From the replicate samples collected at sites L3 and L4, considerable spatial variability in total activity and activity distribution with mass depth within the detector field of view is evident. For example, a 2σ

Site No.	In-situ Gamma Spectrometry Estimates		Soil Core Derived Estimates			In-situ derived erosion rate estimates	
	^{137}Cs kBq m^{-2}	Q_{Cs}[b]	Activity kBq m^{-2}	ß g cm^{-2}	δ g cm^{-2}	Directly proportional mm a^{-1}	Kachanoski Power func. mm a^{-1}
Ref. Site (not eroded)			2.4 ± 0.3[c]			0.0	0.0
L 2	1.85 ± 0.10	2.6 ± 0.1	1.9 ± 0.3[e]	22.8 ± 2.8[e]	40.0 ± 3.8[e]	-1.1 ± 0.14	-1.24 ± 0.13
L 3	1.94 ± 0.10	2.3 ± 0.1	1.91 ± 0.13	24.0 ± 1.7	39.4 ± 2.4	-0.91 ± 0.12	-1.0 ± 0.13
L 4	1.75 ± 0.10	2.5 ± 0.1	1.64 ± 0.15	17.7 ± 1.2	31.0 ± 4.0	-1.3 ± 0.16	-1.5 ± 0.21
L 5	1.36 ± 0.10	3.0 ± 0.2	1.37 ± 0.18[a]	19.6 ± 2.5[a]	33.0 ± 4.0[a]	-2.1 ± 0.33	-2.69 ± 0.42
L 6	1.78 ± 0.10	2.5 ± 0.1	1.48 ± 0.20[a]	25.5 ± 3.0[a]	41.0 ± 4.0[a]	-1.23 ± 0.16	-1.42 ± 0.18
L 7	1.53 ± 0.13	2.6 ± 0.3	1.44 ± 0.20[a]	[d]	[d]	-1.73 ± 0.33	-2.1 ± 0.4

Poisson errors on Q_{Cs} are calculated from 1 σ errors within each region and are dominated by the error on full energy peak A. Error on *in situ* ^{137}Cs are estimates are controlled by the error on A and initial calibration site error (site 3). Spatially weighted standard errors are quoted on soil core activity estimates. Erosion rate estimates incorporate additional error from the reference site estimate and the dry specific mass per unit area. [a] Estimated from a single core/soil pit. [b] Not sufficient core data or range in values to calibrate to ß or mass depth of ploughed layer. [c] Estimated from 1995 data set. [d] Laboratory sample analyses incomplete

Table 16
Comparison of erosion rates derived from *in situ* spectrometry and soil core samples.

coefficient of variation of about 30% for total ^{137}Cs activities estimated from soil cores is observed at each site. Table 16 shows a comparison of activities determined by laboratory and *in situ* methods and activity distributions in terms of mean mass depth distributions (β) and mass depth of the ploughed layer (δ). There is excellent agreement between the ^{137}Cs activity measurements from both techniques when the analytical and sampling errors are considered. Changes in the observed QCs, whilst not yet calibrated to β or δ, demonstrate changes in the mass depth distribution of activity. As expected, a comparison between QCs and the mass depth functions for sites 3 and 4 (estimates derived from five cores each) suggests an increase in QCs with decrease in β or δ. Without the complete set of results it is difficult to define the relationship between mass depth distribution of activity and QCs. The incorporation of a spectrally derived calibration correction coefficient would improve the relationship between core derived ^{137}Cs activity and in situ derived ^{137}Cs activity estimates.

Conversion to erosion rates used exactly the same methodology as given above.

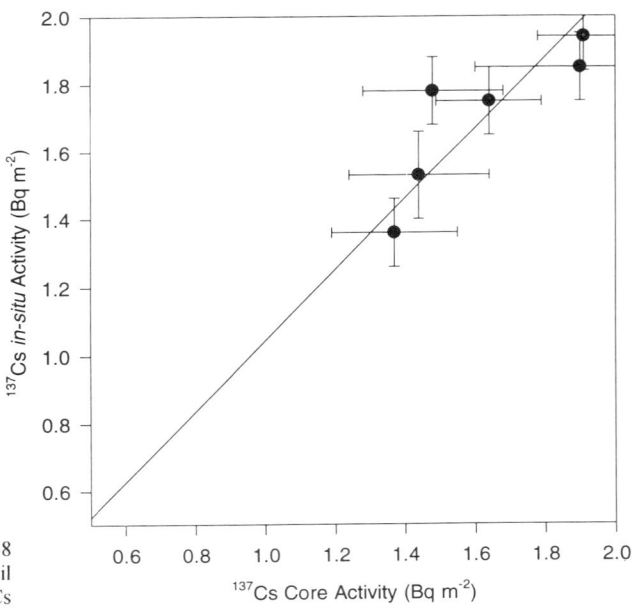

Illus 68 Relationship between full soil core and *in situ* derived ^{137}Cs activity estimates (Bq m^{-2}).

DISCUSSION

Within the field studied at Littleour, redistribution of soil over the last 43 years has resulted in a pronounced spatial pattern of erosion and deposition. The maximum erosion rate of just over 2mm a^{-1} was found on the slope and the maximum deposition of just over 2mm a^{-1} was found at the base of the slope in the southern corner of the field. Both the directly proportional and power function calculations indicate a similar pattern and this is consistent with the downslope variations shown by the *in situ* measurements. The location of the zone of maximum accumulation can also be seen from the aerial photograph (illus 65) to be directly downslope from the dominant direction of ploughing within the field, further confirming the relationship between ploughing direction and soil redistribution.

By interpolation from this spatial pattern, an erosion rate of at least 0.5mm a^{-1} can be proposed for the area of the cropmark since about 1953. This estimate is based on the redistribution of ^{137}Cs activity since the start of atomic weapon testing which peaked in 1964. Even taking into account the errors associated with this estimate, as discussed earlier, the erosion rate at the crop site is markedly higher than the soil loss tolerance value of 0.1mm a^{-1} which Evans (1981) considers appropriate to UK conditions. Thus the immediate and obvious implication from the Littleour investigation is that, if the average erosion rate which has been present for the last c43 years continues, the net result will be an overall thinning of the depth of topsoil. Further ploughing at the site will have the effect of penetrating to an increasing depth into the Bs horizon and this will lead to damage to, and ultimately loss of, the archaeological features cut into it.

Looking at the pattern in more detail, however, it can be seen that at comparable locations to the cropmark, just above the edge of the slope (eg at L2 and CL2) annual loss rates of 0.93mm and 1.94mm per annum have been recorded. This may confirm the suggestion that sites close to the edges of slopes are the most vulnerable to soil erosion effects thus it is conceivable that the erosion rate experienced over the cropmark site is closer to 1mm a^{-1} than to 0.5mm a^{-1}.

The depth of the topsoil (Ap horizon) on the excavated site ranges from 0.2m to 0.3m. In the lower part of the field where deposition is dominant, the depth of topsoil (Ap and A horizons) is between 0.5m and 0.6m. A simple calculation thus suggests that a loss of 0.15m from the area of the cropmark could account for the observed increase in thickness in the lower part of the field. On the basis of the estimated erosion rate of at least 0.5mm a^{-1} the accumulation of soil in the lower part of the field could have been achieved over a period of up to 300 years. It seems likely, however, that an acceleration in erosion rate has occurred during this time, with greater erosion rates following the introduction of new cultivation and cropping techniques since 1945. The recent pattern of increasing rainfall during the winter months in central Scotland may also have contributed to greater erosion rates in the recent past (Davidson, DA & Harrison 1995).

CONCLUSIONS

1. The erosion rate of at least 0.5mm per annum within the past few decades has important implications for cropmark sites on erodible soils derived from fluvio-glacial sands and gravels. Such sites must be deemed to be subject to potentially serious erosion in both the short and long term under current conditions.

2. Considerable spatial variability in rates of erosion within the field was identified and this demonstrates the need for detailed *in situ* investigations of soil erosion rates at such sites.

3. The *in situ* method provides estimates of the underlying spatial change at temporal scales appropriate for field systems. It has the additional advantages of being non-invasive and, by integrating activity measurements over a relatively large area, avoiding the errors associated with spatial variability of soil cores.

4. The potential reliability of the *in situ* method is clear from the close agreement between the erosion and deposition rate estimates derived from this method and those derived from detailed field sampling and laboratory analysis of soil cores.

5. Rapid methods using *in situ* gamma ray spectrometry thus have the potential to quantify soil erosion rates which can then be considered as part of a wider policy to conserve archaeological sites and landscapes.

CURSUS MONUMENTS AND BANK BARROWS OF TAYSIDE AND FIFE

Kenneth Brophy

In this section, I will discuss two monument types—cursus monuments and bank barrows—the physical characteristics of which define the Cleaven Dyke. Although both types occur throughout Britain, I will consider mainly the sites closest to the Cleaven Dyke, those in Tayside and Fife.

These monument classes (mainly appearing as cropmarks) are currently defined solely by their morphology, based on often arbitrary length and width limitations. Only two sites within these classifications have been excavated in the study area: the Cleaven Dyke, and a pit-defined rectilinear enclosure at Douglasmuir, Angus (Kendrick 1995); little more than superficial examination of the general landscape locations has been undertaken for any of the other sites (Brophy 1995).

The concentrated programme of aerial reconnaissance in Scotland which began in the 1970s, along with the re-interpretation of existing photographs, and a growing awareness on the part of those interpreting and taking aerial photographs that these sites exist in Scotland, has increased the known number of possible cursus and bank barrow sites from one or two to over 40. This cropmark record has flaws–it is inevitably biased towards gravel lowlands and river valleys, and the drier east of Scotland, where cropmarks more often appear (Hanson & Macinnes 1991). However, it has also shown the wide variety of sites regarded as belonging to these monument classes within Scotland.

I will consider first the cursus monuments, looking in turn not only at the archaeological characteristics of each site but also at its location within the general topography. I will then describe the only bank barrow identified in the study area, Kilmany in Fife, and look more generally at these sites across Scotland. Finally, I will briefly consider the relationships between these linear monuments and the natural world in their construction and usage. The Cleaven Dyke, which has the characteristics of both bank barrow and cursus, must be considered as only one aspect of the 'ritual' life of the Neolithic of this area, to be viewed against a rich and varied background of linear monumentality.

6.1 THE CURSUS MONUMENTS

WHAT IS A CURSUS MONUMENT?

Cursus monuments are found across Britain, primarily located in lowland river valleys or the chalklands of southern England. It was not until the early 1970s that their existence in Scotland was recognised (Williams & Anderson 1972). The 30 or so cursus sites now identified in Scotland (illus 69), including the few excavated examples, have shown a wide variation in size and form of definition, more so than that in the sites across the rest of Britain.

All cursus monuments share the common feature of being long, or even very long, rectilinear enclosures, usually defined either by a ditch enclosing the site with a bank running along the inner edge of the ditch, or, in many cases in Scotland, by pits (which may or may not have held wooden posts). Length and width can vary greatly, from the Dorset cursus, roughly 10km long, to the Douglasmuir enclosure, only 65m long. The common linear form does not, of course, mean that they were all used in the same way and for the same purpose, nor that they had the same meaning for the people who built them. Furthermore, in their builders' eyes, members of different archaeological categories may have been quite closely related in meaning or function.

Loveday and Petchey (1982) attempted to classify cursus monuments by length (and to a lesser extent, width), and shorter sites were removed from the class altogether. It seems difficult to class together monuments which appear so different in character, and perhaps it is better first to look at monuments individually, rather than part of a larger class. I will therefore make no attempt to break

THE CURSUS MONUMENTS OF TAYSIDE AND FIFE ◆ 93

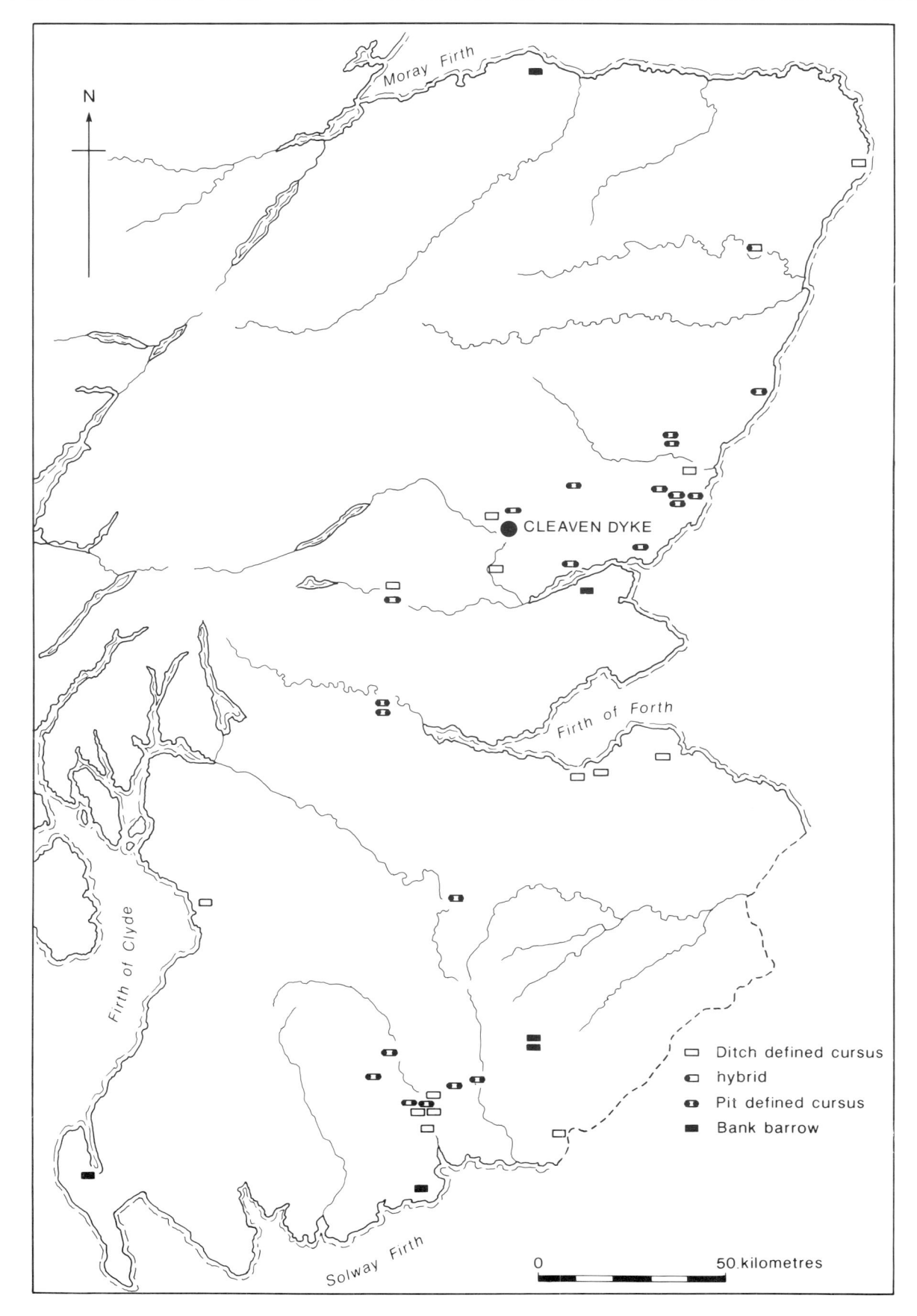

Illus 69
Distribution map of cursus monuments and bank barrows in Scotland.

down the 'cursus' label any further in the study area, but rather, will consider instead the individual properties of each site.

I have already mentioned that some cursus sites are defined by posts or pits. This appears at present to be a purely Scottish phenomenon. Maxwell (1979) was the first to suggest that these sites were cursus monuments. Morphologically, they are 'cursus-like' in form, but have no visible earthwork component (although there is no surviving evidence for banks at many ditched sites). Two excavated pit-defined enclosures in Scotland have been shown to have held posts, and have produced Early Neolithic dates (Douglasmuir, Kendrick 1995; Bannockburn 2, Stirlingshire, Rideout forthcoming), while another (Bannockburn 1) has been shown to consist of pits with complex histories of re-use and deliberate backfilling. In other periods of prehistory alignments of pits have been shown to be quarry pits for accompanying continuous earthen banks (Strong 1988).

Construction dates in Britain seem to vary from the Early to the Late Neolithic, although unequivocal dating evidence is scarce, and increasingly it is recognised that some sites may have had several phases of construction. Many show evidence for being foci for activity long after the initial building, in the form of later burials and through the continued construction of monuments, either around the cursus or sharing its alignment. Most cursus monuments are associated in some way with other sites, including causewayed enclosures and henges, round barrows and ring-ditches, long barrows and 'long mortuary enclosures', timber circles and stone circles. These relationships range from alignments and intervisibility, to actually being incorporated in the monument itself.

The location within the landscape is a further common feature which these sites seem to share. They are usually located within river valleys, on low-lying gravel river terraces and flood plains: there are very few cursus monuments which are not very close to a river. Even the few sites which are situated on the chalk uplands in England are closely associated with rivers and dry valleys. In Scotland, this is certainly the case (see below).

The range of functions represented by cursus monuments remains unclear after over 60 years of excavation. Early antiquarians suggested that the long Wessex cursus monuments were Roman chariot racing arenas (hence the name *cursus*). Atkinson felt that the Dorset cursus and other cursus monuments might have been ritual avenues: 'it is clear that the function must have been religious or ceremonial, rather than domestic, and the activity which took place in them was of a processional, or at least a linear pattern' (1955, 9). This has been the accepted view for some time, although it is now more than ever being embellished and elaborated. Tilley (1994) studied the Dorset cursus from within the site itself, moving along and through it, experiencing the relationship of monument to landscape. He saw the cursus as playing host to a rites of passage ceremony, involving water, a series of 'surprise' encounters for subjects passing along the cursus, and long barrows incorporated into the cursus itself. In similar fieldwork in Scotland I have also suggested that topography and water were involved in the experiences of moving along cursus monuments (Brophy 1995).

Harding (1995) has suggested that cursus monuments represented an increasing degree of control over the landscape, and movement through the landscape, as the Neolithic went on. They were one aspect of wider social changes, illustrated also by changes in funerary practice from communal to individual graves. The idea of control on the landscape echoes Bradley's suggestion (1993) that cursus monuments were some form of boundary, perhaps between 'wild' and 'domesticated' land. On a more immediate level, cursus monuments have been associated with mortuary activity, partly because of the close relationship both physically and morphologically with 'long mortuary enclosures' and long barrows. Secondary burials have been discovered at several cursus sites.

Many of the new approaches to the so-called 'cursus problem' (Hedges & Buckley 1981) are very personal, indeed subjective, interpretations, reflecting the current trend towards an interpretative archaeology. These interpretations involve looking closely at individual sites, and on a more descriptive than interpretative level, I will now go on to look at the cursus monuments of Tayside: as yet, none are known of in Fife.

THE CURSUS MONUMENTS OF TAYSIDE

Of the 16 cursus monuments in Tayside, 11 are pit-, and five ditch-defined. In particular, the pit-defined sites dominate the known cropmark record of Angus, nine to two. All sites (save one) have low-lying locations, near or on river flood plains and terraces. Only one has been excavated, Douglasmuir, which I will look at first, along with other cursus monuments in the Friockheim area.

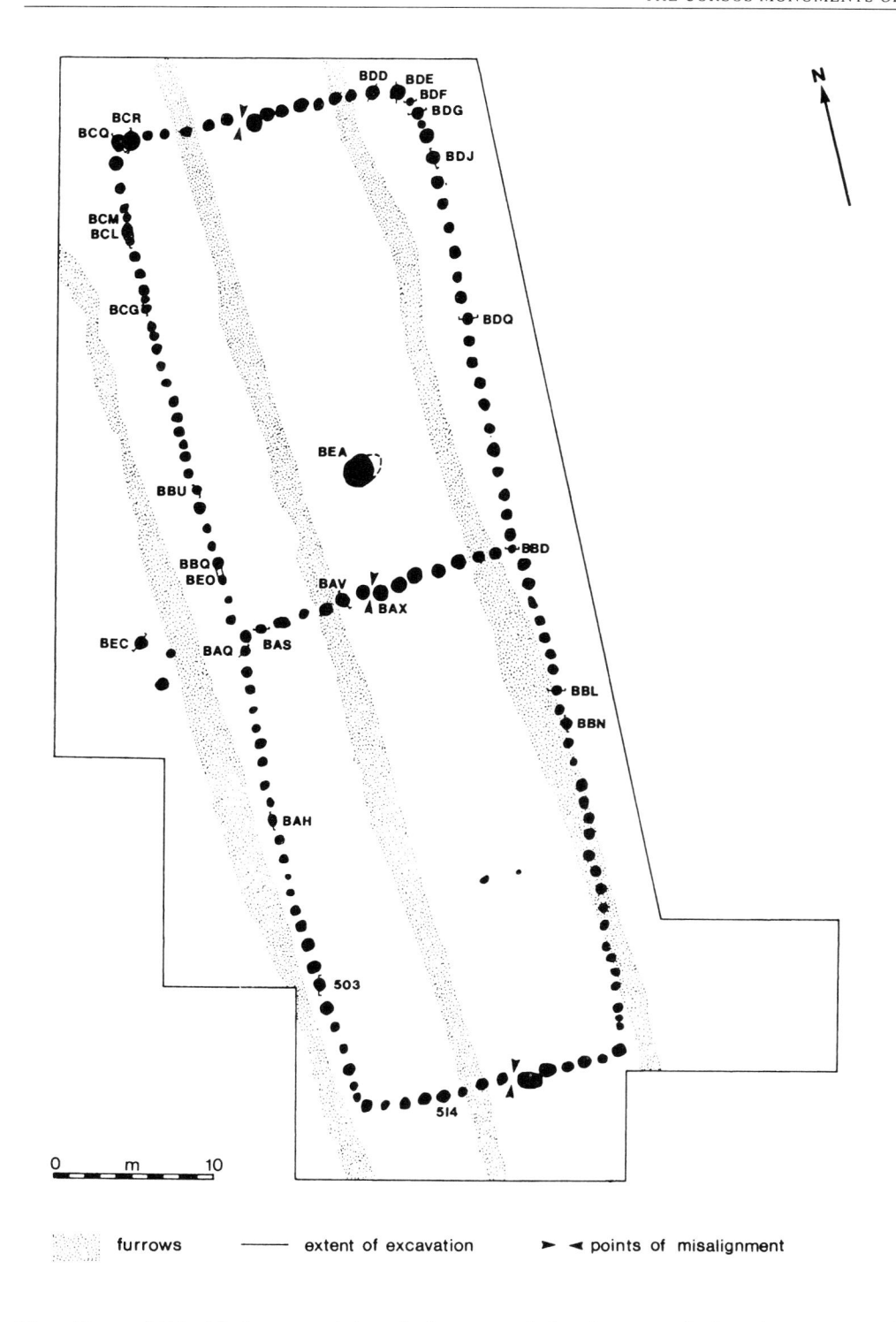

Illus 70
Plan of the enclosure at Douglasmuir, Angus.

The village of Friockheim, near Arbroath, is surrounded by cropmark sites of many periods, including two of the longest known pit-defined cursus monuments, Milton of Guthrie and Balneaves Cottage, close to the substantially smaller enclosure just to the south at Douglasmuir.

The Douglasmuir enclosure was excavated in 1979 and 1980 (Kendrick 1995) in advance of development on the site (illus 70). The pit-defined enclosure was originally identified in one set of aerial photographs from 1970, and excavation revealed an enclosure, 65m x 20m, defined by large postholes. A transverse line of pits divided the enclosure roughly in half. The enclosure itself was fairly irregular, and postholes showed a variety in both spacing and size. Some posts were burnt *in situ*, and radiocarbon dating of some of this burnt material placed the site within a period of c 4000-3350 cal BC (GU-1210, GU-1469, GU-1470; Kendrick 1995, 33). A large pit lies on the axis of the monument in the northern half.

Artefacts found included sherds of decorated Neolithic pottery and some Beaker sherds (Cowie 1993). Some of these finds came from a group of pits and postholes to the east of the enclosure. Barclay (1995) interpreted the site as being defined by free-standing timbers, with no roof, perhaps constructed in two stages, the transverse post-line initially being a terminal. He also suggests, however, that alternative explanations might exist, for example, perhaps in two phases laterally (as opposed to transversely), leaving an open 'E'-shaped structure at one point. The function and meaning of the site remains unclear.

The nearby monuments, Balneaves Cottage and Milton of Guthrie, both have a width only a little larger than Douglasmuir (25m), straight, occasionally oblique, terminals (where visible) and internal divisions. They are, however, both much longer than Douglasmuir. Balneaves Cottage cursus is visible for 500m, running NE-SW. One terminal is visible, at the NE end, and c 100m short of this is the only visible internal division (illus 71). The enclosure this defines, just over 100m long, is slightly wider than the rest of the cursus, suggesting two phases of construction, perhaps beginning as a relatively small Douglasmuir-type enclosure, with the longer cursus added later (Loveday 1985). The cursus lies amidst many varying cropmarks, and runs across a gravel terrace above the Lunan Water, terminating short of both sides of the terrace.

Milton of Guthrie, just over 1km to the NW of Balneaves Cottage, is a straight-sided, rectilinear, pit-defined enclosure, almost 600m long, with three visible internal divisions splitting the enclosure into four 'compartments' 100-200m long. Both terminals are square (illus 72a; 72b). It is cut by both the A933 and a railway embankment, and has a low-lying location, on the flood plain of the Lunan Water. The eastern terminal lies within 40m of the current course of the river, and is within 150m of the confluence of the Lunan Water and the Vinny Water. This site was originally interpreted as two individual cursus monuments, known as Milton 1 and 2.

There are a further six pit-defined cursus sites in Angus, about which very little is known of any of them. At Newbarns, a few hundred metres from the current coastline, and barely visible on aerial photographs, is a narrow rectilinear enclosure which appears to have at least one internal division, and lies alongside a series of other cropmarks, including an unenclosed settlement and souterrains (presumably much later than the cursus). It runs across a level area, and is lost from visibility at the top of a 'fossil cliff' (Pollock 1985).

Further to the north, and inland again, near the village of Inchbare, lies a series of parallel pit-alignments, all with a very similar ENE-WSW alignment (illus 73). These appear to form two pit-defined cursus monuments,

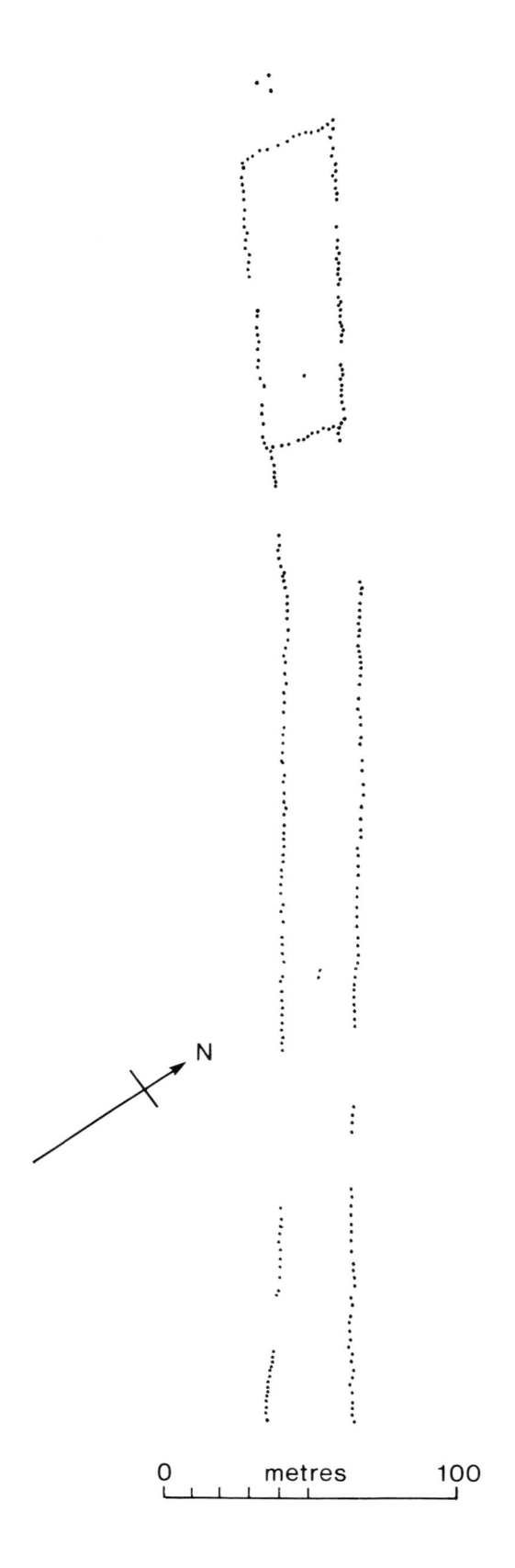

Illus 71
The cursus monument at Balneaves. Based on a computer-generated plot of the cropmarks prepared by RCAHMS.

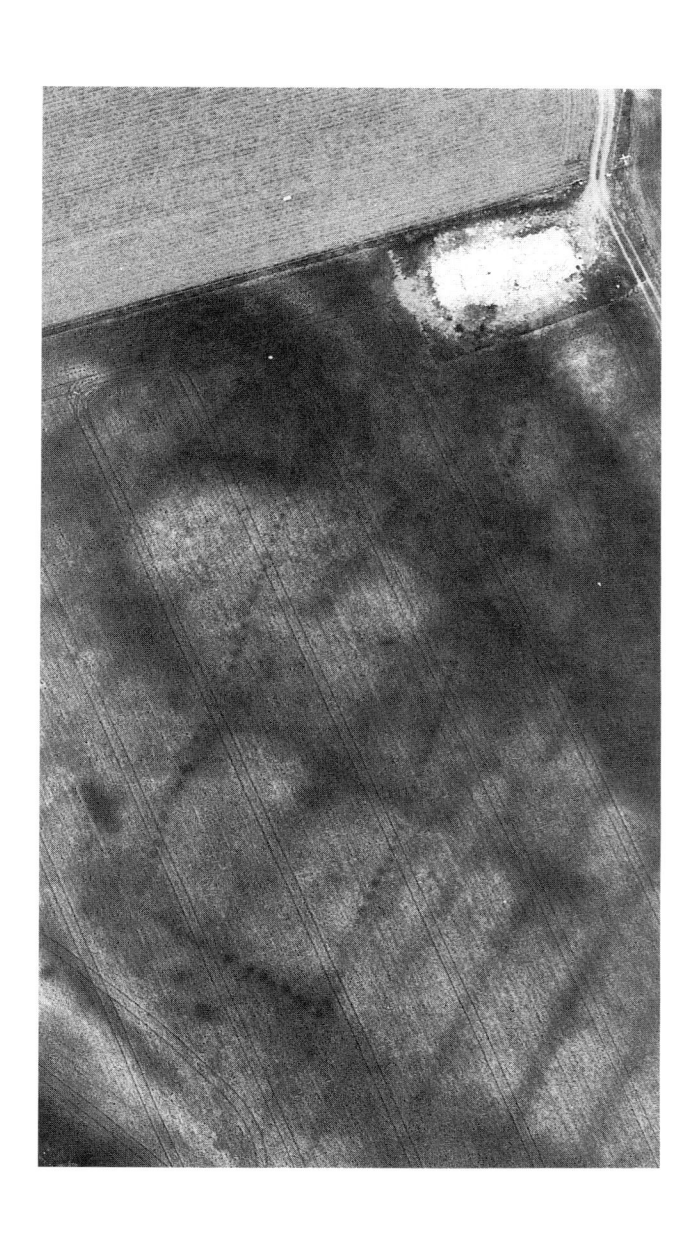

Illus 72
The cursus monument at Milton of Guthrie: a) view (*Crown Copyright: RCAHMS*); b) plan based on a sketch plot prepared by Gordon Barclay.

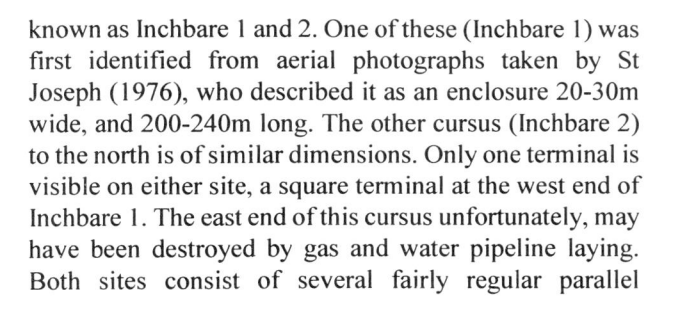

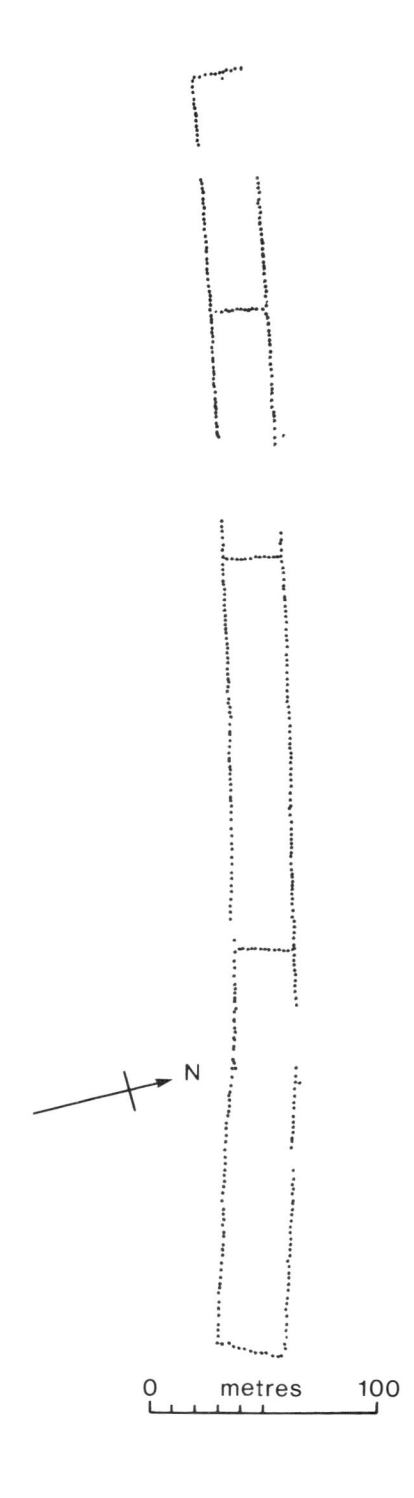

known as Inchbare 1 and 2. One of these (Inchbare 1) was first identified from aerial photographs taken by St Joseph (1976), who described it as an enclosure 20-30m wide, and 200-240m long. The other cursus (Inchbare 2) to the north is of similar dimensions. Only one terminal is visible on either site, a square terminal at the west end of Inchbare 1. The east end of this cursus unfortunately, may have been destroyed by gas and water pipeline laying. Both sites consist of several fairly regular parallel pit-lines; Inchbare 2 is defined by at least six such lines which all follow the same orientation. It is not entirely clear which two actually define the enclosure, if indeed the boundaries were single lines. Another interpretation, that of multiple boundaries, has already been noted for two ditch-defined sites in Scotland–Monktonhall, Edinburgh (Hanson 1984) and Carmichael Cottages, Longforgan (Armit 1996). Like these cursus sites, Inchbare 1 and 2 have been interpreted as Neolithic,

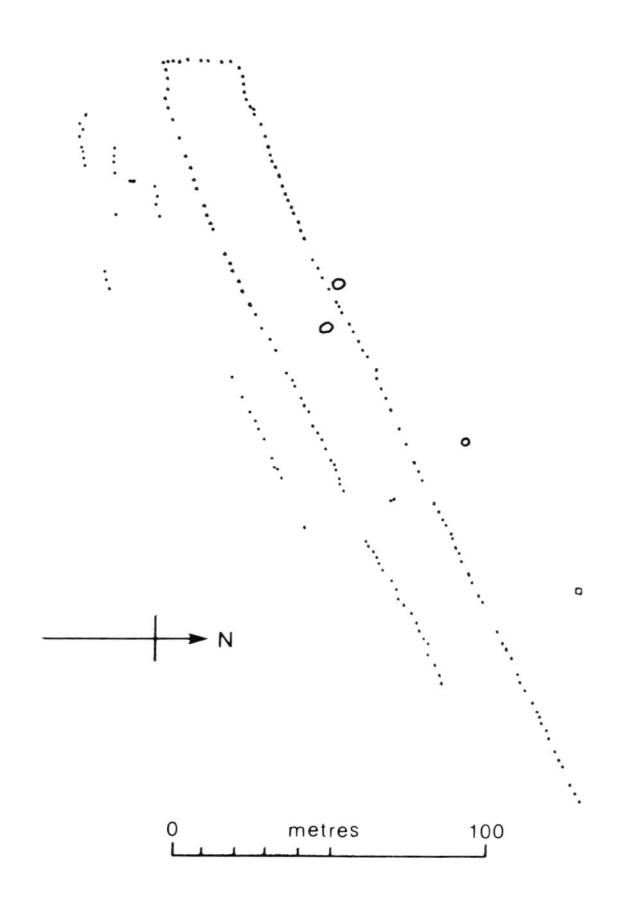

Illus 73
Plan of the cursus monument at Inchbare. Based on a computer-generated plot of the cropmarks prepared by RCAHMS.

Illus 74
Plan of the cursus monument at Star Inn. Based on a computer-generated plot of the cropmarks prepared by RCAHMS.

less than 100m (illus 74). They are roughly 35m apart, and appear to be joined at one end by a curving terminal. A series of cropmarks in and around this 'cursus' includes two circular enclosures on the northern lateral pit-line, and an oblong enclosure within the 'cursus' itself.

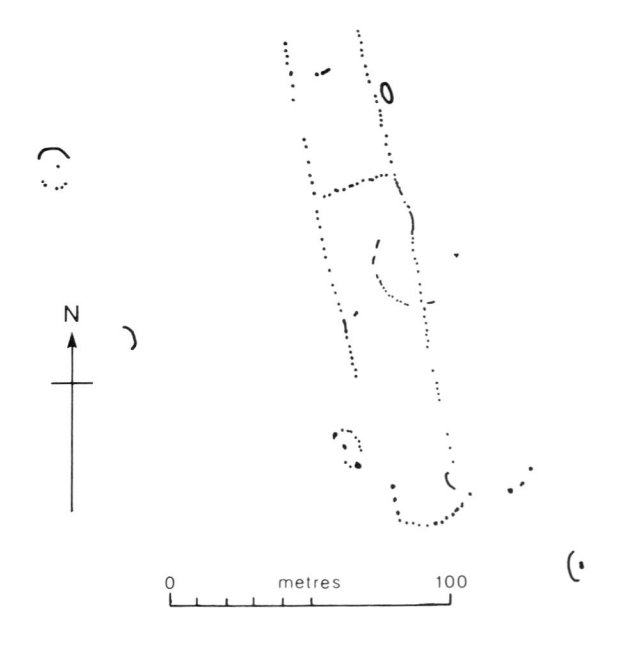

Illus 75
Plan of the cursus monument at Kinalty. Based on a computer-generated plot of the cropmarks prepared by RCAHMS.

although St Joseph (1976) suggested that they may have had Early Historic origins.

Both Inchbare 1 and 2 lie on the flat gravel flood plain of the West Water, just 1.5km west of its confluence with the North Esk. Both cursus sites are very close to the West Water, and Inchbare 2 is last visible just a few tens of metres from the current course of this river.

Further pit-defined sites in Angus include a wide enclosure at Woodhill, east of Dundee. It is far wider than any pit-defined site which I have mentioned—at least 50m wide—and is visible for over 100m. It is orientated roughly SW-NE, and only the rounded SW terminal is visible. The only internal division is slightly curved also, giving the appearance of being a terminal of a smaller earlier enclosure. The irregular sides curve in to meet the internal division, adding to this effect.

To the west of Dundee, near the village of Longforgan, are two further cursus sites—Star Inn and Carmichael Cottages—one pit-defined, the other ditch-defined. The site at Star Inn Farm (also known as Greystanes Lodge) consists of two short parallel pit-alignments, visible for

West of Star Inn Farm at Carmichael Cottages is a possible ditch-defined cursus, discovered recently through the re-interpretation of old aerial photographs. The cursus consists of two lateral ditches, 300m long, 60m apart, and with a transverse straight ditch running across the cursus near its west end. There is a double ditch at one point. Armit (1996, 97) notes that: 'the site occupies a well-defined natural plateau with a moderately steep drop around three sides', a location shared by many cursus sites.

By way of contrast, one final pit-defined cursus in Angus, Kinalty, near Kirriemuir, sits on slightly higher land (80m above sea level) with no nearby rivers. It is visible as a cropmark for almost 200m, defined by pit-lines 30m apart, with a rounded southern terminal, and one internal division. The lateral pit-lines curve outwards, and then into the junction with the internal division (illus 75), again suggesting at least two phases of construction. It runs across the brow of a ridge, ending at the top of a downward slope. A circular ditched enclosure lies just to the south, on the alignment of the east side, and a few other pit features (enclosures and arcs) are visible in and around the cursus.

To the west of Montrose and the Montrose Basin, south of the village of Barnhead, lies a large cropmark complex (illus 76). Lying on a level plateau in the centre of the valley of the River South Esk (contained within an area defined by the 15m contour line), the cropmarks include a large ditch-defined cursus, square and round barrows, ring-ditches, an unenclosed settlement, a circular enclosure, and a very large subrectangular enclosure (not illustrated: possibly a 19th-century horse-racing track, according to local information: Armit pers comm).

The cursus, known as Old Montrose (or Powis), runs eastward from the western edge of the plateau for just over 600m; it is 75m wide, and has one internal division near the west end. The western terminal, facing up the valley of the South Esk, is obscured by a circular enclosure overlapping it, but appears to consist of short straight sections of narrow ditch, giving the impression of a rounded terminal. The eastern terminal, however, is straight, although set at an angle to the main axis. The cursus widens towards this end, the ditch of the south side describing an outward curve in this sector, in contrast to the much straighter northern ditch. A few breaks are visible along the ditches of this cursus, including two or three around the western terminal ditch, a long stretch of the northern lateral ditch (where the cursus passes through a field which appears to show no cropmarks), and in the centre of the septal ditch. Whether these represent true 'causeways' cannot be properly established from aerial photography alone (cf Buckley 1988). The relationship of the Powis cursus with the other cropmark sites is unclear. Several barrows and ring-ditches lie within the line of the cursus, as does part of the large circular enclosure. Excavations at other cursus sites have shown such barrows to be later than the cursus construction (Christie 1963; Reaney 1966). A scatter of flint tools and agate and chalcedony flakes was discovered less than 1km to the south of the cursus (Sherriff 1982) and a flint borer was found to the NE (Stuart pers comm). Certainly, there is much to suggest a long history of activity in this area, possibly from the Mesolithic onwards.

A relationship with barrows has also been noted at Blairhall cursus (Loveday forthcoming), just north of Scone in Perthshire. There are fewer known cursus monuments in Perthshire and Kinross, the majority of which are ditch-defined. These include Blairhall, which

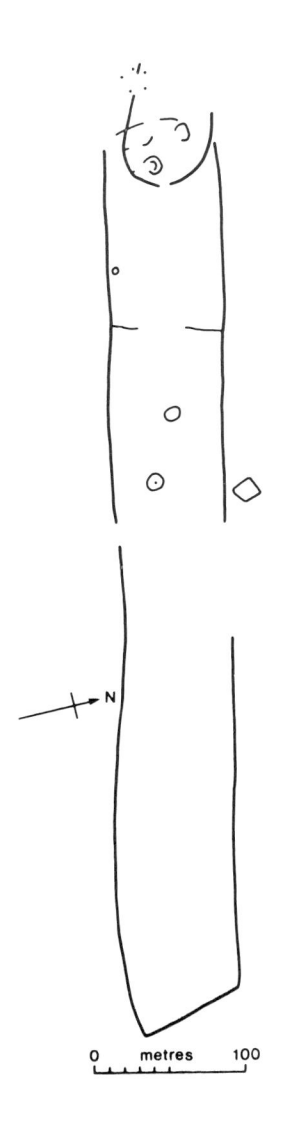

Illus 76
Plan of the cursus monument at Barnhead, also known as Old Montrose. Based on a computer-generated plot of the cropmarks prepared by RCAHMS.

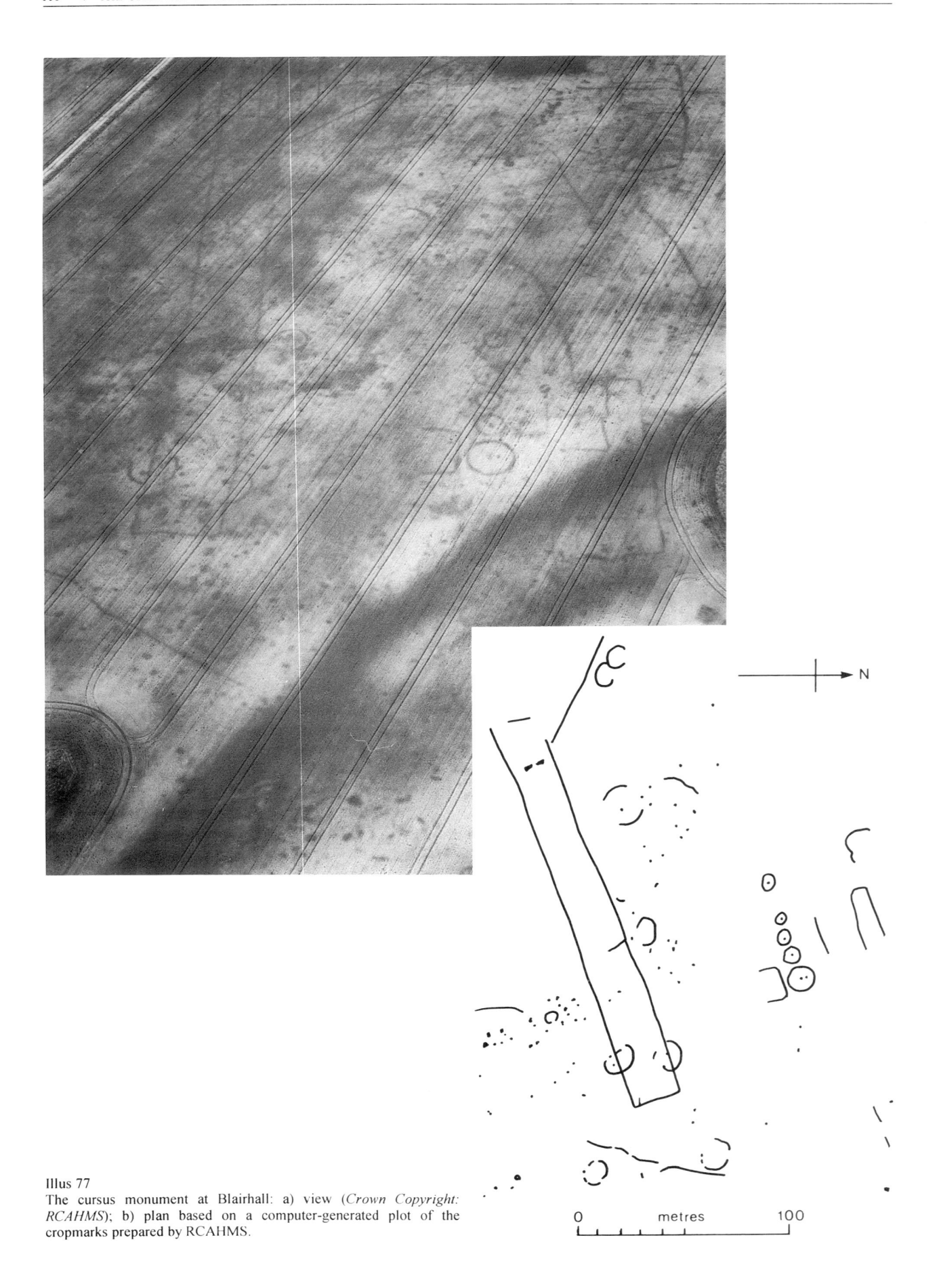

Illus 77
The cursus monument at Blairhall: a) view (*Crown Copyright: RCAHMS*); b) plan based on a computer-generated plot of the cropmarks prepared by RCAHMS.

lies within a field full of fascinating cropmarks. The complex is captured best in a series of excellent aerial photographs taken in 1992 (illus 77a). The cursus itself is defined by a pair of narrow 'wobbly' ditches 24m apart, and 190m long (RCAHMS 1994a). Both terminals are visible and straight (although the western terminal is not completely clear), and there appears to be one internal division. Two ring-ditches intersect the side ditches towards the east end of the cursus. The cursus may have had two phases of construction, the eastern half being wider and on a slightly different alignment (illus 77b).

At least five ring-ditches, which have been identified as round burial mounds because they appear to have central burials (King 1993), lie in a line, parallel to the cursus which sits less than 100m to the south. Further similar round enclosures lie within this same field, along with a series of confusing linear cropmarks. All lie on a low plateau, cut to the north and east by a stream. The River Tay flows southwards 1.5km to the west.

To the south of Crieff two cursus monuments face each other across the River Earn; both lie on terrace edges above and overlooking the flood plain of the river. The northern of the two, Broich, is defined by two widely-spaced parallel ditches, both running N-S, up to 80m to 100m apart, and is visible for perhaps 900m, running from the river terrace edge to the town itself, curving slightly and then disappearing beneath school buildings at the edge of the town (Maxwell pers comm). No terminals are visible.

The eastern ditch line is intersected by the edge of a large circular enclosure, c 100m in diameter, with a narrow bounding ditch, near the edge of the river terrace. This enclosure has been partly destroyed in the last few years by development. A small ring-ditch lies within a gap in the western ditch, and this ditch may also pass through the general location of Crieff Barrow, now excavated and destroyed (Childe 1946, 109). A standing stone was located c 100m west of the side of the Barrow.

The cursus itself seems to have been constructed in this particular place partly to exploit the local topography. It terminates at its south end on the edge of the terrace, in a very prominent location. Approaching both southern terminal and terrace edge within the cursus line, one must pass between two large natural hollows, one on the line of each ditch. Standing within them, the view in most directions is obscured other than towards the river and cursus interior. The cursus lies within a large 'U' shape formed by the River Earn and a small tributary, the Hoolet Burn, and structurally it mimics the general flow of water, N-S, in this area.

Across the Earn, 1km to the south, on the opposite terrace at Bennybeg, lies a pit-defined cursus. Its orientation is

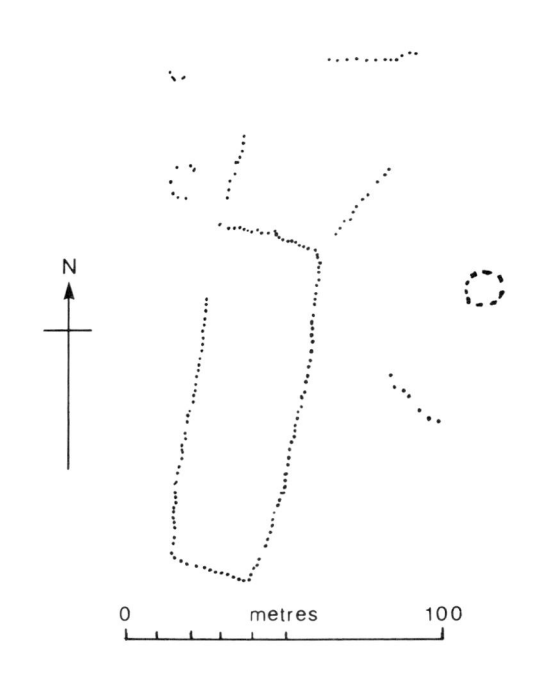

Illus 78
Plan of the cursus monument at Bennybeg, based on a computer-generated plot of the cropmarks prepared by RCAHMS.

almost the same as that of Broich, and both lie just above the 40m contour. This cursus enclosure is c 110m long, and 30m to 35m wide. The sides are bowed and both terminals are roughly squared (illus 78). At the N end, an irregular line of pits projects from each of the corners, forming what appear to be 'horns'. Around this enclosure is a series of pit-defined features, including a clearly-defined pit-circle (Tolan 1988), two short pairs of pit-lines and a few circular and subcircular enclosures. A presumably complete oval/circular enclosure to the E is partially obscured by woodland.

Two further sites near the Cleaven Dyke again illustrate the varied nature of the cursus class in this area. To the north at Milton of Rattray, just outside Blairgowrie, lies a pair of straight parallel pit-lines (illus 79). The pits, in contrast to all other known pit-defined cursus sites, are widely-spaced (4m apart), set in opposing pairs (18m apart), and can be traced for just over 100m (RCAHMS 1994a). This site lies on the flood plain of the River Ericht, within 100m of the river itself, and closer still to a stream just to the N. Recent small-scale excavation revealed that at least the pit excavated was shallow and elongated (Brophy 1998).

Four kilometres NW of the Cleaven Dyke, at Mains of Gourdie, aerial photography has revealed an unusual pair

Illus 79
View of the cursus monument at Milton of Rattray, defined by two lines of widely-spaced pits. (*Crown Copyright: RCAHMS*)

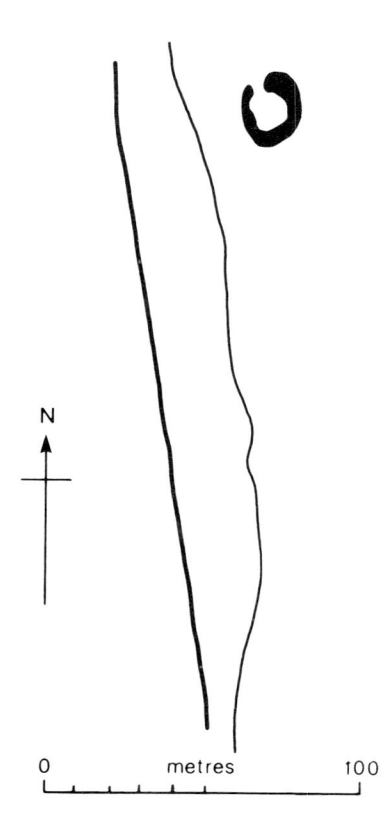

of linear cropmarks. Running N-S, the western ditch is straight and regular, whilst the eastern ditch is very irregular, the distance from the other varying from 12m to 25m. The linear cropmarks run for over 200m and no terminals are visible (illus 80). A small hengiform enclosure lies to the east. Nothing more is known of these sites, and it is difficult to speculate what, if any, relationship they may have had with the Cleaven Dyke. It is interesting to note, however, that Mains of Gourdie lies at the foot of the Hill of Lethendy, on which the Cleaven Dyke aligns to the NW.

Illus 80
Plan of the cursus monument at Mains of Gourdie. Based on a computer-generated plot of the cropmarks prepared by RCAHMS.

6.2 THE BANK BARROWS

WHAT IS A BANK BARROW?

In contrast to cursus monuments, very little has been written about bank barrows, and even less is understood about their function. The name itself is slightly misleading, in that not all identified bank barrows have been associated with primary burial deposits. Like cursus monuments, however, excavation and associations have shown these to be monuments of the earlier Neolithic, probably contemporary with cursus monuments (Bradley 1983).

Essentially, in physical appearance they are massively elongated long barrows, usually with a length well over 100m. When appearing as cropmarks (as most of Scotland's examples do), they are usually differentiated from cursus monuments by their width; bank barrows are much narrower than ditch-defined cursus sites because the ditch lies close to the single central mound, which is built from material quarried from them. Cursus monuments enclose an open rectangular space, bank barrows consist of a single long mound.

Very few of these sites have been identified in Britain. The Cleaven Dyke (which shares features of both bank barrow and cursus monument) and the monument (or pair of monuments?) known as Tom's Knowe/Lamb Knowe, Eskdalemuir, Dumfries and Galloway, are among the best preserved examples known anywhere in Britain (and certainly the longest). Crawford (1938) listed only three bank barrows, all in Dorset, when discussing parallels he had come across in Germany. These included the first excavated bank barrow, at Maiden Castle, which runs through a slightly earlier causewayed enclosure (Wheeler 1943) and for many years served as a type-site, having provided evidence of mortuary practice (although it has been suggested that it pre-dated the barrow (Sharples 1991, 53)). Radiocarbon dating of material from the primary fills of the ditch of the Maiden Castle bank barrow suggests it was built by *c* 3100 cal BC (OxA-1146) (using calibrations expressed at the 95% level of confidence) (*ibid*, 103-5).

Bradley (1983) listed six bank barrows across Britain, three outwith Dorset, including the supposed cursus at Scorton, Yorkshire, which after excavation was shown to enclose an axial central mound (Topping 1982) and perhaps offers the closest known parallel to the Cleaven Dyke, particularly as the central mound appeared on aerial photographs as 'a contiguous series of mounds', suggesting segmentary construction. A further narrow rectilinear enclosure, North Stoke, Oxfordshire, has also been excavated (Case 1982). This enclosure, 225m x 9-12m, was visible only as a cropmark (as was Scorton). The silting pattern of the ditches showed no clear evidence of mounds adjacent to their inner edges, leaving little or no room for anything else within the enclosure other than a single central mound. Radiocarbon dating of antler on the bottom of the western ditch has produced a calibrated range of 3620-3350 cal BC (BM-1405), broadly comparable to the estimated date of the Cleaven Dyke.

Loveday defines bank barrows as having 'a length greater than normal, sides parallel, mound of a uniform height....' (1985, 236). He included eight sites as bank barrows, in addition to North Stoke and Scorton. Amongst these was a 100m-long mound of turf and topsoil running through an earlier causewayed enclosure at Crickley Hill, Gloucestershire. A large post stood at one end, and slabs lined the side of the mound (Dixon 1988). Yet Loveday later questioned the validity of this site as a Neolithic bank barrow, suggesting it also possessed the characteristics of an artificial rabbit warren, or 'pillow mound', a type of structure generally built between AD 1600 and 1800, to encourage or establish local rabbit populations. Crickley Hill, in particular, shares several constructional features with pillow mounds, and the unusual location—within a natural gully—again is ideal for encouraging rabbits (Williamson & Loveday 1988). In the absence of full presentation of the excavated evidence this matter remains unresolved.

I will now turn to the only bank barrow so far identified within the study area (save for the Cleaven Dyke), and then consider other sites in Scotland, including the well-preserved earthworks at Eskdalemuir.

KILMANY: A BANK BARROW IN FIFE

Near the small village of Kilmany in north-east Fife, on a valley side overlooking the course of the Motray Water, is the cropmark of a narrow rectilinear enclosure. The enclosure is roughly 180m long, and less than 10m wide, and both terminals are rounded. Although classified as a cursus monument in the NMRS, it is perhaps more aptly described as a bank barrow (Brophy forthcoming). A ring-ditch lies just beyond the eastern terminal, just offset from the line of the bank barrow (illus 81).

The interpretation of this site as a bank barrow is made on a morphological basis–it is very narrow in appearance, narrower than perhaps we would expect a cursus to be. Its location on a fairly steep valley side differs from that of most cursus monuments. Although the greater part of the length of the enclosure runs along the contour and is level for much of its length, it is still on a higher and more undulating piece of land than most of the monuments described above. It is, however, as with the cursus monuments, close to water.

A closer look at the site itself, and the landscape in which it sits reveals much of interest. The west end of the bank barrow appears to kink slightly to the south. This may be partly because 30m or so of the land on that side of the site drops away dramatically, presumably leaving neither end of the site visible from the other. Nevertheless, similar 'kinks' have been found at the end of other bank barrows in Scotland, at the NW terminal and on the SE side of Section-break Y on the Cleaven Dyke, and the Tom's Knowe terminal of the Eskdalemuir site(s) described below. Changes of alignment can also be seen at two further cropmark bank barrows, Springbank and Redbank, in Dumfries and Galloway, and further afield, the Maiden Castle bank barrow.

The location of Kilmany offers outstanding views upstream, along the valley to the west. Indeed, the structure may align on a gap between two hills a few kilometres to the west, through which the modern A914 road passes. The view downstream—eastwards—is completely obscured from the western end of the site, and only becomes partially clearer as one moves eastward. The Motray Water is visible from anywhere on the bank barrow.

Illus 81
View of the probable bank barrow at Kilmany. (*Crown Copyright: RCAHMS*)

THE BANK BARROWS OF SCOTLAND

The possible bank barrow at Eskdalemuir, first recognised by RCAHMS (1997), consists of two long mounds, known as Tom's Knowe and Lamb Knowe, on opposite valley sides of the River White Esk. They run approximately N-S, and have the same general alignment. If originally one monument, they would have formed an earthwork running in a slight curve for over 2km, running down either valley side, and crossing the valley floor and river. Unfortunately, evidence for any central section is now obscured or lost as the result of land improvement and fluvial activity.

Both long mounds consist of a bank 5.5m to 6m wide, up to 0.5m high, flanked by a ditch (*c* 2.75m to 3m across) on each side, 3.5m from the base of the bank. The Tom's Knowe sector of the monument can be traced for 255m, Lamb Knowe intermittently for 650m. In each case only the upper terminal has survived. Both terminals have recently been surveyed (RCAHMS 1997), the results making interesting comparisons with some of the Cleaven Dyke's section terminals.

The Tom's Knowe terminal occupies the southern end of

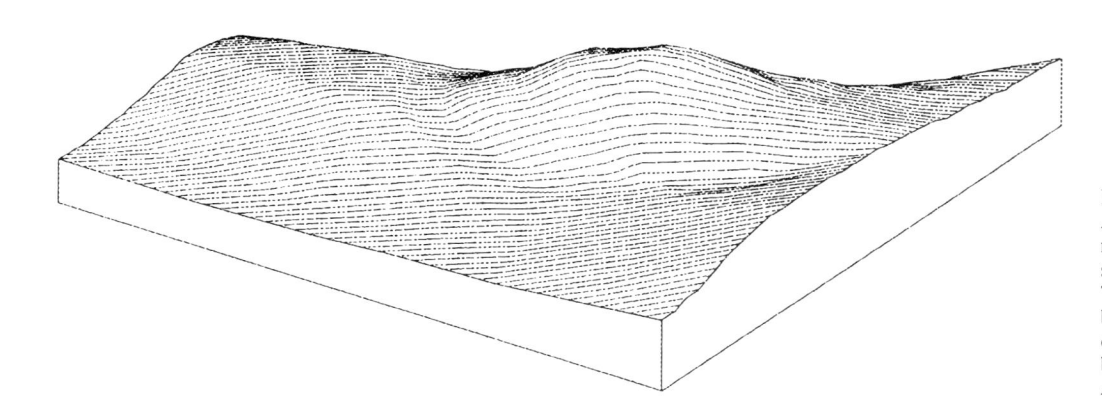

Illus 82
A three-dimensional representation of the southern terminal of the Tom's Knowe bank barrow. The vertical dimension is multiplied by 2. (*Crown Copyright: RCAHMS*)

a natural promontory, set back from its edge and overlooking lower lying land to both the north and south. It consists of a large subcircular mound (interpreted when first discovered as a free-standing burial cairn (Yates 1984, 91-2, No. ED 5)) with an average diameter of 10m, which tails off into a long mound (illus 82). The chronological relationship here is unclear - which came first? The oval mound is offset from the alignment of the long mound at a slight angle. The ditch continues around this terminal mound.

To the north, the Lamb Knowe terminal occupies a less dominant location, on a hillside with a series of natural spurs of similar appearance to the terminal. The long mound runs gently northwards uphill, gradually narrowing in width until it meets a prominent circular mound, 9.7m in diameter, at the terminal. Again, the ditch surrounds the terminal mound. At both ends, the circular, barrow-like terminals are much more substantial than the adjoining banks.

The phenomenon of bank barrows running towards, or joining, mounds and enclosures has been noted at several other sites across Britain, including Crickley Hill (Dixon 1988, *pace* Williamson & Loveday 1988), North Stoke (Case 1982), and Pentridge 21 and 22 on Cranborne Chase, Dorset (Bradley 1983). The Cleaven Dyke runs from the relatively massive circular mound at its NW end (and possibly towards another mound at Section boundary **Y** - section **7.1** below) and Kilmany runs to or from a ring-ditch at its east end. Loveday (1985) suggested that in the cases he identified this was the result of a three-phase linear sequence of development, with enclosures having a long mound added, then a subsequent enclosure constructed at the further end.

Two further cropmarks, interpreted as possible bank barrows, have been discovered recently in Dumfries and Galloway. One of these, Springbank, near Stranraer, appears to have a circular enclosure, roughly 30-40m in diameter, at the single visible terminal. Very little is known of this site and, as a cropmark, it appears as a pair of parallel ditches, fairly close together, with perhaps a major change of alignment near the terminal. Further east along the Solway Firth coastline, at Redbank, is a further pair of ditches, visible as a cropmark for up to 200m. The narrow enclosure they form is fairly sinuous, and appears to define a low mound on the ground (Gannon pers comm). It sits on the lower slopes of Drumbuie Hill, and narrows towards the east end, perhaps being joined to a rounded terminal, where it overlooks a stream.

Illus 83
View of the possible bank barrow at Muirton, Moray, which is marked by the two closely-spaced, broadly parallel ditches. At the further end of the monument the cropmarks of a large pit can be seen. (*Copyright: Aberdeen Archaeological Services*)

Illus 84
View of the extremely long cairn at Auchenlaich. (*Crown Copyright: RCAHMS*)

The final Scottish example was found in 1996 at Muirton in Moray, just south of Lossiemouth (illus 83). A pair of ditches, parallel and fairly regular, runs across two fields for several hundred metres. Muirton is similar in appearance to the North Stoke bank barrow, and lying between the ditches, at what appears to be each end, a large pit is visible. There is a possible circular enclosure nearby.

The very long cairn at Auchenlaich, Callander deserves mention here, as a possible bank barrow-type monument, but built in stone. I am grateful to Dr Sally Foster and Mr J B Stevenson for the following description:

'Early in 1991, fieldwork by Mrs Lorna Main led to the discovery of a long, apparently artificial, stony mound at Auchenlaich, near Callander, Perthshire. Subsequent examination by staff of the Royal Commission on the Ancient and Historical Monuments of Scotland confirmed Mrs Main's identification of the mound as the remains of a remarkable chambered long cairn (illus 84) (Foster & Stevenson, forthcoming).

It comprises a trapezoidal chambered cairn, aligned NNW-SSE, with, at its NNW end, a very long stony mound. The mound measures 342m in length overall and varies in width from a maximum of 15m at the SSE end to 11m at the NNW. On the NNW the original mound appears to have been extended by about 20m, on a slightly different alignment, by the addition of a considerable amount of field-cleared stone (although it resembles the 'terminal deviations' noted on the Cleaven Dyke and elsewhere), and at three points the mound has been breached by relatively recent trackways. The chambered cairn which forms the SSE end of the mound, has been much-disturbed by stone-robbing, and its original length is difficult to determine, but it was probably trapezoidal on plan, measuring up to 48m in length by 15m in breadth at the SSE end, narrowing to about 11m on the NNW, and now standing to a maximum height of 1.6m (although a pronounced narrowing at c 80m along the length of the monument may mark the end of the 'normal' cairn and the beginning of a further phase of construction). There is an apparent swelling of the cairn near its SSE end which corresponds with an increase in the height of the mound, but it is uncertain whether this merely indicates a section of the mound where less stone-robbing has occurred, or suggests that the cairn is of multi-period construction, parallels for which are not hard to find. About 118m from the SSE end of the cairn there are the disturbed remains of a lateral chamber opening from the west side of the mound.'

6.3 DISCUSSION

In this section I have attempted to show the wide range of elongated rectilinear enclosures and mounds, of which the Cleaven Dyke is one. This disparate group of sites classed morphologically as 'cursus monuments' and 'bank barrows' shares two defining physical characteristics–linearity and, often, extreme length. It would be difficult to argue that sites as contrasting as Douglasmuir, Old Montrose, Blairhall and the Cleaven Dyke had the same function and meaning to the people who built them. Yet, this author would argue that they display sufficient similarity for it to be legitimate to consider them together. There are three particular aspects already discussed in relation to individual sites–location, linearity, and the use of natural features of the landscape in both the siting and use of the enclosures.

The Neolithic period across Britain saw the development and construction of many monument types, generally considered to be of a ritual or mortuary nature. This has included a large variety of linear monuments, including 'mortuary houses', 'long mortuary enclosures', long barrows, houses, small pit-defined enclosures, pit-alignments, avenues, bank barrows and cursus monuments. These have been viewed as parts of a continuum (Loveday & Petchey 1982), defined and broken down into groups by length, or as part of a developing trend of larger and larger linear monuments. Thus, Loveday (1985) saw a link between long mortuary enclosures at one end of the range, and cursus monuments at the other. Bank barrows could thus be seen as simply massively extended long barrows (Ashbee 1970). Loveday (forthcoming) has suggested that cursus monuments may in some cases be intended to represent the idea of field boundaries and rectilinear houses.

Certainly, a degree of overlapping between these 'fixed' categories can be discerned. Bradley (1983) suggested bank barrows and cursus monuments were interchangeable within the Neolithic of Dorset, and Barclay (1995) suggested the same regarding pit-defined and ditch-defined cursus monuments in Scotland. The Cleaven Dyke, as discussed elsewhere in this volume, shares characteristics of both a bank barrow and a cursus monument, and does indeed have a connection with a more conventional long barrow (Herald Hill), which aligns on the same low hill on which the Cleaven Dyke seems to end. The Neolithic rectilinear pit-defined enclosure at Littleour (described in **4** above) sits within view of the cursus. Elsewhere in Scotland, a cursus enclosure at Mill of Fintray, Aberdeenshire, consists of a series of connected enclosures, one pit-defined, the others ditch-defined. The Holywood North cursus, Dumfries, is ditch-defined, but a line of posts follows the interior edge of the ditch.

The Cleaven Dyke fits into this pattern of ambiguity very well, and it may suggest that the linear nature of such defined spaces may have been more important than how the site was defined. The apparent connections of mortuary practice, ritual, domesticity and control of movement suggests that perhaps we should not so readily break down social life into these distinct categories, but rather see cursus monuments as places where, perhaps through ritual activity, control of movement and exclusion of certain people, any such boundaries in people's minds were blurred. The linear form may have encouraged movement from one experience to another, bringing them together in the participants' minds.

The inclusion of natural features within the architecture of cursus monuments may add a further dimension to this overall view of social life, and add to the complexity of meaning of the sites. The location near rivers has been explained as a factor of practicality–ease of construction on river gravels, and flat space in river valleys and terraces (Loveday 1985). Yet it is difficult to dismiss this constant relationship. Amongst the sites discussed, there are structures aligned on watercourses and on the direction of water flow, dominant terminal locations overlooking rivers and flood plains, sites actually on flood plains, or close to rivers and river confluences, and even one site (Eskdalemuir) possibly crossing water or aligned on a river crossing.

Other features of the natural landscape have also been incorporated into the structure and alignments of cursus monuments–terminals on the edges of plateaux or on promontories, alignments on hilltops or points on the horizon, and subtle changes in topography such as hollows and mounds along the course of cursus and bank barrow sites.

Such relationships—which are only those which we can still observe today—may have been deliberately exploited (and sought after) by those who built the sites. They incorporated the natural world into the humanly constructed architecture of cursus monuments and bank barrows. Recent studies (Bender 1992; Bradley 1993; Tilley 1994, 1996; Richards 1996) have highlighted the significance of places within the natural landscape, places given significance and histories by local people, part of an increasingly culturally defined landscape. Rivers, hilltops, trees, rock outcrops, ridges and valleys may have become parts of ritual pathways and cultural biographies. Later architectural formalisation brought them further into a controlled ritual landscape.

In this brief discussion, I have suggested that cursus monuments and bank barrows were part of increasing attempts, through monumentality in Scotland's Neolithic, to connect aspects of social life from burial to domestic life and ritual, and to merge the natural with the cultural. This may have been done through ritual activity contained within, and controlled by, linear enclosures. Connections with water (and so fertility and agriculture), topography, burial and rectangular groundplan may have been drawn together at such sites as the Cleaven Dyke, a focus for generations of users and builders. It is perhaps through programmes of research such as the Cleaven Dyke Project that we can hope to capture most of the elements to which these sites may have imparted a cumulative significance.

7

THE CLEAVEN DYKE AND LITTLEOUR: CONTEXT, FORM AND PURPOSE

Gwendolen [glibly]: "Ah! that is clearly a metaphysical speculation, and like most metaphysical speculations has very little reference at all to the actual facts of real life, as we know them.' Oscar Wilde *The Importance of Being Earnest*, 1895.

7.1 CLEAVEN DYKE: THE CONSTRUCTION OF THE MONUMENT

THE BUILDING SEQUENCE

From the evidence of the new survey and the excavations we suggest that construction of the monument began at the NW terminal, and that the first element was an oval or subcircular burial mound (its axis E-W) of a type common in the area in the Neolithic (eg Pitnacree: Coles & Simpson 1965). Subsequently, a *c* 80m-long barrow was added to the SE (with defining ditches a few metres from the base of the mound on both sides), but not on the apparent axis of the oval barrow; this mound may itself have been built in two episodes. From the SE end of this mound (segment-boundary A1) the nature of the monument alters; it seems to us that only at this point does the cursus/bank barrow proper begin.

The bank was continued at first on the same line as the long barrow but then re-aligned slightly to the south. It was accompanied by regular quarry-ditches, set further back from the foot of the bank, with the familiar cursus-like spacing. The monument was then constructed in segments, towards the SE, possibly over a prolonged period. Eventually, at a point about 300m along its length, the overall alignment of the Dyke settled down (later perturbations notwithstanding) appearing to point at the hill to the SE where we believe it terminated (illus 85).

The builders felt it necessary, at certain points, to leave gaps in bank and ditches, breaking the monument into

Illus 85
Extract from the RAF vertical aerial photograph (CPE/SCOT/303-3070) of the Cleaven Dyke flown 26 September 1947. The road near the left-hand edge of the photograph is the Perth-Blairgowrie road. To the right (SE) of the road the irregular course of Section **C** can be seen clearly. Section break **Y** also shows clearly, as does the more recent circular enclosure overlying the northern ditch at that point. The soil mark of Section **E** is visible towards the right-hand edge of the photograph. (*Crown Copyright: RCAHMS*)

five Sections which varied in structural character and scale, and also to leave gaps only in the ditches at certain points. Section **C** was, in comparison with **A** and **B**, very irregular, and terminated at its SE end in a long mound with an oval swelling strongly reminiscent of the NW terminal of the Dyke. That the oval portion of this feature may have had a separate existence, with its own defining ditch, lends strength to such a comparison, especially as it occupies the summit of a local eminence lying squarely on the adopted alignment of the bank.

After this possible mirroring of the 'founding' monuments the segmentary construction of the monument was resumed. The penultimate Section, **D**, which measures only c 175m long, displays a disuniformity of construction similar to that of **C**, although it resumes the asymmetrical bank cross-section of Sections **A** and **B** of the monument. The ditches of the final Section are visible on aerial photographs for more than 350m, extending as far as the top of the low hill to the SE. The bank of this Section has been recorded for only c 240m, as an earthwork by the Ordnance Survey in 1864, and more recently by aerial photography; its omission in this final sector would, of course, accord with our hypothesis of progressive departure from the earlier uniformity of standards of construction.

The present-day appearance of the Cleaven Dyke as a unitary monument naturally inspires our expectation that its primary function was related to its elongated, linear character. However, it is clear from the excavation and detailed survey of this monument, that it developed into its present form piecemeal, possibly over a prolonged period. Of the five Sections, four, **A-D**, are upstanding, exhibiting 28 identifiable segments. If Section **E** had the same number of segments as Section **B**, which is of the same length, then the Dyke would have had 34 segments. If each segment represented, say, an annual construction event, then the building of the whole of the Dyke from segment-boundary A1 to the SE terminal could have been encompassed within a lifetime.

It is possible that the less regular construction of the SE part of the Cleaven Dyke reflects a weakening in the traditions of construction, or a change in the perceived needs of the builders later in the possibly prolonged construction process. The differentiation between segments—into narrow and broad—may be a deliberate way of emphasising the separateness of constructional events, while not prejudicing the continuous nature of each Section. In this context the breaks between Sections may take on a greater significance. They clearly represent deliberate punctuations, but what determined that such breaks should occur? While one might speculate on the causes—the passage of time, the death or birth of an individual, the occurrence of a natural phenomenon—the arguments concerning lengths of Sections (in **3.2** above) suggest a more deliberately planned programme of construction. We must note that there are occasionally more pronounced segment boundaries, which may themselves have had more than normal significance (eg segment-boundary B3).

THE CHOICE OF TERRAIN AND ALIGNMENT FOR THE DYKE

The character of the ground occupied by the Cleaven Dyke is so striking as to suggest it provides strong evidence for the intentions of the monument's builders. It is the only extensive area of very level ground for some distance around the confluence of the Rivers Tay and Isla; it adjoins and is defined by four watercourses, including the two rivers, but is itself well-drained and dry. From the NW terminal to a point barely 50m beyond Section boundary **X** (a distance of 1400m), the changes in ground level are scarcely perceptible. To the SE, however, gradients are more acute, especially in the first 220m of Section **C**, where the Dyke crosses a broad gully, or in the last 150m, where it obliquely ascends the flank of a low hill. Not surprisingly it is in this SE sector that the monument also displays its greatest irregularity. We therefore consider it not unreasonable to suggest that, when work started on the Dyke proper, those responsible already intended to exploit a great part of this level expanse, although not necessarily all at once. This exploitation of level ground may be considered standard practice in the location of cursus monuments. Elsewhere in Britain (Brophy, **6** above) level river terraces near confluences evidently represent preferred sites. It hardly needs to be emphasised that the conception, planning and laying out of such extensive monuments would be facilitated not only by level terrain but also by the absence of dense vegetation. It is significant therefore that the palaeoenvironmental evidence offered above (**1.2** and **2.4**) indicates that the monument was built over a landscape probably already cleared of woodland, but probably not in intensive agricultural use. It should be noted that conditions were also suitable for the stripping of turf during construction.

The question then arises: what factors influenced the adoption of the main alignment, which differs sharply from the orientation of the original oval barrow (c 80° magnetic) and slightly from that of the secondary long barrow (c 118° magnetic)? To the NW, the Dyke aligns on the rounded summit of the Hill of Lethendy, a relatively undistinguished hill; on the SE it appears to terminate near the highest point of a sinuous hill. Neither feature seems an irresistible target, and it is possible that other significant objectives (or indeed none) were in view. The long barrow on Herald Hill is aligned on the same sinuous hill at the SE end of the Dyke; it is unclear whether the barrow was aligned on the terminal of the Dyke (making it later than the construction of the whole monument) or whether both barrow and Dyke were aligned on the same hill.

There is another possibility: that the Dyke originally had an intermediate objective. At the SE end of Section **C**, the line of the bank closes with what may be a composite long/oval mound possibly reversing the order of construction where the Dyke began at the NW end. The possible interpretation of the disjointed stretch of the southern ditch opposite the oval element as an indication of an independent existence need not imply anything other than phased construction of a unitary whole; and, indeed, the immediate approach to this terminal over the awkward terrain and the glaring disuniformities of Section **C** scarcely proclaims the working out of a grand design, rather the stuttering addition to a monumental statement already clearly enunciated. Moreover, such an assessment fairly characterises the Dyke for the remainder of its course.

It therefore follows that we might seek the proximate objective further to the NW. Suitable candidates include the conspicuously enlarged terminals of Sections **A** and **B**, both noticeably regular and uniform in appearance and local alignment, although both the result of aggregated construction. Of these, special attention should be directed at the terminal of Section **B**, where the final segment (B5) is not only much more massive than the preceding portion of the bank, but is also linked to it by an uncharacteristic double change of alignment. The precise significance of this change may resist interpretation without excavation, but, as noted above, only 50m or so to the SE, the Dyke leaves the level ground for less even terrain. It could thus be argued that at a comparatively early stage, it was intended that the Dyke went no further than this, terminating on a perhaps pre-existing long mound at the limit of favourable terrain. It might be argued that Richmond's excavation in 1939 had demonstrated that this portion displayed the standard internal structure and asymmetrical profile, and was thus part of the original design. However, the oval mound at the NW end of the Dyke seems to show the same pattern of construction–the gravel mound held in place by a turf toe; this, however, is merely a constructional technique.

On the other hand, the mound on the NW side of most of the Section boundaries (**W, X, Y**, and the end of the bank of the Dyke as surveyed by the Ordnance Survey in 1864) is broader. Thus, the marking of one or both terminals of each Section with an enlargement of the bank, however effected, appears to be part of the overall plan, and there may have been a purpose other than monumentality–for example, provision of elevated platforms for a range of purposes, perhaps including viewing of the previously constructed portions.

THE ENVIRONMENT OF THE CLEAVEN DYKE'S CONSTRUCTION

We are fortunate in having palaeoenvironmental evidence from three sources, providing background to the construction of the Cleaven Dyke. The column from Rae Loch (**1.2** above) provides a general picture of the area to the north of the Dyke; the soil micromorphology (**2.4** above) tells us about the soil and vegetation conditions immediately under the bank; and the pollen in the soils buried below the Dyke (**2.5** above) gives us an idea of the vegetation cover in the vicinity.

The portion of the Rae Loch pollen sequence that relates to the period of the Dyke's construction is RAE-5, the beginning of which is defined by the elm decline at c 4010 cal BC. The expansion of grasses and other species, perhaps indicative of Neolithic pastoral activity, was noted in zone RAE-5a, although the landscape was still (in the vicinity of the loch at least) dominated by woodland. Possible podsolisation of the soils may also be indicated at this time. Cereal-type pollen appears at c 3040 cal BC. At around 2510 cal BC the percentage of tree pollen drops from 80% to 67%, showing continuation of the clearing of woodland.

The soil micromorphology results (**2.4** above) confirm that podsolisation of the sandy soils in the area was indeed underway when the Dyke was built. The presence of phytoliths in the thin sections suggests that grassland was a component of the ground cover. The lack of morphological indicators of major anthropogenic activities such as cultivation, intensive burning and substantial woodland vegetation clearance in the immediate area of the excavated sections of the Dyke was also noted. It seems that construction of the monument did not require or attract major ground preparation. The absence of substantially disturbed soils and lack of infilled tree root channels also supports the view that all that was required was the removal of a light brush vegetation from the line of the construction.

The interpretation of soil pollen is notoriously difficult. Bearing in mind the caveats expressed by Edwards and Whittington (**2.5** above) we can consider the evidence presented. The results seem to suggest that the vegetational landscape which confronted the builders of Cleaven Dyke would have consisted of an intermixture of light birch-hazel woodland, perhaps of a secondary nature, heath and grassland. At face value, this seems to have been achieved through the simple progression from birch-hazel woodland to heath, as might be expected to result from human interference with woodland for pastoral purposes in an area of sandy soils.

Taking the three strands of evidence together then, the picture that emerges is as follows:

1. Much of the major woodland cover in the immediate area of the Dyke, and possibly in the area around, had been removed some time prior to the construction of the Dyke.

2. The area was in use at a low enough intensity to allow birch and hazel secondary woodland to develop, but at a high enough intensity to continue the process of change towards a grass/heathland vegetation. However, parts of the landscape in the area of the Dyke were still dominated by woodland.

3. No significant ground preparation was necessary for the construction of the Dyke, and the area had not been cultivated. However, the soil micromorphology indicated some light burning, perhaps indicating the removal of scrub immediately prior to construction of the Dyke.

It may be suggested that the Dyke was constructed on the fringes of a settlement area largely in use for cattle or sheep herding. Cereal pollen was not noted in the Rae Loch column until after the period proposed for the construction of the Dyke. However, cereal-type pollen is both low in quantity and disperses only a short distance; therefore its absence from the pollen diagrams before this period may tell us little about the extent of arable activity in the area. Indeed, many herbaceous plants found as weeds in arable and pastoral habitats become consistently present within zone RAE-5a, contemporary with the building of the Dyke, and there is evidence elsewhere in lowland Scotland for cereal cultivation at this time. All that can be said is that cereals were not being grown in the immediate vicinity of the Dyke.

7.2 THE CLEAVEN DYKE IN ITS CONTEXT OF CURSUS MONUMENTS AND BANK BARROWS

Cursus monuments and bank barrows have traditionally been assigned to the mid or even the late Neolithic; in the latter period they have been equated to henges in the analyses of distributions (Bradley 1984, 43; Barnatt 1996, 52). What seems certain is that construction began in the earlier part of the Neolithic–there is a convincing series of dates in the range 4000-3300 cal BC. What is not clear is whether the evidence of construction carrying on into the later Neolithic in southern Britain is paralleled in the north.

Brophy (**6.1** above) deals in detail with the cursus monuments of Tayside and Fife. Here we consider the place of the Cleaven Dyke in the wider context. The only detailed consideration of the British cursus monuments was produced over a decade ago by Roy Loveday as a PhD thesis (1985). When completed, his study proved an immensely useful document, both for its detailed consideration of individual features of cursus monuments and related sites, and its genuinely original approaches to interpretation; the passing years have not reduced its value, and it is to be regretted that circumstances beyond the author's control prevented the planned publication.

Loveday, in being required to discriminate between real cursus monuments and misinterpreted roads, pillow mounds, etc, applied a very critical eye to the evidence. He considered but dismissed the Cleaven Dyke as a classic cursus, accepting the interpretation as a Roman monument. His reasons were: that the monument was too well-preserved; that there was no evidence of turf construction in the comparable site at Scorton; that there were gaps in the mound (unlike most other bank barrows); and that there were no terminals (Loveday pers comm). Of these supposed contra-indications, the first is a function of the subsequent land-use of the site, combined with the method of construction (turf revetting holding the gravel core in place). Given the frequent occurrence of turf in Neolithic mound construction in the Neolithic and Bronze Age in Scotland, the second objection no longer has validity. The third is perhaps more a reflection of the poor preservation (because of subsequent agriculture) of other bank barrows and cursus monuments. The fourth appears to be a consequence of the Dyke being neither classic cursus nor classic bank barrow, although the terminal at the SE end may originally have been closed, but subsequently lost to erosion. No criticism of Loveday's interpretation is implied, particularly as he was working only from, and was misled by, published sources; the present authors believe that the dense tree-cover concealed the true nature of the Cleaven Dyke and it could only become apparent through prolonged and repeated inspection on the ground and from the air.

We agree with Loveday, who also noted (1985, 180) that there are certain discrepancies in the cursus classification. For example, if we propose a new definition of a bank barrow—length greater than normal, sides of mound broadly parallel, ditches closely flanking the bank—we might better interpret the monuments at North Stoke A (200m long, 9-12m wide (Case 1982)) and Llandegai (200m+ long, c 12-13m wide (Houlder 1968)) as ploughed down bank barrows rather than cursus monuments; what evidence there is suggests that at both sites the bank material was on the inner side of the ditches, and there was probably insufficient room at both sites for separate banks running along the edge of both ditches. It is certainly possible to interpret as a bank barrow the excavated site at Scorton, where evidence survives of a bank midway between ditches which are 35m apart (Topping 1982). Since Loveday's consideration of the material, a further site has been excavated, at Sarn-y-bryn-Caled (Gibson 1994) which the excavator has compared to the other narrow sites; the cursus at Sarn-y-bryn-Caled measures 380m long but only 10-13m wide. There is evidence of external banks. Radiocarbon dating of material from just above the primary silts gives a calibrated range of 3960-3550 cal BC (OxA-3997).

Loveday (1985) subdivided cursus monuments and their related structures into three categories according to size.

1 'Long mortuary enclosures'–known examples are up to 140m long and less than 25m wide.

2 'Minor cursuses'–known examples are 180-420m long and 25-50m wide. Upper limit 500m.

3 'Major cursuses'–known examples are between 800m and 5,640m long and 40-100m wide.

He further distinguished five types of cursus monument in terms of plan form: straight, irregular, curved, sinuous and angular. The Cleaven Dyke can be described as 'straight' in overall classification, but sectors, notably Sections **C** and **D**, are notably sinuous in appearance. It is evident that categorisation of this kind may not be the best way to approach the problem.

Moving away from the monuments themselves and looking at their immediate environs, cursus monuments often display complex relationships with other monument types, and these may differ from one region to another (Loveday 1989). For example, long barrows and related sites such as long mortuary enclosures occur repeatedly in the vicinity of cursus monuments, and may occasionally intersect, as in the case of the Dorset cursus. Nearby long barrows and long mortuary enclosures tend to be on the same alignment as cursus monuments, or at right angles to them, while more distantly placed examples tend to be aligned in common, or to point at a cursus terminal, as appears to be the case with the Herald Hill barrow.

It is their sheer size in extreme cases, however, that requires explanation. Loveday (1989) writes of there being some stimulus to gigantism, from long mortuary enclosures to cursus monuments. He suggests that the same pattern can also be seen in the relationship between long barrows and bank barrows, but the stimulus may subsist as much in the landscape which these gigantic monuments traverse. The available evidence points to the landscape of the Cleaven Dyke being on the fringes of settled land: perhaps the builders' perception of the scale of their enterprise in extending the limits of the domestic landscape found concrete form in the great scale of the structural statement made by the construction of the monument–the transformation of the natural landscape through massive, direct cultural intervention (Hodder 1990, 239).

FUNCTION AND PURPOSE

One of Loveday's comments on previous studies of cursus monuments, from the 18th century to the present day, was that too much emphasis had been given to 'the linearity and extended proportions of the monuments at the expense of their enclosure form', placing undue stress on their role as 'processional ways' and 'avenues'. He noted that the rather inaccurate description of the first recognised cursus (Amesbury, by Stukely on 6 August 1723) has continued to determine perceptions of other possible sites (Loveday 1985, 12). That this interpretation continues to hold sway is clear from recent accounts (eg Tilley 1994). Indeed it is fair to say that since Tilley's account was published, work on the interpretation of cursus monuments has taken the 'pathway' model as an accepted fact rather than one of a number of alternatives (cf papers in Barclay & Harding forthcoming).

Although the Cleaven Dyke as a whole appears to relate to features in the surrounding landscape (it appears to terminate on a hill at the SE), we cannot assume either that this alignment is significant or that the monument was planned from the first to be its final length and to have its final form. Indeed, it is possible that the process of construction of the cursus/bank barrow element of the monument may have had a significance as great as the final product, for example, the periodic (annual?) construction of the individual segments having a ceremonial function, related to the continuance of tradition or social relationships; the possibility of modular relationships in the lengths of the different bank Sections makes regular augmentation more likely. Burl (1993, 136) has suggested that the complex stone rows of Brittany may been produced by a similar long-term repetition of small-scale effort, rather than the erection of a complete structure as a single event. Bradley has also noted instances in which the building of a major alignment seems to have been re-enacted. By continuing the construction of an existing alignment the population expressed its continued commitment to the ideas that lay behind it–or at least to their own interpretation of them (Bradley 1993, 57). In the case of the Maxey cursus, likewise the aggregate product of separate construction episodes, he suggests 'it was essentially an idea, a project', the monument being both medium and outcome of successive actions (Kirk 1997) and Relph has postulated (1976, 32) that places can only be kept 'alive' by involving them in practice. Whittle (1992) considered that the three different alignments of the Dorchester-on-Thames cursus might indicate phased construction—'the repetition of costly but important ritual'—or changing meaning over time.

Although we have argued that the Cleaven Dyke's present length is the result of gradual extension and that it was not intended from the first to operate as a long linear 'processional route' in the way the Dorset cursus has been interpreted, we must still consider the possibility that such a use developed. Barrett has suggested that, in the case of multi-chambered cairns there were 'perhaps processional rituals where each element of the monument was visited in turn' (Barrett 1988, 34), and we cannot discount the possibility that prominent parts of the Dyke were visited in this way.

Barrett (1994, 19) has discussed how 'a certain architecture could ... have guided particular forms of discourse'; that is, what is done in and around a ceremonial monument is determined to a great extent by the nature of that monument. Could we suggest that the construction of the Cleaven Dyke presents an architecture which has been guided by a 'form of discourse', involving a 'lengthy and piecemeal programme of construction', a theory advanced by Barrett (*ibid*, 23), referring to the construction of the Durrington Walls south circle? Barrett's consideration of cursus monuments, however, stresses their role as formalised pathways, again echoing the 18th-century view criticised by Loveday (1985, above). However, if we consider cursus monuments in their wider landscape, we can examine their role in separation. Hodder (1990) has discussed the importance of the concepts of *domus* (the home and ideas associated with it), *agrios* (the wild) and *foris* (the 'outside' but used by Hodder to express the emphasis on boundaries and entrances in the Neolithic). It has been suggested that the Dorset cursus passed between open ground on one side and forested land on the other (Barrett 1994, 139); the Cleaven Dyke was built on cleared but not intensively used land, perhaps also on the fringes of the settled area. Could it be that some monuments were constructed across paths between these areas, their locations reflected in the pairs of causeways across the two ditches, as on the Cleaven Dyke? That is, the axis of use of the monument is 90° away from that implied by the 'pathway' model. Brophy (pers comm) has noted that the Holywood 2 cursus appears to align on the Twelve Apostles stone circle: precisely where the projected line crosses the Holywood 1 cursus there are causeways across both of its defining ditches, as though a 'path' projected from the end of one cursus was crossing the other. On the Cleaven Dyke there are six (or seven) pairs of causeways; three of which (or four, if Section boundary **Z** is included) are at the formal breaks in the monument, while three are not (at segment boundaries A11, A13 and B3). It cannot be determined if these are designed to offer formal access to, or through, parts of the monument.

Pryor (1985, 301), in discussing the cursus at Maxey, described it as 'a chronologically extended series of quite separate, short-lived sites, events or episodes' and such monuments as 'episodic sites of significant alignment'. He suggested that there were three types of cursus monument:

1 'Monumental' or continuously used sites: cursuses as originally understood, eg Dorset.

2 Short-lived, single-period sites: small, eg Barnack, or large, eg Springfield?

3 Long-lived episodic ditched alignment sites: eg Maxey; Fornam All Saints.

Unfortunately, the identification of differences between these types may to some extent depend upon the scale and intensity of archaeological investigation (ground or aerial survey, or excavation). On the basis of the results from the Cleaven Dyke we may suggest six overlapping explanations or roles for linear cursiform monuments, where one role does not necessarily exclude others:

1 Structures for formal processions or for orchestrated journeys of experience (cf Tilley);

2 structures linking pre-existing monuments or significant places;

3 structures demarcating an alignment on a place, object or astronomical event, rather than linking anything;

4 symbolic or physical barriers between areas of different significance (eg wild and domestic land);

may involve symbolic control of access between the two; in this respect the possible meaning of the word 'Cleaven' signifying 'dividing' (Simon Taylor pers comm) is particularly interesting;

5 symbolic 'project': the physical expression of a social or ideological need;

6 a *temenos*: an area of land marked off and devoted to the gods (Loveday 1985).

Whittle's (1992) observation that cursus monuments might work to harness and control existing sites may have particular resonance for the Cleaven Dyke, given the presence of a 'founding' monument at its NW end. However, the meaning of monuments changes though time–the meaning and purpose intended at the commencement of construction might well, decades or even hundreds of years later, have changed considerably.

Brophy (above) explores some of the possibly related monuments in Scotland and we do not duplicate his work here. It is clear, however, that the Cleaven Dyke is associated with the local traditions of burial in the Neolithic, as well as with the cursus tradition; Pitnacree-type round barrows, of the kind we believe forms the NW terminal of the Dyke, may be a common feature of the landscape of Perthshire and Angus and a number of long barrows are known in eastern Scotland. The Dyke may itself incorporate three or more burial mounds, both long and oval, or features meant to mimic them–at the NW terminal and at the SE end of Section **C**. Moreover, the tail of the only long barrow known in the area, at Herald Hill, appears to be aligned on the presumed SE terminal of the Dyke.

7.3 OTHER NEOLITHIC MONUMENTS RELATING TO THE CLEAVEN DYKE

ROUND AND OVAL MOUNDS

Two round or oval mounds on the same scale as the Cleaven Dyke terminal mound have been excavated and published in the area, and a third was still under excavation at the time of writing (illus 86). The excavations at Pitnacree (Coles & Simpson 1965) revealed an early Neolithic mortuary structure of the familiar 'linear zone' type, followed by a complex sequence of mound construction, dated to c 4300-2900 cal BC (GaK-601). The excavation of the larger mound at North Mains (Barclay 1983) revealed a circular central burial enclosure, followed by an even more complex sequence of mound development, dated to the early Bronze Age. The mound at Fordhouse has revealed yet another, even more complex, variation on similar themes (**1.1** above; Peterson pers comm).

The most recent overall consideration of round barrows in the Neolithic of Britain is that of Kinnes (1979). In common with more recent regional studies of these sites (eg RCAHMS 1994a) the implications of Pitnacree are not adequately highlighted; in an area containing many mounds on the same scale as Pitnacree, to publish distribution maps which show Pitnacree as the sole Neolithic round barrow in Tayside (Kinnes 1979, fig 4.1) is perhaps misleading. The Royal Commission specifically resisted 'the temptation to assume that many of the large lowland round barrows [were] of Neolithic date' (RCAHMS 1994a, 38); however, to give the clear impression, as their fig. 37a does, that none were, and then to base interpretations on the supposed limited distribution of Neolithic burial mounds in the area, is surely even less appropriate.

The radiocarbon dates from the Dyke place its construction closer to Pitnacree than to North Mains. However, the comparison of the two excavated sites allows us to consider the clearly strong and long-lived tradition of massive round mound building in the area.

The Pitnacree mound was 27.5m by 23.5m across and c 2m high (a height to diameter ratio of (using the average diameter) c 12.7:1). Another excavated and published round barrow of the period, at Fochabers in Moray, measured c 14m in diameter by 1m high (Burl 1984). Both were low, flattish mounds. North Mains, in contrast, was 40m in diameter and 5.5m high, and had the traditional pudding-bowl shape of a Bronze Age mound. In the field, one of the authors (GJB) has observed that individual round barrows in Perthshire, Angus and Fife seem to fall into one class or the other–broad and low, like Pitnacree, or bowl-shaped, like North Mains. We have tried to establish if this observation could be tested more objectively, by taking the measurement data in the NMRS records and trying to separate the two possible types. We are grateful to Patrick Ashmore for his careful analysis of the figures; his doubts about the reliability of many measurements, particularly of height (which seems to have been 'rounded' to an unacceptable degree), are such that any statistical approach would be misleading until better data is available. It is hoped that if consistently reliable measurements can be gathered in future, further work may be possible. However, as an interim measure we have prepared a distribution of 'low flat' mounds which have a diameter of 20m or more and a diameter to height ratio of 12:1 or more (Pitnacree has a

Illus 86
The distribution of certain classes of Neolithic burial and ceremonial monuments in Tayside. The distribution of round mounds must be treated with caution, for reasons discussed in the text.

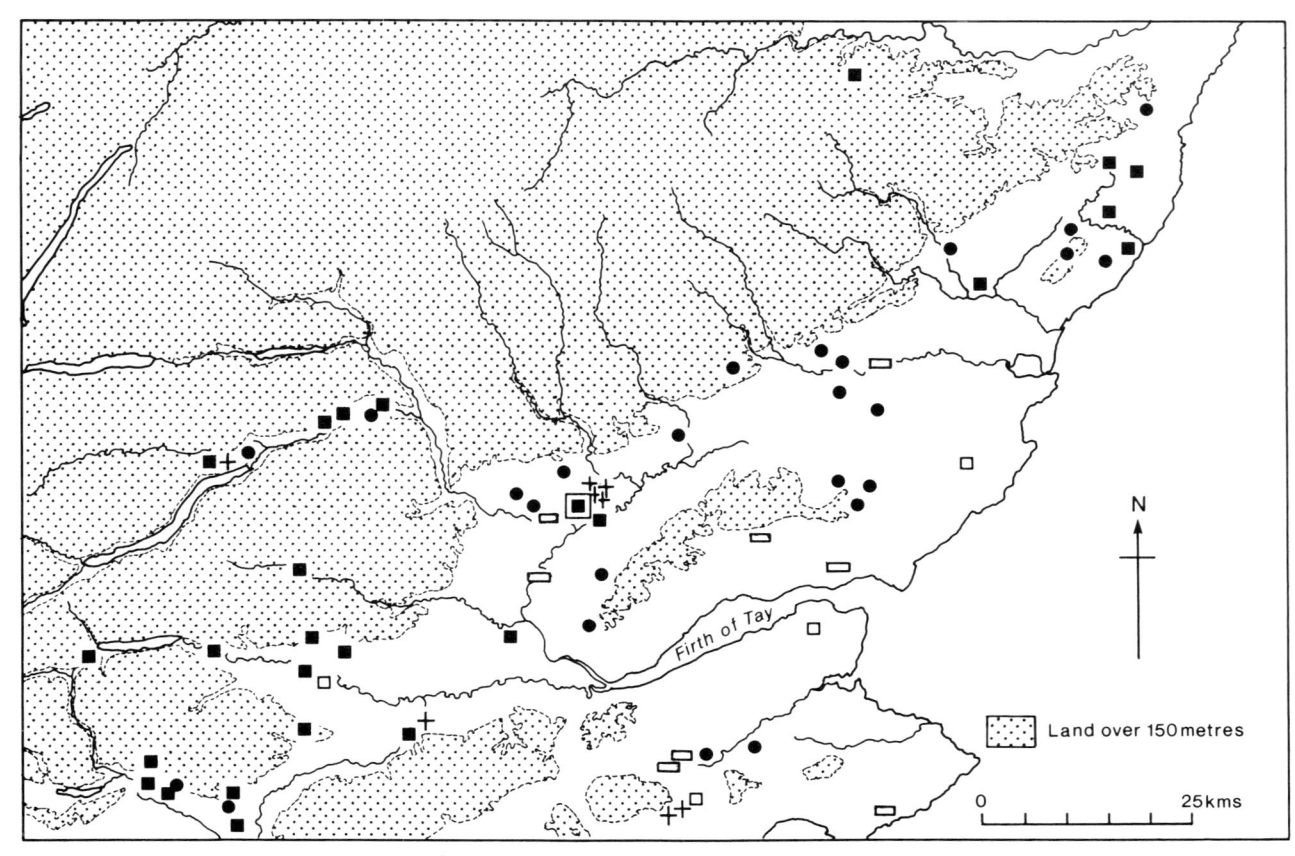

- ■ Long barrow/cairn
- ▢ Possible ploughed down long barrow
- ▭ Narrow ditched enclosure ('long mortuary enclosure')
- + Small pit-defined enclosure
- ● Round mound with diameter to height ratio of 12:1 or more

ratio of c 12.7:1; North Mains 7.3:1), which we feel is a fairly conservative ratio–the sites are indicated on illustration 86. We accept that to attempt this separation on crude morphological grounds is risky, but we feel that the attempt is itself informative and the result of the experiment is no more misleading than previous minimalist approaches. We believe that further research on the round barrows of the area is necessary and would be well worthwhile to test our hypothesis.

Kinnes (1979) placed Pitnacree in his Stage A (early), group 'd' ('linear zone' mortuary structure). The 'linear zone' as defined by Kinnes (*ibid*, 58) is the archetypal early Neolithic mortuary structure, comprising an area usually c 1m wide and up to 10m long, defined at both ends, and often subdivided, by posts. Scott (1992) has recently published a survey of the known sites, giving emphasis to the Scottish examples.

Kinnes comments that the circular mound is '... the most economical way of achieving maximum visual impact from any direction, although it lacks the focal emphasis of the long mound' (Kinnes 1979, 48). Although round mounds are '... the normal type of burial mound in lowland Britain', and are '... integral to Early Neolithic practice in all areas' (Kinnes 1979, 48), long barrows are the normal burial structures of the Neolithic in most of lowland Britain.

LONG MOUNDS

Kinnes (1979, 48) notes, in contrast to round barrows, that the long mound is '... sanctioned by an ancestry leading back to the Bandkeramik longhouse [of continental Europe], its trapezoidal variant being either of comparable derivation or a natural outcome of attention focused at one end'.

Name	Cairn/ Barrow/ Mixed	Overall length (m)	Size of proximal mound	Height of proximal mound
Cleaven Dyke phase 1	B	c.62 m	25 m×22 m	2 m
Cleaven Dyke phase 2 (including phase 1)	B	c.105 m	25 m×22 m	2 m
Herald Hill	B	60-70 m	20 m?	3.5 m
Longmanhill	B	62 m	20 m×18 m	3.4 m
Stirling Farm	M	64 m	19 m	1.2 m
Cnoc Freiceadain	C	67 m	18 m×14 m	1.6 m
Tulach Buaile Assery	C	63 m	20 m	3.7 m
Brawlbin Long	C	62 m	22 m×23 m	2 m
Na Tri Shean	C	71.5 m	19 m	2.2 m
Tulach an t'Sionnaich*	C	62 m	17 m	1.8 m

*3 phase heel-shaped cairn with long tail.

Table 17
Dimensions of some of the mounds mentioned in discussion; none of the Caithness cairns below 60m in length have been included. All dimensions to nearest metre.

Henshall (1963) listed ten apparently unchambered long cairns and barrows in north-east Scotland (approximately the area of the new Aberdeenshire Council). By the early 1970s two further earthen long barrows had been identified at the southern edge of the area, near Dalladies, and one had been excavated (Piggott 1971). There are now 21 long mounds known (extant and destroyed) in Aberdeenshire, Banffshire and Kincardineshire (information culled from NMRS records), in none of which is any chamber visible.

In the old counties of Angus and Perthshire there are both chambered and apparently unchambered long mounds; their distribution was recently mapped by RCAHMS (1994a, 37, fig. B). At first sight there appears to be a pronounced gap, some 80km across, between the mapped distributions of the Aberdeenshire group and the monuments in the hills to the west of Perth; the Cleaven Dyke lies in the middle of this gap. However, there are three reasons for suggesting that the gap may be illusory. First, several examples of long-mounds may exist there unnoticed (eg the Herald Hill barrow, below). Second, the gap may be filled by round mounds of the period (cf Pitnacree), as noted above. And finally, the role of long barrows may have been served by different types of monuments now visible only as cropmarks (eg RCAHMS 1994a, 38). The current distribution of long barrows and cairns, low round mounds and cropmark 'long mortuary enclosures' is shown in illustration 86. Table 17 summarises information on the dimensions of comparitive mounds.

THE 'HERALD HILL' MOUND NATURAL OR ARTIFICIAL?

The sole recognised example of a long barrow, at Herald Hill, measures 70-80m along its axis (its west end has been disturbed) (illus 1; 87a,b; 88). It is c 25m broad and 4.2m high (at the east end), tapering to less than 1m high at the west. It rises steeply from an otherwise fairly flat terrace, in a dramatic position overlooking the confluence of the River Isla and the Lunan Burn, some 1200m east of the Cleaven Dyke. The NMRS record card states that it is a natural mound and that while 'The east end of the mound would make a very impressive terminal for a long barrow ... the crest of the mound runs west in a gentle curve, reflecting the trend of the fluvio-glacial feature that extends some way into the adjacent field to the west.'

There are three reasons why the description and interpretation can be doubted. First, the use and adaptation of pre-existing natural features in the construction of Neolithic mounds is too well-documented for the inclusion of a natural feature to be any objection to the interpretation of the mound as a long barrow. For example, the Capo long barrow, the nearest mound to the NE, is constructed on the raised edge of a river terrace, which gives an enhanced impression of its height and bulk when viewed from the south. Second, the mound, in its shape and orientation, seems a very odd and unaccountable geomorphological feature. The Herald Hill does indeed seem to sit on a very slight fluvio-glacial feature, but the trend of the major features of the topography in the area is different–for example, while the Herald Hill has a bearing of 111° magnetic, the adjacent fluvio-glacial hillock mentioned by RCAHMS has a bearing of 30° magnetic as does the nearest large moraine (c 700m to the SSE). Finally, in 1997 the authors of this report dug a trial trench into the mound c 16m from its summit and 4m to the north of the mound's axis. At this point, the topmost 0.9m of the mound was certainly artificial.

If it is accepted, therefore, that the mound is substantially artificial, although taking advantage of a pre-existing natural feature, certain observations can be made. Perhaps most significantly the west end of the mound aligns on the low hill on which the Cleaven Dyke's SE terminal appears to lie.

118 ◆ THE CLEAVEN DYKE AND LITTLEOUR MONUMENTS

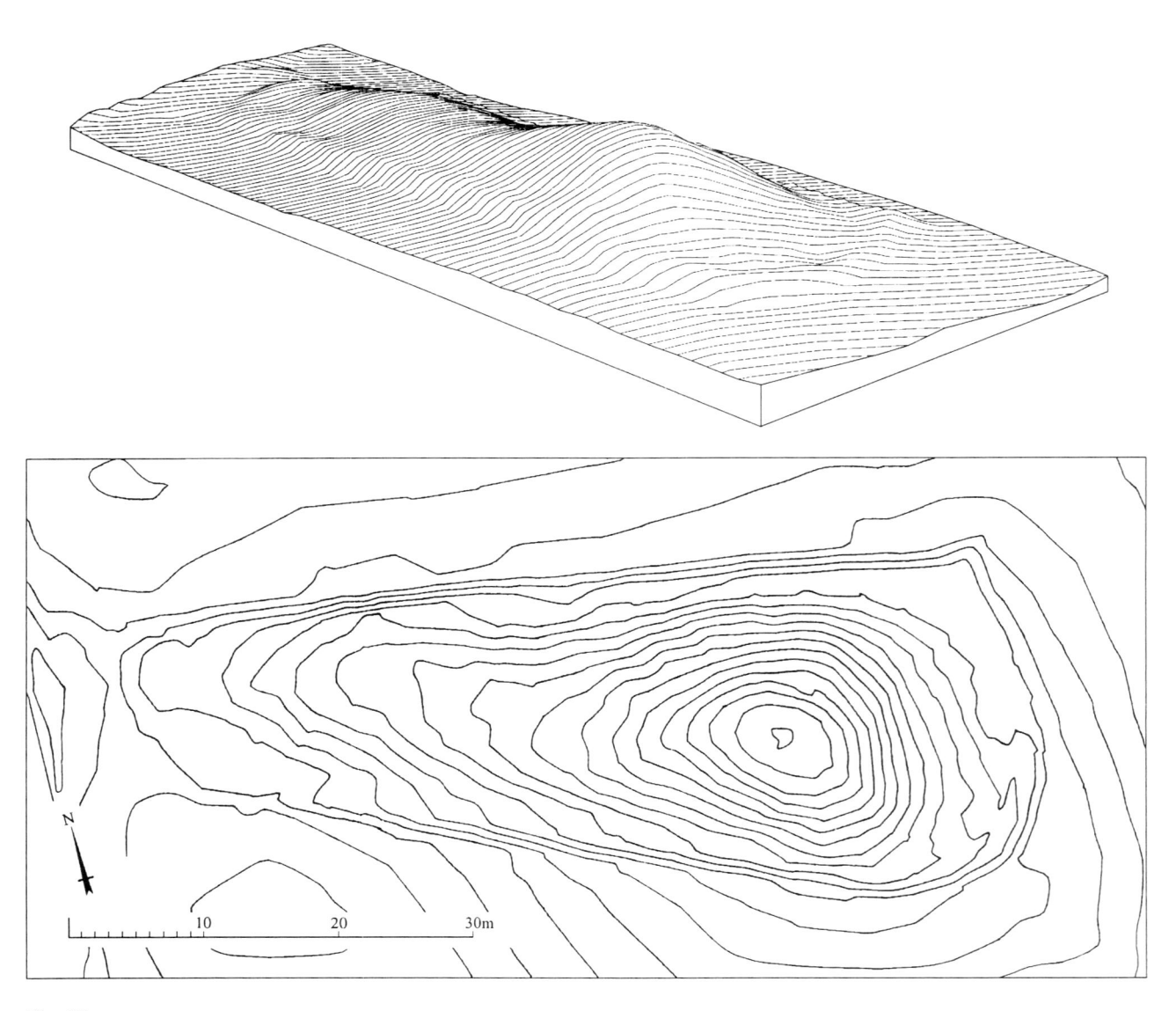

Illus 87
The Herald Hill long barrow: a) three-dimensional view of Herald Hill prepared by RCAHMS. The vertical dimension is multiplied by 2. (*Crown Copyright: RCAHMS*); b)contour survey undertaken by RCAHMS; the contours are at intervals of 0.25m. The impression of regularity is perhaps exaggerated by the modern fence line. (*Crown Copyright: RCAHMS*)

Illus 88
View of the Herald Hill long barrow: from the north.

Illus 89
A photograph of the long barrow at Longmanhill, taken probably in the 1920s. The dip between the proximal mound and the long 'tail' can be seen clearly.

THE PROXIMAL MOUND AND LONG TAIL

Herald Hill has a relatively simple shape: a raised, slightly rounded eastern terminal and a long tail. Three of the Aberdeenshire mounds also have swollen proximal mounds and long narrow tails, a feature shared by the NW terminal of the Cleaven Dyke. Longmanhill Cairn (actually an earthen barrow) in Banffshire is the second longest in the area, at c 62m (illus 89). Its now mutilated NE end has been interpreted as an oval mound c 19.8m by 18.3m and c 3.4m high (Richardson, unpublished plan of 1924 in NMRS) and as a mound with a flat façade (Henshall 1972, 222, fig. 27); field inspection of the damaged remains suggests that the latter interpretation may be more accurate, but neither plan is entirely satisfactory. The terminal mound is separated from its c 40m-long tail by a distinct dip, which is clearly visible on illustration 89. The tail tapers from 11.5m wide and 2.1m high to 8.5m broad and 1.9m high near its SW terminal. There is a further slight dip near the SW end which may mark the edge of a small distal mound. The measurements and the plan in illustration 90 are taken from Henshall's survey. Unauthorised quarrying near the SW end in 1956 revealed that the mound was predominantly of soil or turf. The mound has the distinct appearance of, and has long been interpreted as, a round or oval mound with a later long mound attached. The Blue Cairn of Balnagown (Henshall 1963, 392) has a similar dip between a proximal mound and a tail (illus 90).

The mound (possibly of mixed soil and stone) at Stirling Farm (also in Aberdeenshire) is now severely mutilated and, in part, ploughed down. It is c 64m long, oriented N-S, tapering to a minimum of 7m at its northern end. The southern terminal mound is c 19m in diameter and 1.2m high. Once again it is interpreted as a round mound with a long mound attached.

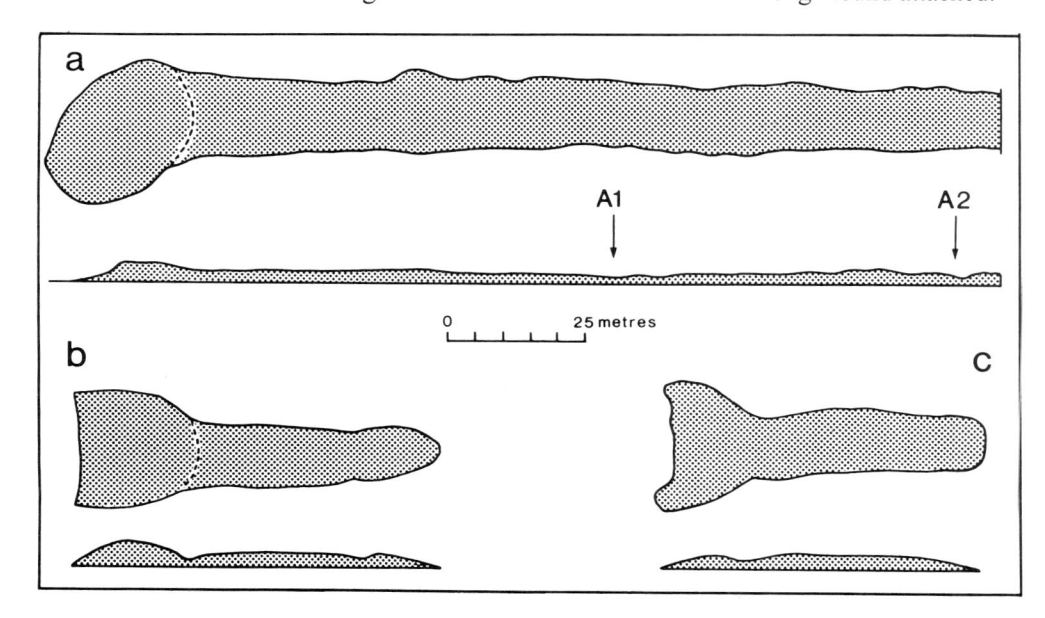

Illus 90
Plans of the long mounds at (b) Longmanhill, Banffshire and (c) Blue Cairn of Balnagowan, Aberdeenshire (both after Henshall), at the same scale as (a) the NW end of the Cleaven Dyke. The possible long barrow at the terminal ends at A1.

At Glenshee the grass-grown cairn c 49m in overall length tapers from 5m to 2.7m. RCAHMS surveyors interpreted it as possibly a long cairn with a round cairn built on its west end, although it was felt that the shape of the mound could be the result of what was described as 'the devastating pattern of robbing'.

This relationship between round mounds and long tails has been observed also in cairns, particularly in Caithness, and has been discussed at length by Henshall (1972) and Davidson & Henshall (1991), who have noted seven cairns with proximal round cairns (1991, 48); they also notes a further four which exhibit traces of both proximal and distal mounds. The latter group (Cnoc Freiceadain, Tulach Buaile Assery, Brawlbin Long and Na Tri Shean) are distinguished by their greater length (62m to 71.5m excluding horns) comparable to two of the Aberdeenshire sites; furthermore, in these sites the proximal round mound seems more clearly-defined than in the other group. In discussing the Caithness material Henshall (1972, 236) notes the examples of composite construction in English long barrows and cairns; she suggests that 'excessive length' (over c 60 m) indicated likely multi-period construction in the Scottish cairns, and that a single-period cairn of over c 45m was unusual. Whether Herald Hill is also a two-period monument could now only be determined by extensive excavation.

Mercer has suggested that the sequence in the Caithness cairns was the reverse of that argued by Henshall, and that in all the round/long mound combinations the long cairn was constructed first and the round mound was subsequently built over its end (Mercer 1992). Although Kinnes suggested that 'while such classic sites as Dyffryn Ardudwy, Mid Gleniron I-II and Tulach an t'Sionnach have a round-long succession, this is not enough to impose the same on other sites where limited excavation or field observation suggests internal complexity' (Kinnes 1992a), he has also seen the round/long succession as 'difficult to resist' (Kinnes 1992b, 67).

However, in the light of the parallels from elsewhere in Scotland and our own observation of the evidence of the long barrows, the suggestion that the NW terminal of the Cleaven Dyke is an oval mound c 25m x 22m, with a tail some 80m long, seems likely (*pace* Mercer). The evidence of Adamson's excavation on the Cleaven Dyke now seems to provide ample confirmation of the sequence: the southern defining ditch of the long mound cuts the oval mound. As has been noted above, there are at least six other multi-period long mounds of greater than average length in northern and north-eastern Scotland. The Dyke terminal mound may be of even more complex construction; at c 38m along the length of the tail, the mound changes angle; it may be that the tail was itself built in two stages (fold-out illus 98).

Looking beyond Scotland, apparently similar relationships between proximal mounds and long tails have been noted at a number of sites, such as Long Low and Great Ayton Moor (Hayes 1967). The former monument is interpreted as a mound linking two pre-existing sites; the latter seems to be a round mound with an added long mound.

'LONG MORTUARY ENCLOSURES'

The very existence of the class of monument known as 'Long Mortuary Enclosures' in Scotland has been brought into doubt (Kinnes 1985, 40). However, the name is still a useful shorthand for rectilinear ditched enclosures, on a scale similar to a long barrow, but with closed-off ends and no trace of a mound. The similarities in scale and construction between many of these sites and long barrows suggest a role in the same burial tradition. Loveday (1985) has argued that these enclosures are the lower end of a continuum of sites which include, at the other extreme of size, the major cursus monuments. Bradley (1984, 31) explicitly saw cursus monuments as developing from long mortuary enclosures. The distribution of possible examples of these sites is shown on illustration 86. Only one example in Scotland has been excavated, at Inchtuthil (Barclay & Maxwell 1991). Inchtuthil, and some of the other examples, show the characteristic wobbly, segmented nature of ditches in the Neolithic of this area, and the radiocarbon determinations from that site suggest that it was constructed and in use at much the same time as the Dyke (4230-3780 cal BC (GU-2760); 3990-3780 cal BC (GU-2761)). A substantial fence was erected in the ditch; it had been burned and, while burning, had fallen or been pushed over.

7.4 COMPARANDA FOR LITTLEOUR: THE BALFARG STRUCTURES

When the two timber structures at Balfarg Riding School were published the Littleour structure, then just discovered, was cited as a possible parallel (Barclay & Russell-White 1993, 175-6). In the Balfarg report the nature of the structures excavated was addressed by the excavator (GJB) and by Hogg (1993, 169-175).

Although constructed of posts of slighter size and twice as closely set, Balfarg Riding School (BRS) structures 1 and 2 are both straight-sided, round-ended enclosures. Care has manifestly been taken with their design: BRS 1 is twice as long as it is broad, a proportion that recurs in Neolithic monuments of this or related classes (cf Balbridie, Raigmore, and Northton), while BRS 2 exhibits an obvious pairing of its side-wall pits; BRS 1, which displays greater spatial irregularity, nevertheless probably had an equal number of posts to each side (14), with eight or nine posts at each end (cf Littleour with seven side-posts and four end-posts). In BRS 2 only the southern portion is available for comparison, but it incorporates an interesting feature: the post-pits forming either end of the gently curving end-wall, roughly twice as large as their neighbours, both lie off the alignment of their respective side-walls, being displaced towards the interior, the western pit most obviously so. The implication is that they were intended to act as terminal supports for the more tightly packed posts of the end-wall rather than as corner-posts of the more slightly built sides. Thus, although in general BRS 2 differed from Littleour in appearance, providing a relatively light framework for screening-panels, its builders seem to have been similarly concerned with the architectural geometry of the end-walls (cf Hogg 1993).

The radiocarbon determinations from Structure 2 at Balfarg Riding School indicated a range of dates for the charcoal of 3030 to 2880 cal BC, close to the dates for the Littleour structure. The Balfarg dates overlapped with those for the Grooved Ware deposits on the site.

The two structures were identified as unroofed palisaded enclosures surrounding settings of two posts. Pollard (in press) has suggested that the platforms were of both two- and four-post construction, and this is accepted. There were three points that underpinned the interpretation presented in the Balfarg report:

1 There is no explanation, if the structures were roofed, for the contrast between the neat parallel layout of the boundary posts and the ragged and irregular layout of the interior posts; this considerable contrast in layout would pose entirely unnecessary problems in roofed construction; a roof could be achieved with far less effort.

2 There is no explanation, if the structures were roofed, for the considerable amount of post replacement in the interior of Structure 2 (where the posts would be protected to a considerable degree from the wet/dry cycle, weathering and bacterial attack) in contrast to the absence of post replacement in the boundary posts, which in a roofed building would be far more exposed; we must therefore seek an explanation of the pattern of use of the boundary feature and the posts in its interior, unrelated to the normal processes of decay and replacement.

3 The relationship between the width of the building and the spacing between the two rough lines of posts in the inner group was very different from the normal spacing of excavated prehistoric rectangular roofed buildings; that is, the two rough lines in the middle of the structure were too close together, and too far from the walls of the hypothetical building.

Barber (1997, 128-9) has suggested that aspects of the analysis of the Balfarg structures were flawed. In particular, he has suggested that Hogg (1993) should not have used parallels with medieval structures to suggest that roofing timbers would have had to have been of a large girth. Barber argues that there are Early Historic structures that relied on lighter superstructures and that roofing the Balfarg structures cannot be ruled out. However, Barber only addresses the nature and analysis of one of the structures (Structure 2) and has not really addressed all the arguments set out above, in particular the patterns of post-replacement in the interior and on the boundary. It can now also be noted that other excavated rectilinear Neolithic buildings in the British Isles do not display such apparently unnecessary complexity in the arrangement of their internal post-settings as the Balfarg structures (Barclay 1996; Darvill 1996; Grogan 1996). A range of comparanda is presented in illustration 91. It has never been our argument that it is impossible to roof the Balfarg structures, only that the balance of evidence is still very much against it.

Whatever the argument about the structures being roofed, there can be little doubt that neither of the Balfarg Riding School structures was domestic. Structure 1 had a ring-ditch/ring-cairn complex built on its axis, over its northern end and had attracted a cremation burial; Structure 2 was sealed under a stony mound containing Grooved Ware.

In summary we believe that the balance of evidence is still very much for an interpretation along the lines set out in the excavation report: that is, unroofed enclosures containing free-standing post-settings, with a ceremonial/ funerary function (Barclay & Russell-White 1993).

One aspect of Balfarg Riding School Structure 2 was not given particular prominence in the original report–an axial feature (F030). At the end of its use the structure was sealed under a mound of soil and stone. The Grooved Ware associated with the structure was found not in primary contexts, but only in the final postholes in its sequence of construction, and in the mound (Barclay & Russell-White 1993, 84-5). All the postholes in the area where the mound survived were buried by the mound, except for one–F030 (Barclay & Russell-White 1993,

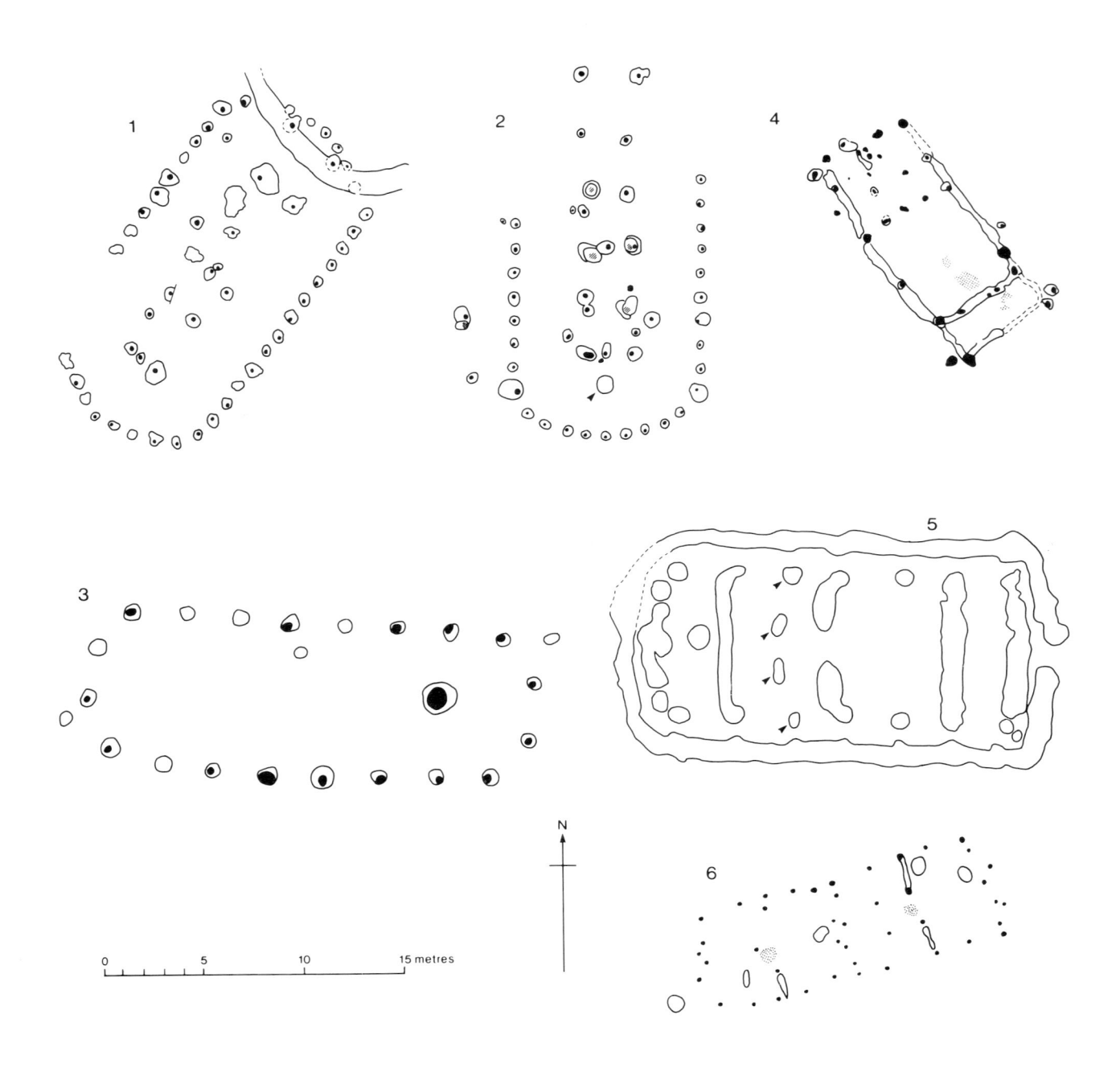

Illus 91
Comparative plans, all at the same scale, of Neolithic timber structures in Britain and Ireland. (1) & (2) the unroofed timber structures, probably of mortuary function, at Balfarg, Fife; (3) the Littleour structure; (4) the house at Ballyglass, Co Mayo (after O' Nuallain); (5) the Balbridie, Kincardineshire building (after Ralston); (6) two buildings end-to-end at Lismore Fields, Derbyshire (after Garton).

83-5), a possible post-setting. The feature lies on the axis of the structure (it is marked by an arrow on illus 91, 2). Its relationship with the boundary of Structure 2 is not clear. Although the mound material also covered the boundary postholes, it is possible that the mound was placed while these features still contained their relatively slight posts, and that the mound later slumped over them.

If F030 did hold a post, did it therefore stand within the enclosure, or did it stand alone on the axis of the mound? The similarity between Structure 2/F030 at Balfarg, and the boundary posts and the axial post L9 at Littleour is therefore even more striking than was suggested at the time of the Balfarg publication (Barclay & Russell-White 1993, 180).

7.5 OTHER TIMBER STRUCTURES RELATING TO LITTLEOUR

The report on the excavation at Littleour provides the occasion for a review of a small group of analogous cropmark enclosures, most of which are situated in eastern Scotland, some only a short distance from Littleour itself; the results of the excavation may also serve to cast light on a number of other sites belonging to different categories, but displaying comparable design features.

Littleour appears to be the most complex example of its own group, the individual site-remains of which typically comprise, as their main element, pairs of widely-spaced upright timbers set in relatively massive pits, defining an oblong or subrectangular area. The example at Fortingall is illustrated here (illus 92). Each side of the enclosure consists of from three to six pits, occasionally displaying a slight medial change of alignment, while the ends are, with the exception of one site (Ardmuir), closed by a single pit or a setting of up to four pits. Apart from the roughly square six-pit setting at Ardmuir, the enclosures vary in length from a maximum of c 22.5m (Littleour) to c 15m at Carsie Mains; in width they show much less variation, between 7m and 9m. All the plans exhibit a degree of dimensional regularity that suggests careful planning, while the size and proportions invite comparison with structures that have been identified as domestic buildings. However, the absence of internal post-pits, apart from the occasional axial example, as at Littleour and Fortingall, strongly suggests that these were not roofed structures; there is thus no close comparison to be made with such sites as Balbridie (Fairweather & Ralston 1993), the smaller examples of contemporary continental houses, or the possible building at The Clash (Foster & Stevenson, forthcoming). Another significant difference is the spacing of the individual posts of each side: at Littleour the posts are disposed at average intervals of c 2.7m, a spacing that appears typical of the group as a whole and perhaps wider than the separation that might be expected in a domestic building. Moreover, the pairing of the post-pits mentioned above was at first presumed to be the product of bilateral symmetry in design, with the object of ensuring structural stability; on closer inspection it may be more significant.

An interesting comparison may be drawn with another pit-defined structure of Neolithic date, the much larger enclosure at Douglasmuir. Although apparently of less regular construction than either Littleour or the Balfarg Riding School enclosures, its sides rarely exhibiting straight alignment, even spacing of posts, or equal length, Douglasmuir appears to have been designed and built with great care. Its even division into a northern and a southern half has already been mentioned, but not the precision with which this was accomplished: the total perimeter numbers exactly 150 posts, including the septal line which comprises 15 posts, or exactly one tenth of the total (a line also extending to a tenth of the peripheral measurement). At first sight, the proportional division of this perimeter seems wholly haphazard: the west side comprises 58 pits, the east only 53, while the width increases from 14 pits at the south end to 15 at the septum, and 16 on the north. However, if we treat the cross-members and sides of each half as independent elements, a distinct pattern emerges. Starting from the south end of 14 pits, the first half is completed with the addition of 68 pits, and precisely the same number has been employed to complete the second. There is, moreover, an internal pattern: the east side of the southern half is built on exactly twice the scale of the adjacent end (28 pits:14 pits; 34m:17m), whereas the west side of the northern half is twice the septal division (30 pits:15 pits). It seems improbable that this closeness of numerical and spatial interrelationship could have resulted without planning.

Such a conclusion is given support by the disposition of possible entrance-gaps in the ends and medial septum. It has been observed (Kendrick 1995) that in each of the ends and the medial division there is a hiatus, represented by a gap or misalignment of the respective row of pits. These gaps fall on the same straight alignment, as if providing a direct, although slightly oblique, means of progress from end to end across the interior of the monument (and passing close by the axial pit that contained the large timber upright). Such an interpretation raises the possibility not only that the

Illus 92
Aerial photograph of the 'Littleour type' structure at Fortingall. (*Crown Copyright: RCAHMS*)

cross-members of the monument were more important than the sides, but even that they could have originally been free-standing–it might be suggested that these 'façades' were similar in appearance to standing stone alignments on the same scale (eg Ballymeanoch in Mid Argyll) and may have been intended to reflect aspects of the façades of long cairns and barrows.

It is only when these details attract the observer's attention–at linear sites in general, as well as at Douglasmuir–that the focus shifts from the fact of linearity to the structural element at which that linearity is directed. The idea of progression from point to point, towards or by way of portals set in 'façades' (which may be obliquely aligned to the main axis of either the monument or the progression) has clear roots in Neolithic ritual and funerary practices, and reflects a more general concern with entrances and access points in contemporary domestic structures (cf Hodder 1990).

Littleour, as also Cleaven Dyke and some of the other monuments described here, may likewise adhere to certain general principles–of design, if not also of ideology.

7.6 THE LITTLEOUR GROOVED WARE: A CONTRIBUTION TO THE SCOTTISH PICTURE

Despite recent statements to the contrary (MacKie 1997), the distribution of Grooved Ware is no longer restricted to the far south of England and the far north of Scotland (MacSween 1995a). The discovery of the cache of Grooved Ware at Littleour (illus 93) extends the distribution in Fife/Tayside only a little to the north, from Beech Hill House (Stevenson 1995), leaving a considerable gap in the known distribution before the next, isolated, findspot to the north at Raigmore, Inverness (Simpson 1996). However, this gap may represent nothing more than the very restricted amount of archaeological excavation done in eastern Scotland; on the other hand, it may reflect real differences in social structure or ritual practice, perhaps reflecting the almost exclusive distribution of, on the one hand, Recumbent Stone Circles in north-east Scotland and, on the other, henges to the south and north-west of them. Grooved Ware, like henges, may not have developed any sort of significant role in that area (Barclay 1997a). Saville's caution (**4.6** above) in interpreting the presence of the flint in L23 as being the result a 'ritual' structured deposition, in the absence of surviving surface deposits, is understandable. However, the circumstances of the deposition of portions of Grooved Ware vessels, and unused high-quality flint in pit L23, apparently within or on the site of an earlier structure, probably of ceremonial function, seems to give us little option but to see them as confirming the very clear pattern (albeit from few excavated sites) that Grooved Ware is (in this part of Scotland) a phenomenon associated with ceremonial sites (Mercer 1981; Barclay & Russell-White 1993).

Birch charcoal from the homogenous fill of pit L23 seems likely to reflect fairly accurately the date of deposition of that material in the range 2350-2030 cal BC. The relatively near, but stylistically unrelated, material from Balfarg Riding School (Barclay and Russell-White 1993) produced a significantly earlier range of dates–from 3300-2920 cal BC (GU-1670/1904 combined) in the ditch to 3100-2550 cal BC in pit F1002 (GU-1902); on the henge at Balfarg excavated by Mercer (1981) the combined calibration of the dates from posthole A11 was 2930-2660 cal BC (GU-1161-3; using amended errors as suggested by Ashmore 1997). The Littleour date is substantially later; however, given the sparse dating evidence for Grooved Ware in southern Scotland we cannot say whether this date is anomalous. As noted above (**4.4**): 'a better way to understand Grooved Ware in north Britain is to regard it as a long-lived ceramic tradition with a basic "vocabulary" of design elements, with chronological, regional, local, and site-specific variations on a few basic themes' (MacSween 1995a). Littleour perhaps begins to provide a little of the chronological depth so far missing in the consideration of Grooved Ware in Scotland south of Orkney.

Illus 93
Grooved ware Pot *6 in situ* in pit L23 at Littleour.

The results of Long's thorough analysis of the residues on the Grooved Ware (**4.5** above) were relatively disappointing, compared to Moffat's analysis of the material from Balfarg Riding School (Moffat 1983), where pollen and seeds of black henbane were reported. It has not been possible to replicate Moffat's findings on the Balfarg Riding School material, however, (Long *et al* forthcoming) and until similar results are obtained from other Grooved Ware assemblages, it would be unwise to interpret all Grooved Ware from ceremonial sites in eastern Scotland as having a function related to the consumption of hallucinogens.

POSTSCRIPT

SITE CONSERVATION ISSUES

Gordon Barclay

The Cleaven Dyke illustrates a number of conservation problems faced in the past and in the present by earthwork monuments in woodland and in arable land.

LEGAL PROTECTION

The preservation of ancient monuments was to a great extent problematic before the implementation (in 1981) of the Ancient Monuments and Archaeological Areas Act 1979. Protection was applied under the Ancient Monuments Consolidation and Amendment Act 1913, as amended by the Ancient Monuments Act 1931, and the Historic Buildings and Ancient Monuments Act 1953 (MacIvor & Fawcett 1983).

Parts of the Cleaven Dyke were first given legal protection in 1960, under the terms of the 1953 Act. However, the limitations of pre-1979 ancient monuments legislation, and the lack (until relatively recently) of means to avert damage to ancient monuments by state-supported forestry and agricultural improvements, meant that little protection could be applied in reality. There was certainly no automatic presumption that scheduled monuments would be protected–the Dyke was therefore replanted with trees in the late 1960s.

In 1981 the Ancient Monuments and Archaeological Areas Act 1979 came into effect. This significantly strengthened the protection of scheduled monuments, introducing the requirement for the prior written consent of the Secretary of State for a range of works, including the planting of trees and other woodland operations. Additionally, in the late 1970s and 1980s an increasing body of evidence was gathered to demonstrate the damage being done to archaeological sites by forestry (Jackson 1978; Proudfoot 1989) and since 1988 important archaeological monuments have been protected through arrangements agreed between the Forestry Commission and the three state heritage agencies (Barclay 1992c). With the protection of the 1979 Act and the clearly expressed policy of the Forestry Commission, it is almost unthinkable that the Dyke could now suffer further forestry damage. In 1991 the Meikleour Estate Trust responded positively to an offer from Historic Scotland of a management agreement under the 1979 Act to arrange for the trees in an area near the middle of the Dyke to be removed. As the block adjoined a ride left for a power line, the total length now left clear was 350m. In 1996 a length of c 280m at the NW end of the Dyke was cleared; the Scots pine in the area had reached maturity. It, like the area felled earlier, was felled under a Scheduled Monument Consent issued under the terms of the 1979 Act.

TREE ROOT DAMAGE

It is widely accepted that the afforestation of archaeological features causes damage, through deep cultivation (fortunately avoided on the Dyke), the development of root systems, and the effects of windthrow (Barclay 1992c), although in the 1992 paper the effect of roots was not discussed in detail. However, it is still occasionally suggested that so-called 'shallow-rooting' species will not damage sites, the implication being that some species, including Scots pine, which until recently covered parts of the Dyke, might be acceptable as a tree crop on archaeological features.

The effect of the development and penetrative power of roots has been considered in some detail (Dobson & Moffat 1993, 15-28); although the purpose of this research was to assess the vulnerability to trees of thick polyethylene membranes sealing landfill sites, the data and their interpretation are of considerable use in discussing archaeological features.

The conclusions of the paper of relevance to archaeological conservation are as follows (with observations by GJB in italics):

1 Mature trees have 99% of their root biomass in the top metre of soil (80-90% in the top 0.6m) and the majority of roots are no deeper than 0.3m. The root mat of common trees in Britain is typically 0.5m to 1.5m deep.

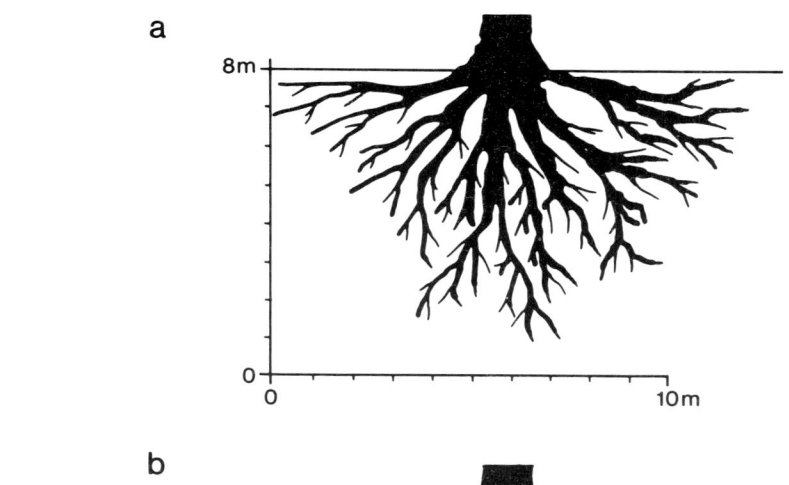

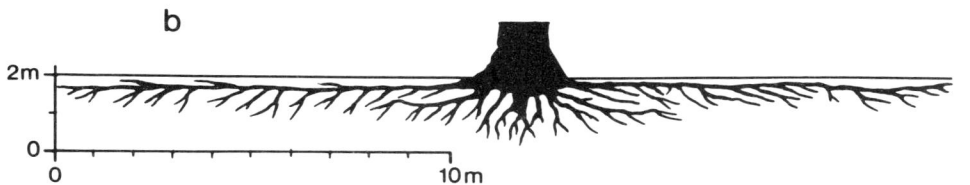

Illus 94
The 'mythical' (a) and more normal (b) distribution of tree roots. After Dobson 1995.

2   Even in waterlogged soils root systems will penetrate to c 0.4m.

It should be noted that many archaeological deposits at risk from trees lie within 0.3m of the surface. Most lie within the range 0.3m to 1m.

3   Tap roots are not the predominant root form. Illustration 94a (after Dobson 1995) shows what is described as a 'mythical' representation of a tree root system, illustration 94b showing the more normal structure. *While the normal tree root system is that shown as (b), the supposedly 'mythical' representation of a mature tree's system does appear on some archaeological sites, where growing conditions can be ideal (cf the North Mains mound (Barclay 1983)). Both major root patterns on illus 94b would cause damage to archaeological features.*

4   Although roots are small, they are numerous and exert axial and radial force. Only very compact soil layers and pans will prevent penetration: penetrative force increases exponentially as soil strength decreases. When roots hit an obstruction, they can stop moving forward and start 'spiralling' behind the tip, increasing turbation. They are deflected along the surface of impenetrable layers. *Archaeological features are often made up of or are filled with relatively loose, well-aerated soils, often lying over harder natural deposits and have less strength than these natural deposits, and observation has shown that soil-filled pits dug into subsoil are more heavily 'colonised' by roots than the surrounding subsoil with consequent loss of meaningful structure in archaeological deposits.*

Therefore, in the range of dry land archaeological sites in Scotland every mature tree regardless of species (including the main trees of regeneration in Scotland–birch and Scots pine) will normally have a root system which will penetrate sufficiently far, cover a large enough area, and have enough penetrative force to cause severe damage to buried archaeological features not protected by very dense layers of soil (eg dense re-deposited gravel).

DAMAGE BY AGRICULTURAL PLOUGHING

Although the damage caused to archaeological features in arable land has been appreciated for many years (various papers in Hinchliffe & Schadla-Hall 1980), little has been done to tackle the problem. Government rescue archaeology funding was for many years concentrated on sites threatened by commercial development, and on other, more visible and dramatic, threats (eg coastal erosion). It is clear, however, that much of the archaeology of the arable lowlands of Scotland, mainly from Inverness-shire round the east coast to the border with England, and in the south-west of the country, has been severely damaged by ploughing and other agricultural operations, and that much of the rest is being eroded, at varying rates from site to site (cf Tyler *et al* above).

Damage to sites in arable land arises from a number of processes.

1   The insertion of drains.

2   Subsoiling, undertaken to disrupt the subsoil to a greater depth than achieved during normal cultivation

to improve drainage and root penetration, by breaking up natural or man-made restricting layers (eg plough pans).

3 Erosion, leading to thinning of the topsoil layer; if this is followed by normal ploughing to the accustomed depth, it is inevitable that the plough will cut into the subsoil and any archaeological features at the same depth.

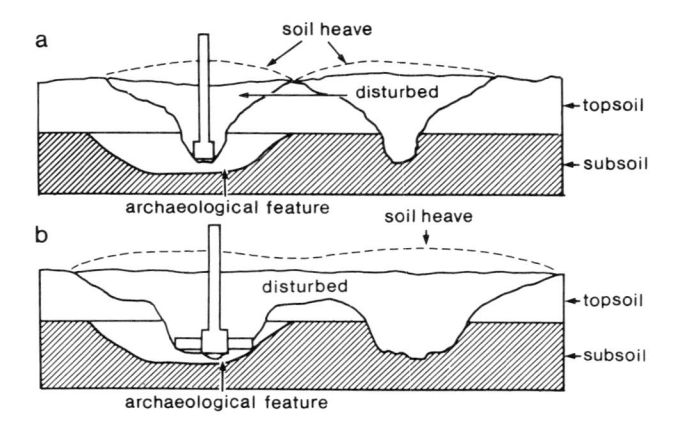

Illus 95
The effects of subsoiling using (a) a normal and (b) a winged tine subsoiler, at c 1m intervals and 0.4m depth. The topsoil is c 25cm deep. After Spoor 1980.

The effects of the use of a subsoiler and a particular type of subsoiler with 'wings' fitted to the bottom of the blade in relation to buried archaeological features are illustrated below (illus 95) (after Spoor 1980).

The area of the Cleaven Dyke ditch excavated in an arable field near the SE end of the monument produced clear evidence of the effect of repeated episodes of subsoiling prior to the scheduling of the monument. Illustration 96 shows the parallel tracks of two episodes of subsoiling - the combined effect has been to remove all coherent archaeological information in an area up to 0.25m below the subsoil surface (that is, 0.55m below the topsoil surface) and 0.5m across. These pairs of tracks were repeated at c 1.8m intervals across the site. Sites are at risk of being severely damaged by a handful of episodes of subsoiling, perhaps over a decade or two; where a site is made up of relatively shallow features subsoiling may completely remove its archaeological content.

Just as damaging in the longer term, but even more difficult to control, is the erosion of topsoil; if a farmer ploughs to the same depth every year, but the topsoil depth is reducing, it is inevitable that the plough will cut deeper and deeper into the subsoil, and into archaeological features cut into it. Soil erosion in Scotland has been exacerbated by poor soil management and autumn ploughing (cf Tyler *et al* above). Sites like Littleour may be at risk over a longer period—30 to 50 years—from unacceptable levels of erosion.

Illus 96
The side of the ditch of the Cleaven Dyke in this section in excavation area I/1 has been removed by channels cut by two parallel episodes of subsoiling. The two channels run away from the viewer, under the scale, which lies on the subsoil surface.

Although subsoiling and the deepening of ploughing are operations that specifically require consent under the Ancient Monuments and Archaeological Areas Act 1979, this provision is very difficult to police, particularly where land is let on short-term contracts. It is possible to take scheduled cropmark sites out of cultivation, although the owner or tenant of land would have a valid claim for compensation for the losses incurred. It is clear, however, that if that part of Scotland's archaeological heritage represented by the cropmarks of the lowlands is to be protected effectively, more sites will have to be withdrawn from cultivation. This could be undertaken either through the powers available under the Act, or, more positively, the schemes available from The Scottish Office to promote environmentally sensitive farming (SOAEFD 1997).

... AND FINALLY

The survey and excavation of the Cleaven Dyke has proved conclusively that it is not a Roman monument. It can now be seen to be an extraordinarily well-preserved linear monument of the early to mid Neolithic, related to the cursus monument and bank barrow traditions of the late 5th to mid/late 4th millennia cal BC. As such it takes its place as one of the foremost monuments of its kind and date in mainland Britain.

Excavation of the Littleour structure has given us a further Neolithic rectilinear structure of probably ceremonial function, and apparent confirmation of the ceremonial context of Grooved Ware in eastern Scotland. It has extended the date range of this pottery type. Equally useful, the results of the dating programme confirm the dangers of assuming that superficially simple structures have a simple building history.

The projects involved ground-breaking research into soil-loss from lowland archaeological sites, the development of contour survey methodologies to deal with the largest survey of this kind yet undertaken in Scotland, and a detailed consideration of the problems faced by geophysical survey on the fluvio-glacial gravels covering much of lowland Scotland.

The results of the detailed contour survey of the Cleaven Dyke suggest that some other major monuments might benefit from our approach. The Maiden Castle bank barrow and the Stonehenge cursus (both of which appear from field inspection to have a segmented character, and both of which suffer from publication of their surveys at too small a scale) perhaps deserve more detailed survey of the kind undertaken on the Dyke, to bring out its subtleties, and it may be that a contour plan (Burgess **5.1**,

Illus 97
The bank of the Cleaven Dyke, shrouded in trees. (*Crown Copyright: Historic Scotland*)

above) would be more productive of information. In the case of the Stonehenge cursus, the monument is being actively eroded by cattle and the information that could be recovered using a microtopographical survey is being degraded. Likewise, while the larger scale irregularities of the enormously elongated Dorset cursus (which is visible largely as a cropmark) have been noted, lesser irregularities, hinted at in small-scale published plans, have been relatively neglected. Detailed cropmark plotting might reveal more details of the sequence of construction of that monument.

We would not suggest for a moment that all linear monuments were built in the way we have suggested for the Cleaven Dyke, but perhaps more were than we have so far realised. It might also be suggested that more detailed recording and interpretation of linear monuments could reveal information of equally complex, if not comparable, sequences or patterns in construction.

FUTURE WORK

The investigation of the Cleaven Dyke and its surroundings could keep the two main authors and any number of collaborators busy for many more years. However, we both feel that to spend the rest of our active fieldworking years teasing out more detail on the constructional sequence of the Dyke would be relatively unproductive. One of us was asked how we could possibly abandon the Dyke before we had answered every question we felt we could answer, and how we dared to publish without clearing up all areas of doubt that were in reach of 'just a few more seasons of work'. The answer is two-fold: first, the Dyke is a scheduled monument, and we should not lightly destroy further portions in one episode of investigation; Second, is the cliché 'one can obtain 80% of the information for 20% of the effort'; in this case we could claim perhaps to have got 40% of the information for 5% of the work, a fair return? Scottish archaeology has perhaps seen too much detailed (perhaps even obsessive) dissection of a small number of sites, while the broad picture remains even to be sketched in for much of the country (Barclay 1997b). Let what we have done suffice; other generations can have the challenge of proving us wrong.

What is needed now is further investigation of the rich landscapes of lowland Scotland. The story told in this volume concerned the recovery of a previously lost Neolithic landscape which has been hidden, not so much physically, as through lack of recognition. Much work remains to be done.

'Scotland should be able to afford data for the solution of several most fascinating problems in British...prehistory'
Childe *The Prehistory of Scotland* (1935)

REFERENCES

Abercromby, J, Ross, T & Anderson, J 1902 'Account of the excavation of the Roman station at Inchtuthil, Perthshire, undertaken by the Society of Antiquaries of Scotland in 1901', *Proc Soc Antiq Scot*, 36 (1901-2), 182-242.

Adamson, H 1979 'Cleaven Dyke [Interim Report]', *in* DJ Breeze (ed) *Roman Scotland: Some Recent Excavations*, 45. Edinburgh: Inspectorate of Ancient Monuments.

Adamson, HC & Gallagher, DB 1986 'Excavations at the Cleaven Dyke, Perthshire, 1975', *Glasgow Archaeol J*, 13 (1986), 63-8.

Aitken, MJ 1972 Physics and Archaeology. Oxford.

Armit, I 1996 'Carmichael Cottages', *Discovery Excav Scot* 1995 (1996), 97.

Armit, I, Cowie, T & Ralston, I 1994 'Excavation of pits containing Grooved Ware at Hillend, Clydesdale District, Strathclyde Region', *Proc Soc Antiq Scot*, 124 (1994), 113-27.

Ashbee, P 1970 *The Earthen Long Barrow in Britain*. London: Dent.

Ashmore, PJ 1996 *Neolithic and Bronze Age Scotland*. London: Batsford.

Ashmore, PJ 1997 *Radiocarbon Dates for Archaeological Sites in Scotland*. Edinburgh: Historic Scotland.

Atkinson, RJC 1955 'The Dorset cursus', *Antiquity* 29, 4-9.

Atkinson, RJC 1965 'Wayland's Smithy', *Antiquity* 39, 126-33.

Barber, J 1997 *The Archaeological Investigation of a Prehistoric Landscape: Excavations on Arran 1978-1981*. Edinburgh: Scottish Trust for Archaeological Research.

Barclay, GJ 1982 'The excavation of two crop-marks at Huntingtower, Perthshire', *Proc Soc Antiq Scot*, 112 (1982), 580-3.

Barclay, GJ 1983 'Sites of the third millennium bc to the first millennium ad at North Mains, Strathallan, Perthshire', *Proc Soc Antiq Scot*, 113 (1983), 122-281.

Barclay, GJ 1992a 'Sair Law', *Discovery Excav Scot 1991* (1992), 73.

Barclay, GJ 1992b 'The Scottish gravels: a neglected resource?', *in* M Fulford & E Nichols (eds) *Developing Landscapes of Lowland Britain. The Archaeology of the British Gravels: A Review*, 106-24. London: Society of Antiquaries of London.

Barclay, GJ 1992c 'Forestry and archaeology in Scotland', *Scottish Forestry*, 46 (1992a), 27-47.

Barclay, GJ 1995 'Discussion', *in* J Kendrick 1995, 36-9.

Barclay, GJ 1996 'Neolithic buildings in Scotland', *in* T Darvill & J Thomas (eds) *Neolithic Houses in Northwest Europe and Beyond*, 61-75. Oxford: Oxbow. (= *Neolithic Stud Grp Seminar Pap*, 2)

Barclay, GJ 1997a 'The Neolithic', *in* KJ Edwards & IBM Ralston (eds) *Scotland: Environment and Archaeology, 8000 BC - AD 1000*, 127-49. Chichester: Wiley.

Barclay, GJ 1997b *State-funded Rescue Archaeology in Scotland: Past, Present and Future*. Edinburgh: Historic Scotland. (= *Ancient Monuments Division Occas Pap*, 2)

Barclay, GJ & Maxwell, GS 1991 'Excavation of a long mortuary enclosure within the Roman legionary fortress at Inchtuthil, Perthshire', *Proc Soc Antiq Scot*, 121 (1991), 27-44.

Barclay, GJ & Maxwell, GS 1993 *The Cleaven Dyke Project 1993: Interim Report*. Privately circulated paper.

Barclay, GJ & Maxwell, GS 1995 *The Cleaven Dyke Project 1995: Interim Report*. Privately circulated paper.

Barclay, GJ & Maxwell, GS 1996 *The Cleaven Dyke Project: Interim Report on the Excavations at Littleour 1996*. Privately circulated paper.

Barclay, GJ & Maxwell, GS forthcoming 'The Cleaven Dyke: survey and excavation 1993-1996: a summary account', *in* A Barclay & J Harding (eds) *Pathways and Ceremonies: the cursus monuments of Britain and Ireland*. Oxford: Oxbow.

Barclay, GJ & Russell-White, CJ (eds) 1993 'Excavations in the ceremonial complex of the fourth to second millennium BC at Balfarg/Balbirnie, Glenrothes, Fife', *Proc Soc Antiq Scot*, 123 (1993), 43-210.

Barclay, GJ, Maxwell, GS, Simpson, IA & Davidson, DA 1995 'The Cleaven Dyke: a Neolithic cursus monument/bank barrow in Scotland', *Antiquity*, 69 (1995), 317-26.

Barnatt, J 1996 'Moving beyond the monuments: paths and people in the Neolithic landscape of the Peak District', *in* P Frodsham (ed) *Neolithic Studies in No-man's Land* (=*Northern Archaeol* 13/14) 1996, 43-59.

Barrett, JC 1988 'The living, the dead and the ancestors: Neolithic and Early Bronze Age mortuary practices', *in* JC Barrett & IA Kinnes (eds) *The Archaeology of Context in the Neolithic and Bronze Age: Recent Trends*, 30-41. Sheffield: Univ Sheffield, Dept Archaeol.

Barrett, JC 1994 *Fragments from Antiquity*. Oxford: Blackwell.

Barrett, JC, Bradley, R & Green, M 1991 *Landscape, Monuments and Society: the Prehistory of Cranbourne Chase*. Cambridge: Univ Press.

Bender, B 1992 'Theorising landscape and the Prehistoric landscape of Stonehenge', *MAN* 27, 735-55.

Bennett, KD 1994 *Annotated Catalogue of Pollen and Pteridophyte Spore Types of the British Isles*. Cambridge: Dept Plant Sci, Univ Cambridge.

Bertok, G 1997 *Antonine Fortlet System in South West Scotland*. Unpub M Phil Dissertation.

Billcliffe, R 1987 *James McIntosh Patrick*. London: The Fine Art Society.

Birks, HJB 1989 'Holocene isochrone maps and patterns of tree-spreading in the British Isles', *J Biogeography*, 16 (1989), 503-40.

Bohncke, S 1983 'The pollen analysis of deposits in a food vessel from the henge monument at North Mains', *in* Barclay 1983, 113 (1983), 39-47.

Bradley, R 1983 'The bank barrows and related monuments of Dorset in the light of recent fieldwork', *Dorset Nat Hist Archaeol Soc Proc*, 105 (1983), 15-20.

Bradley, R 1984 *The Social Foundations of Prehistoric Britain*. Harlow: Longman.

Bradley, R 1986 *The Dorset Cursus: the Archaeology of the Enigmatic*. Salisbury: Counc Brit Archaeol.

Bradley, R 1991 'The evidence of the earthworks', *in* J Barrett, R Bradley & M Green (eds) *Landscape, Monuments and Society: the Prehistory of Cranborne Chase*, 35-58. Cambridge: Univ Press.

Bradley, R 1993 *Altering the Earth: the Origins of Monuments in Britain and Continental Europe*. Edinburgh: Soc Antiq Scot. (= *Soc Antiq Scot Monogr Ser*, 8)

Bradley, R 1994 *Strath Tay Field Survey, 1994. Interim report*. Privately circulated paper.

Bradley, RJ & Chambers, R 1988 'A new study of the cursus complex at Dorchester on Thames', *Oxford J Archaeol*, 7 (1988), 271-89.

Brodie, J 1796 'Parish of Kinloch', *The Statistical Account of Scotland*, vol 17, 469. Edinburgh.

Brophy, K 1995 *The landscape archaeology of Scotland's cursus monuments*. Unpubl BSc thesis, Univ Glasgow.

Brophy, K 1998 'Milton of Rattray', *Discovery Excav Scot 1997* (1998), 65.

Brophy, K forthcoming 'The cursus monuments of Scotland', *in* A Barclay & J Harding (eds) *Pathways and Ceremonies: the Cursus Monuments of Britain and Ireland*. Oxford: Oxbow.

Buckley, D 1988 'Springfield', *Current Archaeol*, 10, 6-11.

Bullock, P, Federoff, N, Jongerius, A, Stoops, G, Tursina, T & Babel, U 1985 *Handbook for Soil Thin Section Description*. Wolverhampton: Waine Research Publications.

Burgess, C & Henderson, J 1996 'Close contour survey of submerged sites using datalogging software with particular reference to Scottish crannogs', *Int J Nautical Archaeol*, 25 (1996).

Burl, A 1984 'Report on the excavation of a Neolithic mound at Boghead, Speymouth Forest, Fochabers, Moray, 1972 and 1974', *Proc Soc Antiq Scot*, 114 (1984), 35-73.

Burl, A 1993 *From Carnac to Callanish: the Prehistoric Stone Rows and Avenues of Britain, Ireland and Brittany*. London: Yale Univ Press.

Callander, JG 1928 'A collection of stone and flint implements from Airhouse, parish of Channelkirk, Berwickshire', *Proc Soc Antiq Scot*, 62 (1927-28), 166-80.

Callander, JG 1929 'Scottish Neolithic pottery', *Proc Soc Antiq Scot*, 63 (1929), 29-98.

Case, HJ 1982 'The linear ditches and southern enclosure, North Stoke', *in* HJ Case & AWR Whittle (eds) *Settlement Patterns in the Oxford Region: Excavation at the Abingdon Causewayed Enclosure and Other Sites*, 60-75. London: Counc Brit Archaeol.

Caseldine, CJ 1980 *Aspects of the Vegetation History of South-east Perthshire*. Unpubl PhD thesis, Univ St Andrews.

Childe, VG 1930 'Excavations in a chambered cairn at Kindrochat, near Comrie, Perthshire', *Proc Soc Antiq Scot*, 64 (1929-30), 264-72.

Childe, VG 1946 *Scotland Before the Scots*. London: Methuen.

Christie, PM 1963 'The Stonehenge cursus', *Wilts Archaeol Natur Hist Mag*, 58 (1963), 370-82.

Clark, AJ 1990 *Seeing Beneath the Soil: Prospecting Methods in Archaeology*. London: Batsford.

Clark, JGD 1932 'The date of the plano-convex flint knife in England and Wales', *Antiq J*, 12 (1932), 158-62.

Clark, RL 1982 'Point count estimation of charcoal in pollen preparations and thin sections of sediments', *Pollen et Spores*, 24 (1982), 523-35.

Coles, JM & Simpson, DDA 1965 'The excavation of a Neolithic round barrow at Pitnacree, Perthshire, Scotland', *Proc Prehist Soc*, 31 (1965), 34-57.

Collingwood, RG & Richmond, IA 1969 *The Archaeology of Roman Britain*. London: Methuen.
Cormack, WF 1963 'Prehistoric site at Beckton, Lockerbie', *Trans Dumfries Galloway Nat Hist Antiq Soc*, 41 (1963), 111-15.
Courty, MA, Goldberg, P & Macphail, RI 1989 *Soils and Micromorphology in Archaeology*. Cambridge: Univ Press.
Coutts, H 1970 *Ancient Monuments of Tayside*. Dundee: Dundee Mus Art Gallery.
Coutts, H 1971 *Tayside Before History*. Dundee: Dundee Mus Art Gallery.
Cowie, TG 1993 'A survey of the Neolithic pottery of eastern and central Scotland', *Proc Soc Antiq Scot*, 123 (1993), 13-41.
Crawford, OGS 1938 'Bank barrows', *Antiquity*, 12 (1938), 228-32.
Crawford, OGS 1949 *Topography of Roman Scotland North of the Antonine Wall*. Cambridge: Univ Press.
Cushing, AJ 1967 'Evidence for differential pollen preservation in Quaternary sediments in Minnesota', *Rev Palaeobot Palynology*, 4 (1967), 87-101.
Dalland, M 1997 'Maryton Law', *Discovery Excav Scot 1996*, (1997), 13.
Darvill, T 1996 'Neolithic buildings in England, Wales and the Isle of Man', *in* T Darvill & J Thomas (eds) *Neolithic Houses in Northwest Europe and Beyond*, 77-111. Oxford: Oxbow. (= *Neolithic Stud Grp Seminar Pap*, 1)
Darvill, T & Thomas, J 1996 *Neolithic Houses in Northwest Europe and Beyond*. Oxford: Oxbow. (= *Neolithic Stud Grp Seminar Pap*, 1)
Darwin, T 1996 *The Scots Herbal: the Plant Lore of Scotland*. Glasgow: Mercat Press.
Davidson, DA & Harrison, DJ 1995 'Water erosion on arable land in Scotland: results of an erosion survey', *Soil Use and Management*, 11 (1995), 63-8.
Davidson, JL & Henshall, AS 1983 'A Neolithic chambered long cairn at Edinchip, Perthshire', *Proc Soc Antiq Scot*, 113 (1983), 35-9.
Davidson, JL & Henshall, AS 1991 *The Chambered Cairns of Caithness*. Edinburgh: Univ Press.
Dickson, JH 1978 'Bronze Age mead', *Antiquity*, 52 (1978), 108-13.
Dimbleby, GW 1962 *The Development of British Heathland and their Soils*. Oxford. (= *Oxford Forestry Memoir*, 23.)
Dixon, P 1988 'The Neolithic settlements on Crickley Hill' *in* C Burgess, P Topping, C Mordant & Maddison M (eds), *Enclosures and defences in the Neolithic of Western Europe*, 75-87. Oxford: Brit Arch Rep. (= *Brit Arch Rep Int Ser*, 403)
Dobson, MC 1995 *Tree Root Systems*. Alice Holt: Arboricultural Advisory and Information Service.
Dobson, MC & Moffat, AJ 1993 *The Potential for Woodland Establishment on Landfill Sites*. London: HMSO.
Dockrill, S & Gater, J 1992 'Tofts Ness: exploration and interpretation in a prehistoric landscape', *in* P Spoerry (ed) *Geoprospection in the Archaeological Landscape*, 25-31. Oxford: Oxbow.
Douchafour, P 1982 *Pedology: Pedogenesis and Classification*. London: George Allen & Unwin.
Edmonds, M, Sheridan, A & Tipping, R 1992 'Survey and excavation at Creag na Caillich, Killin, Perthshire', *Proc Soc Antiq Scot*, 122 (1992), 77-112.
Edwards, KJ 1979 'Palynological and temporal inference in the context of prehistory, with special reference to the evidence from lake and peat deposits', *J Archaeol Sci*, 6 (1979), 255-70.
Edwards, KJ 1993 'Models of mid-Holocene forest farming for north-west Europe', *in* FM Chambers (ed) *Climate Change and Human Impact on the Landscape*, 133-45. London: Chapman & Hall.
Edwards, KJ 1996 'A Mesolithic of the Western and Northern Isles of Scotland? evidence from pollen and charcoal', *in* T Pollard & A Morrison (eds) *The Early Prehistory of Scotland*, 23-38. Glasgow: Univ Glasgow.
Edwards, KJ & Hirons, KR 1984 'Cereal pollen grains in pre-elm decline deposits: implications for the earliest agriculture in Britain and Ireland', *J Archaeol Sci*, 11 (1984), 71-80.
Edwards, KJ & Rowntree, KM 1980 'Radiocarbon and palaeoenvironmental evidence for changing rates of erosion at a Flandrian stage site in Scotland', *in* RA Cullingford, DA Davidson & J Lewin (eds) *Timescales in Geomorphology*, 207-23. Chichester: J Wiley & Sons.
Edwards, KJ & Whittington, G 1990 'Palynological evidence for the growing of Cannabis sativa L. (hemp) in medieval and historical Scotland', *Trans Inst Brit Geogr*, NS 15 (1990), 60-9.
Edwards, KJ & Whittington, G 1997 'Vegetation history', *in* KJ Edwards & IBM Ralston (eds) *Scotland: Environment and archaeology, 8000BC-AD1000*, 63-82. Chichester: J Wiley & Sons.
Evans, R 1981 'Potential soil and crop losses by erosion', *in Proceedings SAWMA Conference in Soil and Crop Loss: Developments in Erosion*. Stone Leigh: National Agricultural Centre.
Faegri, K & Iversen, J 1989 *Textbook of Pollen Analysis*. Chichester: J Wiley & Sons.
Fairweather, AD & Ralston, IBM 1993 'The Neolithic timber hall at Balbridie, Grampian Region, Scotland: the building, the date, the plant macrofossils', *Antiquity*, 67 (1993), 313-23.
Finlayson, B 1989 *A Pragmatic Approach to the Functional Analysis of Chipped Stone Tools*. Unpubl PhD thesis, Univ Edinburgh.

FitzPatrick, EA 1993 *Soil Microscopy and Micromorphology*. Chichester: Wiley.

Frost, CA & Speirs, RB 1996 'Soil erosion from a single rainstorm over an area in East Lothian, Scotland', *Soil Use and Management*, 12 (1996), 8-12.

Gibson, A 1994 'Excavations at the Sarn-y-bryn-Caled cursus complex, Welshpool, Powys, and the timber circles of Great Britain and Ireland', *Proc Prehist Soc*, 60 (1994), 143-223.

Girling, MA & Greig, J 1985 'A first fossil record for *Scolytus scolytus* (F.) (elm bark beetle): its occurrence in elm decline deposits from London and the implications for Neolithic elm disease', *J Archaeol Sci*, 12 (1985), 347-51.

Göransson, H 1986 'Man and the forests of nemoral broad-leaved trees during the Stone Age', *Striae*, 24 (1986), 145-52.

Green, HS 1984 'Flint arrowheads: typology and interpretation', *Lithics*, 5 (1984), 19-39.

Grieve, IC, Davidson, DA & Gordon, JE 1995 'Nature, extent and severity of soil erosion in upland Scotland', *Land Degradation and Rehabilitation*, 6 (1995), 41-55.

Grimm, EC 1991 *TILIA and TILIA•GRAPH*. Springfield: Illinois State Mus.

Grogan, E 1996 'Neolithic houses in Ireland', *in* T Darvill & J Thomas (eds) *Neolithic Houses in Northwest Europe and Beyond*, 41-60. Oxford: Oxbow. (=*Neolithic Stud Grp Seminar Pap*, 1)

Haldane, ARB 1973 *The Drove Roads of Scotland*. Newton Abbot: David & Charles.

Hanson, WS 1984 *Monktonhall, Inveresk [interim report]*. Glasgow: Univ Glasgow.

Hanson, WS & Macinnes, L 1991 'The archaeology of the Scottish Lowlands: problems and potential', *in* WS Hanson & EA Slater (eds) *Scottish Archaeology: New Perceptions*, 153-66. Aberdeen: Univ Press.

Harding, J 1995 *'Pathways to new realms: cursus monuments and symbolic territories'*. Unpublished paper delivered to Theoretical Archaeology Group conference, Reading, December 1995.

Havinga, AJ 1984 'A 20-year experimental investigation into the differential spore corrosion susceptibility of pollen spores in various soil types', *Pollen et Spores*, 26 (1984), 541-58.

Hayes, R 1967 *The Chambered Cairn and Adjacent Monuments at Great Ayton Moor, North-east Yorkshire*. Scarborough: Scarborough & District Archaeol Soc.

Hedges, J & Buckley, D 1981 *The Springfield Cursus and the Cursus Problem*. Chelmsford: Essex County Counc.

Henshall, AS 1963 *The Chambered Tombs of Scotland, vol 1*. Edinburgh: Univ Press.

Henshall, AS 1972 *The Chambered Tombs of Scotland, vol 2*. Edinburgh: Univ Press.

Henshall, AS 1993 'The Grooved Ware', *in* Barclay and Russell-White (eds), 1993, 94-108.

Henshall, AS & Mercer, RJ 1981 'Report on the pottery from Balfarg, Fife', *in* Mercer 1981, 128-39.

Henshall, AS & Stewart, MEC 1956 'Excavations at Clach na Tiompan, Wester Glen Almond, Perthshire', *Proc Soc Antiq Scot*, 88 (1956), 112-24.

Hinchliffe, J & Schadla-Hall, RT 1980 *The Past under the Plough*. London: Dept Environment.

Hodder, I 1989 'Writing archaeology: site reports in context', *Antiquity*, 63 (1989), 268-74.

Hodder, I 1990 *The Domestication of Europe*. Oxford: Blackwell.

Hogg, D 1993 'Analysis of the timber structures', *in* GJ Barclay & Russell-White (eds), 1993, 169-75.

Houlder, C 1968 'The henge monuments at Llandegai', *Antiquity*, 42 (1968), 216-21.

Hulme, PD & Shirriffs, J 1985 'Pollen analysis of a radiocarbon-dated core from North Mains, Strathallan, Perthshire', *Proc Soc Antiq Scot*, 115 (1985), 105-13.

Huntley, B & Birks, HJB 1983 *An Atlas of Past and Present Pollen Maps for Europe: 0-13000 years ago*. Cambridge: Univ Press.

Jackson, A 1978 *Forestry and Archaeology: a Study in the Survival of Field Monuments in SW Scotland*. Hertford: Rescue.

Jenny, H 1980 *The Soil Resource: Origin and Behaviour*. New York: Springer.

Kachanoski, RG 1987 'Comparison of measured soil ^{137}Cs losses and erosion rates', *Can J Soil Sci*, 67 (1987), 199-203.

Kachanoski, RG 1993 'Estimating soil loss from the changes in soil Caesium-137', *Can J Soil Sci*, 73 (1993), 629-32.

Kearey, P & Brooks, M 1984 *Introduction to Geophysical Exploration*. Oxford: Blackwell.

Keith-Lucas, M 1986 'Vegetation development and human impact', *in* A Whittle, M Keith-Lucas, A Milles, B Noddle, S Rees & JCC Romans (eds) *Scord of Brouster: an Early Agricultural Settlement on Shetland. Excavations 1977-1979*, 92-118. Oxford: Oxford Univ Comm Archaeol. (= *Oxford Univ Comm Archaeol Monogr*, 9)

Kendrick, J 1995 'Excavation of a Neolithic enclosure and an Iron Age settlement at Douglasmuir, Angus', *Proc Soc Antiq Scot*, 125 (1995), 29-67.

Keppie, LJF 1986 *Scotland's Roman Remains*. Edinburgh: John Donald.

King, M D 1993 'Blairhall–cursus, ring-ditches', *Discovery Excav Scot 1992* (1993), 79-80.

Kinnes, I 1979 *Round Barrows and Ring-ditches in the British Neolithic*. London: Brit Mus. (= *Brit Mus Occas Pap*, 7)

Kinnes, I 1985 'Circumstance not context: the Neolithic of Scotland as seen from the outside', *Proc Soc Antiq Scot*, 115 (1985), 15-57.

Kinnes, IA 1992a 'Balnagowan and after: the context of non-megalithic mortuary sites in Scotland', *in* N Sharples & A Sheridan (eds) *Vessels for the Ancestors*, 83-103. Edinburgh: Edinburgh University Press.

Kinnes, I 1992b *Non-Megalithic Long Barrows and Allied Structures in the British Neolithic*. London: British Museum.
Kirk, T 1997 'Towards a phenomenology of building: the Neolithic long mound at La Commune-Seche, Colombieres-sur-Seulles, Normandy', *in* G Nash (ed) *Semiotics of Landscape: Archaeology of Mind*, 59-70. Oxford: Brit Archaeol Rep. (=*Brit Archaeol Rep*, Int Ser 661.)
Kirkbride, MP & Reeves, AD 1993 'Soil erosion caused by low-intensity rainfall in Angus, Scotland', *Applied Geogr*, 13 (1993), 299-311.
Knox, J 1831 *The Topography of the Basin of the Tay*. Edinburgh: John Anderson.
Long, D, Holden, TG, Milburn, P, Bunting, MJ & Tipping, R forthcoming 'Black henbane (*Hyoscamus niger L.*) in the Scottish Neolithic: a re-evaluation of palynological findings from Grooved Ware pottery at Balfarg Riding School and Henge, Fife', *J Archaeol Sci*.
Longworth, IH 1967 'Further discoveries at Brackmont Mill, Brackmont Farm and Tentsmuir, Fife', *Proc Soc Antiq Scot*, 99 (1967), 60-92.
Longworth, IH 1971 'The Neolithic pottery', *in* GJ Wainwright & IH Longworth (eds) *Durrington Walls: Excavations 1966-1968*, 48-155. London: Soc Antiq London.
Loveday, R 1985 *Cursuses and related monuments of the British Neolithic*. Unpubl Ph.D. thesis, Univ Leicester.
Loveday, R 1989 'The Barford ritual complex: further excavations (1972) and a regional perspective', *in* A Gibson (ed) *Midlands Prehistory: Some Recent and Current Researches into the Prehistory of Central England*, 51-84. Oxford: Brit Archaeol Rep. (=*Brit Archaeol Rep Brit Ser*, 204)
Loveday, R forthcoming 'Dorchester-upon-Thames–Ritual complex or ritual landscape?' *in* A Barclay & J Harding (eds). Oxford: Oxbow.
Loveday, R & Petchey, M 1982 'Oblong ditches: a discussion and some new evidence', *Aerial Archaeol*, 8 (1982), 17-24.
Lye, D 1977 'Nethermuir of Pittendreich: flints', *Discovery Excav Scot 1976*, (1977), 43.
Lye, D 1983 'Nethermuir of Pittendreich: flints', *Discovery Excav Scot 1982*, (1983), 33.
Lye, D 1984 'Nethermuir of Pittendreich: flints', *Discovery Excav Scot 1983*, (1984), 37.
MacIvor, I & Fawcett, R 1983 'Planks from the shipwreck of time: an account of ancient monumentry, then and now', *in* M Magnusson (ed) *Echoes in Stone*, 9-27. Edinburgh: Scott Devel Dept.
MacKie, E 1997 'Maeshowe and the winter solstice: ceremonial aspects of the Orkney Grooved Ware culture', *Antiquity*, 71 (1997), 338-59.
Macphail, RI, Romans, JCC & Robertson, L 1987 'The application of micromorphology to the understanding of Holocene soil development in the British Isles; with special reference to early cultivation', *in* N Federoff, LM Bresson & M A Courty (eds) *Soil Micromorphology*, 647-56. Plaiser: AFES.
MacSween, A 1992 'Orcadian Grooved Ware', *in* N Sharples & A Sheridan (eds) *Vessels for the Ancestors*, 259-71. Edinburgh: Univ Press.
MacSween, A 1995a 'Grooved Ware from Scotland: aspects of decoration', *in* I Kinnes & G Varndell (eds) '*Unbaked Urns of Rudely Shape*': *Essays on British and Irish Pottery for Ian Longworth*, 41-8. Oxford: Oxbow.
MacSween, A 1995b 'Pottery, bronze and bone artefacts', *in* Stevenson 1995, 209-19.
Manby, TG 1974 *Grooved Ware Sites in Yorkshire and the North of England*. Oxford: Brit Archaeol Rep. (=*Brit Archaeol Rep Brit Ser*, 9)
Marshall, T 1776 'Of certain antiquities in the neighbourhood of Perth', *in* Pennant, T, *A Tour in Scotland 1772*, 451-3.
Marshall, JN 1915 'Preliminary note on some excavations at Dunagoil fort and cave', *Trans Buteshire Natur Hist Soc*, 8 (1914-15), 42-9.
Maxwell, GS 1979 'Air photography and the work of the Royal Commission on the Ancient and Historical Monuments of Scotland', *Aerial Archaeol*, 2 (1979), 37-43.
Maxwell, GS 1983a 'Air photographs 1982: Strathmore', *Popular Archaeol*, (July) (1983a), 33-4.
Maxwell, GS 1983b 'Recent aerial survey in Scotland', *in* GS Maxwell (ed) *The Impact of Aerial Reconnaissance on Archaeology*, 27-40. London: Counc Brit Archaeol.
McOmie, J (1784): *Plan of the Roman Wall and Camp near Mickleour*. MS copy in Perth Museum.
Mercer, RJ 1981 'The excavation of a late Neolithic henge-type enclosure at Balfarg, Markinch, Fife, Scotland', *Proc Soc Antiq Scot*, 111 (1981), 63-171.
Mercer, RJ 1992 'Cumulative cairn construction and cultural continuity in Caithness and Orkney', *in* N Sharples & A Sheridan (eds) *Vessels for the Ancestors*, 49-61. Edinburgh: Univ Press.
Moffat, B 1993 'An assessment of the residues on the Grooved Ware', *in* Barclay & Russell-White (eds) 1993, 108-110.
Moore, PD, Webb, JA & Collinson, ME 1991 *An Illustrated Guide to Pollen Analysis*. Oxford: Blackwell.
Murphy, CP 1986 *Thin Section Preparation of Soils and Sediments*. Berkhampstead: AB Academic.
Pennant, T 1776 *A Tour in Scotland 1772*. London.

Peterson, R & Proudfoot, E 1997 'Fordhouse Barrow', *Discovery Excav Scot 1996*, (1997), 12.

Piggott, S 1962 *The West Kennett Long Barrow Excavations 1955-6*. London: HMSO.

Piggott, S 1971 'Excavation of the Dalladies long barrow, Fettercairn, Kincardineshire', *Proc Soc Antiq Scot*, 104 (1971), 23-47.

Piggott, S & Simpson, DDA 1971 'Excavation of a stone circle at Croft Moraig, Perthshire, Scotland', *Proc Prehist Soc*, 37 (1971), 1-15.

Pitts, LF & St Joseph, JK 1985 *Inchtuthil: the Roman Legionary Fortress excavations 1962-65*. London: Soc Promotion Roman Stud.

Pollard, A in press 'Excavation of a Neolithic settlement and ritual complex at Beckton Farm, Lockerbie', *Proc Soc Antiq Scot*, 127 (in press).

Pollock, D 1985 'The Lunan Valley Project: medieval rural settlement in Angus', *Proc Soc Antiq Scot*, 115 (1985), 357-99.

Proudfoot, E 1989 *Our Vanishing Heritage: Archaeology and Forestry*. Edinburgh: Counc Scott Archaeol.

Pryor, F 1985 'Aspects of the archaeology in the Lower Welland region', *in* F Pryor (ed) *Archaeology and Environment in the Lower Welland Valley*, 299-310. Cambridge: Cambridge Archaeol Comm.

Quine, TA 1995 'Estimation of erosion rates from Caesium-137 data: the calibration question', *in* IDL Forster, AM Gurnell & BW Webb (eds) *Sediment and Water Quality in River Catchments*, 307-29. Chichester: J Wiley & Sons.

Rackham, O 1990 *Trees and Woodland in the British Isles*. London: Dent.

RCAHMS 1990 *North-east Perth: an archaeological landscape*. Edinburgh: HMSO.

RCAHMS 1994a *South-east Perth: an archaeological landscape*. Edinburgh: HMSO.

RCAHMS 1994b *Braes of Doune: an archaeological survey*. Edinburgh: RCAHMS.

RCAHMS 1997 *Eastern Dumfriesshire: an archaeological landscape*. Edinburgh: The Stationery Office.

Reaney, D 1966 'A Beaker burial at Aston-upon-Trent', *Derbyshire Archaeol J* 86, 103.

Reid, A 1985 'Nethermuir of Pittendreich: flints', *Discovery Excav Scot 1984*, (1985), 40.

Relph, E 1976 *Place and Placelessness*. London: Pion.

Richards, C 1994 'Barnhouse, Stenness, Orkney', *Archaeometry*, 36(2) (1994), 355.

Richards, C 1996 'Henges and water: towards an elemental understanding of monumentality and landscape in late Neolithic Britain', *J Material Culture* 1/3 (1996), 313-36.

Richmond, IA 1940 'Excavations on the estate of Meikleour, Perthshire, 1939', *Proc Soc Antiq Scot*, 74 (1940), 37-48.

Romans, JCC & Robertson, L 1975 'Soils and archaeology in Scotland', *in* JG Evans, S Limbrey & H Cleere (eds) *The Effect of Man on the Landscape: the Highland Zone*, 37-9. London: Counc Brit Archaeol.

Romans, JCC & Robertson, L 1983 'The environment of North Britain: soils', *in* JC Chapman & HC Mytum (eds.) *Settlement in North Britain 1000BC - AD 1000* 55-79. Oxford: Brit Archaeol Rep. (=*Brit Archaeol Rep*, 118.)

Romans, JCC, Durno, SE & and Robertson, L 1973 'A fossil brown forest soil from Angus', *J Soil Sci* 24, 125-8.

Ruggles, CLN forthcoming a *Astronomy in Prehistoric Britain and Ireland*. New Haven and London: Yale Univ Press.

Ruggles, CLN forthcoming b 'Astronomical alignments and cursus monuments' *in* A Barclay & J Harding (eds) *Pathways and Ceremonies: the Cursus Monuments of Britain and Ireland*. Oxford: Oxbow.

Ruggles, CLN & Burl, HAW 1985 'A new study of the Aberdeenshire Recumbent Stone Circle, 2: Interpretation', *Archaeoastronomy*, 8 (=suppl *J Hist Astron*, 16) (1985), S25-60.

St Joseph, JKS 1976 'Air reconnaissance, recent results', *Antiquity* 50 (1976), 55-7.

Saville, A 1994 'Exploitation of lithic resources for stone tools in earlier prehistoric Scotland', *in* N Ashton & A David (eds) *Stories in Stone*, 57-70. London: Lithic Stud Soc. (=*Lithic Stud Occas Pap*, 4)

Scollar, I, Tabbagh, A, Hesse, A & Herzog, I 1990 *Archaeological Prospecting and Remote Sensing*. Cambridge: Univ Press.

Scott, JG 1992 'Mortuary structures and megaliths', *in* N Sharples & A Sheridan (eds) *Vessels for the Ancestors*, 104-19. Edinburgh: Univ Press.

Sharpe, L 1996 *The Cleaven Dyke Project: an Aerial Photographic and Geophysical investigation*. Unpubl MPhil thesis, University of Glasgow.

Sharples, N 1991 *Maiden Castle: Excavation and Field Survey 1985-6*. London: Historic Buildings Monuments Commission England.

Sherriff, J 1982 'Bonnyton Farm: flints', *Discovery Excav Scot 1981*, (1982), 46.

Simmons, IG 1996 *The Environmental Impact of Later Mesolithic Cultures*. Edinburgh: Univ Press.

Simpson, DDA 1996 'Excavation of a kerbed funerary monument at Stoneyfield, Raigmore, Highland, 1972-3', *Proc Soc Antiq Scot*, 126 (1996), 53-86.

Simpson, DDA & Coles, JM 1990 'Excavations at Grandtully, Perthshire', *Proc Soc Antiq Scot*, 120 (1990), 33-44.

Skinner, RJ & Chambers, BJ 1996 'A survey to assess the extent of soil water erosion in lowland England and Wales', *Soil Use and Management*, 12 (1996), 214-20.

SOAEFD 1997 *Countryside Premium Scheme*. Edinburgh: Scott Off Agric Environ Fisheries Dept.

Spoor, G 1980 'Agronomic justification and technique for subsoil disturbance', *in* J Hinchliffe & R T Schadla-Hall (eds), *The Past Under the Plough*, 4-31. London: Dept Environ.

Stace, C 1991 *New Flora of the British Isles*. Cambridge: Univ Press.

Startin, DW 1982 'The labour force involved in constructing the causewayed enclosure', *in* HJ Case & AWR Whittle (eds) *Settlement Patterns in the Oxford Region: Excavation at the Abingdon Causewayed Enclosure and Other Sites*, 49-50. London: Counc Brit Archaeol.

Stevenson, S 1995 'The excavation of a kerbed cairn at Beech Hill House, Coupar Angus, Perthshire', *Proc Soc Antiq Scot*, 125 (1995), 197-235.

Stewart, MEC 1959 'Strath Tay in the second millennium BC–a field survey', *Proc Soc Antiq Scot*, 92 (1959), 71-84.

Stewart, MEC 1973 'The prehistory of Perthshire in the fourth, third and second millennia, BC', *Proc Perth Natur Hist Soc*, (1973), 5-13.

Stobie, J 1783 *Map of the Counties of Perth and Clackmannan*.

Strong, P 1988 'Pit alignment and earthworks between Marygoldhill Plantation and Drakemire, Berwickshire', *Proc Soc Antiq Scot*, 118 (1988), 111-29.

Stuiver, M & Reimer, PJ 1993 'Extended ^{14}C database and revised CALIB 3.0 ^{14}C age calibration program', *Radiocarbon*, 35 (1993), 215-30.

Sturludottir, SA & Turner, J 1985 'The elm decline at Pawlaw Mire: an anthropologenic interpretation', *New Phytol*, 99 (1985), 323-9.

Ten Hove, HA 1968 'The *Ulmus* fall at the transition Atlanticum-Subboreal', *Palaeogeography, Palaeoclimatology, Palaeoecology*, 5 (1968), 359-69.

Thomas, J 1991 *Rethinking the Neolithic*. Cambridge: Univ Press.

Tilley, C 1994 *A Phenomenology of Landscape: Places, Paths and Monuments*. London: Berg.

Tilley, C 1996 'The powers of rocks: topography and monument construction on Bodmin Moor', *World Archaeol*, 28 (1996), 161-76.

Tipping, R 1994a 'The form and fate of Scotland's woodlands', *Proc Soc Antiq Scot*, 124 (1994a), 1-54.

Tipping, R 1994b '"Ritual" floral tributes in the Scottish Bronze Age–palynological evidence', *J Archaeol Sci*, 21 (1994b), 133-9.

Tipping, R 1995 'Holocene landscape change at Carn Dubh, near Pitlochry, Perthshire', *J Quaternary Sci*, 10 (1995), 59-75.

Tipping, R, Carter, S & Johnston, D 1994 'Soil pollen and soil micromorphological analyses of old ground surfaces on Biggar Common, Borders Region, Scotland', *J Archaeol Sci*, 21 (1994), 387-401.

Tolan, M 1988 *Cropmark Pit Circles in Scotland*. Unpubl BA thesis, Univ Newcastle.

Topping, P 1982 'Excavation at the cursus at Scorton, North Yorkshire 1978', *Yorks Archaeol J*, 54 (1982), 7-21.

Tyler, AN, Davidson, DA & Bradley, S 1995 *Preliminary Investigation of Soil Erosion Rates from ^{137}Cs Activity Distributions on a Tilled Site at Littleour, Perthshire: report to Historic Scotland*. Privately circulated paper.

Tyler, AN, Sanderson, DCW & Scott, EM 1996a 'Estimating and accounting for ^{137}Cs source burial through *in situ* gamma spectrometry in salt marsh environments', *J Environmental Radioactivity*, 33(3) (1996a), 195-212.

Tyler, AN, Sanderson, DCW, Scott, EM & Allyson, JD 1996b 'Investigations of spatial variability and fields of view in environmental gamma ray spectrometry', *J Environmental Radioactivity*, 33(3) (1996b), 213-35.

Vyner, B 1984 'The excavation of a Neolithic cairn at Street House, Loftus, Cleveland', *Proc Prehist Soc*, 50 (1984), 151-95.

Wainwright, GJ & Longworth, IA 1971 *Durrington Walls: Excavations 1966-1968*. London: Soc Antiq London.

Walling, DE & Quine, TA 1991 'The use of caesium-137 measurements to investigate soil erosion on arable fields in the UK: potential applications and limitations', *J Soil Sci*, 42 (1991), 147-65.

Wheeler, REM 1943 *Maiden Castle, Dorset*. London: Soc Antiq London.

Whittington, G 1993 'Palynological investigations at two Bronze Age burial sites in Fife', *Proc Soc Antiq Scot*, 123 (1993), 211-13.

Whittington, G & Edwards, KJ 1990 'The cultivation and utilisation of hemp in Scotland', *Scott Geogr Mag*, 106 (1990), 167-73.

Whittington, G & Edwards, KJ 1993 '*Ubi solitudinem faciunt pacem appellant*: the Romans in Scotland, a palaeoenvironmental contribution', *Britannia*, 24 (1993), 13-25.

Whittington, G & Edwards, KJ 1997 'Climate change', *in* KJ Edwards & IBM Ralston (eds) *Scotland: Environment and Archaeology, 8000BC-AD1000*, 11-22. Chichester: J Wiley & Sons.

Whittington, G, Edwards, KJ & Caseldine, CJ 1991a 'Late- and post-glacial pollen-analytical and environmental data from a near-coastal site in north-east Fife, Scotland', *Rev Palaeobot Palynol*, 68 (1991a), 65-8.

Whittington, G, Edwards, KJ & Cundill, PR 1991b 'Late- and post-glacial vegetational change at Black Loch, Fife, eastern Scotland - a multiple core approach', *New Phytol*, 118 (1991b), 147-66.

Whittington, G, Edwards, KJ & Cundill, PR 1991c 'Palaeoecological investigations of multiple elm declines at a site in north Fife, Scotland', *J Biogeogr*, 18 (1991c), 71-87.

Whittle, A 1992 'Excavations in the Neolithic and Bronze Age complex at Dorchester-on-Thames, Oxfordshire, 1947-1951 and 1981', *Proc Prehist Soc*, 58 (1992), 143-201.

Williams, J & Anderson, G 1972 'Gallaberry: cursus', *Discovery Excav Scot 1971*, (1972), 16.

Williamson, T & Loveday, R 1988 'Rabbits or ritual? Artificial warrens and the Neolithic long mound tradition', *Archaeol J* 145 (1988), 290-313.

Wilson, DR 1982 *Air Photograph Interpretation for Archaeologists*. London: Batsford.

Yates, MJ 1984 *Bronze Age round cairns in Dumfries and Galloway: an inventory and discussion*. Oxford: Brit Archaeol Rep. (=*Brit Archaeol Rep*, 132)

FOREIGN LANGUAGE SUMMARIES

RESUME

Cet ouvrage décrit l'étude et les fouilles réalisées sur un long monument linéaire datant du début de l'époque néolithique, le 'Cleaven Dyke', ainsi que les fouilles effectuées sur un autre site voisin, à savoir l'enceinte de bois de Littleour datant de la fin du néolithique.

L'historique de l'étude du 'Cleaven Dyke' depuis le 18e siècle jusqu'à nos jours est exposé ici et les deux monuments sont placés dans leur contexte régional et national.

LE 'CLEAVEN DYKE'

Le 'Cleaven Dyke' se compose de deux fossés parallèles, largement espacés de part et d'autre d'un talus central qui s'étend du nord-ouest au sud-est sur environ 2 kilomètres à travers une zone boisée et des terres arables, au nord du village de Meikleour, près de Blairgowrie dans le Perthshire, en Ecosse. Pendant 200 ans, on a cru que le monument était d'origine romaine comme la forteresse de légionnaires située non loin de là, à Inchtuthil. L'un des auteurs (Gordon Maxwell) avait remis en question l'interprétation romaine et, dans les années 80, la version qui associe le monument aux 'cursus' du néolithique a commencé à se répandre. Les auteurs ont étudié le site entre 1993 et 1997 et y ont effectué des fouilles en 1993 et en 1995 dans le but de définir le monument.

L'interprétation de leur étude des courbes de niveau et des fouilles effectuées dans le passé laisse supposer que la première partie du monument était un tumulus ovale construit à l'endroit qui allait devenir l'extrémité nord-ouest du 'Dyke', aujourd'hui près de l'orée du bois à travers lequel s'étend le monument. Un long tumulus était relié à celui-ci. Le 'Cleaven Dyke' proprement dit, avec ses fossés largement espacés, ne commence qu'après environ 90m. L'extrémité du monument au sud-est semble se situer sur la colline basse où les dernières marques des fossés se distinguent encore.

Les études réalisées en 1993-1997 montrent que le monument n'est pas aussi uniforme et régulier qu'on ne l'avait estimé auparavant mais qu'il est extrêmement varié, complexe et de nature segmentaire. Il comporte clairement quatre clivages principaux (W X Y et Z) qui divisent le monument en cinq 'Sections' (A-E). Le talus ainsi que les fossés présentent des changements de direction non seulement subtiles mais aussi relativement soudains et prononcés. Le sommet du talus présente des élévations et des baisses de niveau et sa largeur varie, ce qui donne l'impression que les sections du talus sont construites en segments formés d'amas de terre joints. Les sections A à D du talus se composent de 28 segments (on a pu voir lors des fouilles qu'ils ont été construits du nord-ouest au sud-est). Le talus s'élève et atteint une largeur exceptionnelle en des points apparemment significatifs à l'extrémité nord-ouest ainsi qu'aux clivages principaux. Sur une grande partie de sa longueur, mais particulièrement dans les sections A et B, le talus est fortement asymétrique en coupe transversale.

L'étude du paléoenvironnement suggère que la zone où se situe le 'Dyke' et peut-être les alentours ont été largement déboisés quelques temps avant la construction du 'Dyke' et que le degré d'activité dans la zone était assez faible pour qu'une seconde poussée de bouleaux et de noisetiers se développe, mais tout de même assez intense pour permettre la poursuite du processus de transformation en une végétation constituée d'herbe/de lande.

La datation au carbone 14 d'un foyer situé sous le talus ajoutée à l'interprétation de la micro-morphologie du sol semble indiquer que, dans ce secteur, le talus a été construit entre la fin du 5e et le milieu ou la fin du 4e millénaire avant Jésus-Christ.

LITTLEOUR

La structure de Littleour, qui se situe à environ 250m au nord-est du 'Cleaven Dyke' en son point le plus proche (section limite Z), a été découverte lors d'une prise de vue aérienne. Elle constitue l'une des structures aux caractéristiques apparemment similaires qui ont été repérées au moyen de photographies aériennes dans le Perthshire ces dernières années. Elle présente une ressemblance superficielle avec les structures probablement mortuaires du néolithique et, du point de vue des dimensions, avec un édifice couvert d'une toiture datant de la même période et situé à Balbridie dans l'Aberdeenshire. Les fouilles de Littleour laissent supposer que l'édifice avait des fonctions cérémoniales plutôt que domestiques.

La structure (qui a 22m de long) consistait en deux rangées plus ou moins parallèles de huit excavations destinées à recevoir des poteaux, écartées de 7 à 8m. Les deux extrémités étaient formées d'une paire d'excavations. Des matières brûlées en quantités diverses ont été retrouvées dans toutes les conduites formées par les poteaux, ce qui implique la présence de matières brûlées à la surface pendant le processus de pourriture des poteaux. Une excavation massive était située dans l'axe de la structure près de son extrémité est. Un gros poteau était planté dans la cavité. Il est possible que le poteau soit tombé ou bien qu'il ait été extrait et qu'alors des matières brûlées ou en feu y aient été placées. A l'intérieur de l'enceinte, il y avait une petite cavité circulaire, L23, qui contenait un tas homogène de terre brune riche en terreau. Dans ce tas se trouvaient, sans qu'ils ne touchent le fond ni les côtés, les tessons de huit ou neuf récipients ('Grooved Ware': poterie de la fin du néolithique décorée de cannelures et d'applications) ainsi que dix pièces de silex (dont trois grandes pièces travaillées en silex translucide gris foncé de haute qualité).

La datation au carbone 14 place la construction et l'utilisation de la structure de Littleour entre la fin du quatrième et le début du troisième millénaire avant Jésus-Christ: le dépôt des récipients et du silex dans la cavité L23 semble s'être produit environ mille ans plus tard.

──────── ♦♦♦ ────────

KURZE ZUSAMMENFASSUNG

Dieser Band beschreibt die Untersuchung und Ausgrabung eines langen, geradlinigen Denkmals aus dem frühen neolithischen Zeitalter, dem *Cleaven Dyke*, und der Ausgrabung einer anderen Stelle in dessen Nähe, der spätneolithischen Holzeinzäunung bei Littleour.

DER CLEAVEN DYKE

Der *Cleaven Dyke* besteht aus einem Paar weit auseinander plazierten, parallelen Gräben, die einen zentralen Wall flankieren, etwa 2km NW-SO durch Wald und bebaute Felder verlaufend, nördlich des Dorfes Meikleour, in der Nähe von Blairgowrie in Perthshire, Schottland. 200 Jahre lang wurde er zuversichtlich als römische Stätte identifiziert, in Verbindung mit dem naheliegenden Legionärsfort bei Inchtuthil. Einer der Authoren (Gordon Maxwell) hatte die römische Interpretation herausgefordert, und die Interpretation des Denkmals als den neolithischen *cursus* Denkmälern verwandt, wurde in den 1980er Jahren populär. Die Authoren führten zwischen 1993 und 1997 Untersuchungen, und in 1993 und 1995 Ausgrabungen aus, mit dem Ziel, das Monument zu definieren.

Die Interpretation ihrer Konturenuntersuchung und früherer Ausgrabungen deutet darauf hin, daß der erste Teil des Denkmals ein ovaler Hügel war, errichtet wo später das NW Endstück des *Dykes* geformt wurde. An diesen angeschlossen war ein länglicher Hügel. Erst nach etwa 90m fängt der richtige *Cleaven Dyke*, mit seinen weit auseinander angeordneten Gräben, an. Das Ende des Denkmals im SO scheint an dem niedrigen Hügel zu liegen, wo zuletzt die Umrisse im Feld sichtbar sind.

Die 1993-97er Untersuchung zeigte, daß das Denkmal nicht so einheitlich und regelmäßig ist, wie frühere Eindrücke annahmen, sondern daß es vom Typ her höchst variiert, kompliziert und unterbrochen ist. Es hat vier Hauptunterbrechungen (W X Y und Z), welche das Denkmal in fünf 'Sektionen' (A-E) spalten. Es zeigt sowohl in den Anhöhen, wie auch in den Gräben, nicht nur leichte, sondern auch relativ plötzliche und substanzielle Richtungswechsel. Die Fläche oben auf dem Hügel steigt an und fällt ab, und ihre Breite ist unterschiedlich, welches den Eindruck vermittelt, daß die Sektionen des Hügels in Abschnitten von verbundenen Erdaufhäufungen konstruiert wurden. Es gibt 28 Hügelabschnitte in den Sektionen A bis D (wo diese ausgegraben wurden, zeigte sich, daß sie von NW nach SO gebaut wurden). Der Hügel steigt an und erreicht außergewöhnliche Breite an scheinbar besonderen Punkten am NW-Ende und an den Hauptunterbrechungen. Für die meiste Länge, aber besonders in Sektionen A und B, ist der Hügel deutlich asymmetrisch im Durchschnitt.

Die Untersuchung der Umgebung deutet darauf hin, daß die größere Waldbedeckung in der unmittelbaren Nähe des *Dykes*, und eventuell im Umfeld, einige Zeit vor dem Bau des *Dykes* entfernt wurde, und daß die Gegend mit solch niedrieger Intensität genutzt wurde, daß sekundärer Birken- und Haselwald sich entwickeln konnte, aber mit genügend hoher Intensität, um den Fortschritt des Übergangs zu einer Gras/Heide-Vegetation weiterzuführen.

Radiocarbon-Datierung einer Feuerstelle unter dem Hügel, zusammen mit der Interpretation der Erdmikromorphologie, deuten darauf hin, daß der Hügel in diesem Teil im späten 5. bis mittlerem/spätem 6. Jahrtausend v. Chr. gebaut wurde.

LITTLEOUR

Die Struktur zu Littleour, etwa 250m zu NO des *Cleaven Dyke* an ihrer nähesten Stelle (Sektionsgrenze Z), wurde durch Luftaufnahmen entdeckt. Sie ist eine von einer Gruppe von scheinbar ähnlichen Strukturen, die durch Luftaufnahmen in Perthshire in den letzten Jahren gefunden wurden. Sie hat eine oberflächliche Ähnlichkeit mit sowohl wahrscheinlichen Begräbnisstrukturen der Neolothik, wie auch, in Ausmaßen, mit einem überdachten Gebäude aus derselben Periode in Balbridie in Aberdeenshire. Die Ausgrabung der Littleour-Struktur deutet an, das sie zeremonielle, und nicht häusliche, Funktionen hatte.

Die Struktur (welche 22m lang ist) besteht aus zwei hauptsächlich parallelen Linien von acht Pfostengruben, mit 7m - 8m Abstand. Beide Enden wurden durch Paare von Pfostengruben bestimmt. Veschiedene Mengen von verbranntem Material wurden in allen ausgegrabenen Pfostengrubeninhalten gefunden, welche auf die Anwesenheit während dem Pfostenverfaulen von verbranntem Material auf der Oberfläche hindeuten. Eine besonders massive Pfostengrube lag auf der Achse der Struktur nahe dem östlichem Ende. Ein großer Pfosten war in die Grube gesetzt. Es ist möglich, daß der Pfosten umfiel oder entfernt wurde, an welchem Zeitpunkt verbranntes oder brennendes Material in die Grube gelang. Innerhalb der Umzäunung war eine kleine kreisförmige Grube, L23, die eine einzelne, homogene Füllung von braunem Lehm enthielt. In dieser Füllung, allerdings nicht den Boden oder die Seiten berührend, befanden sich Scherben von acht oder neun *Grooved Ware*-Behältern (spätneolithische Keramik von gerillter und aufgesetzter Verziehrung) und zehn Feuersteine (drei große, überarbeitete Exemplare aus dunkelgrauem Feuerstein von hoher Qualität).

Radiocarbon-Datierungen setzen die Konstruktion und den Nutz der Littleour-Struktur in das späte vierte bis frühe dritte Jahrtausend v. Chr.; die Ablagerung der *Grooved Ware* und Feuersteine in Grube L23 scheint etwa eintausend Jahre später stattgefunden zu haben.

◆◆◆

RESUMEN DEL CLEAVEN DYKE Y LITTLEOUR

Este tomo describe el estudio y la excavación de un monumento largo y lineal del Neolítico Inicial, el 'Cleaven Dyke' (el Terraplén de Cleaven), y la excavación de otro emplazamiento cercano, una empalizada de madera del Neolítico Final en Littleour. Se presenta la historia de las investigaciones del 'Cleaven Dyke' desde el siglo 18 hasta la actualidad, y se definen a ambos yacimientos en un contexto regional y nacional.

EL 'CLEAVEN DYKE'

El 'Cleaven Dyke' está compuesto de un par de zanjas paralelas y bien espaciadas, que flanquean un terraplén central, recorriendo 2 km en dirección noroeste a sudeste, atravesando bosque y campo sembrado, al norte del pueblo de Meikleour, cerca de Blairgowrie en Perthshire, Escocia. Durante 200 años se lo clasificó con confianza, como un emplazamiento de la época romana, relacionado con la cercana fortaleza de legionarios en Inchtutchil. Uno de los autores (Gordon Maxwell) cuestionó la versión aceptada, y en los años '80 ganó vigencia la interpretación que sugiere un vínculo con las 'avenidas' Neolíticas. Los autores llevaron a cabo investigaciones en 1993 y 1997, y excavaron en 1993 y 1995 con el propósito de poder definir al monumento.

El estudio topográfico y las excavaciones pasadas sugieren que la primera porción del monumento habría sido un túmulo ovalado construído en lo que vendría a ser la terminal noroeste del terraplén, actualmente al lado del bosque que el emplazamiento atraviesa. Acoplado a éste habría un túmulo alargado. Solo después de unos 90 metros comienza el terraplén de Cleaven propiamente dicho, con sus zanjas espaciadas. La terminal sudeste del emplazamiento parece situarse sobre un pequeño montículo donde se disciernen por última vez las huellas de las zanjas.

Las investigaciones de los años 1993 al '97 han demostrado que el monumento arqueológico no es ni tan uniforme ni tan regular como lo habría parecido anteriormente, y que al contrario, tiene un carácter mucho mas variado, complejo y segmentado. Tiene cuatro cortes formales (W, X, Y y Z) que dividen al monumento en cuatro 'Secciones' (A-E). Las zanjas y el terraplén muestran cambios en dirección, a veces imperceptibles y otras bruscas y grandes. El nivel del terraplén sube y baja, y varía de ancho, dando la impresión de que las Secciones se construyeron con depósitos de tierra vertidos en tramos empalmados. El terraplén se eleva y llega tener un ancho excepcional en lo que aparentan ser puntos claves como la terminal noroeste y los cortes formales. Por la mayor parte de su largo, pero especialmente en las Secciones A y B, el terraplén es notablemente asimétrico en corte transversal.

El trabajo paleoambiental sugiere que la principal aforestación en la zona imediata al 'Dyke', y posiblemente en los alrededores, se habría quitado un tiempo antes de la construcción del terraplén, y que la zona estaba bajo uso poco intensivo como para permitir el desarrollo de un bosque secundario de abedules y avellanos, pero a la vez suficientemente intensivo como para que continuara el proceso de cambio hacia una situación de praderas y brezales.

Datación por radiocarbono de un foco de fuego encontrado debajo del terraplén, combinado con la interpretación de la micromorfología del suelo indican que en este sector, el terraplén se construyó entre finales del 5to. milenio a.C., y mediados o fines del 4to. milenio a.C (calibrado).

LITTLEOUR

La estructura en Littleour, a 250 metros aproximadamente al noreste del Cleaven Dyke en el punto mas cercano (límite de la Sección Z), se halló de forma aérea. Es parte de un grupo de emplazamientos aparentemente similares descubiertos en los últimos años a través de aerofotos en Perthshire. Superficialmente se asemeja a un emplazamiento funerario del Neolítico, y en tamaño se parece a un edificio con techo de la misma época en Balbridie, Aberdeenshire. La excavación de la empalizada de Littleour sugiere que tuvo una función ceremonial más que doméstica.

La estructura (de unos 22 metros de largo) consistió de dos líneas casi parallelas, a siete u ocho metros de distancia, con ocho hoyos para postes cada una. Ambas puntas estaban compuestas por un par de hoyos. Se hallaron cantidades variables de residuos quemados en los ductos vacíos para los postes dentro de los hoyos, insinuando que habría depósitos calcinados sobre la superficie durante la pudrición de los postes. Cerca de la punta este de la estructura y sobre su axis se encontró un hoyo grande. En él habría un poste de madera enorme. Es posible que el poste se cayó o se sacó, permitiendo que el agujero se llenara con depósitos ya calcinados o en el proceso de quemarse. Dentro de la empalizada se halló un pequeño pozo circular, L23, relleno de un solo depósito homogéneo de tierra marga marrón. Dentro de este relleno, pero sin tocar el fondo ni los costados, se encontraron fragmentos de ocho o nueve vasijas del estilo *Grooved Ware* (cerámica con acanaladura), y diez piezas de sílex (tres grandes, con retoque, en sílex gris oscuro traslúcido de alta calidad).

La construcción y el uso de la estructura de Littleour se datan por medio del radiocarbono entre finales del 4to. milenio a.C. y comienzos del 3er. milenio a.C. (calibrado). Parece que la cerámica *Grooved Ware* y el sílex se depositaron en el pozo L23 aproximadamente mil años mas tarde.

INDEX

Italicised references at the end of an entry denote illustration numbers

aerial photography xvi, 5, 13, 14, 15, 18, 53, 60, 82, 92, 95, 97, 101, 102; *2, 3, 20*
    significance of 2, 3
alignment
    of Cleaven Dyke 49, 110
    of cursus monuments 3, 114
Ancient Monuments Acts 126, 129
artefacts *see* arrowheads; axes; flint; lithic scatters; pottery
arrowheads, flint 24
Auchenlaich, Perthshire, long cairn 106; *84*
axes
    Bronze Age 5
    stone 24
        extraction and manufacture 4

Balbridie, Kincardineshire (Aberdeenshire), Neolithic timber structure xvi; *96*
Balfarg Riding School, Fife, ceremonial complex xvi
    pottery from 121, 125
    radiocarbon dates *Table 1*
    timber structures 120-2; *91*
Balneaves Cottage, Angus, cursus monument 96; *71*
    phases of construction 96
Barnhead (Old Montrose), Angus, cursus monument 99; *76*
barrows xvi, 99
    bank 49, 92, 103-106, 112; *83*
        definition of 103
        distribution of 103
        radiocarbon dating of 103
    long 13, 48-50, 109
    round 1, 2, 3, 20, 94, 115-7, 119, 120
Bennybeg, Perthshire, cursus monument 101; *78*
Blairhall, Perthshire, cursus monument 99-101; *77*
Blue Cairn of Balnagowan, Aberdeenshire 119; *90*
buildings *see also* timber structures
    ridged 54, 60
burials 2, 3, 94 *see also* mortuary structures
    cist 2
    cremation 2
    monuments 1-2
    secondary 4
    traditions, Neolithic 115
burning, evidence of 31, 54, 58, 67 *see also* charcoal

cairns 1, 2, 120
    chambered 1, 2, 4, 114, 116
    long 2, 106; *84*
chambered tombs 2
charcoal 2, 37, 42, 47, 58, 59; *43, 46*
    birch 58, 61
Cleaven Dyke xv, 4, 13-52, 92, 124; *2, 11-37, 85, 97, 98, 99*
    18th- and 19th-century references to 14, 15; *12*
    20th-century accounts of 15-24
    alignment of 49, 110
        astronomical 49, 50-52; *Tables 8; 9*
    as Roman monument xv, xvi
    bank of 13-15, 18-29, 30-36, 47, 48, 82; *13-15, 17-19, 22-27, 29, 30, 32-34, 97*
        turf-toeing of 17, 19, 31, 35
    barrows within xvi, 50
    burning beneath bank 31
    choice of terrain 110, 111
    construction
        dumps 26
        labour required for 52
        patterns of 48, 49
        sequence of 109-110, 113, 114
    context 112, 113; *Table 17*
        interpretation of 112, 113, 115
    dating of 11, 47, 112
        Long 13, 49
    design of 47
    ditches xv, 13, 14, 18-20, 24, 30-36, 47-50, 75, 81-83; *26-29*
    environment of 111, 112 *see also* pollen; vegetational history
    excavation of 15, 17-22, 30; *13, 15*
        strategy 30-36
    function of 114, 115
    mounds 19
        long 20
        oval 13, 50
        proximal with tail 119, 120
    orientation of 26
    palaeosols 36-42; *Tables 3-6; 36, 37*
    pollen 12
        soil 42-46; *38-40*
    postholes 31, 35
    radiocarbon dates 47
    segmentation of 14, 25-29, 76, 110, 111, 114; *Table 7; 24, 55*
    spatial relationships of 48
    setting of 4, 13, 110-111; *1*
    survey of xvi, 15, 22, 24-27; *22, 24, 98, 99*
        contour 22, 75, 76
        geophysical 80-83; *57-61*
conservation issues 126-129; *96*
Craig na Caillich, Perthshire, stone quarry site 4
cropmark sites 5, 14, 15, 18, 20, 21, 22, 77, 81, 83, 92, 95, 96, 98, 99, 101, 103-105, 123; *2, 3, 20, 71, 77, 92*
cursus monuments 92-102, 112, 113; *71-80 see also* monuments, ceremonial; enclosures; *and under individual monuments*
    alignment of 3, 114
    and relationship to water 94
    as landscape control 94, 107
    barrows, relationship with 99, 113
    classification of 112, 113, 115
    causeways 99
    dating of 94, 113
    description 92
    distribution of 92; *69*
    ditch-defined 94, 97, 98, 99, 101; *77*
        interpretation 97
    function and purpose of 94, 113, 114, 115
    of Tayside 94-102
    pit-defined 94-99, 101; *73-76, 78*
    setting in landscape 94, 107

daub 62, 67; *52*
deposition
    of lithics 73
    of pot 67
ditches 2, 13, 15, 17
    parallel xv, 5
    ring 99, 101, 103
Douglasmuir, Angus, cursus monument 4, 92, 94, 95, 123; *5, 70*
    interpretation of 96, 123, 124

radiocarbon dating of 95
enclosures 2, 5, 60, 62, 94, 101, 103, 106, 123, 124; *5, 79 see also* cursus monuments
    henges and hengiform 3, 102
    lobate 5
    mortuary 4, 113
    Neolithic 52, 62
    palisaded 3, 121
environment
    evidence 68-70
    of Cleaven Dyke 111-112
environmental change, indicators of 4, 5-12
Eskdalemuir, Dumfriesshire, bank barrow *see* Tom's Knowe

flint 22, 24, 58, 70-73; *Table 10*; *46, 53*
    scatters 22
fortresses, Roman 2, 5

geophysical surveys *see* surveys, geophysical
Grandtully, Perthshire, pit group 2
Grooved ware
    dating of 124
    distribution of in Scotland 124
    from Littleour 58, 62-9, 124-5; *48-52, 93*

hearths 37, 42
henbane, Neolithic occurrence of 125
Herald Hill, Perthshire, long barrow 107, 111, 117, 119; *2, 87, 88*

Inchbare, Angus, cursus monument 97, 98; *73*
Inchtuthil, Perthshire xv, 2, 15, 18; *4*
    lobate enclosure at 5
    Neolithic long mortuary enclosure 2, 4, 5, 22, 120; *4*
    pit-circles 5, 22
    plateau, archaeology of 5
    radiocarbon dates from 2
    Roman fortress 2, 5

Kilmany, Fife, bank barrow 92, 103, 104; *81*
kilns, corn-drying 2
Kinalty, Angus, cursus monument 99; *75*

lithic scatters 22-4 *see also* flint
Littleour, Perthshire xvi, 4, 22, 53-73, 107; *3, 42, 45*
    ceremonial function of xvi
    comparisons with Balfarg 120-123; *91*
    excavation of 54-59
    flint artefacts from 58, 70-73, 124; *Table 10*; *53*
        microwear analysis of 72
    location of 53, 61; *1*
    postholes 54-60; *Table 10*; *42-48*
        alignment of 60-62
        dimensions of ??
    postpipes 54; *43, 44*
    pottery 58, 62-69, 124, 125; *Table 10*; *48-52, 93*
        analysis 62-68
        ceremonial use 67, 68
        dating 67
        residues on 67-70; *Table 13, 14*
    pollen from pot residues 68-70
    radiocarbon dating 54, 58, 60, 61; *Table 12*
    survey of 53, 77-79; *56, 57, 62 see also* survey, methodology
    timber structure 53, 54, 60-62; *3, 41, 91*
        analysis 62
        comparisons with 123, 124
        whether roofed 60
Longmanhill Cairn, Banffshire (Aberdeenshire) 119; *89, 90*

Mains of Gourdie, Perthshire, linear cropmark site 101-2; *80*
Milton of Guthrie, Angus, pit-defined enclosure 96; *72*
Milton of Rattray, Perthshire,
monuments
    burial xvi
    ceremonial xvi
    cursus monuments xv, 3, 18, 22, 24, 49-51, 62 *see also* individual monuments
    distribution in Tayside *86*
    ditch-defined 3, 49
    funerary 49
    linear 107
    mortuary structures xvi, 2, 61, 115 *see also* monuments, burial
mounds 4, 103 *see also* barrows; cairns
    burial 4, 101, 109
    complexity 115
    distribution 117; *86*
    long 2, 20, 105, 116-120, *Table 17*
    morphological classification of 115, 116
    oval 13, 50, 105, 115-117
    proximal with long tail 119, 120; *89, 90*
    round 2-4, 50

North Mains, Strathallan, Perthshire, round mound 3, 4, 6, 115, 127

Old Montrose cursus monument *see* Barnhead

palaeosols, Cleaven Dyke 36-42; *Tables 3-6*; *36, 37*
pit
    alignments 48, 53, 54, 95-98, 101; *79*
    -circles 5, 22, 101
    -defined cursus 62, 92, 94
    -defined enclosures xvi, 3, 48, 49, 92, 94, 95, 123, 124; *70, 92*
Pitnacree, Perthshire, Neolithic round mound 2, 115
    radiocarbon dates from 2, 58, 115
pits 2, 3, 36, 53, 58, 60, 94, 121; *Table 10*; *46, 48,*
plant remains *Table 11, 13, 14 see also* henbane
pollen
    content in pottery residues 68-70, 125; *Table 13, 14*
    diagrams *6-8, 10, 38-40*
    isopollen maps 11
    from Rae Loch 5
    from Stormont Loch 6, 12
    soil, from the Cleaven Dyke 42-46; *38-40*
postholes 54-62, 95
posts
    penannular setting of 2
    pits 121
    spacing 123
pottery *Table 10*
    Beaker 95
    ceremonial use 67, 68
    Flat rim (flat-rimmed) ware 2
    Grooved ware 2, 4, 58, 62-69, 121, 124, 125; *46, 48-52, 93*
        comb-impressed 67
    Neolithic decorated, from Douglasmuir 95
    Neolithic impressed ware from Grandtully 2
    residues on 68-70
    urns, cinerary 5

quarrying, stone 4
quartz industry in Strathtay 4

radiocarbon dating xvii, 1, 2, 3, 4, 9-12; *Table 1, 2, 12 see also* individual sites
    calibration xvi, 61
    of bank barrows 103
Rae Loch, Perthshire 5-12
    location of 6
    pollen data 5-9; *6-8, 10*
    radiocarbon dating of sediments from 9; *Table 2*
ramparts
    circular 15
Richmond, IA, excavation of the Cleaven Dyke 16-18; *13-16*
ring-banks 2
    Bronze Age 4
ring ditches 3
roads, post-medieval 3
roofing 60-1, 123

Sarn-y-bryn-Caled, Powys, cursus complex 113
segmentation 18, 22, 26, 47, 48-9, 103, 110, 113-4
site conservation issues 126-9; *94-96*
soil loss
    at Littleour 85; *62, 65, 67, Table 16*
    causes of 84

erosion rates 86; *65*
estimates of, using ^{137}Cs 83-91; *Table 15; 68*
soils *see also* palaeosols
    charcoal-stained 58; *43, 46*
    fire-reddened 58
standing stones 2, 101
Star Inn, Angus, cursus monument 98; *74*
stone circles 2
structures
    at Douglasmuir 96
    at Littleour 60-62
    Neolithic roofed 60
    timber 4, 120-124; *91*
surveys 2, 4
    by Royal Commission on the Ancient and Historical Monuments of Scotland 1, 2, 4, 22, 75; *22*
    digital terrain modelling (DTM) 74, 75; *54*
    geophysical 77
    methodology of 74-6, 78
    of Cleaven Dyke 15, 22, 24-2, 80-3; *22, 24, 55, 57-61, 98/99*
        contour 22, 75, 76
    of Littleour 53, 77, 78, 79; *56*
    of rock art 4

Tayside
    Neolithic and Early Bronze Age 1
timber structures 4
Tom's Knowe, Dumfriesshire, bank barrow 104, 105; *82*
tools *see* artefacts

urns *see* pottery

vegetational history of Cleaven Dyke area 9-11

wood *see also* pollen
    birch 59, 61
    oak 59
    pine 59, 61

SOCIETY OF ANTIQUARIES OF SCOTLAND MONOGRAPH SERIES

Editor ALEXANDRA SHEPHERD

Previous volumes in the series

1	CL Curle *Pictish and Norse finds from the Brough of Birsay 1934-74.*	ISBN 9 903903 01 6
2	JC Murray (ed) *Excavations in the medieval burgh of Aberdeen 1972-81.*	ISBN 0 903903 02 4
3	H Fairhurst *Excavations at Crosskirk Broch, Caithness.*	ISBN 0 903903 03 2
4	JR Hunter *Rescue excavations on the Brough of Birsay 1974-82.*	ISBN 0 903903 04 0
5	P Holdsworth (ed) *Excavations in the medieval burgh of Perth 1979-1981.*	ISBN 0 903903 05 9
6	JA Stones (ed) Three Scottish Carmelite friaries: excavations at Aberdeen, Linlithgow and Perth 1980-86.	ISBN 0 903903 06 7
7	C Wickham-Jones Rhum: Mesolithic and later sites at Kinloch. Excavations *1984-86.*	ISBN 0 903903 07 5
8	R Bradley *Altering the earth. The origins of monuments in Britain and Continental Europe.*	ISBN 0 903903 08 3
9	B Ballin Smith (ed) *Howe: four millennia of Orkney prehistory.*	ISBN 0 903903 09 1
10	JH Lewis & GJ Ewart Jedburgh Abbey. The archaeology and architecture of a border abbey.	ISBN 0903903 10 5
11	J & B Coles *Enlarging the past. The contribution of wetland archaeology.*	ISBN 0 903903 11 3
12	ST Driscoll & PA Yeoman *Excavations within Edinburgh Castle in 1988-91.*	ISBN 0 903903 12 1